*If you are looking for a hands-on approach to acceptance and commitment therapy, this book is must! Very well organized and written in clear, concise terms, Luoma and colleagues spell out the essentials of doing ACT, with annotated narrative in session transcripts demonstrating key points. You will leave this book with not only a set of clinical skills, but also with the knowledge of when and how to apply them in therapy.*

—Kirk Strosahl Ph.D., coauthor of *Acceptance and Commitment Therapy: An Experiential Approach to Behavior Change* and *A Practical Guide to Acceptance and Commitment Therapy*

*Learning ACT is by far the best practical skill-building work book produced so far in the ACT literature. Teaching psychotherapy skills is complicated, and this book serves as a model for how it can be done. This book breaks down the ACT core process into bite-size portions making these skills visible, understandable and doable. The book is organized around core competencies but uses an ingenious system of therapist-client dialogue where the reader is encouraged to interact and respond applying each core skill. Besides all the cutting edge skill training abundant in this book, you cannot miss the compassionate vital spirit that these extraordinary ACT therapists bring into the therapy room. This book will surely be a classic for teaching psychotherapy!*

—JoAnne Dahl, Ph.D, associate professor in the Department of Psychology at Uppsala University in Uppsala, Sweden

# Publisher's Note

Acceptance and commitment therapy (ACT) has an extensive literature. The theory and philosophy that comprise ACT were first formulated and presented in book form by Steven C. Hayes, Kirk D. Strosahl, and Kelly G. Wilson in 1999.

The book you hold is addressed to clinicians who wish to apply the principles of ACT in their practices. This book goes beyond the philosophy, theory, concepts, and techniques of ACT, and addresses the acquisition of skills and competencies by the practitioner. *Learning ACT* is a practical rather than theoretical book.

For that reason, this book does not take the place of the ground-breaking theoretical and philosophical text that first introduced the ACT treatment model, *Acceptance and Commitment Therapy: An Experiential Approach to Behavior Change*, by Hayes, Strosahl, and Wilson (Guilford Press). The authors strongly encourage their readers to consult and use this indispensable foundational book and the other important works on ACT that are referenced in *Learning ACT*.

New Harbinger is proud to present *Learning ACT* as a valuable new addition to the ever-growing literature of ACT.

# Learning ACT

An Acceptance & Commitment Therapy
Skills-Training Manual for Therapists

JASON B. LUOMA, PH.D.
STEVEN C. HAYES, PH.D.
ROBYN D. WALSER, PH.D.

New Harbinger Publications, Inc.

Distributed in Canada by Raincoast Books

Copyright © 2007 by Jason B. Luoma, Steven C. Hayes, and Robyn Walser. All Rights Reserved.
New Harbinger Publications, Inc.
5674 Shattuck Avenue
Oakland, CA 94609
www.newharbinger.com

Image of flying fish on page 61 used with permission of J. Ciarrochi & D. Mercer. Images for conducting Acceptance and Commitment Therapy Interventions (part 1), 2005. University of Wollongong, Australia.

Printed in the United States of America

Acquired by Catharine Sutker; Cover design by Amy Shoup; Edited by Jude Berman

Library of Congress Cataloging-in-Publication Data

Luoma, Jason B.
  Learning ACT : an acceptance and commitment therapy skills-training manual for therapists / Jason B. Luoma, Steven C. Hayes, and Robyn D. Walser.
       p. cm.
  Includes bibliographical references.
  ISBN-13: 978-1-57224-498-6
  ISBN-10: 1-57224-498-4
  1. Acceptance and commitment therapy--Handbooks, manuals, etc.  I. Hayes, Steven C.  II. Walser, Robyn D.  III. Title.
  RC489.A32L86 2007
  616.89'142--dc22
                                                  2007031814

13  12  11

15  14  13  12  11  10  9  8

To my partner, Jenna LeJeune, for your support, your sacrifice, and your faith in me.

    —JBL


I would like to dedicate this book to David H. Barlow, and to my fellow interns (Peter M. Monti, Kelly D. Brownell, A. Toy Caldwell-Colbert, and Carol Heckerman Landau) who worked under him in the first class of clinical psychology at Brown University, Department of Psychiatry and Human Behavior, 1975–1976 and who such showed patience and kindness in shaping up a wild man to be able to work with people.

    —SCH


I would like to dedicate this book to Susan L. Pickett. Thanks for the encouragement over the years and for always having faith in me.

    —RDW

# CONTENTS

Dear Reader:

Welcome to New Harbinger Publications. New Harbinger is dedicated to publishing books based on acceptance and commitment therapy (ACT) and its application to specific areas. New Harbinger has a long-standing reputation as a publisher of quality, well-researched books for general and professional audiences.

*Learning ACT* is a great tool to help readers learn how to become and be ACT therapists. Without going into too much detail about the scientific and conceptual underpinnings of ACT, this workbook provides brief and concise explanations of the six core therapist processes and treatment targets. Throughout the book you will find actual client-therapist transcripts occasionally accompanied by a commentary about the therapist's overall strategy and reasons for specific word choices.

The book does not focus on learning ACT for specific disorders or problems. Instead, it provides you with the conceptual knowledge, the general tools, and the therapeutic stance that will help you become a good ACT therapist. Other workbooks and therapist guides in the Acceptance and Commitment Therapy Series are more problem-specific and provide detailed descriptions of specific ACT techniques such as metaphors, acceptance and mindfulness meditations, and how to implement value-guided behavioral activation. This book will help you avoid applying these techniques in a mechanistic bag-of-trick-type fashion because it teaches you the fundamental skills of being an ACT therapist—the ACT therapeutic stance.

ACT has developed quite an extensive list of core therapist competencies that therapists should strive to acquire. This workbook provides many opportunities to help you develop those competencies. Specific exercises in each chapter will give you some valuable immediate feedback about whether you're on your way to learning what the authors want you to learn. You will also learn to conceptualize cases from an ACT perspective using an easy-to-use case conceptualization form.

For many people—therapists included—ACT goes against the grain because it is so counterintuitive. ACT also challenges some of the cultural mantras of western society: pain is bad and must be gotten rid of, and feeling good is more important than just about anything else in life. As therapists we sit in the same boat as our clients. We're all part of this culture and caught up in similar struggles and mind games with difficult thoughts and feelings. We get caught up in old storylines and unworkable solutions as much and as often as our clients do. For this reason, the authors give you ample opportunity to recognize and experience this similarity. Exercises will help you notice and observe your reactions to the presented material so you won't get sidetracked by your evaluative mind and cultural programming.

The therapeutic relationship is very important in ACT. The authors make very helpful suggestions on how to approach difficult situations you may experience with clients when applying ACT (e.g., "resistance" to ACT). Novice therapists in particular can easily get caught up in struggles and arguments with clients trying to convince them that ACT is right and what clients have been doing and thinking is wrong. ACT applied in this top-down, noncompassionate fashion can easily backfire. Apart from devoting a whole chapter to this issue, the authors share with you many suggestions and examples in each chapter to help you acquire an ACT therapeutic stance that will likely benefit the people you work with. You may even benefit yourself in no small way.

As part of New Harbinger's commitment to publishing sound, scientific, clinically based research, Steven C. Hayes, Georg H. Eifert, and John Forsyth oversee all prospective ACT books for the Acceptance and Commitment Therapy Series. As ACT Series editors, we review all ACT books published by New Harbinger, comment on proposals and offer guidance as needed, and use a gentle hand in making suggestions regarding the content, depth, and scope of each book. We strive to ensure that any unsubstantiated claim or claims that are clearly ACT inconsistent are flagged for the authors so they can revise these sections to ensure that the work meets our criteria (see below) and that all of the material presented is true to ACT's roots (not passing off other models and methods as ACT).

Books in the Acceptance and Commitment Therapy Series:

- ✓ Have an adequate database, appropriate to the strength of the claims being made

- ✓ Are theoretically coherent—they will fit with the ACT model and underlying behavioral principles as they have evolved at the time of writing

- ✓ Orient the reader toward unresolved empirical issues

- ✓ Do not overlap needlessly with existing volumes

- ✓ Avoid jargon and unnecessary entanglement with proprietary methods, leaving ACT work open and available

- ✓ Keep the focus always on what is good for the reader

- ✓ Support the further development of the field

- ✓ Provide information in a way that is of practical use to readers

These guidelines reflect the values of the broader ACT community. You'll see all of them packed into this book. They are meant to ensure that professionals get information that can truly be helpful, and that can further our ability to alleviate human suffering by inviting creative practitioners into the process of developing, applying, and refining a more adequate approach. Consider this book such an invitation.

Sincerely,
Steven C. Hayes, Ph.D., Georg H. Eifert, Ph.D., and John Forsyth, Ph.D.

# ACKNOWLEDGMENTS

This book was a team effort. To all those who read and provided feedback on drafts of these chapters, thank you. The exercises were particularly improved by those who piloted chapters of this book, including Mary Englert, Anne Shankar, Lianna Evans, Ross Leonard, Brendan Sillifant, Kevin Handley, Laura Meyers, Joanne Hersh, Jennifer Boulanger, and Jennifer Plumb. Thanks to the Portland ACT peer consultation group for their ideas about how to organize the book, exercises, and accompanying DVD. Thanks to Joe Parsons for discussions about shaping therapist behavior, which influenced the exercises in this book, to Jason Lillis for allowing us to adapt his ACT case conceptualization form, and to Jonathan Weinstein for allowing us to create a vignette based on a session where he was the therapist.

To all of our clients who have honored us with their presence, trust, and courage. Without all of you, this book would not have been possible.

Thanks to those students and professionals who allowed themselves to be supervised by us and who taught their supervisors so much.

Thanks to our editor, Jude Berman, who corrected our poor grammar, removed many parentheses, and made gentle course corrections.

Acknowledgment from individual authors:

Thank you to all those who helped me (JBL) learn ACT. When I first began studying ACT, I was blown away by the rigor and scope of the theory and was thoroughly confused by the technical language. I was rapidly able to utilize many of the metaphors and exercises, but didn't really understand how it all tied together. I needed a book about the in between moments. This is my attempt to write that book.

I (SCH) would like to thank my wife, Jacqueline Pistorello, for her support, advice, and patience throughout, and to thank my lab for their input and encouragement.

I (RDW) would like to thank my mom for providing some of the illustrations in this book. They look great, Mom! We appreciate your willingness and action on short notice. I would also like to thank my husband, Mark Castoreno, for being a supportive partner and for providing numerous massages throughout the writing of this book.

# INTRODUCTION

Whenever Richard Cory went down town,
We people on the pavement looked at him:
He was a gentleman from sole to crown,
Clean favored, and imperially slim.

And he was always quietly arrayed,
And he was always human when he talked;
But still he fluttered pulses when he said,
"Good-morning," and he glittered when he walked.

And he was rich—yes, richer than a king—
And admirably schooled in every grace:
In fine, we thought that he was everything
To make us wish that we were in his place.

So on we worked, and waited for the light,
And went without the meat, and cursed the bread;
And Richard Cory, one calm summer night,
Went home and put a bullet through his head.

—Edwin Arlington Robinson (1922)

It is impossible to construct a human life untouched by suffering. Edwin Arlington Robinson's well-known poem reminds us that every day someone who seemingly has all the things a person could ever want, at least as viewed from the outside, ends his or her existence rather than bear up under another moment. As a human species, we encounter many of the same painful events as do other species; humans and nonhuman animals alike are faced with loss, unexpected upsets, and physically painful experiences. Yet we do something with these encounters that they do not: we "mind" about them, and through this process we amplify our suffering and we bring it with us.

The human ability to think and reason is truly amazing. Our system of language is unlike any other; as an ongoing process, it fills our awareness with a never-ending stream of verbal connections. This ability is both a wonderful and a terrible thing. It sustains the capacity for human achievement: our ability to communicate, build, plan, and problem solve. It is part of our ability to love deeply and to commit to others, to dream of hoped-for futures and work toward their realization. However, the same cognitive and verbal building blocks that enable these possibilities also allow us to struggle in the midst of plenty. They allow us to *be* Richard Cory.

Human beings struggle in a number of ways that can be painful and life changing. When events occur that bring us into contact with difficult emotions and thoughts, we often work very hard to rid ourselves of these experiences, both by trying to avoid the event that triggered them and by attempting to remove the negatively evaluated emotions and thoughts that accompany the experience. We don't want, for instance, to feel anxiety about failure or sadness about loss, so when an event occurs that might occasion those emotions, we work to avoid the event and the resulting emotional reactions.

It is not unexpected that we take these steps. If something is unpleasant, it makes sense to figure out how to fix it. The problem with this strategy lies in the paradoxical effects of language—those symbolic abilities that make up what we call the "mind"—as we attempt to use these abilities to avoid that which cannot be avoided. When it becomes important that we not think or feel a certain way, and we nevertheless find ourselves thinking or feeling that way, our minds can become consumed with efforts to eliminate these experiences. However, in the focused effort to eliminate these experiences, we tend to actually propagate and grow the very demons we wish to destroy.

Acceptance and commitment therapy (ACT, which is said as one word, not as A.C.T.; Hayes, Strosahl, & Wilson, 1999) offers a possible antidote to the harmful functions of this verbal capacity and its role in human suffering. ACT is a contextual cognitive-behavioral intervention designed to create psychological flexibility by helping us come into closer contact with our sense of experiential wisdom, while undermining the verbal difficulties that trap us in suffering. ACT addresses the paradoxes inherent in human cognitive processes and actively works to help clients live meaningful and valued lives. ACT employs a number of strategies, including contact with the present moment, acceptance of self and others, defusion and deliteralization, contact with a transcendent sense of self, values-based living, and committed action, as means to help clients move in valued directions. Each of these processes is applied with warmth and compassion for the client's struggle and for the difficulties that unwanted experience can bring. ACT is a constructive approach to psychotherapy that helps people learn to embrace compassionately their internal experience for all that it is, while also focusing on building repertoires of constructive behaviors that are values oriented.

ACT, informed by its related basic theory, Relational Frame Theory (RFT; Hayes, Barnes-Holmes, & Roche, 2001), explores how language functions to keep human beings stuck in painful psychological material, and how this leads to increased suffering and misery. This relationship has been written about extensively in previous books, and we summarize it briefly in a more clinical way in this volume. We describe in some detail how ACT approaches these problems. The main part of this book shows how the core therapeutic processes of ACT are applied, and does so in a way that is useful and understandable to the reader.

It is our hope that, by reading the book, clinicians will be empowered to begin to apply the techniques in their practices. That is what is most unique about this volume. It is designed to go beyond the philosophy, theory, concepts, and verbal knowledge of techniques to the actual production of skills and competencies. We have deliberately written it in a style that is lightly referenced and accessible because our focus is on the practical.

This workbook:

- ✓ Is about helping clinicians help their clients to live more rewarding, full, vital lives

- ✓ Provides discrete chapters, each designed to target a different major core therapeutic process in the work of ACT

- ✓ Is about training clinicians to reach sufficient knowledge and skill levels so that they can begin to implement the therapy as a result of reading about and engaging with the material

- ✓ Is intended as a skill-building companion for other ACT texts that provide much more detail about the theory, philosophy, data, metaphors, exercises, and application of ACT, and about its relevance to various client problems, such as anxiety, depression, chronic pain, and psychosis (see For More Information at the end of this introduction)

- ✓ Attempts to help build clinicians' skills in the core competencies associated with the respective therapeutic processes so they can be more effective, regardless of client presentation

We do not mean to imply that we think of this as a cookbook. ACT is not that kind of therapy. We not only want to provide practitioners with a clear sense of how ACT is conducted, but we would also like to convey the vitality this therapy can bring to human experience. Personal involvement in the book, including engaging in practice and homework, is encouraged. We ask this for a number of reasons, but most importantly, so you as the therapist can experience what it means to personally engage ACT, just as you will be asking your clients to do. This therapy can be difficult to do if you are not applying the same approaches in your own life. Take, for example, your own personal experience with emotion: what do you do when confronted with what is most painful to you? If your answer includes many efforts to eliminate or control, you would hear us asking, "To what end?" Perhaps for you, as it is for most, the end is to feel better. However, if your answer is to experience the pain for what it is, and you are able to live better by doing so, then you are ahead of the game in learning the ACT approach.

Many therapies focus largely on helping people feel better. The hope is that, at the end of the therapy, the client will have fewer symptoms and will feel better emotionally. The focus in ACT is explicitly on living better. Although this may involve feeling better, it also may not. Sometimes living better actually calls for *feeling* the pain; if doing so promotes connection, choice, and living with vitality, then ACT tries to provide the skills needed to feel pain without needless defense. The key goal of ACT is to support clients in feeling and thinking what they directly feel and think already, while also helping them move in a chosen, personally valued direction.

# HOW TO USE THIS BOOK

*Learning ACT* is designed to be used with other books on ACT concepts and methods. We recommend in particular the following:

Hayes, S. C., Strosahl, K. & Wilson, K. G. (1999). *Acceptance and commitment therapy: An experiential approach to behavior change.* New York: Guilford Press. [This is still the seminal ACT book and no ACT clinician should fail to have it and to read it.]

Hayes, S. C. & Strosahl, K. D. (2005). *A practical guide to acceptance and commitment therapy.* New York: Springer-Verlag. [Shows how to do ACT with a variety of populations.]

Eifert, G. & Forsyth, J. (2005). *Acceptance and commitment therapy for anxiety disorders.* Oakland: New Harbinger. [Although this is nominally for a specific population, it is also a strong, generally useful ACT protocol that shows how to mix ACT processes into a brief therapy for anxiety disorders.]

Hayes, S. C. & Smith, S. (2005). *Get out of your mind and into your life.* Oakland, CA: New Harbinger. [A general purpose ACT workbook. Can be useful in helping therapists new to ACT contact the work experientially and can readily be used as homework for clients.]

Hayes, S. C. (2007). *ACT in action.* Oakland, CA: New Harbinger. [A six DVD series with some of the best ACT therapists showing how to do ACT.]

In addition, there are many ACT books for specialized populations, both for therapists and for individuals. You can find a list at the website of the Association for Contextual Behavioral Science (www.contextualpsychology.org), which is *the* gateway to ACT research, clinical and theoretical publications, online discussions, trainings, institutes, conferences, manuals, protocols, metaphors, and networking. It is not only a valuable resource when learning and implementing this intervention, but is also useful for ongoing training and use of ACT.

In addition, www.learningact.com is specifically intended to support this book. It allows you to interact with other readers and contains additional guidance on learning ACT. The books and resources above are listed only to help readers find out more about ACT. *Learning ACT* is not endorsed by or affiliated with the other publishers of ACT books (e.g., Guilford Press; Springer-Verlag).

# ORGANIZATION OF THIS WORKBOOK

The introduction and first chapter of this workbook provide an overview of the theory behind ACT and some tools to help you think about cases from an ACT perspective. Specifically, chapter 1 outlines the ways in which basic learning processes, combined with the problematic effects of language, lead to increased suffering for humans. The ACT theory of change is also outlined in chapter 1. Chapters 2 through 7 and chapter 9 focus on the core competency areas to be learned by the ACT clinician. The first six of these chapters focus on the six core therapeutic processes, and the last one focuses on the therapeutic relationship in ACT. Each chapter includes a description of basic metaphors, stories, and techniques used in connection with that competency, as well as client/clinician demonstrations of each technique, and ends with a practical writing assignment in which you are asked to apply the principles you have learned to various sample client materials. Each chapter also addresses when to use the process discussed, how to address common problems that arise when implementing that process, and at least one experiential exercise. Chapter 8 begins the process of integrating all you have learned in the previous chapters by guiding you through case conceptualization and treatment planning from an ACT perspective and giving you an opportunity to apply an ACT model to practice cases.

In chapters 2 through 7, each of the ACT processes is presented largely as if it were separate. In actual sessions with clients, however, a single competency is rarely focused on alone; rather, multiple processes are explored and worked on within each session. Chapter 10 is intended to help you integrate use of the various ACT processes in sessions and to be flexible in doing so. Just as ACT attempts to build psychological flexibility in clients, we hope this workbook will increase your flexibility as a clinician in the application of ACT. Chapter 10 provides various exercises to help you develop this flexibility and also includes answers to some frequently asked questions about ACT.

The appendices form the last section of this workbook. Appendix A provides guidance to people learning ACT as a group, such as in a study group, classroom setting, or practicum. Experience has shown us that it is important to have a community to support therapists in their ACT work. Whether it is a group of friends or colleagues, a virtual community accessed through the Internet, a temporary course, or a relationship with a supervisor or mentor, this social/verbal community is essential in keeping you on track as a clinician, particularly as an ACT clinician. Fortunately or unfortunately, many of the ways of speaking or thinking that are part of the repertoire of an effective ACT clinician are not commonly seen in the culture. Many of the messages of the mainstream Western culture are so dominant and automatic, particularly those fostering "feelgoodism" (i.e., experiential control) and literal ways of interacting with thought, that without support from a social/verbal community versed in ACT, newer, less practiced repertoires of behaving and thinking based on ACT are less likely to be maintained over time.

# COMPANION DVD

The DVD complements the book by providing role-played examples of the core competencies, with trained actors playing the clients. We have created these examples to show both relatively skilled and relatively unskilled applications of the ACT methods and principles. Not all the competencies are covered on the DVD, but with the exception of chapter 8 (case conceptualization), examples are provided for chapters 2 through 10.

The DVD provides models of exercises and techniques in a manner that could not be adequately demonstrated in written form. One good way to use it is to play each clip and then pause the playback before the narrator describes what was being done. Try to determine what fit or did not fit with the ACT model in the clip, and only then let the narrator describe his or her thinking. This start-and-stop method is especially recommended for workshops or classroom use of the book and DVD package. We recommend reading the corresponding chapter in the book before watching a section of the DVD.

# USING THE PRACTICE EXERCISES IN THIS BOOK

Although reading about ACT techniques and skills is important, it is even more important to practice these skills in order to become an effective ACT clinician. Having extensive mental knowledge about a therapy can clearly set the stage for implementation; however, we ask you to go further with ACT. In ACT, it is not only verbal knowledge that will guide you through the therapy; knowing by experience (i.e., experiential knowledge) is also key to understanding and to providing quality implementation. Learning ACT is like attempting to learn the violin. You can read a book about how to hold the bow or how the musical scales function. However, simply reading about playing does not make you a violinist. Practice is essential. Although reading (verbal knowledge) can teach you "how to hold the bow," the exercises in this book are designed to help you begin to play the violin (experiential knowledge).

At the end of each of the chapters 2 through 7, we have included a section entitled Core Competency Practice, in which we provide practice exercises based on transcripts of hypothetical clients. Many of the cases presented in this book are based on actual clients or amalgamations of clients; in every case, certain aspects have been changed to protect the person's identity. These exercises give you the opportunity to formulate and practice responding to hypothetical clients prior to doing so with real clients. In the exercises, you are asked to generate your own responses and then to compare them with the suggested responses consistent with ACT that are given at the end of that chapter.

In addition to the practice exercises, experiential exercises are presented in each chapter. These exercises are intended for you to do as practice and are of a personal nature. By "experiential," we mean that their purpose is to help you find the ACT space, stance, or psychological posture from which you as an ACT clinician are likely to be most effective. The nature of these exercises is deeply connected to the nature of the therapy.

In ACT, we ask clients to engage fully in the process of being willing to experience all that is offered experientially, including the difficult and the negative. We ask them to do this with the goal of living rich and valued lives. We would like to ask you to do the same by engaging the experiential exercises presented in this workbook fully and openly, interacting with them in a way that connects you to yourself. We have attempted to include as many interactive exercises in this book as possible, and we encourage you to use all of them. Although it may be tempting to skip ahead to learn other material, we encourage you to notice that curiosity, stick with the material at hand, and engage in the exercises in the order they are presented in the book. If you do skip ahead, we suggest you later come back and complete the exercises so that you can extract the full value of this volume.

# BEGINNING TO USE ACT

We have several recommendations about beginning to use this therapy. First, before you begin to put this approach into practice with your clients, we recommend that you have a good sense of the entire ACT model. Although, as we mentioned, the therapeutic processes are presented as if they were separate, they are actually interdependent. Missing a basic understanding of one process could lead to difficulties implementing other processes, to confusion, and to dead ends in therapy. In addition, without an overall understanding of the approach, the therapist can easily introduce inconsistencies that might undermine the overall thrust of the intervention. For most clinicians, it is helpful to have read the original ACT book (Hayes et al., 1999) to establish a good sense of understanding about the whole model. If you have done that carefully, you may find it workable to begin to apply methods in this book as you go. If this is your first book on ACT, however, you should read it cover to cover before using these methods with your clients.

Second, we recommend allowing time for a period of growth with the theory and therapy. You may experience some disruption in your practice when you begin to use these approaches, particularly if you have been operating from control-based theories of intervention. It is not at all uncommon for practitioners drawn to this work to initially feel awkward, confused, and anxious in applying ACT. A recent effectiveness study with beginning therapists in general outpatient practice showed that, compared with traditional cognitive behavioral therapy (CBT), doing ACT tended to produce more anxiety in therapists, slower reduction of anxiety with experience in applying these methods, and significantly better clinical outcomes in patients (Lappalainen et al., in press). Especially because this seems to suggest that clinician anxiety and awkwardness do not eliminate effectiveness, we recommend you try to "make room" for the discomfort you may experience in implementing ACT and continue to apply the new techniques. Self-help ACT books, such as *Get Out of Your Mind and Into Your Life* (Hayes & Smith, 2005), may be of use in applying ACT to this process. Time and effort, combined with openness, will eventually produce a greater sense of wholeness, but we do caution that the sense of vulnerability in doing ACT never completely disappears. ACT asks clinicians to stand with another human being, undefended and open. There is a rawness and richness to this process that cannot be avoided without undoing the work itself.

Third, we recommend two basic ways to begin to incorporate ACT into your practice. One is to begin by implementing ACT based on one of the standardized manuals available in a variety of forms, including the books listed under "How to Use This Book" and on the website www.contextualpsychology .org. Ideally, you can follow the manual from beginning to end with a client who presents with problems matching the specific treatment discussed in that manual. A second approach is to begin implementing ACT with a client with whom you find yourself struggling. If it is a difficult client, which is often the case, this may be a counterintuitive place to begin; however, because your old repertoire has already been failing in an important way, you will find yourself in the same place as the client: stuck. Giving ACT a try can allow you to see whether something new can happen to free up the therapy process.

Fourth, we recommend attending an experiential ACT workshop. This is truly one of the best ways to learn this particular intervention. ACT is centered on living fully with all experience—both negative and positive—and on the freedom and richness that purposeful living can bring. Attending a workshop can help create these events in your life, both in your personal way of being in the world and in your work with clients, and can provide an intuitive guide for the *function* of ACT processes, not just the *form* of these processes. ACT trainings and workshops are listed at www.contextualpsychology.org.

Finally, you should know that ACT is based on a large body of scholarly and research work in the fields of philosophy of science, basic psychology, psychopathology, and clinical intervention. In this book, we deliberately use relatively informal language because our purpose is intensely practical and skills focused. As your skills in ACT grow, you may find reading the broader body of research deepens your understanding. Practitioners who attend their first ACT conference are often startled to find workshops and sessions on RFT, behavioral principles, and contextualistic philosophy of science. Perhaps even more startling, after gaining some experience, clinicians themselves begin to demand these sessions and are often enthusiastic about their practical usefulness. In this book, we use clinical and common sense terms, generally without stopping to link them to basic principles. For example, we speak easily of mind, without delving into the work done in RFT labs to identify the component behavioral skills involved in this commonsense domain. You can satisfy your interest by reading more in the ACT and RFT literature.

If you connect deeply to the work, you will eventually learn that ACT is part of an attempt to restructure psychology itself. If you are concerned with immediate practical purposes, this book can help you learn enough about ACT to care about that larger context. Most important, we hope that reading—or perhaps the word would be "doing"—this book will help you learn enough about ACT to begin to use these methods with clients who can benefit from them.

# CHAPTER 1

# THE SIX CORE PROCESSES OF ACT AND THEIR COMMON TARGET

*Pay no attention to that man behind the curtain.*

—The Wizard of Oz

The blessing and the curse of human existence is language. All of the processes in ACT flow from this insight, and from the basic research that led to it.

From an ACT point of view, the primary source of psychopathology and human unhappiness is the way language and cognition interact with the circumstances of our lives to produce an inability to persist or to make changes that are in the service of long-term valued ends. This kind of psychological inflexibility emerges when people use language tools in instances when those tools are not helpful, or use them in ineffective or problematic ways. Language and logical or rational thinking are useful in so many ways that it is easy to overextend their use into areas of living in which they are neither needed nor helpful.

There is no doubt that language is a blessing. Imagine you were in a room where all the exits were locked, and you were offered one and only one chance to attempt to escape. Your task in this scenario would be to decide on a course of action, but you would not be allowed to take this action until you had announced your plan. Under this circumstance, you would probably put your mind to work evaluating your various options and their predicted consequences, and then you would announce the one most likely to succeed. If you took a moment to reflect on the plan your mind developed, you might discover you had such ideas as using a cell phone to call for help, kicking down the door, calling to your spouse in the next room, or breaking the window and jumping to the ground. Using only thought, you could consider the risks associated with each of these plans. For example, you could consider such questions as, "What if the door is too stout to be kicked in?" or "What if no one answers the phone?" Using only your mind, you could fully formulate your plan and explain why this plan would be most likely to succeed.

This example contains all the elements humans need to do well in the external world by using their verbal and cognitive skills. A complex situation is broken down into its components and features. Those components and features set the occasion for imagined actions, predictions, and evaluations, and a plan is chosen based on likely outcomes.

This process of verbal problem solving offers a huge evolutionary advantage: it has allowed human beings to take over the planet even though they are weak, slow, and poorly defended. These same powerful abilities, however, can easily bestow a huge disadvantage. Suppose, instead of being trapped in a room, you were trapped in a feeling of intense anxiety or impending doom. Again, your task would be to find a way out. The same problem-solving abilities could be brought to bear that would provide solutions (e.g., take a tranquilizer, suppress the anxiety, or engage in self-injury) and would deliver possible outcomes, such as escaping from the feelings. This time, however, ACT research suggests that the very solution designed to solve the problem would become the problem (Hayes, Luoma, Bond, Masuda, & Lillis, 2006). You would now be engaging in a core pathological process known in the ACT model as *experiential avoidance*. Yet this "curse" would be virtually identical to the blessing in the locked room example.

The work on which this book is based makes it clear that the same things that work well in the external world can easily create harm when turned toward the internal world. For example, if we don't like peeling paint, we can scrape the wall and put on a fresh coat. On the other hand, if we don't like thinking of a past trauma and try to "scrape it away," we may make it more central, more salient, and more influential. If we fear a future drought, we might save water to quench our future thirst. But if we fear future rejection and try to make sure no one will ever hurt us in that way again, we may detune our relationships or avoid making commitments, thus amplifying the role of rejection in our lives.

ACT is based on basic behavioral principles and their expansion into human language and cognition, as explained by Relational Frame Theory (RFT; Hayes et al., 2001). RFT explains the origin of our verbal abilities. We need to understand this theory in general terms because all of ACT is linked to it. This understanding also clarifies why ACT, which is in one sense part of cognitive behavioral therapy (CBT), differs so dramatically from traditional CBT.

RFT explains that we learn as small children to relate events to each other based on social convention. By an "event" we mean any experience a person has, such as seeing an object, smelling an odor, touching another person, having a thought, or feeling an emotion. As a result of training by the social/verbal community, we learn to respond to an event based on its ascribed relation to another event, rather than simply based on the physical properties of those events. An example illustrates this concept. Before language abilities are strong, a small child will prefer a nickel over a dime because the nickel is bigger, and will cry when given a dime instead of a nickel. A more verbally mature child will prefer a dime over a nickel because the dime is purportedly "bigger," and will cry when given a nickel instead of a dime, even if the child has never actually used a dime to acquire goods. Thus, the functions of the coins (the events in this example) are based solely on social whim or convention, which arbitrarily declares that a nickel is "smaller" than a dime.

The flexibility of relational skills in humans allows us to go beyond the nonarbitrary relations that exist in the physical world, but we do this so seamlessly that the world itself becomes thoroughly entangled in our relational actions. We can say "skinny is better than fat," and the "better than" in this statement seems to be the same as "bigger than" in the statement "the elephant is bigger than the mouse." The relation (in this example, an evaluation) seems to be in the object itself, rather than in the arbitrary history of social training. Once these abilities gain strength, we create vast relational networks and increasingly live in a world whose functions are verbally acquired, not based on direct experience. This can trap us into culturally and socially derived modes of living and relating that are not chosen and that may not always be workable. In this way, language works behind the scenes to structure our world.

ACT, on the other hand, works to reveal the illusion of language and to uncover "the man behind the curtain." What we refer to as the "mind" is, from the perspective of RFT, not a "thing" at all, but rather a collection of relational abilities. Although this ability to relate events—for example, by thinking, planning, judging, evaluating, or remembering—has both a light and a dark side, the process is remarkably similar on both sides. What is different are the context and the targeted domain. Literal language and cognition are tools, but they are not fitting tools for all purposes.

Fortunately, RFT suggests not just how language and higher cognition develop and why they are a help and a hindrance, but also how to rein in these abilities so we can use them and not be used by them. RFT points to the source of verbal and cognitive excesses. Researchers are increasingly able to use the insights RFT provides to train important verbal and cognitive skills, such as teaching children to make logical comparisons (Berens & Hayes, in press) or to establish a sense of self as perspective (McHugh, Barnes-Holmes, & Barnes-Holmes, 2004; Rehfeldt, Dillen, Ziomek, & Kowalchuck, 2007).

RFT concepts provide a foundation for the core processes that are thought to lead to psychopathology from an ACT point of view. In essence, the problem is that literal language leads to increases in pain and the tendency to overextend a problem-solving mode of thinking as a way to solve that pain. As a result, we try to escape and avoid our feelings, we become entangled in our thinking, we lose contact with the present, and we begin to believe and defend our own stories about ourselves. Meanwhile, what we really want is put on hold or drifts to the background, and committed action is made more difficult. In short, an overextension of human language leads to a rigid, psychologically inflexible way of living. From an ACT/RFT point of view, these core processes produce or exacerbate human suffering. We turn now to a more detailed examination of these processes.

# THE ACT MODEL OF PSYCHOPATHOLOGY

The overall ACT model of psychopathology can be illustrated in the form of a hexagon (figure 1-1), with each point on the hexagon corresponding to one of the six processes hypothesized to contribute to or cause much of human suffering and psychopathology (Hayes et al., 2006). At the center of this diagram is psychological inflexibility, which is simply a term used to refer to the interaction of all these processes. Although ACT acknowledges that specific pathological processes are associated with particular disorders, it also holds that these general processes cut across traditional boundaries of what we call *psychopathology* and may account for much of the comorbidity in what many describe as discrete disorders.

## Experiential Avoidance

*Experiential avoidance*, also called *experiential control*, is the attempt to control or alter the form, frequency, or situational sensitivity of internal experiences (i.e., thoughts, feelings, sensations, or memories), even when doing so causes behavioral harm (Hayes, Wilson, Gifford, Follette, & Strosahl, 1996). From an ACT/RFT point of view, experiential avoidance emerges naturally from our abilities to evaluate, predict, and avoid events. In other words, it is fed by an entanglement with language and cognition. Language is useful in the external world, in part because external events can be predicted, evaluated, and avoided. Nothing prevents these language skills from expanding from the external world to the world within. There is essentially no difference between the cognitive processes involved in escaping a locked room and those used to escape an urge to use drugs, or between the cognitive processes used to predict an absence of food and those used to predict a panic attack.

Our predictive and evaluative abilities lead us to sort emotions, thoughts, bodily sensations, and memories into positive and negative categories. These experiences are then sought or avoided, in part, on this basis. Unfortunately, direct attempts to avoid or alter experiences can have paradoxical effects in certain contexts.

Let's begin with the process of avoiding a negative thought. Suppose it is very, very important not to think something. Deliberate attempts to control the emergence of this thought involve a verbal rule: do not think "X." Whatever the X may be, however, specifying X will tend to evoke X. Not thinking of a lake evokes thoughts of a lake; not thinking of a baby evokes thoughts of a baby. This happens simply because these verbal events are related to the actual events, and because some of the properties of the actual events transfer to the verbal event (e.g., when you hear the word "baby," you might see an image of a baby in your mind).

The same thing tends to occur with emotions. Part of this is due to the verbal rule we just discussed. Thus, trying to control anxiety involves thinking of anxiety, which tends to evoke anxiety. But part of it is due to the verbal reasons behind these control efforts. Usually, anxiety is said to be something to avoid because of a long list of undesirable consequences; you may think, "I will make a fool of myself" or "I will go crazy" or "I will have a heart attack" or "I will not be able to function." But the natural emotional response to such consequences includes (you guessed it) anxiety.

For these reasons and several others, experiential avoidance tends to be both unhelpful and self-amplifying over the long term, although not, sad to say, over the short term. A person handling anxiety

## Figure 1.1: An ACT Model of Psychopathology

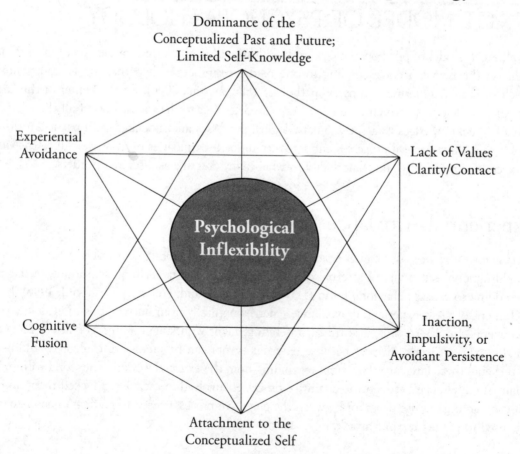

by drinking may "get away with it" for years; a person avoiding fearful situations may feel relieved in the moment and only gradually notice the constriction of his or her life space. Furthermore, some experiential avoidance seems to feed and be fed by cultural processes. A person avoiding fear of rejection by buying fashionable clothes is seemingly supporting the culture and its economic engines. Perhaps for similar reasons, experiential avoidance is often amplified by the social/cultural community, which promotes the idea that healthy humans do not have psychological pain (e.g., stress, depression, memories of trauma) and specifies the actions that need to be taken to avoid such negative private events. In Western culture, at least, the general social focus is on "feeling good." Sometimes it even goes further than this: not only should we feel good, but we're *entitled* to feel good! Avoidant solutions, such as alcohol, drugs, and mindless sex, are modeled in television shows, commercials, and other media, and a general "feel goodism" is promoted by the culture.

Sadly, perhaps, feeling good is often at the very heart of the mental health model. The very names of our disorders and treatments reveal this connection. We diagnose disorders based upon the presence of particular configurations of private events and experiences. For example, self-critical thoughts, suicidal thoughts, and feelings of fatigue are part of depression. Then we construct treatments designed to eliminate these symptoms, ostensibly with the goal of returning the person to good health. Unfortunately, all of this has the risk of feeding the message of "feel goodism."

## Cognitive Fusion

In general terms, *cognitive fusion* refers to the tendency of human beings to get caught up in the content of what they are thinking so that it dominates over other useful sources of behavioral regulation. By "thinking" we mean anything that is symbolic or relational in an arbitrarily applicable sense; this includes, for example, words, gestures, thoughts, signs, images, and some properties of emotions.

The word *fuse* comes from a word that means "to pour." Metaphorically, it is as if the content of cognition and the world about which we are thinking are poured together until they are one, in much the same way that lemons, water, and sugar can together become lemonade. But when thinking and the world about which we are thinking are treated as one thing, thinking habits can dictate how we react to the world, and we can miss that the structure being imposed on the world by thought is an active process. It is something we *do*.

It has long been known that behavior controlled by some verbal rules tends to be rigid and inflexible (see Hayes, 1989, for a book-length review). Most forms of psychological intervention realize this, and following a logical path, try to solve the problem by changing the verbal rules (i.e., changing the thoughts). Unfortunately, that misses the core of the problem. It is not so much that an incorrect rule is being used, but rather that a verbally interpreted event is two things appearing to be one: the event and the interpretation of the event. We conflate the meaning of thoughts with the literal events thought about, missing the ongoing process of thinking itself. From an ACT/RFT point of view, it is not *what* we think that is most troublesome; it is *how* we relate to what we think.

Imagine that thoughts are like a pair of sunglasses you forgot you were wearing. They color your view of the world, and you are unaware it is being colored. The trouble with this is that thoughts are then free to present you with a world structured through thought—a world seen through this color. You are dealing with the world as it is directly experienced to be, and missing that you are "languaging" about it. For example, when people with obsessive-compulsive disorder think, "If I don't wash my hands, my family will be contaminated," they can become so focused on the world colored by that thought that they are seemingly not interacting with a thought at all. They are dealing with contamination and its consequences (e.g., that their family will die), not with a thought.

All languaging occurs in a context, and language and cognition only have particular functions within particular contexts. Because symbolic thinking is so broadly useful to human problem solving and to ecological success, however, most successful cultures have vastly overextended the contexts that give language its automatic functions. For most practical purposes, it is useful to treat words as if they were what they said they were. When you think of walking on the beach, it usually does not do any harm to experience reactions that are like that of an actual walk on the beach, but in a less vivid form. You may "see" the water in your mind's eye and "feel" the wind on your skin. This process is helpful in most contexts, such as the one experienced when you thought about how to escape from a locked room. Because of social training and support, we typically see the world from the vantage point of thoughts, rather than observing thoughts directly. Seeing the world as structured through thought is fine for activities such as doing your taxes or fixing a car or planting crops. It is often not as helpful, however, when appreciating sunsets or figuring out how to achieve peace of mind.

Think back to the earlier example of wondering how to escape from a room. If you really became engaged in the task, you were probably not aware of what you were physically doing at the moment. You probably did not particularly notice your foot or the chair in which you sat or the texture and color of the paper on which these words are written. Your attentional focus narrowed: you were focused on planning your escape.

This is what happens with cognitive fusion. Verbal/cognitive constructions substitute for direct contact with events. We forget we are interacting with thoughts, rather than with the real thing. The past can present itself as if occurring now, although it is dead and gone. The future can become present here and now, even though it is there and then. The present moment is lost to the mind's focus on the past and the future. We are constantly interacting with the world as cognitively organized, without noticing that we are constantly organizing it.

When a depressed client imagines how he or she might fall apart because of the stress of another day at work, that person is seemingly dealing with the problem of literally falling apart, just as you were moments ago seemingly dealing with a locked room. If the literal functions of that thought dominate over all other possible functions, the issue may become how to avoid falling apart, and not any of a thousand other possible responses or situational issues. Thus, psychological and behavioral flexibility are lost. This might result in the client not going to work, oversleeping, or withdrawing from challenges or colleagues at work—all typical behaviors that are part of what we call *depression*. The danger is that when a client fuses with verbal content, that content can have almost total dominance over the person's behavior, limiting other possible sources of influence, such as the therapist, newer and weaker verbal repertoires, or direct contingencies in the environment.

The overextension of language has several important contextual sources. Initially, language begins within a *context of literality*, which is the social/verbal context that establishes certain sounds we hear (the spoken word "lemon") and certain pictures we see (an image of a lemon) as words or thoughts with meaning. The social community expands this repertoire in other ways, as well. For example, most children are exposed to early demands to justify and explain their actions. This helps the social/verbal community have access to children's reasoning skills, and helps keep children's actions within the bounds of what can be verbally justified within a cultural community. Children and adults are expected to have reasons to justify and explain their actions. These often take the form of verbal statements of cause and effect, such as saying, "I stayed in bed *because* I was depressed."

Unfortunately, this context of literality also tends to support the idea that reasons are literal causes; for example, we think depression *caused* staying in bed. After all, this notion of a literal cause is what answers to "why" questions seem to address. In effect, verbally constructed why answers are considered "real" simply because the verbal community treats them that way. Reasons that begin as explanations for behavior later come to exert control over our behavior because of this social context of reason giving. Our lives become entangled with an ever-larger network of verbal formulations, as every aspect of our lives is analyzed and categorized (Addis & Jacobson, 1996).

In addition, many answers to why questions point to difficult private experiences. For example, meetings are missed because "they were forgotten" or tasks are avoided "because we are afraid." This formulation is rarely challenged. It is almost rude to ask, "Why did you forget?" or "Why didn't you just feel the fear and still do it?" Thus, the context of reason giving quickly expands into a context of experiential control. The logical next step is to try to remove troublesome private experiences in order to gain more behavioral control by, for instance, getting rid of forgetting and of being afraid. The dominant Western culture teaches us that private experiences can be dangerous and thus need to be controlled. For example, think of the father who tells his son, "Don't be afraid. Only babies are afraid."

Cognitive fusion is combined with culturally supported messages of the causal effect of private events, their dangerous nature, and the need and supposed ability to control them. For example, a person thinking "I will fall apart" will believe that this thought is part of the process of literally falling apart—thoughts are causes. We are taught such things as "anxiety is bad," as if feelings themselves were dangerous. We are told as youngsters to "stop crying or I will give you something to cry about," as if emotional control were reasonable and obvious. It would be interesting if, as children, we were able to respond to the adult and show the stupidity of the command by saying, "Stop being bothered by my crying or I will give you something to be bothered about." All of these cultural messages only serve to give thoughts an even more dominant and excessive effect on action.

## Dominance of the Conceptualized Past and Future; Limited Self-Knowledge

Fusion and avoidance tend to pull us out of the present moment. This is problematic in two ways. First, the ongoing, flexible awareness of private experiences is reduced. Knowledge about what we are feeling, thinking, sensing, and remembering in the moment will often be punished because such an awareness will lead to contact with experiences of fear, anger, sadness, and so on, given the breadth of human responding. It is for these reasons that experiential avoidance and alexithymia and related processes are highly correlated (Hayes et al., 2004; Hayes et al., 2006).

Second, fusion, in particular, leads to less contact with the present moment. We noted earlier that, as we enter the world as conceptualized, we tend to lose awareness of our nonconceptual, direct, and current experience. Metaphorically, getting out of the locked room becomes more central, and the awareness of breathing and other sensations becomes less so. The conceptualized past or future dominates over the present. A client may ruminate about past wrongs or fearful futures. Daydreaming takes the place of effective action. Pouring over every minor hurt stands in the place of intimacy and connection in the moment. Without adequate contact with the present moment, behavior tends to be dominated by historically programmed thoughts and reactions, resulting in more of the same behavior that occurred in the past. New possibilities are foreclosed.

## Attachment to the Conceptualized Self

Probably nothing is as great a focus of verbal processes as oneself. From an early age, children are asked many questions about themselves such as how old they are, what they like, what they want to be when they grow up, and what they enjoy in school. Children are harassed into answering why questions, as if the answers were already available and only shyness prevented full and revealing answers. In fact, children have little to say at first about such things. Why questions are met honestly with the answer "just because," and other complicated queries about self-knowledge lead to an equally honest "I don't know." Eventually, however, more coherent and entertaining stories are told. The past is formulated and described. The future is predicted and evaluated. Within this storytelling process is a *conceptualized self* (Hayes et al., 1999): the individual and his or her attributes are described and analyzed. Because children quickly learn that changing stories without good cause is frowned upon, the stories become more stable over time. By the time a client comes in for therapy, this process has woven a spider's web of categories, interpretations, evaluations, and expectations regarding the self.

We have stories to tell about what we've done and what we like, about why we have problems and what would function as solutions, and about how we are and how we differ from others. Typically, all of these stories have some truth to them. The problem is that the truth about which we are speaking is not necessarily useful or helpful; rather, it is a truth that can be justified by the correspondence between the verbal formulations and the supposedly objective facts of the matter. In other words, these stories are considered true because they are "right," not necessarily because they are helpful in living.

Consider a typical client who comes in saying, "I am an agoraphobic. I've been this way for twelve years, ever since my husband beat me and then abandoned me with my then two-year-old child. My parents tried to help, but they were so critical that it only made it worse. Ever since, I have had terrible anxiety. I cannot function as a result of it, and I'm too fearful to handle it. I am thinking about anxiety all the time." All of these events could be 100 percent true, but what is more important is that the person has fused with a self-focused story and is trying to solve problems within that story. Instead of a flexible, complex human being, we are dealing with a self-created cartoon: "I *am* an agoraphobic." It is not that "I feel fear," but that "I *am* a diagnostic category." In the statement "I *am* too fearful," the word "too" implies that "who I am" is somehow illegitimate.

The problem is that real solutions may not exist within this story, and yet the story is so well supported that all possible ways out of it would be experienced as invalidating. The conceptualized self has become narrow and cage-like, and inflexible behavior patterns are the unavoidable result.

## Lack of Values Clarity/Contact

Values are chosen qualities of life that are represented by ongoing patterns of behavior. Ultimately, values are about living in a chosen and meaningful way; they are the compass heading we can use to guide our lives. Values are not to be evaluated themselves, but serve as the chosen standard by which other things can be evaluated. Valuing is a partially verbal process, not a logical or rational one; it involves choosing, assuming, creating, and postulating. This is not how we typically set life goals. Often goals are established mindlessly or are created through evaluating reasons (e.g., lists of pros and cons) and then selected based on the "best" ones. Although this may be useful in many cases, unfortunately many of these reasons are tied to ultimately unimportant process goals (e.g., being right, avoiding pain, or pleasing others), rather than to pursuing a meaningfully chosen path in life.

To the extent that behavior is tied up in experiential avoidance, a person will have a hard time contacting what really matters in his or her life. It's painful to care, and if one has a life history filled with losses, regrets, or failures, it might be easier to avoid caring. In particular, people who were raised in chaotic families, in which life was unpredictable and often disappointing, may avoid constructing valued futures in order to avoid more loss and pain. They may never have solidly established a behavioral repertoire of verbally constructing valued futures, or such values may have been suppressed by pain. Either way, valuing is absent or weak.

# Inaction, Impulsivity, or Avoidant Persistence

Associated with fusion, avoidance, a conceptualized self, and loss of the present moment is the inability to behave effectively with regard to chosen values. Impulsivity or rigid persistence is manifested instead of flexible actions directed toward long-term ends.

Short-term goals, such as feeling good, being right, and defending a conceptualized self, can become so dominant that the long-term desired qualities of life (i.e., values) take a backseat. People lose contact with what they want in life, beyond relief from psychological pain. A whole life can be consumed by process goals, such as defending oneself from anxiety, handling depression, or defending one's self-esteem, rather than many other possible outcome goals that could have greater meaning, depth, and vitality. A person is metaphorically consumed with always sharpening the axe, never getting the chance to actually put it to use chopping trees and building the home in which they longed to live.

Patterns of action can emerge that are detached from long-term desired qualities and gradually dominate in a person's repertoire. Sometimes this appears in the form of a weak overall life direction. For example, a person may lack effective involvement in work, close relationships with family and friends, healthy exercise and nutrition habits, recreation and leisure activities, or meaningful spiritual practices. Often, the pattern presents itself as a lack of vitality and a sense that the person has "checked out" of his or her own life.

Behavioral repertoires narrow and become less sensitive to the possibilities for valued action in the current environment. Persistence and change in the service of effectiveness is less likely.

# SIX CORE THERAPEUTIC PROCESSES OF ACT

ACT targets each of the core problems just described, with the general goal of increasing *psychological flexibility*; that is, the ability to contact the present moment more fully as a conscious human being, and based on what the situation affords, to change or persist in behavior in order to serve valued ends (Hayes & Strosahl, 2005). Psychological flexibility is established through six core ACT processes, as shown in figure 1-2. Each of these areas is conceptualized as a positive psychological skill, not merely as a method of avoiding psychopathology.

## Acceptance

*Acceptance* of private events is taught as an alternative to experiential avoidance. It involves the active and aware embrace of private events that are occasioned by our history, without unnecessary attempts to change their frequency or form, especially when doing so would cause psychological harm. For example, clients experiencing anxiety are taught to feel anxiety as a feeling, fully and without defense; clients experiencing pain are given methods that encourage them to let go of their struggle with pain.

Acceptance in ACT is not an end in itself. Rather, acceptance is fostered as a method of increasing values-based action. Acceptance methods in ACT involve exercises that encourage rich, flexible interaction with previously avoided experience. For example, emotions are turned into described objects, complex reactions are broken down into experiential elements, and attention is given to relatively subtle aspects of an avoided event. These look to a certain extent like exposure exercises, but with the additional purpose of increasing willingness and response flexibility, rather than diminishing emotional responding.

# Cognitive Defusion

ACT is one of the cognitive and behavioral therapies, but like other so-called third generation CBT approaches (Hayes, 2004), it does not embrace the theoretical core of traditional CBT—namely, that clients need to rid themselves of negative feelings and distorted or unrealistic thoughts before profound behavior change is likely. From an RFT point of view, the problem is this: efforts to change relational networks (i.e., patterns of thinking) generally expand these networks and make the event (e.g., the thought or emotion) on which the person is focused even more important. In technical terms, a relational context is generally also a functional context.

Generally, clients are overly focused on negative private experiences. They have, in effect, narrowed their behavioral repertoire. Focusing even more attention on this area may not be maximally helpful. The job of permanently and thoroughly changing cognitive content is difficult because thoughts are historical; often automatic; and in clinical areas at least, generally well established. Altering them can take a long time even when successful, and they are still not really gone—as shown by the tendency for older verbal/cognitive networks to reemerge under stress (Wilson & Hayes, 1996). Furthermore, clients are quite prepared to attempt to suppress or eliminate negative thoughts and feelings, which may result in paradoxical effects, at times actually increasing the frequency, intensity, and behavioral regulatory powers of these experiences (Wenzlaff & Wegner, 2000). Although cognitive change techniques are typically not meant to be suppressive, this tendency adds risk to the use of cognitive change strategies. Very little data suggest that cognitive disputation and change are either helpful or a key pathway to behavior change; to date, studies suggest these methods are relatively inert, or in some cases even harmful (Dimidjian et al., 2006; Jacobson et al., 1996).

Fortunately, RFT suggests that we do not need to change the content of thought in order to change the function of thought in our lives. The typical contexts of literality, reason giving, and emotional control normally determine the function of thought on behavior. In this normal context, the effects of thinking on action are machine-like; that is, thoughts or feelings seem to cause actions just as one billiard ball striking a second causes the second ball to move. Therefore, to change the action, we must change the thought. However, with a contextual view, we can see that the effects of thinking are only mechanical-seeming: they *seem* to cause actions, but in truth do not. Rather, particular thoughts are tied to particular actions or thoughts only within a given context. Thus, by creating other contexts (e.g., through defusion or experiential acceptance), the impact of thoughts can be altered without first having to change their form. There is no need to change the thought. Indeed, studies are beginning to suggest that contextual strategies may more quickly lead to lasting behavior change than will strategies directly targeting the content of thoughts and feelings (Hayes et al., 2006). From an ACT perspective, when clients engage in struggling with their own private experiences as if their lives depended upon it (as appears to be the case when thoughts are taken literally) and create stories to justify and explain their actions, the result can be an amplification of suffering and a rigidity of responding, both of which can be difficult to overcome. A major reason for this effect is that these very efforts create pervasive and rigid contexts of literality, reason giving, and emotional control. It is these contexts that ACT techniques target.

*Defusion* is an invented word meaning to undo fusion, or "de-fusion," and refers to the process of creating nonliteral contexts in which language can be seen as an active, ongoing, relational process that is historical in nature and present in the current moment. That is, language can be observed in the moment as language: we can watch what the mind says, rather than be a slave to it. A word is viewed as a word, not as what it seems to mean. Creating this nonliteral context loosens the relationship to thought, creating greater flexibility. We do not have to be driven by our words.

Technically, defusion is perhaps one of the most unique features of ACT. Scores of defusion techniques have been developed for a wide variety of clinical presentations. For example, a negative thought can be watched dispassionately, repeated out loud until only its sound remains, or it can be treated as an externally observed event by giving it a shape, size, color, speed, or form. The result of defusion is usually a decrease in believability of or attachment to the thought, rather than an immediate change in its frequency. Additionally, defusion is not a process of eliminating thinking or the impact of thoughts. The point is to have a more mindful perspective on thoughts, which increases behavioral flexibility linked to chosen values. We are not speaking of mindlessness or intuition or the elimination of rationality.

Defusion techniques all have the goal of catching language processes in flight and bringing them under contextual control, so that when needed, they can be looked *at* rather than looked *from*.

## Being Present

ACT promotes ongoing, nonjudgmental contact with psychological and environmental events as they occur. The goal is *present moment awareness*. When in contact with the present moment, humans are flexible, responsive, and aware of the possibilities and learning opportunities afforded by the current situation. Compared with living in the conceptualized past or future, present moment awareness is more direct, less conceptual, less fused, and more responsive. Without adequate contact with the present moment, behavior tends to be more dominated by fusion, avoidance, and reason giving, resulting in more of the same behavior that occurred in the past. New possibilities are foreclosed.

A sense of self called *self as process* (Hayes et al., 1999) is actively encouraged, and is characterized by the defused, nonjudgmental, ongoing description of thoughts, feelings, and other private events. An open sense of mindfulness is encouraged as well, so we can learn to notice more fully the rich set of interactions that are afforded in any given moment.

## Self as Context

From an RFT perspective, it is argued that language training (i.e., deictic relational frames, such as "I versus you," "now versus then," and "here versus there") establishes a sense of self as a boundaryless locus. From this perspective, self is more like a context or arena for experience, than like an experience itself. In the words of Hayes et al. (1999),

When people are asked many questions about their history or experience, the only thing that will be consistent is not the content of the answer, but the context or perspective in which the answer occurs. "I" in some meaningful sense is the location that is left when all the content differences are subtracted. (p. 185)

For example, consider what is common among the following questions: "What did you eat?" "What do you want?" "To whom did you talk?" "When did you do that?" "Why did you do that?" Only the location of the answer: the same I who will answer all the questions.

Through experiential exercises and metaphor, ACT helps us contact this sense of *self as context*—a continuous and secure I from which events are experienced, but that is also distinct from those events. This process helps us disentangle from the word machine. The goal is to help us develop a more solid sense of ourselves as observers or experiencers, independent of the particular experience being had at the moment.

# Figure 1.2: Six Core Therapeutic Processes of ACT

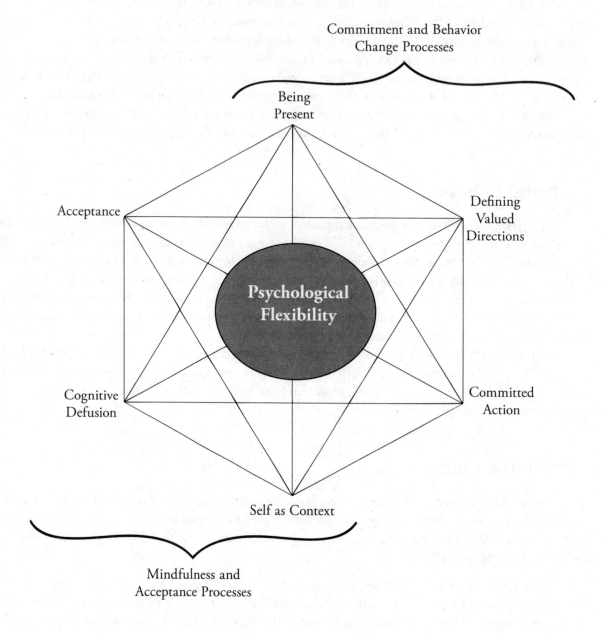

Commitment and Behavior
Change Processes

Being
Present

Defining
Valued
Directions

Acceptance

Psychological
Flexibility

Committed
Action

Cognitive
Defusion

Self as Context

Mindfulness and
Acceptance Processes

Additionally, because the limits of consciousness and awareness cannot be contacted within consciousness or awareness, human language leads to a sense of transcendence, a spiritual aspect of normal human experience. Establishing this transcendent sense of self can also be helpful in decreasing attachment to content. This idea was one of the seeds from which both ACT and RFT grew (Hayes, 1984), and there is evidence of its importance to the language functions that underlie such phenomena as empathy, compassion, and theory of mind (Barnes-Holmes, Hayes, & Dymond, 2001; Barnes-Holmes, Hayes, & Gregg, 2001; McHugh et al., 2004). In ACT, a transcendent sense of self is important, in part, because we can be aware from this standpoint of our own flow of experiences, without attachment to them. Defusion and acceptance are thus fostered by this naturalistic, spiritual side of human experience.

# Defining Valued Directions

The previously described ACT processes are mostly aimed at undermining language in areas of l    ̣    ̣
in which language is relatively ineffective. The processes of values clarification and commitment are focused on strengthening language in those areas in which language is most likely to be effectively applied. Values clarification asks us to step back from everyday problems of life and take a look at what gives our lives meaning, to look for the larger possibilities that dignify our struggles and can guide constructive action.

Values are chosen actions that can never be obtained as an object, but can be instantiated moment by moment. They are combinations of gerunds and adverbs, not nouns (e.g., to relate *lovingly* or to participate *honestly*). ACT uses a variety of exercises to help clients choose life directions in various domains (e.g., family, career, spirituality), while undermining verbal processes that might lead to choices based on experiential avoidance, social compliance, and cognitive fusion. For example, none of these are values in the ACT sense: "I would feel guilty if I did not value Q," "I value Z because my mother wants me to," "I should value X," and "A good person would value Y." The first is avoidant, the second compliant, and the last two fused. Values are choices. Values are the answer to the question, "In a world where you could choose to have your life be about something, what would you choose?" (Wilson & Murrell, 2004, p. 135).

Values are the lynchpin of ACT because the truth and utility of ACT depend on them. In ACT, acceptance, defusion, being present, and the other core processes are not ends in themselves; rather, they clear the path for a more vital, values-consistent life.

ACT takes a stance toward truth that is based on a particular form of pragmatic philosophy called *functional contextualism*. Truth is defined on the basis of workability, and workability in turn is linked to chosen values. In the more typical, mechanistic worldview, literality is the context that defines truth, and that truth is a type of correspondence-based truth. Using the metaphor of a map, if the marks on the map accurately indicate where things are in the "real world" in relation to each other, the map is true. Pragmatic truth looks for truth only within a certain context, based on the workability of whatever is being evaluated in that context. So, while a map of the world might work (be true) in order to figure out to which city to fly if you are flying around the world, it is going to be pretty useless (not true) for finding your way around New York City. Is one map less true than the other in the normal correspondence-based sense? No. But certainly one map works better in the context of trying to find your way around New York. This is the sense in which truth is defined in ACT. ACT swaps the truth that emerges from a context of literality (i.e., correspondence) for truth defined by what is useful in empowering us to live rich, meaningful lives, guided by our values.

This radical stance toward truth allows ACT therapists to step around common therapeutic traps with clients who get caught in arguments about whether their own particular stories are right or wrong, or whether their views of the world are accurate or inaccurate. When it comes to clients, truth is local and is defined in terms of whether a particular way of thinking or behaving is helpful or unhelpful in the pursuit of a valued life. For example, suppose a client thinks he or she is inherently unlikable; life has gone down the tubes; and it will never be possible to have a life with caring relationships and a family, even though these are felt to be deeply important. An ACT therapist will not focus on the rational or irrational nature of these thoughts or on the evidence for and against them. Instead, the focus will be on what they are in the service of, and whether experience shows them to be helpful in leading toward a life that reflects chosen values. The issue in the room probably will be about whether the client is willing to have these thoughts when they occur and move in the direction of his or her chosen values, not literally what the thoughts purport to indicate about the state of the world or themselves.

## Committed Action

Finally, ACT encourages the development of larger and larger patterns of effective action linked to chosen values. In this regard, ACT looks very much like traditional behavior therapy, and almost any behavior change method can be fitted into an ACT protocol, including exposure, skills acquisition, shaping methods, and goal setting. Unlike values, which are constantly instantiated but never achieved as an object, concrete goals that are values consistent can be achieved. ACT protocols almost always involve homework linked to short-, medium-, and long-term behavior change goals. Behavior change efforts, in turn, lead to contact with psychological barriers, which are addressed through other ACT processes (e.g., acceptance, defusion).

## A DEFINITION OF ACT

The six core ACT processes are both overlapping and interrelated. Taken as a whole, each supports the other and all target psychological flexibility—the process of contacting the present moment fully as a conscious human being, and persisting or changing behavior in the service of chosen values. The six processes can be chunked into two groupings. First, the *mindfulness* and *acceptance* processes involve acceptance, defusion, contact with the present moment, and self as context. Indeed, these four processes provide a workable behavioral definition of mindfulness (Fletcher & Hayes, 2005). Second, the *commitment* and *behavior change* processes involve contact with the present moment, self as context, values, and committed action. Contact with the present moment and self as context occur in both groupings because all psychological activity of conscious human beings involves *the now* as known.

Now that the six processes have been defined, we can define ACT very simply. ACT is a psychological intervention based on modern behavioral psychology, including RFT, that applies mindfulness and acceptance processes, and commitment and behavior change processes, to the creation of psychological flexibility.

ACT is thus a model, not a specific technology. It contains a model of psychopathology and a model of intervention processes and health. It is an *approach* to psychological intervention and human functioning, defined in terms of six specific theoretical processes, grounded in basic principles. It is to the first of these six processes we now turn.

## FOR MORE INFORMATION

For an overview of the research about outcomes, and evidence of the processes of change that underlie ACT, see Hayes et al. (2006).

For an introductory overview of RFT, the theory of language and cognition that underlies ACT, see the excellent four-hour online tutorial at www.contextualpsychology.org/rft_tutorial.

For a briefer introduction to RFT, you can read the introductory article by Blackledge (2003).

For a book-length treatment of RFT—be warned, it's a tough read—see Hayes et al. (2001).

# CHAPTER 2

# DEVELOPING WILLINGNESS/ ACCEPTANCE

*When suffering knocks at your door and you say there is no seat for him, he tells you not to worry because he has brought his own stool.*

—Chinua Achebe, from *Arrow of God* (1967, p. 84)

Key targets for willingness/acceptance:

- ✓ Help clients let go of the agenda of control as applied to internal experience.
- ✓ Help clients see experiential willingness as an alternative to experiential control.
- ✓ Help clients come into contact with willingness as a choice, not a desire.
- ✓ Help clients to understand willingness as a process, not an outcome.

A great deal of struggle and suffering is found in the denial of the inevitability of human pain. When we feel fear, anxiety, sadness, hopelessness, or other negative emotions, or when we think of ourselves as less than or unworthy, we often engage in efforts to undo these experiences. A battle with our internal experience begins. Often without awareness of another option, we pick up the experiential control agenda and go to work. Unfortunately, because we are largely the products of our history and we cannot simply eliminate our history or the content it contains, the agenda of experiential control is largely ineffective and it backfires, entrapping us in an unsuccessful war with ourselves and creating a self-amplifying loop, which creates additional suffering. The result can be years of human life consumed by fruitless effort and destructive behavior, directed toward unworkable ends.

This tendency toward experiential avoidance is natural and a basic part of being human; it is born out of language and amplified by our culture. We all try to control painful experience, and a fair number of us work feverishly at times to avoid painful events. However, because pain is also a basic part of the human condition, we do not have a long-lasting or viable way to escape the experiences that are elicited when we encounter loss, unmet desires, or other similar conditions. Although control methods sometimes work in the short run, they tend to have the paradoxical effect of actually increasing suffering over the long run. Amplification of suffering can occur both through the basic properties of language—as for example, when trying not to think about a bad memory evokes that memory—and through the loss and pain that result from living outside our closely held values, as in the case of a person with social anxiety who wants to be with people but who avoids them for fear of embarrassment and thus suffers from isolation.

ACT specifically targets letting go of misapplied control, or control that is aimed at getting rid of experiences that cannot be gotten rid of in a healthy way. Rather than increase suffering by engaging in control efforts, ACT offers an alternative that helps the client contact negative experience, and to do so without excessive or rigid efforts to make the experience be other than what it is. This alternative is willingness.

## WHAT IS WILLINGNESS?

*Willingness* can be defined as being open to one's whole experience while also actively and intentionally choosing to move in a valued life direction. Developing willingness occurs through a process of contacting the present moment as it is, with whatever internal experience is present, while simultaneously taking action that is guided by valued intention. The opposite of willingness also points to what we are exploring when working with clients on this process. If a client is unwilling, then he or she makes choices based on the avoidance of internal experiences, rather than on his or her personal valued direction.

Willingness is an action and has an all-or-none quality to it. It is like a leap. For an action to be a leap, part of the time we need to be completely in the air, with no part touching the ground, allowing gravity to do its work. Leaping has a different quality than does stepping, in which each moment is controlled. A step can be a large step, but it is still a step, and a step can only take us so far. We can step from a chair, but not from a roof. Conversely, leaps can be small, but a leap is a leap and has no upper limit. The motion involved in a leap from a chair is identical to the motion involved in a leap from a roof. We are either in the air or we are not—just as we are either willing or we are not.

Although having tolerance can bring us a step closer to being willing, tolerance implies that negative experience is to be withstood until something better comes along. It still has a "step" quality to it. Willingness, on the other hand, has the qualities of openness, allowing, and being present with what is there to be felt, sensed, or witnessed. Willingness is experienced as an ongoing process, not as a waiting for something to change to a better thing if we are tolerant enough.

Clients often confuse willingness with a feeling. One does not have to feel willing in order to be willing. Willingness is also not about wanting. A client does not have to *want* to feel or think something in order to be willing to do so. The question is whether the client would be willing to experience these feelings or thoughts fully and without defense if that meant new possibilities would be created in his or her life.

Willingness is inherently active. Depending upon clients' values, willingness can be found in making a telephone call to the friend who hurt their feelings, having a conversation with their spouse when they don't feel like it, laying down defenses when they want to argue for something, or saying "I love you" when they are scared to say the words.

For the purposes of this book, we use the terms *acceptance* and *willingness* interchangeably. Unfortunately, the term "acceptance" can carry a lot of cultural baggage, which makes it less useful with some clients, particularly those who have been lectured by others about how they have to accept something. It is useful for the therapist to keep an eye out for negative connotations that may be associated with any of these terms. We want to use terms with connotations that are predominantly life affirming, empowering, and vitalizing. Acceptance and willingness are not about loss or resignation. For some people, acceptance sounds like resignation, and indeed the literature has sometimes defined it that way. This is not the kind of acceptance we are talking about in ACT (Hayes et al., 1999), and if a client reacts to the term "acceptance" in this way, it is better to use the term "willingness."

We can catch a glimpse of what ACT means by acceptance by examining the historical origins of the word. Acceptance can be traced back to a Latin word meaning "to take or receive what is offered." This implies an action of embracing, holding, or taking what life offers—willingly. Acceptance is ultimately a choice to embrace what is and what life offers; to say yes to life. This is the sense in which acceptance is understood in ACT.

# WHY WILLINGNESS?

Willingness is one of the key functional goals of the ACT intervention. Acceptance and willingness cannot just be described to the client in the hopes that this will have benefits (i.e., the client will "be accepting" or "be more willing") because it is a skill to be learned, not a concept. In ACT, the therapist attempts to build the behavior of acceptance by engaging clients in specific activities that structure the possibility of choosing to experience difficult thoughts, feelings, emotions, and so on. Acceptance can be thought of as one component of mindfulness, along with self as context, defusion, and contact with the present moment. All of these processes are designed to help clients come into the present as conscious human beings in an open, nonjudgmental fashion. Clinically, all these methods are tied together, and they are in turn linked to the ability to make values-based choices.

Rigid and misapplied attempts at controlling and managing unpleasant, unwanted, and difficult internal experiences can cost us in at least two ways. One is that the things we do in attempts to reduce or remove our painful emotions, thoughts, sensations, and memories often backfire, and ironically can produce even more distress. The pain caused by the effort to not have pain is referred to in the ACT community as "dirty pain." In contrast, "clean pain" refers to pain that is the natural and automatic result of living life. In fact, research has shown that attempts to suppress troubling thoughts or emotions tend to result in rebound effects, wherein the emotion or thought is even more prominent (Hayes et al., 1996). Efforts to not think about a bad memory often tend to elicit that same memory (e.g., in post-traumatic stress disorder; PTSD). The depressed person who stays in bed all day to escape from the meaninglessness of life only further confirms fears about the meaninglessness of his or her life. Panic is at least in part the result of a person's struggle *not* to have anxiety. Many more examples of the ironic effects of experiential avoidance can be seen in other ACT texts (Eifert & Forsyth, 2005; Hayes et al., 1999).

Second, a life lived in pursuit of feeling good is not lived in the service of our most deeply held values. Often, doing what is important or what matters is painful, or at least creates a sense of vulnerability, precisely because caring shows where we can be—and often have been—hurt. This connection between pain and values is part of why experiential avoidance has such a cost. It can lead us to turn aside from valued directions, relationships, or activities so we can modulate, control, or avoid certain experiences. For example, as we discussed in the previous chapter, a person with social anxiety may have no friends because of the desire to avoid embarrassment, yet that very anxiety is an indication of how important people are to the person. Similarly, a person engaging in chronic, persistent experiential avoidance may never develop a sense of what he or she desires in life because the person is so caught up in not feeling. In the end, a life lived in pursuit of feeling good may not feel very good.

# THE LINK BETWEEN WILLINGNESS
# AND DEFUSION

Willingness is particularly closely linked to cognitive defusion (see chapter 3), and some extended discussion of this link seems warranted here. Because humans tend to become fused with literal language, we often do not distinguish between the world as it is verbally conceptualized and the world that is directly experienced. The world simply occurs as it does, and we do not see that this is actually a result of a blending of direct experience and thought. We are fused with our minds. Under these circumstances, the verbal content of the mind dominates over behavior, and the direct contingencies of experience are lost. For example, with fusion, a client saying, "I can't stand this feeling another moment" believes the ideas that he or she will fall apart, cease to exist, or be damaged if the experience of that feeling continues. However, when defused, the client is able to attend to direct experience, and can and will stand the feeling for another moment, and will also experience that he or she does not cease to exist. Furthermore, with attention to the ongoing flow of present experience, the client will learn that this feeling will pass and another will come along.

One of the main problems with fusion, as it pertains to this chapter, includes getting fused with culturally supported messages that negative thoughts and emotions are bad and should be removed, as well as messages that wholeness and well-being are defined largely by feeling okay, and we should do what it takes to feel okay. When these messages are wholly bought, behaviors are set in motion that are designed to eliminate negative thoughts and emotions, and thus supposedly attain well-being. Additionally, we are taught that if we don't like something, we should figure out how to get rid of it and then get rid of it. This makes sense in the world outside the skin. If you don't like something, fix it. For instance, if you don't like the way the room is arranged, rearrange it. If you don't like dirty dishes in the sink, wash them and put them away. If you don't like long hair, get a haircut. Figure out how to fix the problem, and fix it. When this strategy is applied to internal negative experience, however, the very efforts to fix it actually sustain and sometimes increase the experiences we are trying to fix. "If you don't like anxiety, figure out how to get rid of it, and get rid of it" may actually cause the anxiety to linger and grow because not wanting anxiety is itself something about which to be anxious. What we conclude is that we need more strategies to try to fix the problem: we need more control.

The goal of the ACT therapist, then, is to undermine this strategy as a workable strategy when applied to internal private events. The therapist appeals to experience in this undertaking, not to logic. Logic is part of the same self-perpetuating system because logic "tells" clients they should be able to control emotions and thoughts.

# WHAT SHOULD TRIGGER THIS PROCESS?

The clearest sign for use of willingness elements in the session is experiential avoidance. When difficult material is touched on in a session, the client may change the topic, become superficial, joke, deny issues are present, or use words that seem incongruent with his or her affect. In early sessions, the need for this element is often reflected in client inaction, a sense of struggle, rumination, or the like. Later in therapy, the need to revisit this process can be indicated by argumentativeness, excessive logic, lack of motivation, passivity, or a sense of trying to hand over responsibility to the therapist.

The clinician's own reactions can also be an effective guide to the presence of experiential avoidance in the client, and perhaps in the therapist. Avoidance can be revealed when the therapist feels boredom, feels a frustrated urge to push the client, has a sense of arguing with the client, or feels a need to convince the client.

# WHAT IS THE METHOD?

The process of developing acceptance usually involves two major clinical foci: 1) undermining experiential control as a dominant method of relating to one's self and the world, in order to create an initial openness and as a precursor to the rest of the work; and 2) structuring opportunities for the client to actively practice and intentionally develop willingness skills in the presence of previously avoided internal experience. Both of these steps are intended to foster psychological flexibility; that is, the ability to contact the present moment more fully as a conscious human being, and to change or persist in behavior when doing so serves valued ends.

## Undermining Control

Experiential avoidance and control can be so well practiced that they occur virtually without awareness. For many people, managing and controlling their internal experience is not a choice, but just "the way it is." The idea that they might willingly *choose* to have anxiety, sit with pain, rest in sadness, embrace fear, or relax into uncertainty is so unusual and novel that they may feel it is a bit like suggesting they could live without breathing. Particularly for clients with pervasive and chronic histories of experiential avoidance, substantial work is needed to clear a space wherein willingness, acceptance, and compassion can grow. Therapists doing ACT often begin therapy with the process of undermining experiential control, and in particular by focusing on two issues:

1.  Helping the client, by "drawing out the system," to become aware of the ways in which he or she attempts to avoid and control his or her own experience

2.  Examining the workability of these strategies in terms of a more extended timeline and larger life goals, and guiding the client to a place where he or she can begin to let go of unworkable strategies

The outcomes of the process of undermining control are a loosened attachment to and confidence in the eventual success of the experiential control agenda, and some space to practice willingness and acceptance in a way in which these new strategies are less likely to get pulled back into the old system. The term *confronting the system* is also used to describe this process and helps orient the therapist to the idea that this therapy is not about confronting the client, but rather about confronting the social-verbal-cultural system of experiential control in which the client is stuck. The confrontation is not between the client and the therapist; rather, the confrontation occurs between the client's lived experience and his or her mind's proposed solutions to problems that are the result of social-cultural conditioning.

Let's look at how this occurs.

### DRAW OUT THE SYSTEM

Undermining control begins with developing an understanding of what the client is trying to control with respect to his or her internal experience. This is usually discovered in the presenting problem (e.g., "I'm too anxious," "I don't want to be sad anymore"). The therapist might ask, "With what are you struggling?

What brings you to therapy?" Almost always, clients will report a struggle with some emotion, memory, or self-evaluation (e.g., pain, anxiety, fear, emptiness, self-doubt, worthlessness). Once the therapist has a good idea of what the client is trying to control, it is possible to move on to explicitly draw out the strategies the client has used in an effort to "solve" the presenting problem. By the use of the term "strategy," we are not necessarily implying that the client is conscious of or intentionally choosing a particular behavior, but rather we are highlighting the fact that his or her behavior does have a purpose. For example, with an anxious client, the therapist can talk about the things that client does when feeling anxious. Similarly, with a depressed client, the therapist can identify what that person has done to try to be rid of or manage the depression. A client with drug addiction can be helped to see what unpleasant internal reaction drug use was intended to fix, and to see other possible ways of solving the problem. All methods of solving the problem should be explored, including seemingly healthy ones, such as help received from others, psychopharmacology, and counseling.

Clients often are not aware of the variety and extent of ways in which they struggle to control their private experience and cannot describe or identify the purpose of their behavior. Thus, part of the therapist's job is to identify the function (i.e., purpose) of a client's attempts at solutions, and to suggest these to the client. For example, a client with depression may not immediately see how oversleeping or overeating are typically intended to avoid or modulate a mood state or to decrease unpleasant rumination. Being able to better track the purpose of their own behavior can help clients develop present-moment awareness and become better observers of their behavior.

## EXAMINE WORKABILITY

Concurrent with drawing out the system, the therapist's job is to examine the workability of the client's behaviors, particularly over the long term. The basic question asked here is whether the various solutions to the client's problems really turned out as his or her mind said they would.

One sphere of workability is found in examining whether the client's change attempts have actually resulted in long-term decreases in suffering. For example, has what the client did to reduce or eliminate anxiety really reduced or eliminated anxiety in the long run? Have steps taken to manage depression really reduced depression to a seemingly manageable level? Many clients will realize the ironic effects of experiential control in this domain relatively easily, and see that as they tried to cope with and control their suffering, it actually increased over time or at least remained unaffected. However, some clients will not see the cost of experiential control as strongly in this sphere, even though they may have experienced lingering suffering—think, for example, of the flat, wiped out, anhedonic, depressed client, who while not suffering very acutely, has a lingering sense of meaninglessness and loneliness in his or her life.

The second sphere of workability is found in the ways the client has constricted or limited his or her life in an effort to deal with whatever problems have been identified. This is basically workability with respect to the client's lived values. To draw out this aspect of workability, the therapist might ask questions such as, "What has happened to your life over time? Have you done more or less with your life? Have your options increased, or has your life space narrowed over time?" (Eifert & Forsyth, 2005, p. 135). "What would you be doing with your time if you were not busy managing your (insert whatever difficult feelings, thoughts, sensations, images, urges, or memories here)? What have you given up in an attempt to deal with this problem? Have you found yourself moving in the direction of the kind of life you most want to live, or perhaps even found yourself moving farther from it?"

The reason to explore both of these spheres is because the two are linked in the experiential control agenda (Hayes et al., 1999). The most obvious promise of the experiential control agenda is that through deliberate, conscious control we can have more, better, or different emotions, self-evaluations, thoughts, sensations, images, and so on. The first sphere of workability examines whether this promised outcome has been achieved. However, we don't *merely* want to feel good. We also want to live well, and have full, rich, meaningful, vital lives, as defined by our particular dreams and life aspirations (i.e., values). The most enticing promise of the experiential control agenda is what it can deliver in the second sphere: better living. The cultural story says that once we are able to feel more happy, joyful, and energetic, and feel less anxious, depressed, sad, regretful, tired, and angry—or have different self-evaluations, history, and thoughts—then we will be able to chase our dreams, have better relationships, lead a more vital life, live our values, find more meaningful work, and so on. Unfortunately, the reality is often the opposite, and whole lives can be consumed in trying to achieve the first goal of experiential control, apparently in service of the second goal of a valued life, but actually at its cost.

A few notes are important regarding the stance of the therapist during this process of examining the workability of the client's behavior. First, the therapist's stance should take the position that whatever the client has done is understandable and reasonable—which indeed it is, given his or her history (Hayes et al., 1999). It is also important to focus thoroughly on the issue of workability, not on whether the therapist or client is right. This is not about proving to the client that the therapist has a better way. That would be fundamentally antithetical to the basic ACT stance. Rather, the job of the therapist is to help the client begin to apply the criterion of workability, given his or her own life goals and aspirations.

A word about pitfalls. As a therapist doing this work, it can be hard not to get caught up in the content of what the client is saying. When focusing on undermining control, the therapist's job is to consistently return to the issue of whether these strategies have worked in the client's life. Because clients' verbal formulations are well practiced and cherished, clients can feel threatened and begin to defend their actions or reasons for what they have done. This is a normal and understandable reaction to this process. One way to respond to this is to ask the client in a nonjudgmental and nondefensive way (which cannot be faked) to step back for a moment and consider "defending the rightness of my views" as a strategy, and to see if it has worked in his or her life (Eifert & Forsyth, 2005). For example, the therapist might say, "And what you are doing right now—defending this approach—has that worked in the long run? Not whether it's right or wrong, but has taking this position worked to get you where you want to be in your life?" When saying something such as this, it is important for the therapist not to speak from a place of trying to be right and making the client wrong, but from an honest examination of whether this take on things, which is probably strongly believed, has worked for the client.

Another common pitfall is the client saying that a particular strategy has worked. In this context, the client is usually referring to its short-term effect, and the therapist's job is to help the client examine its longer term workability. If even the latter is defended, the therapist can *gently* inquire about the need for therapy, saying, for example, "Then why are you still here?" (Eifert & Forsyth, 2005).

For more about drawing out the system and examining workability, see Hayes et al. (1999, pp. 92–98).

## VALIDATE THE CLIENT'S EXPERIENCE

The discussion about past experiential control and avoidance efforts is likely to show that the old solutions have not worked very well. These efforts also may have come at considerable personal cost (Eifert & Forsyth, 2005). To help clients move from seeing these patterns to beginning to actually let go of experiential control or avoidance efforts, the therapist tries to pull this all together and foster a sense of *creative hopelessness* (Hayes et al., 1999, pp. 87–112). The term "creative hopelessness" has created some problems because readers can mistakenly take it to refer to a feeling. It is actually a stance of self-validation. Therapeutically, it refers to the process of validating clients' experience of the futility of the struggle in which they have been caught, and of beginning to open up to the entirely new possibilities that come from self-validation. Clients know what they have been doing was not working. The possibility ACT therapists add to the mix is that this experience may be valid: perhaps it *can't* work.

Once the experience of the workability of many different behaviors has been explored, and both the client and the therapist have a sense of the extensiveness of the problem and the attempts at a solution, the therapist attempts to develop creative hopelessness in the moment of the session. Any of a number of stories and metaphors can be used about times when a great deal of effort is put forward with little payoff. The client's situation can be compared with that of a hamster on an exercise wheel that goes nowhere, a person struggling to get out of quicksand, a gambler playing a rigged game, or a person investing with a bad investment adviser (Hayes et al., 1999, p. 97). Additional stories include a person who gives meat to a tiger to make it go away, only to find the tiger returning bigger and stronger and hungrier (Eifert & Forsyth, 2005); and a person who has fallen into a hole, with only a shovel to dig out (Hayes et al., 1999, pp. 101–104). The Person in a Hole is a key ACT metaphor that suggests that the tools (shovels) the person has do not create a way out of the hole, but rather make it larger; thus, the goal is to drop the shovel. The client is asked to examine the unworkable change agenda and notice that he or she is stuck in a hole. As therapy continues, the images from this or a different metaphor can be referenced again when the client gets caught up in another control strategy. The therapist can then playfully ask, "Are you digging again?" or "Are you on the hamster wheel again?"

## SAMPLE TRANSCRIPTS

Two transcripts demonstrate portions of the process of undermining control. We have chosen these transcripts to give examples of the process at two ends of the spectrum. The first demonstrates creative hopelessness with a client who has a long and pervasive history of experiential avoidance, and thus the process is intense, prolonged, and emotional. The second transcript is a gentler, more tentative version with a client who has less of an attachment to and history with experiential avoidance, and who also has less experience of the costs of such behavior.

The first transcript begins after the therapist and client have had a couple of sessions to form a therapeutic relationship and have talked a bit about the client's values and about how the client has tried to manage anxiety.

# TRANSCRIPT 2.1

| | **Commentary** |
| --- | --- |
| *Client:* Wow, I have really tried a lot of different things. I guess I've also tried therapy and I've tried just to ignore it. | The therapist continues to draw out as many examples as possible. |
| *Therapist:* Let's add those to the list—therapy and ignoring. What else? | |
| *Client:* Well, I guess I've tried to hide it by not letting people see my hands shake. | |
| *Therapist:* Okay, hiding … Other things? | |
| *Client:* I'm sure there are others, I just can't think of them right now. | |

*Therapist:* There are probably a lot more. We may come across them as we keep working and we can add them to the list then. So, here we have this pretty extensive list ... One thing is clear: You've definitely put a lot of effort into fixing your anxiety.

When working on this process, you want to validate the effort the client has put into this, and at the same time, this begins to undermine "more of the same" as a solution.

*Client:* Yeah, I guess I have. Maybe I just haven't put enough effort in yet. I need to try harder?

*Therapist:* Let me ask you, have you tried hard? It seems you have. The list of things you have tried is long. I wonder if we need to add "try harder" to the list of things you have tried?

While, on a literal level, any solution probably requires hard work, functionally, "trying harder" is currently linked to the control agenda, and therefore needs to be undermined.

*Client:* [chuckles] Yeah, I guess we do.

*Therapist:* So, now we have "try harder" in this long list. So, again, I want to be clear, it's not that you haven't put in enough effort ... But something is funny here. Look at all of these things you've tried, and yet here you are, still struggling with anxiety. In fact, can you name one thing on this list that has solved your anxiety problem in any long-term kind of way?

The therapist asks the client to look at the workability of this in a long-term framework, rather than in the short term, where it may appear to work better.

*Client:* [puzzled] Well, I guess anxiety management worked.

*Therapist:* [also puzzled] It seems if that had worked, you wouldn't be here right now. Why not just do more anxiety management and call it good?

The therapist appeals to the client's experience: why is the client in therapy if these solutions worked in a long-term sense?

*Client:* I need you to remind me. I've forgotten most of it.

*Therapist:* Let's look at that. Have you been reminded before?

*Client:* Yeah, lots of times.

*Therapist:* I'm going to go ahead, then, and add that to the list of things that haven't worked. I could remind you, but it seems you would need to be reminded again, and then again. Does that seem true to you?

The therapist identifies what the client is doing right now as something he tried before, and therefore it must not have worked because he is here.

*Client:* [laughs] Yeah, I do forget a lot. Can you see what a pain this is for me? I just need to figure it out.

A common response is figuring it out.

*Therapist:* How long have you been trying to figure this out?

The therapist addresses how long this strategy has been applied.

*Client:* Oh, about thirty years.

*Therapist:* Then we should probably add "figuring it out" to the list of things that don't work. If you've been trying to figure it out for thirty years, it seems that would have worked by now.

The therapist identifies the functional category of the response and gives it a label.

*Client:* [getting slightly impatient] You're the therapist, you tell me what works.

*Therapist:* Ah, that's a great strategy: get information from someone else about how to solve this. Yet here we are. You said you've been to therapy and you've read books. You've tried to get information, and that didn't solve it. So let's add that one to the list, too. The list is growing.

*Client:* This is frustrating. There must be something that works, right?

*Therapist:* This is going to sound funny, but we're still in the same place. You asked me a question about what works. So, two things are present: a question and getting information again ... We already know that getting information hasn't worked. How about questions? How many questions have you asked about anxiety?

*Client:* Tons.

*Therapist:* So asking questions goes on the list.

*Client:* Something must work. Why would people go to therapy? You just need to help me understand.

*Therapist:* I see. So, if you understand anxiety better, then that will solve your problem.

*Client:* [pause] I understand anxiety pretty well.

*Therapist:* So, it seems understanding this better isn't working, either, and ...

*Client:* I know, that goes on the list. [pause] Well, maybe I should just go home if nothing works.

*Therapist:* Maybe. But let me point out that staying at home is already on your list. So just going home won't solve anything. That's an unworkable strategy, too.

*Client:* Well, hell then, there is nothing left to do. I give up.

*Therapist:* Have you given up before?

*Client:* Yes. [sounds frustrated] Go ahead, put that one on the list, too.

*Therapist:* Yeah, giving up hasn't solved this problem, either.

*Client:* This is frustrating.

*Therapist:* I can imagine.

*Client:* I guess I just have to accept it.

*Therapist:* Have you tried just accepting it before?

*Client:* Oh no, not again. Isn't this called acceptance and commitment therapy?

*Therapist:* Sure is. But have you tried acceptance before?

*Client:* Yes.

Again, the therapist identifies the functional category of the client's current behavior and labels it. The therapist may be feeling anxious here, too, but with an entrenched client, it's important to stick with it.

Frustration at this stage isn't necessarily a bad reaction.

Responding to the client's statement literally would not be useful here. The therapist instead labels this as another example of the kinds of things the client does.

The therapist continues to label the function of the client's behavior.

Often, giving up or resignation comes up as a strategy, but as a strategy within the old agenda. Although its form may look like acceptance, it is probably a control strategy in disguise. Behind resignation is the hope that someday things will change.

Expressing frustration has probably led to people backing off before. The client would probably feel better in the moment if the therapist simply backed off or gave some suggestion for a solution (e.g., some sort of relaxation exercise). However, functionally, this would be feeding the old agenda. The therapist assumes that for this very stuck, pervasively avoidant client, anything the client is offering at this point is not new behavior and must be part of the old agenda.

*Therapist:* And it didn't work to solve your anxiety, or you wouldn't be here. We're kind of getting to a place where nothing works. Here you have tried all these things and nothing has worked to solve your anxiety. And you don't have to believe it because I'm saying it. Look back across the years and tell me, based on your experience with all of these strategies, what has worked?

Therapist asks the client to check his experience. We are trying to shift the client over to a way of responding more in contact with his experience and less rule bound, even (or especially) to rules generated by the therapist.

*Client:* Well, some of them work a little bit.

*Therapist:* Sure. You can try a little of this here and a little of that there and feel better for a bit. You can even drink and feel better for a bit. But then what happens?

The therapist again draws the client's attention to the longer term pattern. Clients usually want to focus on the short term.

*Client:* It comes back.

*Therapist:* And then you have to do what?

*Client:* Try harder.

*Therapist:* But we already know that trying harder doesn't work. It isn't because of lack of effort that you're sitting here before me today.

Suggesting that it isn't about "not trying hard enough" helps keep the client away from useless self-blame.

*Client:* I'm lost. I don't know what to do.

*Therapist:* What do you bump up against when you feel lost?

Contact with the present moment occurs when the client is asked to notice what is showing up now.

*Client:* It's hopeless. There is nothing to be done.

*Therapist:* Now we're getting somewhere.

*Client:* You must be kidding me. I'm lost, and you think we're getting somewhere?

This is clearly not an expected response. It steps outside the bounds of literal discourse, where if taken literally, "hopeless" and "lost" are really bad places to be. However, for this client, moving away from feeling hopeless and lost is part of what keeps him stuck.

*Therapist:* Lost is a good place to be, at least right now. Not knowing means that perhaps something different can take place. If you knew, then I suspect we'd have to add it to the list of things that don't work. And I don't want to take you back to what hasn't worked. So, for now, perhaps lost is a place to be. But it is a creative place because it is from this place that maybe, just maybe, something new can happen.

## EXPERIENTIAL EXERCISE: ACCEPTANCE

As you read the transcript, what were your reactions? How did you feel? Was it uncomfortable for you in any way? If so, how? What emotions did you notice? Did you have any evaluations? Make a note of these.

It is important to be respectful and humble when working in a lengthy, confrontational fashion; otherwise it can appear as if you are playing a game with the client or as if you are invalidating him or her. The idea is to validate the client's actual experience of control not working, and to suggest that the social message he or she was given might be incorrect, rather than that the client is incorrect. It is also important to point out before the end of this kind of session that you are suggesting that the agenda is hopeless, not that the client is hopeless.

The creative piece in creative hopelessness refers to an openness that comes when needless experiential control is finally abandoned and attention is focused instead on living a life that comports with chosen values. The goal is not a feeling of hopelessness or belief in hopelessness; in fact, usually this process feels hopeful. The goal is to speed the process of abandoning what is not working (Hayes et al., 1999). Often when old control agendas are stripped away, the client experiences a sense of being lost or confused. This is not a negative sign; it is a sign the old control behaviors are beginning to fall away. Other common reactions include the client slowing down or being more thoughtful; periods of silence; a sense of lightness in the room; laughter; and starting and stopping the dialogue, as if the client were catching habitual patterns of thinking.

Other guidelines are important to keep in mind. A very common mistake by the therapist is trying to convince the client that avoidance is not working or that he or she must give up the experiential avoidance agenda. The therapist can also try to push the client beyond where he or she is ready to go. It is important that the *client's experience be the absolute arbiter*. Creative hopelessness will only function as it should if the confrontation is between the client's mind/system of experiential control and his or her experience, not between the therapist and the client. The therapist is simply there to guide this process of helping the client examine his or her own experience and determine whether the solutions that have been put forward by his or her mind have actually worked out as they were supposed to, or whether experience has shown otherwise.

It is important for the therapist not to get caught up in the content of what clients say. It is a mistake, for example, to encourage a client who offers a seemingly logical or healthy solution without first thoroughly exploring its actual function. This mistake is especially tempting if what is put forward is similar or formally identical to ACT methods. However, the purpose is not to list formally correct methods; it is to explore the functional impact of any and all solutions and to let go of what is not working. Typically, what is not working is the client's cognitive entanglement and the resulting unseen control agenda, which may not be seen easily or logically. Client experience is the biggest ally.

It is also important to note that creative hopelessness is not a one-time, all-or-nothing shift in behavior, but rather is about establishing the possibility of something other than control—in this moment, and the next moment, and then the next moment. It is about eventually helping clients see that each moment of existence offers an opportunity to say no to their experience and feed the agenda of experiential avoidance, or to say yes and feed the vitality of a life embraced.

The relative emphasis on undermining control largely depends upon the pervasiveness of experiential avoidance and control in the client's life. For some clients, experiential control has been their dominant way of living for many years and they are very entrenched in the pattern; for other clients, experiential control is less pervasive, less practiced, or less dominant, and they are more ready to give it up as a solution. The higher the chronicity and pervasiveness, the more likely it is that this part of ACT needs to be emphasized. The therapist can probably move through this step more rapidly with clients who have relatively less pervasive patterns of experiential avoidance and can move into helping them develop mindfulness and acceptance skills in the context of pursuing their values.

The following transcript comes from an early session with a bright, young, relatively functional client with social anxiety.

# TRANSCRIPT 2.2

*Therapist:* [after reviewing how the client has tried to deal with anxiety] Let me suggest something. If this were any easy, obvious thing to do, you would have figured it out.

*Client:* I think, yeah.

*Therapist:* You're a smart, capable person. You've been struggling with this a good portion of your life. And you know directly that there is something inherently tricky about this problem. So, for example, even noticing that something is not there is enough to create it. It's like, "Oh, I'm feeling better,... oh no,... oh no I'm not." Like that. Let's look at what was on this list of things you've done to manage anxiety. There was distracting, reassurance, talking yourself out of it, avoiding it, and perhaps some other things we haven't talked about yet. See if they all have this characteristic in common: They can, at certain times, be a little helpful, and ... ultimately they're not that helpful.

*Client:* Yeah.

*Therapist:* They don't solve it.

*Client:* No. I know that. [laughs]

*Therapist:* And see if even this isn't true. They can work for a short period of time, and they might even make it worse in a moderate or longer period of time. Like this. If you do something to distract yourself, sooner or later you have to check to see if it worked. And then when you check to see if it worked, it'll remind you of what you were trying to forget ... and it's back.

*Client:* Yeah, sometimes I'll be thinking, "Okay, I'm going to distract myself. Let's think about something fun. So I think ... skiing, riding down the hill, getting to the lodge, hanging with friends at the lodge— crap! Okay, start over."

*Therapist:* Yeah.

*Client:* Or sometimes it happens like, gosh, I'll notice I'm feeling better, and then it'll be back.

*Therapist:* Yeah. And here's the problem. You talked about the tricks your mind plays on you, right? The problem is, your mind is in the room, not just you. So you're doing a lot of stuff your mind is telling you to do. And it works however it works, and in the long term, it doesn't seem to work, and here you are. And yet it's in the room, listening to what we're saying.

*Client:* It knows. [giggles]

*Therapist:* Yeah, it knows what's going on, right?

*Client:* Yeah.

*Therapist:* But it doesn't seem to be able to give you ultimate, final answers. If anything, it seems to torment you. It reminds you of some random memory you don't want to think about.

*Client:* And I can't logically make it go away. I think I understand what you're saying. I know what I'm thinking isn't logical, but it just doesn't get through.

*Therapist:* Right, because this isn't just a logical deal, it's a psychological deal. And that's not the same thing. So let's put these things together. We need to carve out some space here in which to work. I want you to consider the possibility that the things that seem logical, reasonable, sensible you've pretty much exhausted. They pay off like this. [spreads hands] They don't pay off in some other way.

*Client:* [laughs] No, they don't.

*Therapist:* They pay off like this. And if that's the case, then we're going to have to open up the possibility that a whole other attack on it is what's needed. And yet we've got a mind in the room that'll say, "Oh yeah, I get that. That's like that," and will try to pull it back into the same system. [pause] So, you know what quicksand is?

*Client:* Yeah.

*Therapist:* When people step in it, they do the normal, logical, reasonable, sensible thing: they try to get out of it.

*Client:* Which makes it worse.

*Therapist:* Yeah. So the normal way to get out of things is you push to get out of it. The problem is, when you do that with quicksand, it just sinks you in deeper. The one foot didn't work, so you push on the other. Now you've got two of them in there. Maybe it's like that. Maybe the things you've been doing are like the normal, logical, reasonable, sensible things people do when they are stuck in suction mud. And, in fact, it's not liberating you; if anything, it's making you more stuck. So, if that's true, then we have to find something that might work that's outside the set of all the things that might work. You know what I mean?

*Client:* [laughs] Yeah. [pause] So, what are we going to do, then?

*Therapist:* [pauses, smiles] Well, your experience is telling you, "I do something, and it doesn't pay off. It pays off short term and it doesn't pay off long term." And, really, the problem just keeps hanging around. Sometimes it's better, sometimes it's worse, but here it is. And you're trying not to let it grow. But it's still here, and you're stuck.

*Client:* [murmurs agreement]

*Therapist:* Well, I want to open the door and say, "You know that sense that you have that you're stuck? Well, maybe you have that because you really are stuck." This game is a stuck game. It's not going to work some other way. It works like this. You know in your experience how things have worked. If you back up and look at it, it looks almost as though this were a rigged game. In other areas of your life, you put in the effort and get the outcome. Not here. So, we will need to do something really different.

## CONTROL AS THE PROBLEM

In the second example just presented, you can see the therapist transition from working on the sense of creative hopelessness to more explicitly outlining how experiential/emotional control might be part of the problem, rather than the solution to the client's current difficulties. Many clients come to therapy believing they need more control over their internal experience. However, what happens instead is that misapplied control lands them in an unworkable agenda—and does so at the expense of their lives, as they put their lives on hold while they work to get their emotions or thoughts under control.

We've all heard clients make statements such as, "When I get my anxiety under control, I will get a job" or "When the pain stops, I will find another relationship" or "When I don't feel guilty anymore, I will reconnect with my children. I don't want to subject them to my guilt." These kinds of statements come in all shapes and sizes, and are all about the client beginning to live only after his or her internal experience is under control. Of course, the problem with this is that life is occurring in the present moment, and it is very difficult to change what happens internally in any lasting and meaningful way. Additionally, efforts at control can lead to more problems and costs. This can happen in obvious ways: a client drinks heavily to avoid feeling sad, for instance. Misapplied control can also be problematic in more subtle ways. Imagine a client who subtly changes the topic whenever you begin to talk about painful issues, yet desires to have intimacy. The following transcript points to this issue.

*Therapist:* So you had a good time this weekend at the lake?

*Client:* Yes, it was a lot of fun. I water-skied and swam. I really got to catch a break… But I was alone, and that was kind of a bummer.

*Therapist:* You were alone? I know it has been hard for you to be alone. Was it painful?

*Client:* Yes, but I was also able to go hiking, and you would not believe what happened. I came across a bear on the side of the trail …

*Therapist:* [interrupts] I noticed that you skipped past that painful part.

*Client:* Yeah, but I wanted to be sure and tell you about the bear.

*Therapist:* It seems it just happened again. What do you think would happen if you showed up to the pain?

*Client:* [gets tearful] I would start to cry and I don't want to do that.

Here you can see how the client is avoiding vulnerability at the expense of intimacy. The goal of the therapist is to point out the cost of this kind of control: loss of valued living. For this client that means, for instance, loss of intimacy, connecting, and lovingly participating in relationship.

Misapplied control can be tackled by both an appeal to experience and by use of metaphor. Creative hopelessness appeals to experience; the therapist might ask, for example, "In your experience, has control worked?" Additional flexibility can be fostered through metaphors that model the problem of control. The ACT literature is replete with them: the Chinese Handcuffs metaphor, the Driving with the Rearview Mirror metaphor, the Feedback Screech metaphor, the Box Full of Stuff, the Tug-of-War with a Monster metaphor, the Jelly Doughnut metaphor, the Falling in Love exercise, and the Polygraph metaphor (Hayes et al., 1999, pp. 104–105, 108, 136–138, 109, 123–124). All illustrate the paradox of control: the more you try to control your internal experience, the more you lose control.

This paradox is captured by the message "If you aren't willing to have it, you've got it" (Hayes et al., 1999, pp. 120–122), or its variant, "If you are not willing to lose it, you've lost it." If you are not willing to have anxiety, then anxiety is something about which to be anxious, and even more anxiety will be created. If you're not willing to lose love, then you cannot have love because you will constantly be trying to control your beloved.

Many of these examples are focused on experiential control related to emotions, but this kind of paradox also can be applied to thoughts. If you try to control what the mind is thinking, an immediate problem arises: you have to contact what you would like to control in order to know that you want to control it. As an example, you can ask clients *not* to think about a banana. What will happen is that they will immediately think about a banana. And the harder they try not to think about a banana, the more they will be thinking "banana," and then perhaps even about banana splits and the color yellow and batches of bananas and the banana they had for breakfast. You might discuss how this effort is likely to backfire when applied to thoughts that seem particularly important to control. Distracting ourselves from thinking about a banana might work unless we see a banana or hear the word "banana." The seriousness of thinking about a banana is probably miniscule for most people. However, other thoughts can have quite a strong impact; for example, thoughts the client really wants to eliminate, such as, "I'm damaged goods" or "There is something wrong with me" or "I've wasted my life." These are weighty thoughts, and distraction will be much more difficult. In other words, clients don't generally try to control or get rid of happiness or good thoughts. Those are welcomed and stay as long as they stay. Efforts to control are applied to that which we don't want: the negative stuff. This is where the paradox shows up. Exploring this issue with the client can be useful when he or she points to distraction as a technique to control unwanted private experience.

In the following transcript, the therapist returns to the Quicksand metaphor (Hayes et al., 1999), but this time for a slightly different purpose—as a way to begin to point to what willingness is like.

*Therapist:* You remember that metaphor of falling into quicksand?

*Client:*  Yeah. You mean how the harder I try to get out, the worse it gets?

*Therapist:*  Exactly ... The harder you try to get out, the faster you sink. We didn't talk about it before, but this metaphor also points to what to do when you get stuck in a situation like this—besides struggle. With quicksand, in order to not sink, what you need to do is the opposite of what you would think to do. In order to stay afloat in quicksand, you have to gently spread out and let as much of your body contact the sand as possible. The more surface area is in touch with the sand, the more you will float and not drown. What if this getting rid of anxiety thing is like drowning in quicksand? The harder and faster you try to get out of it, the more you get into it, the worse things get. And maybe the thing to do is to stop struggling, to get in contact with the emotion, to float in it.

*Client:*  But floating in it doesn't get me out of it, either.

*Therapist:*  That's right. What you feel is still there to be felt, you have just given up the struggle. Is that something you would be willing to do if it means you don't drown?

*Client:*  Yes, but how?

This is just one example of how to introduce the idea of willingness as an alternative to control. This process is further outlined in the next section.

# Developing and Practicing Acceptance

After the initial work has been completed to help loosen the client's attachment to the agenda of experiential control, the focus of therapy turns to helping the client bring willingness to the events that occur in his or her life. In the previous section, the focus was mainly on undermining a well-practiced set of behaviors: experiential control. In this section, we turn clinical attention toward an explicit focus on building new behaviors that are about embracing, holding, and compassionately accepting one's experience. Clients usually enter therapy with the agenda of directly wanting to feel *better*. Acceptance is the work of helping them to *feel* better (i.e., get better at feeling; Hayes et al., 1999) in the service of living better. The job of this part of therapy is to guide clients in practicing willingness in various contexts, with various private events, and with the goal of developing the ability to apply it broadly to their lives. Occasionally, clients come to session ready and open to learning how to more effectively accept their own experiences, and the therapist can jump right to this step. Where you start with the client is determined by your case conceptualization (see chapter 8).

Clients are generally unsure what will happen if they are willing to experience their emotions. Letting go of control of internal events can and does feel as though we are taking a step into the unknown. Being willing to accept emotional content is a bit like closing our eyes, taking a step, and hoping that our foot finds the ground. The therapist's job is to teach the client what willingness is, to stick with the client, and to gently encourage the client to take these steps. The therapist helps the client to do this in two ways: 1) teaching what willingness is, and 2) actively practicing willingness by embracing the current moment.

## TEACH WHAT WILLINGNESS IS

Willingness is an inherently compassionate act of self-validation in which the person embraces the moment, in the here and now, as it unfolds. We explore the notion of the here and now more thoroughly in chapter 4. Here we only note the importance of actively practicing moment-to-moment awareness, fully and without defense. What we mean by "fully" is broad and inclusive: all emotions and mind content are there to be experienced—not just some of it and not just specifically the parts we like. This is an issue of contact; that is, to show up to all parts of experience or to spread out into our experience, as in the Quicksand metaphor. What we mean by "without defense" is nonjudgmental, nonevaluative awareness: to observe dispassionately. Awareness of this kind requires ongoing practice. For many clients, practicing mindfulness in and out of session can be helpful.

**Willingness is a choice:** Choice means making a selection simply because we can. Therefore, the choice to be willing is present every moment. Often clients will assume they don't have a choice and will list several if not many reasons they cannot choose to be willing. You can work with these clients to help them defuse from or observe their reasons and still take action. There are a couple of quick ways to demonstrate this for the client. First, you can give the client a choice between two similar objects. For instance, you might ask the client, "Tea or coffee, which would you choose?" After the client has made a choice, ask him or her to generate as many reasons as possible to explain why that choice was made. When you have a fair number of reasons for drinking coffee, let's say, even if they are really good ones, such as "I'm allergic to tea" or "The taste of tea makes me sick," ask if it is not true that the client could still choose tea and drink it, despite all the good reasons. The answer is, of course, yes. It is not the reason that chooses, but the person who chooses. You can then bring this back to the larger issue at hand. You could, for instance, ask, "Would you be willing to choose willingness if it meant you got to live your life?"

The following metaphor (Hayes et al., 1999, p. 240) can be useful in this type of situation.

*Therapist:* Imagine you've just purchased a new home and you decide to hold an open house. You make invitations that say, "All are welcome," and post them around the neighborhood. You're excited about the party and you begin to get ready by making everything look nice and by preparing the food and drinks. The big day comes, and everything is going well. The guests are arriving and enjoying themselves; everyone is laughing and having a good time. More guests are arriving. Then you hear a knock at the door. You open it with a smile, which rapidly changes to a look of disgust. There, before you, stands Edna, your annoying new neighbor. Edna makes obnoxious noises, is often rude to people, smells bad, and has terrible manners. You've only been in your new home for a month, yet you've already learned a lot about her. You quickly try to close the door, but realize Edna has placed her foot between the door and the jamb, and you can't close the door. You ask Edna to leave, but she slowly shakes her head and shows you one of the invitations you posted around the neighborhood. She repeats the words written in large letters: "All are welcome." She also tells you she's not leaving and will sit right there until you let her in. Given the situation—she's not leaving and you are missing your guests—you decide to let Edna in, but you insist she needs to stay away from the guests and remain in the kitchen. You rapidly escort her to the kitchen and admonish her to stay there. You close the door to the kitchen and begin to walk away … and right behind you is Edna. She follows you out of the kitchen. You turn and say, "No, Edna, you must stay in the kitchen," and you escort her back. Once again, you turn to join the party, and guess what happens?

*Client:* Edna comes pushing through the door again.

*Therapist:* Right! And what you find is that you have to prop your foot right up against the kitchen door to keep Edna out of sight. You're locked in. What is the problem here?

*Client:* I don't get to be at the party.

*Therapist:* Yes. So, the big question is, would you be willing to let Edna wander the house if it meant you got to be at the party, too?

*Client:*      It would be hard.

*Therapist:*   Yes, but could you choose to do it, and be at your party?

*Client:*      Yeah, that's what I'd want to do.

Working with the client in this area boils down to a simple question: are you willing to feel what you feel; have the thoughts you have; let the sensations be there, fully and without defense; and do what works for you according to what you value?

**Willingness is an action:** Throughout this chapter, we have provided multiple descriptions of willingness. Willingness is not a feeling and is not something that can be directly instructed or described, just as one can't directly describe how to ride a bicycle, play an instrument, or perform a skilled sport. This can be captured, in part, by comparing willingness to something that happens when skiing.

*Therapist:*   Have you ever gone skiing?

*Client:*      Yeah, a few times.

*Therapist:*   Have you noticed how, when you're skiing and you're afraid you are going too fast, the natural tendency is to want to lean away, to lean back into the hill? The problem is that, as soon as you do that, you lose control of the direction in which you're headed, and in fact, you even increase the chance of wiping out. In this situation, the natural response—to lean back—doesn't work very well. What if this situation in regard to your own thoughts and feelings is similar: what if the natural reaction—to lean away from your own experience—is actually part of the problem? What if what we need here is to practice leaning downhill, leaning into your experience, so you can have more control over where you're headed in your life?

## PRACTICE WILLINGNESS

Ideally, willingness is practiced throughout therapy and interwoven with all the other ACT processes. A very basic way in which willingness is practiced is when ACT therapists give clients a choice whether or not to do an exercise or discuss a difficult topic. This happens whenever an ACT therapist has an idea to do an exercise or to discuss a topic that might evoke difficult content for the client, and the therapist asks the client whether he or she is willing to do the exercise before beginning that piece of work.

A large number of in-session and out-of-session exercises have been described that are in large part about structuring opportunities for clients to practice willingness. Many examples are described in various texts. Examples include the Tin Can Monster exercise, the Eyes On exercise, the Looking for Mr. Discomfort exercise (Hayes et al., 1999, pp. 171–174, 244–247), and exposure exercises (Eifert & Forsyth, 2005). These usually occur later in treatment, after the therapist has worked on defusion and self as context.

Although willingness tends to have an all-or-none quality, the context in which willingness is practiced can be chosen, at least in part (Strosahl, Hayes, Wilson, & Gifford, 2004). For example, clients can choose to be willing for five seconds or for an hour. They can choose to be willing in the mall, but not in the bookstore. They can work on willingness with one emotion, but not another. This ability to choose the situation (but not the level of willingness) allows therapists to titrate willingness work to the client's current level of willingness. Just as therapists conducting exposure create an exposure hierarchy, ACT therapists usually encourage clients to start with small acts of willingness, perhaps for moments in a session or with relatively less difficult private events. From there, they can move to larger acts of willingness, such as calling a sibling with whom the client has not talked in several years and willingly feeling whatever shows up during that call. Willingness exercises often take the form of in-session exposure exercises in which difficult material is elicited; the therapist and client work with this material together in the session.

## Willingness Depends Upon the Other ACT Processes

Willingness is a process and not an outcome, and it is integrated into all aspects of ACT. It isn't as if we "get willing" and we are finished. There is always more willingness to do—in life and throughout a course of treatment.

Willingness is not fully possible without the other elements of the ACT model. Thus, at this point in the book, it is only possible to broadly outline the application of willingness later in therapy. Because willingness involves embracing the moment, as it unfolds in the here and now, willingness is an important subtext when we address these topics in chapter 4. Willingness is a choice—which means letting go of fusion with reasons, while simultaneously selecting among alternative courses of action. Thus, willingness, in its fully developed form, incorporates defusion as a necessary component, as discussed in the next chapter. Willingness to experience difficult thoughts, feelings, and experiences is put in the service of our values. This is what makes willingness different from wallowing. This is explored further in chapter 6. Finally, important strategies are available for implementing willingness in the context of committed action and exposure. These are addressed in chapter 7.

# CORE COMPETENCY PRACTICE

This section is intended to provide practice in using willingness in response to sample transcripts based on ACT sessions. Listed here are the ten ACT core competencies for willingness/acceptance. For each core competency, you are presented with a description of a clinical situation and a section of a transcript. The overall transcript is intended to illustrate the core competency. Most transcripts also include other elements of the ACT protocol because one process is seldom used in isolation. The transcript ends after a client statement, and you are asked to provide a sample response that reflects that competency. You are also asked to describe the basis for your response. After you provide each response and explanation, you should turn to the end of the chapter, where you can compare your response with the two model responses.

The model responses are not the only right responses. Often there are scores of good, ACT-consistent alternatives. The main purpose in providing models is to give you a sense for good, ACT-consistent responses. If you sensed the possibility of one of the models, that is an especially good sign. If your response seems to fit the explanation and competency just as well as the models do, then you are doing fine. If you think the models might have been more powerful, try to learn from them. If you do not understand the model responses, or they suggest your response does not fit, you will want to reexamine this chapter or other texts again. If you aren't sure, you can post a question to the bulletin board to ask about it (www.learningact.com/forum/).

Notice that some of the transcripts continue across multiple competencies. In these cases, we have provided text to guide you in finding where the next section and its associated exercise pick up.

We recommend you not read the model responses until after you respond with your own ideas. Creating your own responses first allows the greatest opportunity for learning and allows you to benefit maximally from the feedback. You may even want to write down multiple possible responses to increase your flexibility. It's also important to focus on providing responses that illustrate the particular competency in each section and to describe steps that lead toward implementing the competency most effectively, rather than providing responses that are consistent with ACT in general.

Here is an example of how you might complete the exercises.

---

COMPETENCY: **The therapist helps the client make direct contact with the paradoxical effects of emotional control strategies.**

## COMPLETED SAMPLE EXERCISE

The client is a nineteen-year-old female college student who complains of social anxiety and a general sense of lack of color or excitement in her life. She feels this is related to her history of sexual abuse as a child. Through therapy, she has been able to see how memories of this abuse surface when she finds herself feeling close to people. In response, she distances or numbs herself. This dialogue occurs in the sixth session.

*Therapist:* So, let me see if I get the sequence. You're sitting around with your boyfriend; he touches you; you start to feel anxious, really unsafe; and then feel ashamed that you feel that way. Right? Then you find some excuse to get out of there and go home and drink so you don't have to think about it? Is that the sequence?

*Client:* Yeah, I just can't think about it. It's too hard. I'm so tired. I just need a way to get over this.

Write here what your response would be (remember you are using this competency):

*Therapist:* If talking about this experience could make it possible for you to have the open, loving relationship you so want, would you be willing to do that?

*Client:* Yes.

*Therapist:* So let me ask you then: The more and more you've tried to make these anxious and guilty feelings go away, what have you found? Have they gotten less and less over time or have they perhaps even gotten stronger, and in the meantime you still find yourself distant, lonely, cut off?

What are your thoughts in saying this? What are you responding to and what are you hoping to accomplish?

Her avoidance clearly isn't working. I'm linking up this issue with her values and getting permission to talk about what is likely to be a painful and sensitive subject, one in which the client might feel intruded on. Then I'm having her check out whether this strategy has actually worked out the way it was supposed to, or if perhaps it has even, paradoxically, made things worse.

You would then check your responses against the models at the end of the chapter before going on to the next exercise.

# CORE COMPETENCY EXERCISES

**COMPETENCY 1: The therapist communicates to the client that he or she is not broken but is using unworkable strategies.**

## EXERCISE 2.1

A fifty-six-year-old male client has come to therapy seeking relief from his anxiety associated with PTSD. He has been in a number of treatment programs and worked with at least three other therapists and psychiatrists. He complains he cannot do regular, everyday kinds of things because his anxiety is too high. He isolates himself and wishes things would be different, as well as using other avoidance strategies.

Client: [after listing about ten strategies for getting rid of anxiety] What I would really like to do is find a way to get this anxiety under control.

Therapist: It seems you have tried a lot of different things. You've certainly made an effort.

Client: Yeah, I just need to try harder ... to find one thing that will make this different.

Write here what your response would be (remember you are using competency 1):

What are your thoughts in saying this? What are you responding to and what are you hoping to accomplish?

**COMPETENCY 2: The therapist helps the client make direct contact with the paradoxical effects of emotional control strategies.**

## EXERCISE 2.2

*This transcript continues with the same client as in competency 1.*

Therapist: [gives the response found in Sample 2.1b in the Core Competency Model Responses section below]

Client: I see what you mean, but I just want things to be different. I'm feeling anxious all the time. I can't stand being like this.

Therapist: If things were different, what would you be doing?

Client: Everything would be different. I would be able to be around people, I could work. Everything would be a lot better.

Write here what your response would be (using competency 2):

What are your thoughts in saying this? What are you responding to and what are you hoping to accomplish?

---

## COMPETENCY 3: The therapist actively uses the concept of workability in clinical interactions.

### EXERCISE 2.3

*This transcript continues with the same client as in competency 2, but later in the session.*

*Therapist:* How successful have you been at making it different when you try harder?

*Client:* Well, it works for a little while, and then the problems start all over again. The anxiety comes back.

Write here what your response would be (using competency 3):

What are your thoughts in saying this? What are you responding to and what are you hoping to accomplish?

---

## COMPETENCY 4: The therapist actively encourages the client to experiment with stopping the struggle for emotional control and suggests willingness as an alternative.

### EXERCISE 2.4

A forty-one-year-old female client is seeking therapy to alleviate anger and sadness around the breakup of a relationship. The breakup occurred three years prior to entering therapy. The client explained in the initial session that she feels betrayed and unable to move past the pain of the breakup. She notes that her anger is interfering with her ability to move on. She also notes she is angry with herself for "being duped" in the relationship. This dialogue occurs in the fourth session.

*Client:* I feel overwhelmed by my anger ... and I feel stupid. It has been three years. Why can't I get over this? It's embarrassing.

*Therapist:* Somehow getting over this seems like the thing to do, and then embarrassment and "stupid" will go away ... in addition to the anger?

*Client:* Silly, isn't it?

Write here what your response would be (using competency 4):

What are your thoughts in saying this? What are you responding to and what are you hoping to accomplish?

---

## COMPETENCY 5: The therapist highlights the contrast between the workability of control and willingness strategies.

### EXERCISE 2.5

*Let's assume you have the same client as in competency 4, but the session goes like this:*

Client:      I feel overwhelmed by my anger ... and I feel stupid. It has been three years. Why can't I get over this? It is embarrassing.

Therapist:   Somehow getting over this seems like the thing to do, and then embarrassment and "stupid" will go away ... in addition to the anger?

Client:      Silly, isn't it?

Therapist:   I can see you have a lot of judgment about your anger. You think it's silly and stupid.

Client:      It is. I just can't believe I'm still angry about this. It doesn't make any sense to me.

Write here what your response would be (using competency 5):

What are your thoughts in saying this? What are you responding to and what are you hoping to accomplish?

---

## COMPETENCY 6: The therapist helps the client investigate the relationship between willingness and suffering.

### EXERCISE 2.6

*This transcript continues with the same client as in competency 5, but later in the session.*

Therapist:  What kind of effort have you put into making the anger go away?

Client:      A lot. I can't even begin to describe how hard it has been.

Write here what your response would be (using competency 6):

What are your thoughts in saying this? What are you responding to and what are you hoping to accomplish?

---

## COMPETENCY 7: The therapist helps the client make contact with the cost of unwillingness relative to valued life ends.

### EXERCISE 2.7

*This transcript continues with the same client as in competency 6.*

Therapist:   What are some of the things that have happened because of this difficulty? How has your life changed as a result of how hard this has been?

Client:   Well, I am suspicious of men. I think they're all trying to pull the wool over my eyes. I have stopped dating completely. I tried it a couple of times, but found myself being cranky on the dates. I'm incredibly lonely and feel angry at men ... I blame men for that. I'm just out of control about men... How can I ever trust them?

Write here what your response would be (using competency 7):

What are your thoughts in saying this? What are you responding to and what are you hoping to accomplish?

---

## COMPETENCY 8: The therapist helps the client to experience the qualities of willingness.

### EXERCISE 2.8

*This transcript continues with the same client as in competency 7, but in a later session.*

Therapist:   How important is it to you to have another relationship?

Client:   I would really like one, but I just don't think it is possible. Something really significant would have to change.

Write here what your response would be (using competency 8):

What are your thoughts in saying this? What are you responding to and what are you hoping to accomplish?

## COMPETENCY 9: The therapist uses exercises and metaphors to demonstrate willingness as an action in the presence of difficult internal experience.

### EXERCISE 2.9

A fifty-year-old male is in therapy because his wife has insisted he get help for his withdrawn and irritable style of interacting with her. He reports feeling distant and wanting his wife to leave him alone following a misunderstanding during which some of his money was lost. He notes that he is extremely disappointed.

*Therapist:* What would you choose to have happen with this relationship? Are you wanting it to end?

*Client:* No, I don't want a divorce or anything like that. I just can't bring myself to talk to her, I almost can't even look at her. I know the lost money was not her fault, but I still blame her. I want the money back.

Write here what your response would be (using competency 9):

What are your thoughts in saying this? What are you responding to and what are you hoping to accomplish?

## COMPETENCY 10: The therapist models willingness in the therapeutic relationship and helps the client to generalize these skills outside therapy.

### EXERCISE 2.10

*This transcript continues with the same client as in competency 9, but later in the session.*

*Client:* I am ashamed that I'm so focused on the money. It is hard to admit. I am worried you might think I'm an asshole.

*Therapist:* It is hard to admit these things. It can be anxiety provoking.

*Client:* Yeah, I'm having a hard time talking about it with you … I'm not sure you can help.

Write here what your response would be (using competency 10):

What are your thoughts in saying this? What are you responding to and what are you hoping to accomplish?

# Core Competency Model Responses

## COMPETENCY 1

### Sample 2.1a

*Therapist:* Another way to say what you just said is, "I've got to try trying harder." Have you tried to try harder before?

*Client:* Sure. And harder, and harder.

*Therapist:* So, I want you to consider that the problem here maybe isn't that you haven't tried hard enough. Maybe the problem is something about the tools you've been given by society, by your parents, and your history—the things you've been taught to do to deal with this. Maybe they just don't work here. It's as if you've been trying to use a hammer to paint a masterpiece. Now, I'm also not saying I have a different, better tool—because you've done that, too—looked for a better tool. This trap is trickier than that.

**Explanation:** It is important for the therapist to openly recognize that control of internal experience is a socially trained phenomenon. It is not the client's fault that he would try such a maneuver. He has been taught that this maneuver should work.

### Sample 2.1b

*Therapist:* So, trying harder seems like the thing to do? But haven't you tried hard in the past? You have gone to treatment programs, therapists, and a psychiatrist. You've listed numerous things you've tried. You've tried hard, yes? Look at your experience. What do you know from there [points to client's heart] and not there [points to client's head]? What does your experience say about the results of "trying hard"?

*Client:* It hasn't worked so far.

*Therapist:* Right. And what if that is because it can't? What if you really did give it a good attempt, but this is how trying hard actually works in this area?

**Explanation:** Here the therapist validates the client's effort, while pointing to the fruitlessness of this effort. We are not asking the client to believe it is fruitless because the therapist says so, but rather to examine his or her own experience to see whether this effort has paid off.

## COMPETENCY 2

### Sample 2.2a

*Therapist:* So, you would have people around you, and you could work. Things would just be better in general. But something seems funny here. You've been working at making things different for quite some time, and as far as I can tell, things haven't become what you had hoped. In fact, here you are, sitting in front of me seeking yet another way to make your anxiety—to make you different.

**Explanation:** The therapist states that something is "funny," as if to say this is not the client's fault, but the way this works is odd. This is a relatively defused contact with workability. The therapist points out that the client again seems to be doing the same thing he has done in the past. This statement points to the paradox.

### Sample 2.2b

*Therapist:*   Do you see what is happening here? Here you are working to make your anxiety go away, but it stays. In fact, it seems that if you don't want it, you've got it. If you don't want your anxiety, you must have anxiety. In fact, [somewhat playfully] not being able to get rid of your anxiety is something to be anxious about. In your experience, as you've worked on this, has your problem seemed to be getting larger or smaller?

**Explanation:** The therapist shares an idea with the client that reflects the paradox of control that "if you don't want it, you've got it," and asks the client whether this fits with his experience. She also directly points to the issue of what the client's experience says about how this has worked for him in reducing his anxiety over time.

## COMPETENCY 3

### Sample 2.3a

*Therapist:*   In your experience, has there ever been a significant amount of time when you did not experience anxiety?

*Client:*   [shakes head no]

*Therapist:*   And how workable has it been to try to make it go away? Is this struggle opening up your life or closing it down?

**Explanation:** One of the goals of ACT is to help the client move toward a workable agenda that is guided by values. It is from this point forward that the client, while engaging in willingness, takes steps intended to build a better life, not a better feeling. Again, workability is about living well as defined by the client, not necessarily feeling well.

### Sample 2.3b

*Therapist:*   You've hired me, I'm here to work for you, right?

*Client:*   Yeah, I guess.

*Therapist:*   So, part of my job is to tell you what I see, right?

*Client:*   Yeah. What do you see?

*Therapist:*   From what you've told me, you've done many if not most of the reasonable, sensible, logical things you could do to get your anxiety under control. But something seems strange here. It seems like nothing has worked. Bottom line, this—what you've been doing—isn't working. Not in terms of reducing your anxiety: it's still there. And not in terms of your life working: you still aren't around people, still not working.

**Explanation:** The therapist directly addresses the issue of workability, both in the domain of gaining control over emotional experience and also in terms of larger life goals.

## COMPETENCY 4

### Sample 2.4a

*Therapist:* Feeling silly is tied to this, too ... another thing to get over. It really feels as though you've been in a battle for a long time. First, feeling anger, and then feeling you shouldn't have the anger, and then feeling embarrassed and stupid about the anger. This has been a difficult struggle, and also it just seems to be growing. It seems as if you are in a tug-of-war with your emotions. If they win, you lose. And you keep trying to win, but it seems that no matter how hard you pull, your emotions don't seem to lose. I wonder if there is a different way to play this game? Maybe this isn't about winning this tug-of-war, but learning how to drop the rope.

**Explanation:** Here the therapist is working with the client to help her see that the problem is the struggle with emotional content, not the content itself. Feelings of anger and embarrassment, and thoughts of being stupid, are just that: feelings and thoughts. If the client is willing to feel these things as they are, then she can step out of the struggle and get refocused on life direction. This isn't a simple thing, by the way; it is difficult to "drop the rope" because battling to make the feelings go away feels like the thing to do. As the therapist, you will want to be careful to communicate this recognition of the difficulty of the struggle and how easy it is to engage the struggle.

### Sample 2.4b

*Therapist:* Well, let's take a look at the anger for a moment. If I could reach over and peel the anger out of you and see what is left behind, what do you think I'd discover?

*Client:* [hesitates] More anger.

*Therapist:* And if I could peel that away, too? I wonder if I might discover a very powerful feeling of hurt and betrayal ... Is it possible the anger is a way to escape the pain?

*Client:* [nods]

*Therapist:* What if all of this struggle you have been experiencing is about avoiding pain, but the only way to move forward is to turn toward the pain, rather than away from it?

**Explanation:** The therapist is addressing avoidance as part of the struggle. In this example, the therapist is leading the client in the direction of willingness to experience pain as an alternative to the long-standing struggle to escape pain. The goal is to help the client recognize and welcome the hurt, rather than staying focused on escaping the same. If she is willing to experience pain, she has functionally dropped the rope.

## COMPETENCY 5

### Sample 2.5a

*Therapist:* Do you know what would happen if you went inside the anger and tried to see what is there? Maybe it doesn't need to "go away" for you to do something different with it.

**Explanation:** Just raising the possibility of a different approach undermines an avoidance agenda.

**Sample 2.5b**

*Therapist:*   I can see why it doesn't make sense to you... but it seems that it depends on your goal. If your goal is to feel better, to not be angry anymore, then it seems trying harder to fix anger would be a reasonable thing to do. It's logical, right? However, if your goal is to find another relationship, then getting rid of anger may deflect you from doing what is here to be done. There are other things people do to find relationships: go to parties, make phone calls, have friends introduce them to someone—like that. It seems you are trading away finding a relationship for getting rid of anger.

**Explanation:** This response points to how control of internal events is often engaged in at the expense of vitality. The deal is, when the client doesn't feel angry anymore, she will start to find someone. In the meantime, years of her life are drifting by. If she is willing to feel the anger and the hurt, while also making choices about vitality, she might not feel so stuck. It is important to note here that the therapist is not asking the client to be angry. Rather, the therapist is supporting moving forward and creating the opportunity to be in relationship, instead of insisting a different feeling be there first.

## COMPETENCY 6

**Sample 2.6a**

*Therapist:*   What do you think would happen if you stopped putting so much effort into this? It seems like a lot of suffering accompanies this effort. Is there a potential for less suffering?

**Explanation:** By using this kind of questioning, the therapist is pointing out the difference between willingness and suffering. The effort alone has become burdensome and weighs on the client. Simply suggesting "no effort" is both a willingness move and can potentially lead to a decrease in suffering.

**Sample 2.6b**

*Therapist:*   Does the difficulty of trying to make your anger go away make you angry?

*Client:*   [nods and laughs]

*Therapist:*   I thought it might. A strange thing happens when we are working to control certain emotions. If you really don't want to be anxious, for example, then you feel anxious about getting anxious. Or if you really don't want to feel stupid and silly, then you feel stupid and silly about feeling stupid and silly. Do you see what I'm talking about?

*Client:*   [acknowledges the paradox]

*Therapist:*   And now you have anger about your anger. We could call it "clean anger" and "dirty anger." The clean anger is the anger that shows up when you feel betrayed ... and hurt is in there, too. The dirty anger is anger about the anger. So, suffering has been added to your anger. Look to your experience and tell me, are you suffering about your anger?

**Explanation:** Again, the therapist is helping the client investigate the difference between willingness and suffering. Willingness to experience the initial anger and hurt, while also noticing she has thoughts of being duped, is much different from feeling these things and then insisting she does not feel them. The insistence creates more pain.

## COMPETENCY 7

**Sample 2.7a**

*Therapist:* Before we talk about trust, I want to take a look at what has happened to your life. You are suspicious, lonely, and angry, and you've stopped dating. I'm guessing there are other ways in which you have changed your interactions with men—and I bet with women, too, when they are talking about men.

*Client:* Yes, I get mad at my friends when they talk about how great guys are.

*Therapist:* So, now you're lonely, angry, and suspicious, and you have stopped dating and have changed the way you relate to your friends when talking about men. This is getting costly.

**Explanation:** Working to help the client see the cost of unwillingness is often done by focusing on what the client has given up or lost as a result of trying to control emotions. In a sense, the client's life has become smaller. The goal is to help the client see the cost as it relates to the client's own value, and choose willingness as the alternative.

**Sample 2.7b**

*Therapist:* It sounds as though you will have to trust men again before you can have the relationship and life you would like.

*Client:* [agrees]

*Therapist:* The problem is trust doesn't work that way. It doesn't just show up. Trust is a process. In the meantime, while you're waiting to be trusting, you find yourself alone. And I'm wondering if, when you're sitting there feeling lonely, your trust of men is growing or getting smaller?

**Explanation:** Here the therapist is pointing to the difficulty of trying to make a particular feeling show up as a way out of another experience. This, too, can be costly. If the client is waiting to feel trust, she could be waiting a long time. And, as with this example, sitting alone being angry doesn't build trust in men; it builds mistrust. The cost of being unwilling to feel what is there when she goes out with men doesn't allow the process of building trust to happen.

**Sample 2.7c**

*Therapist:* If you were able to trust men, what would you hope would happen?

*Client:* [in a sarcastic tone] Well, I'd then be able to at least have a shot at being in a decent relationship, if I could actually find a decent guy.

*Therapist:* So, what you want is to get over this guy so you can have a decent relationship, right?

*Client:* Yeah.

*Therapist:* So, can I ask you a question about that? And I'd have you check your experience as you answer it. Don't just check your head: notice what your experience has to say. As you work hard to get over this past breakup, are you finding it working out the way you hope it will? You know, as you worked to get over it, are you getting closer to having the kind of relationship with a man that you want, or have you found yourself paradoxically moving further away from it?

**Explanation:** The therapist helps the client to examine the paradox of control in terms of some values the client has in life.

## COMPETENCY 8

### Sample 2.8a

*Therapist:* Well, just notice how your mind pulls you into the future, as if to be, feel, and think what is present you have to change something. What if instead we try to go into *this* moment? What if it were okay to feel what you feel and think what you think? Not "okay" meaning you like it, but "okay" meaning you are present—like "check" or "roger that." Experiencing fear of loss or betrayal will show up when it shows up. We can't predict the future. If this makes sense to you, the question really is this: what is present for you *now*, and are you willing to experience that more fully? What is going on for you as you say this? What is your body doing, for example?

**Explanation:** Willingness is not about the future, but about the present. There are always feelings and thoughts to be experienced. Orienting the client to this notion, and taking the client into the present, helps her see one of the qualities of willingness experientially, not just by instruction.

### Sample 2.8b

*Therapist:* So ... here it is. It feels like something significant would have to occur—like never being duped again. "Duped" would have to go.

*Client:* Yeah, I don't want to feel stupid like that.

*Therapist:* Well, there is another significant thing here that we should look at. It's called "not having relationships." That feels significant.

*Client:* [quietly] Yeah. [pause]

*Therapist:* Can you contact duped? What are the qualities of duped? It sounds like "stupid" is in there. What else is in there? What else is in duped?

*Client:* [thinking] Well, I guess I feel a little shame and embarrassment, like I should have known better.

*Therapist:* So there is betrayal—which is painful stuff—and what comes along with it is embarrassment and a little shame, and your mind is giving you "stupid" and "should have known better."

*Client:* Yeah. I even feel it a bit as we talk about it.

*Therapist:* Ah, as you feel that and think that, is it possible to carry that stuff with you willingly, and to head into a relationship or into the stuff that you do to get a relationship?

*Client:* I suppose I could, but I don't want to.

*Therapist:* Understandable.

*Client:* I mean, I don't want to have to feel that again.

*Therapist:* I hear you. And yet here you are feeling it a little even as we talk about it. You have a good sense of what these experiences feel like.

*Client:* I know them all too well.

*Therapist:*  Will those be the things that keep you out of relationships? Or, given that you know these, could you feel them and think them, and still do the stuff that gets you into relationships?

*Client:*  You mean, like feel embarrassed and still go out with someone?

*Therapist:*  Yeah, would you be willing? I'm not asking you to like it, but if it got you headed toward connection and relationship, would you be willing to hold this stuff as you know it and take some kind of action?

**Explanation:** The client's statement that something would have to change suggests experiential avoidance. The therapist makes a guess at what the client is avoiding by saying, "Duped would have to go." The therapist then proceeds to bring the avoided emotional experience into the room and leads the client to explore it, make room for it, and experience it willingly. At the end, the therapist is careful to differentiate willingness from wanting or liking and also ties willingness to valuing.

## COMPETENCY 9

### Sample 2.9a

*Therapist:*  So, one thing we could do is focus on the money, but that doesn't seem as though it would be useful right now. If you're interested in keeping this relationship, it seems we need to work on the things that would make that happen. You are saying you can't bring yourself to talk to her or look at her, as if the disappointment were holding you back.

*Client:*  [agrees]

*Therapist:*  Is it possible to feel disappointed and actively choose to talk to and look at your wife?

*Client:*  No, I don't think that's possible.

*Therapist:*  If it were possible, would you choose it?

*Client:*  Yes.

*Therapist:*  So here is the deal ... Would you be willing to feel disappointed and talk to your wife if it meant you got to keep the marriage? [pause] Have you ever said something with your mind, but done something different with your action? For example, have you ever said, "I don't feel like getting out of bed today and going to work," and then you did? This is a bit like that— you have the feeling of disappointment and you talk to your wife.

**Explanation:** Multiple things are happening in this response. Establishing willingness as a choice and taking action are both present. The therapist would continue to work with the client on taking action while welcoming the disappointment. The disappointment does not need to be resolved before the client can begin to interact with his wife. And as with the other examples in this chapter, it is likely his disappointment will grow if he continues to choose not to interact with her. Using the Annoying Neighbor Edna metaphor, as described earlier, could be helpful at this point.

### Sample 2.9b

*Therapist:*  [stands up and walks around] I can't stand up and walk around right now. There is no way for me to do this. I am incapable of walking at this moment. [sits back down] And I certainly don't want to sit down. [pause] See how that happened? I had the thoughts that I didn't want to do something, and I did it. You have the thoughts you can't talk to your wife, and you could do it … if you choose to. Now, I know it doesn't seem as easy as what I just did, but I want to point out that this might be both easy and hard at the same time. It is hard because your mind says it is, and it is easy because it is as simple as a chosen action. Probably lots of thoughts and feelings will come and go as you choose to talk to your wife. These things work like that—they come and go, yet they are not the determiners of your behavior. What will you choose?

**Explanation:** This small demonstration helps the client to see that thoughts do not control behavior. They are associated but not causal. The client can choose to take action with respect to his relationship: he can choose to look at his wife and talk to her while also experiencing disappointment and all the other emotions and thoughts that are likely to show up in such a situation. Additionally, pointing to self as an ongoing experiencing being can loosen what seem to be the clutches of inaction as a result of disappointment.

## COMPETENCY 10

**Sample 2.10a**

*Therapist:* I'm not sure I can help, either, especially if the goal is to decrease shame or not feel disappointed. And I feel just a little anxious saying that because I know you really don't want to feel those things … and your goal when we first met was for me to help you not feel those things. However, I think we need to move directly toward them. I'm willing to press forward with this anxiety I'm feeling and see what happens. I'm hoping you will join me.

**Explanation:** This is a small self-disclosure regarding the therapist's own anxiety about being able to help the client. The key is that the therapist continues working while also feeling the anxiety that comes from pressing the client in a direction he has avoided. This is not to say you wouldn't titrate what you do and say as you move toward shame. This merely points out how the therapist can be willing in session. Of note, this should not be contrived. Whatever willingness the therapist shows in session should be genuine.

**Sample 2.10b**

*Therapist:* I can feel myself wanting to move away from this topic because I can see how much pain it is causing you. I can see the tears in your eyes. I almost want to change the subject and talk about the lost money, but I think it's very important to stay with the shame and disappointment. I wonder if we could just take a moment and stay present to what is in the room?

**Explanation:** Here the therapist demonstrates willingness by asking himself and the client to stay present to the different emotions in the room. It would be easy to shift the topic to lost money or conversation about the wife. It is important, however, for both the therapist and the client to remain present to the emotion.

# FOR MORE INFORMATION

For more about acceptance, including exercises and metaphors, see *Acceptance and Commitment Therapy: An Experiential Approach to Behavior Change*, by Hayes, Strosahl, and Wilson (1999), chapters 4 and 5 (pp. 87–147).

For more exercises and worksheets about acceptance to use for yourself and clients, see *Get Out of Your Mind and Into Your Life*, by Hayes and Smith (2005), chapters 3 through 4 (pp. 33–52) and 9 through 10 (pp. 121–152).

# CHAPTER 3

# UNDERMINING COGNITIVE FUSION

*I used to think that the brain was the most wonderful organ in my body. Then I realized who was telling me this.*

—Emo Philips

Key targets for cognitive defusion:

- ✓ Help clients see thoughts as what they are—thoughts—so those thoughts can be responded to in terms of their workability given the client's values, rather than in terms of their literal meaning.

- ✓ · Help clients attend to thinking and experiencing as an ongoing behavioral process, and away from the literal meaning of the contents of the mind.

In relation to their thinking, people are a bit like fish who do not know they are swimming in water. We swim in a river of thought, but rarely notice this fact. And whether we are aware of it or not, language regulates our behavior. ACT works to weaken the unhelpful influence of language in key contexts by helping us to leap out of the river of thought and begin to observe thinking for what it is: a largely automatic, unintentional, and historical process of relating one event to another—in other words, "minding."

"See, that's the stuff I'm talking about."

# WHAT IS COGNITIVE DEFUSION?

ACT argues that the problem with human suffering as it relates to thoughts is not that we have the wrong thoughts, but rather that we spend too much time "in" them or "looking from" them, rather than simply looking at them or observing them. Cognitive defusion attempts to circumvent this problem by drawing the client's attention to thinking as an ongoing behavioral process, and helping clients to spend more time seeing thoughts as thoughts, so those thoughts can be responded to in terms of their workability, rather than their literal truth.

We generally respond to thoughts and feeling as if they directly caused our behavior. For example, in normal discourse, if you ask someone why he or she stood in a corner the whole time at a party, an acceptable answer might be "I was too worried; I thought I might embarrass myself." By this way of thinking, the thought—"I might embarrass myself"—caused the behavior, withdrawal. However, we can easily think of contexts in which this relationship might be quickly altered; for example, if someone at the party shouted "Fire!" At that point, "I might embarrass myself" would no longer be a reason to stay in the corner, but perhaps a reason to leave it. According to ACT, the idea that the thought caused withdrawal is only one way of speaking about the situation, and perhaps a disempowering one. ACT also views human emotion through this same lens. Thoughts and feelings are always seen in context, and only in certain contexts are particular thoughts or feelings tied to particular behaviors. Attention is turned from the specific content of the thoughts and feelings and onto the person's relationship to or the function of those thoughts and feelings. Alter the context, and we alter the function of the thought or feeling.

Thus, in cognitive defusion, rather than trying to directly change the form of thoughts or emotions, or the frequency of thoughts or emotions, the therapist targets the context that relates the thoughts and feelings to undesirable overt behavior, thus creating greater response flexibility. An example of a specific defusion technique can clarify this point (Milk, Milk, Milk exercise, Hayes et al., 1999, pp. 154–155). If a client rapidly says a word over and over again for thirty to sixty seconds, two things usually happen: the word temporarily loses some or most of its meaning, and other functions of the word tend to emerge more dominantly, such as its sound or how it feels to move one's mouth in this manner. You can try it yourself very easily. First, imagine a gallon of milk for a few moments and then repeat the word "milk" for at least sixty seconds. Listen to and notice what happens. This technique can then be repeated with a self-referential word that is difficult for the client—"worthless," for instance. As in some other defusion techniques, the word or phrase is still present, but a nonliteral context is created that diminishes its normal symbolic functions and increases its more direct functions (in this example, its auditory or kinesthetic functions). Stated another way, defusion techniques help clients to see thoughts as thoughts and to be less fused with what the thoughts imply. Additionally, creating defusion is not done through logical argument or instruction, but rather through modifying the context in which thoughts are experienced. As a result, the literal functions of problematic thoughts are less likely to dominate as a source of influence over behavior, and more helpful, direct, and varied sources of control over action can gain ground.

# WHY COGNITIVE DEFUSION?

Defusion techniques are most useful when the client is engaged with thinking in a number of potentially problematic ways. Examples include when the client is holding the literal meaning of a word to be true, when the client is trying to control thinking, when the client is generating reasons to justify behaviors, or when the client is insisting on being right, even at personal expense. The defusion techniques used in ACT include paradox, meditative exercises, experiential exercises, metaphor, and language conventions.

Clients are encouraged to focus on effective action, given the current situation once defusion has been established.

The following hypothetical situation illustrates how this might be helpful. John's alarm does not go off, and he wakes up late. He immediately thinks of his wife, and the thought appears: "She set the alarm wrong." Now, if he does not catch that this is a thought, he may begin to look at the situation as structured by that thought. He does not need to be aware of this process in order for it to occur. If he were, in that moment, aware of the process of thinking and of the fact that he just had a thought, he might not say the next thing he says, which is "You forgot to set the clock again. Now I'm late." His wife now feels blamed. An argument ensues. If John had been able to observe the thought, he might have caught that it was just that—a thought—and been able to respond more flexibly. He might have noticed the thought, and then focused on what would probably be more effective in this situation, and following his values to be open and loving, he might have said, "Honey, do you know what happened with the alarm? Did I forget to set it?" Being able to simply catch the process of thinking in flight and watch it as an observer can begin to create an opening wherein one might be able to step out of habitual patterns and engage in more effective and values-based actions.

Therapists learning ACT can struggle with defusion because there is something inherently difficult in using the main tool at our disposal—language—to weaken language. The situation is similar to how oil well fires are often extinguished. An explosion (itself fire) is created at the source of the oil well fire that momentarily uses up all the available oxygen. The remaining oil is left without oxygen, and thus the fire ceases. Similarly, ACT uses language, and loopholes in its functioning, to extinguish its effects in certain areas of our lives. It's not that language itself is eliminated, but some of its less useful functions are weakened in some contexts, so more flexible ways of knowing can have greater influence over behavior.

It would be nice if fusion could be weakened by simply explaining the dilemma, much as we have done in this chapter so far. Unfortunately this explanation depends entirely upon literal meaning for its impact, and in order to defuse, we must step outside literal meaning. To do this, ACT uses language in nonliteral ways, such as the way a coach might speak to a player, for example, by saying, "See if you can hold that thought like you might hold a butterfly that has landed on your finger."

## WHAT SHOULD TRIGGER THIS PROCESS?

Focusing on this process is most appropriate whenever the therapist finds the client believing, "buying," "holding onto," or clinging to a particular thought or word, and these same actions are limiting or preventing healthy movement in the client's life. This usually shows up when a client seems to be heavily saddled or "trapped" by a thought or feeling and finds himself or herself unable to take valued action based on the same thought or feeling. For instance, a client might say, "I will never be able to find a partner, I am just worthless. Who would want me?" Here, we can see that the client is trapped by the word "worthless." Held to be literally true, it seems that finding a partner would be impossible: who would want a worthless human being as a partner? However, if the client can come to see that "worthless" is a word that is said under certain conditions and given a particular history, and that it is not something he or she literally *is*, then "I can't find a partner because I am worthless" has less control over behavior. This does not mean the client has to stop thinking he or she is worthless or start thinking he or she is worthy; rather, if the client can see the thought as a thought, then its power to control actions is lost, even if that thought continues to occur. The following transcript demonstrates the triggering of use of defusion in session (approximately five sessions into therapy).

*Therapist:* You seem pretty blue today. What's happening for you?

*Client:* It's just always the same story … I try to do something to make things better and it fails … It always fails. It's always like that.

*Therapist:* So there's this place where you get stuck when this same story, "I try and nothing works," shows up.

*Client:* [hangs head and speaks softly] Let's face it, I'm doom and gloom.

*Therapist:* You've mentioned that several times now. You've told me you are doom and gloom.

*Client:* I am doom and gloom.

*Therapist:* I want to recognize the pain of this thought and the struggle that is built around it, but I'm wondering if you might be willing to be a little playful with me for a moment?

*Client:* Sure … might as well.

*Therapist:* This might sound a little silly, but would you sing the words "I am doom and gloom" for me?

*Client:* [chuckles] What?

*Therapist:* Let's just work with this for a minute. Give it a try.

*Client:* [sings the words "I am doom and gloom"; unbeknownst to the therapist, he has quite a good voice and sings solemnly and with heartfelt pain]

*Therapist:* Great … Could you sing it again? Only this time, sing it with great enthusiasm, as if you are in a Broadway play.

*Client:* [chuckles again] Okay. [sings the words, but from the new perspective]

The client was then asked to sing the words from several other perspectives: as a woman, as a small child, as Mickey Mouse. With each new rendition, the therapist could see the client beginning to defuse from the words.

*Client:* The words just seem kind of funny to me now.

*Therapist:* Interesting how that works, isn't it? When you are really trapped in those words, it seems that they paralyze you. But now that we have loosened the trap a little, what do you notice?

*Client:* They don't seem to have the same power. They're kind of funny now.

*Therapist:* From this place, being loosened from those words, I wonder if we can start to work on where you are headed?

This is just one example of the many ways defusion can be brought into session. It is important to note that these exercises are designed to take the meaning out of (*deliteralize*) the words, not to change the number of times the client thinks them, nor to change them into positive words (e.g., "I am great and good"). Also, defusion should be done with a compassionate nature, which can be playful or serious. It should never be done from a position of one-upmanship or from a position that makes the client feel silly or humiliated for having the thoughts.

# WHAT IS THE METHOD?

Already, scores of defusion techniques have been developed for a wide variety of clinical presentations. For example, a negative thought can be observed dispassionately by having the client watch the thought as if watching an uninteresting, nonprovocative television commercial. The thought can be treated as an externally observed event by the client, who gives it a shape, size, color, speed, or form. The client can thank his or her mind for such an interesting thought; label the process of thinking (e.g., "I'm having the thought that I am no good"); or mindfully observe the thoughts, feelings, and memories that occur in consciousness. Such procedures attempt to reduce the literal quality of the thought, weakening the tendency to treat the thought as what it refers to (e.g., the experience "I am no good") rather than what it is directly experienced to be (e.g., the thought "I am no good"). The result of defusion is usually a decrease in the believability of or attachment to private events, rather than an immediate change in their frequency or their form.

## EXERCISE: DEFUSION, PART 1

Bring one of your clients to mind, preferably a difficult one. Think of three thoughts this person has about himself or herself, his or her life, or his or her future that are difficult for this client. Try to be specific. Record these below:

Thought 1:

Thought 2:

Thought 3:

We will come back to these later in the chapter.

In the following sections, we illustrate the major types of defusion techniques, organized by the general therapeutic target. By arranging them in this way, we hope to show what lies beneath the methods themselves. Defusion is not just a specific technique; it is a functional process, and it is this kind of knowledge that moves ACT from a mere collection of procedures to a clinical model. In popular ACT books, such as *Get Out of Your Mind and Into Your Life* (Hayes & Smith, 2005), we even teach ACT clients how to generate their own novel defusion techniques. The purpose of this section is similar. Thus, these are examples; they are not "*the* list" of ACT defusion techniques, nor are they exhaustive. The list is limited only by your own creativity and that of the ACT/RFT community worldwide.

Before we move into the different defusion techniques, it is important to remember that defusion is not confrontational, although it can be powerful. It is an excellent technique to help clients observe their minds. However, clients can report feeling confused, disjointed, or "out of sorts" during and after sessions that focus heavily on defusion. These feeling states are perfectly acceptable. Artful defusion can often have the quality of a light-footed dancer or of a judo master. Both of these experts do not meet partner movements with force, but rather join with and redirect their partner's movements in more useful directions. In defusion, client verbalizations are bounced around, mixed up, and played with in order to see them from varying viewpoints and to explore their many qualities. This is done without direct confrontation or refutation. For example, an ACT therapist might appreciate the beautiful creativity of a client's mind by congratulating him or her for coming to a bleak conclusion. In this case, if the client said, "So then I thought I'd completely blown it," the therapist might respond, "Ah, very nice. That's a good one. Go mind!" Be playful with defusion, but as noted, always maintain compassion.

## Teach the Limits of Language in Rediscovering Experience

"Verbal knowing rests atop nonverbal knowing so completely that an illusion is created that all knowledge is verbal" (Hayes et al., 1999, pp. 153–154). ACT therapists often introduce defusion by pointing to the limits of conscious thought. Various metaphors and exercises are used to demonstrate that our minds do not hold all the answers; that, in fact, there are ways of knowing that operate beyond the mind. One way to do this is to appeal to the client's experience in areas of his or her life in which what the mind knows may not be enough or even can be detrimental. For example, some tasks involve very well-regulated verbal knowledge, such as how to find a certain website on the Internet. Other tasks are less so; for example, learning how to play a musical instrument or a new sport. Clients also may have had experiences with tasks wherein language actually interfered with effective functioning, such as in performance anxiety, sexual behavior, or "choking" on the golf green. The therapist can tentatively suggest, "Although language and rational thought can be helpful in some domains, what if there are other domains of life in which being logical and following what one's mind has to say is actually problematic?"

This basic idea can be demonstrated by asking the client to verbally instruct the therapist to engage in physical movement, as in the case of the following transcript. In it, the therapist responds to the client's instruction by asking the client how to do each move instructed. This exercise nicely points to the arrogance of language because physical movement is generally learned through experience, not through instruction. The basic idea of the exercise is to show the client that some of the things we know how to do are not known through conscious knowledge, but rather were learned through experience (Hayes et al., 1999).

*Therapist:* Tell me how to walk from my chair to the door.

*Client:* Well, first stand up, and then put one foot in front of the other until you are standing over in front of the door.

*Therapist:* Good. How do I do that?

*Client:* What? Oh, push up with your hands on the arm of the chair until you are standing, and then move the muscles in your leg so that you are stepping forward … let your weight move with you.

*Therapist:* Great. How do I do that?

*Client:* [chuckles] Tell your brain to tell your hands and legs to move.

*Therapist:* How do I do that? [continues with the client in a playful way, asking, "How do I do that?" after each instruction, until the client says, "I don't know."] And anything you tell me to do, I am going to say, "How do I do that?" You see, it was a little bit of a trick. I asked you to tell me how to walk, and your mind went to work thinking it knew how to tell me that. All minds do that. But the deal is that neither you nor I learned how to walk by someone telling us how. You probably learned how to walk before you even had words. We learned to walk by experience. We tried to stand up, we fell down, we bonked our heads, but eventually learned how to walk. Experience taught us how. Many things are like that, but we lose touch with them because our minds get so arrogant and think they know everything. There are many things that you know by experience; for instance, you know feelings won't harm you, even if your mind tells you they will.

Following such an exercise, the therapist can suggest something such as, "What if it's a similar case in your struggle with anxiety? Your mind keeps telling you how to solve the problem, but it just doesn't know how to get out of a situation like this. What if we need some other way of responding to the situation you are in, something that's a bit more like learning how to walk than it is like reading about how to do these things?"

Another way to examine the limits of language is to examine how we learn any new skilled activity. For example, the therapist can ask the client to remember how he or she learned how to ride a bike. Clients usually report some combination of simply getting on the bike, trying to find their balance, falling down, and trying again. Having a parent tell us to "stay balanced" doesn't teach us to balance. Knowing with our mind that the pedals turn the wheels doesn't make us a bike rider. Clients tend to easily get the point that logical understanding and knowledge take them only so far. At some point, developing certain skills depends upon getting engaged in the activity, and letting the consequences shape their actions.

Engaging in these kinds of exercises with clients points to something that is often lost to mind, or at least hidden from view: experiential knowledge. We know many things based on this kind of knowledge, and part of what we are trying to do in ACT is get clients back in touch with experiential knowing. It is from the place of experiential knowledge that clients can come to see their emotions, thoughts, memories, and sensations as ongoing events that rise and fall, that come and go and then come and go again. It is also from this place that clients learn that fear and anxiety do not literally kill them, and that they are not "broken"; these are just experiences (e.g., thoughts) they are having at a given moment. Furthermore, it is important to remind clients that these counterintuitive and nonliteral skills require practice. They need to implement what they have learned in session outside of session. Here, the ACT therapist can suggest that coming to ACT sessions and not engaging in exercises outside of sessions is a bit like going to the hardware store, buying a new table saw, and then leaving it at the checkout counter.

Other examples of teaching the limits of language include commanding oneself to have a different history; telling the story about the ancient king who, in his arrogance, sat in the sea and commanded the tide not to come in, and then drowned; and attempting to e-mail orders to a person who does not speak one's language.

## Create Distance Between Thought and Thinker, Feeling and Feeler

When the literal, evaluative functions of language dominate, we are not aware of the distinction between ourselves as the experiencer of these private events and the events themselves. This is the usual human state: "I am what I think and feel." A number of ACT strategies are aimed at helping clients increase the distinction between the experiencing self and those things experienced. That is, thoughts and feelings are something clients *have* rather than something they *are*. Making these distinctions brings forward nondominant qualities of language, such as its aesthetic or functional qualities, and increases the flexibility of ways in which we interact with our own minds. In the next sections we give several examples of ways to apply this principle.

## OBJECTIFY LANGUAGE

We all have a great deal of experience dealing with the objects in the environment as separate from ourselves. In this same way, therapists can teach clients to deal with thoughts and feelings as objects to be viewed. The idea is to create a healthy distance between self and thoughts and other private events held as objects. This is not to say that thoughts are not contacted; they are still present but are viewed from a different perspective. Using metaphors and exercises can help with this process. Objectifying thoughts can help clients interact with their thoughts in more flexible and practical ways, in much the same way that external objects can be used in multiple ways. For example, the therapist might ask the client to consider whether thoughts are like tools in some ways, as seen in the following transcript.

*Therapist:* If thoughts were like a tool, how might we work with them? We don't usually sit around thinking, "I'm not sure this hammer is the right hammer for me. I don't usually use a hammer like this. I think I'm a two-pound hammer kind of person." We just pick up the hammer and start pounding nails or we don't use it at all. In contrast, when you have the thought, "I'm not sure I can do this, I don't usually live my life this way, I'm pretty much a loser kind of person," that thought doesn't seem to you to be like a tool at all. It's more like, "This is true, this is who I am." In this stance, it's like a hammer that you have no choice but to use. Before you know it, the I-am-not-sure-I-can-do-this hammer or the I-am-a-loser-kind-of-person hammer is in your hands and you are pounding away. Now, would it be possible to step back and look at which thoughts are useful as tools for you to construct a life of value for yourself, rather than having to evaluate them in terms of their truth or untruth?

A variety of other ACT exercises are used to objectify thoughts. For example, private experiences can be compared to bullying passengers on a bus (Hayes et al., 1999, pp. 157–158), either as part of a role play, an eyes-closed exercise, or a metaphor. Particular thoughts or feelings can be written down on cards, and then the client can interact with them in various ways, such as fighting to keep them away instead of accepting them (p. 162).

Another way of objectifying language is to introduce the concept of "mind" and help clients see the mind almost as an external entity that follows them around, always commenting on their actions, judging, evaluating, predicting, and influencing them. This serves both to help clients obtain a healthy distance from their own verbal repertoire, with which they are usually heavily identified, and to create the space to begin to discriminate between being present and being caught up in their own chatter.

Often, ACT therapists refer to the client's mind as if it were speaking to the client, or they reframe the client's thoughts to highlight the distinction between the person and his or her mind. For instance, the therapist might say, "So, your mind said to you …" or "Who is talking to me now: you or your mind?" Sometimes therapists or clients playfully give the client's mind a name, as in the case of the therapist who says, "So, what will Bob [the client's mind] say when you get up tomorrow, knowing we're going to do this exposure exercise?"

Experiential exercises can be a powerful way to help clients make this distinction. A core ACT exercise called Taking Your Mind for a Walk (Hayes et al., 1999, p. 163) requires two people to pair up; depending on whether it is group or individual therapy, these could be either two clients or the client and therapist. In this exercise, each person in the pair is assigned a role. Initially, one person plays the role of the *mind*, and the other plays the role of the *person*. In the role of the mind, the job is to continuously speak to the person in an evaluative, second-guessing, wondering, judging, commenting way to demonstrate what the mind is constantly doing ordinarily. In the role of the person, the client is to take a mindful walk, in silence, going wherever the person chooses to go. The mind doesn't get to pick where it goes, and the person doesn't get to lose his or her mind. The pair takes about a five-minute walk and then they switch roles: the person becomes the role of the mind, and the mind takes the role of the person. Again they walk for about five minutes. Finally, they split up and take a mindful walk alone, again for about five minutes, and then return to the session. Generally, what clients learn in this exercise is that, first, minds are busy and have a lot to say, and second, minds are not in charge—they don't get to dictate the direction in which we go. Clients also learn that no matter where they go, their minds go with them. This shows up when they walk alone and begin to hear their own minds babbling on about things.

## LOOKING *AT* THOUGHTS RATHER THAN *FROM* THOUGHTS

A number of strategies are oriented toward helping the client develop the capacity to look *at* thoughts, rather than always *from* thoughts. This is also referred to as the difference between having a thought and buying a thought. One way to begin this process of just observing mental content is to help clients notice the simple fact that we are constantly speaking to ourselves. A therapist can introduce this idea as shown in the following transcript.

*Therapist:* Now, each of us is constantly speaking to ourselves. Often, however, we're not even aware of the fact that we are doing this. In the background, there's a voice constantly narrating things: "I agree with that. I like that. I don't like that. That's true, that's not. I don't know that I like that. What's he saying?" Even right now, check and see if your mind isn't doing that with what I'm saying right now. [pause] It might be saying, "I'm not sure I agree with that." Or "Yup, I am doing that." If you are thinking, "I'm not doing that," then that's the voice! I'd like you to close your eyes for a second and let's just have you notice how you are constantly talking to yourself. Just simply notice what thoughts come up as you close your eyes. [ten-second pause] Notice how your mind has an opinion, comment, or question about everything. I'd like you to think about your car. What comes up around that? [pause] Think about your father or mother. What does your mind have to say about them? [pause] Notice how you don't even need to do anything, yet it constantly keeps going, doing its thing. Think about the part of yourself you like the least. What comments does your mind have about that? [pause] Constantly it's going, and most of the time we aren't even aware of its presence.

The therapist also can introduce the idea that thoughts are like colored bubbles over the head, as illustrated in this transcript.

*Therapist:* You can think of thoughts as similar to see-through, colored, plastic bubbles on your head. These bubbles are really snug and comfortable, and you don't even know they are there. You can't see them. You can only see through them. You forget that you are looking through the bubble of your thoughts, and so the world appears a particular way. Perhaps the view through the bubble isn't so helpful. The view through thoughts such as "I am not okay" or "I am worthless" limits your way of showing up in the world. The point here is not to get rid of the plastic bubbles. The point is to practice taking them off your head so you can see them clearly for what they are. It makes it easier to do what works when the situation calls for it.

Clients also can be taught to practice the Leaves on a Stream exercise, the Soldiers in the Parade exercise (Hayes et al., 1999, pp. 158–162), or other similar exercises.

# Reveal the Hidden Properties of Language

One area in which language disguises important discriminations is in the area of evaluation versus description. All stimuli with which we interact have various properties. Certain properties are primary, experienced directly through the senses. For example, we might see that a rose is red or feel that concrete is rough. These properties belong to the realm of description. On the other hand, secondary properties of stimuli are derived from language and belong to the realm of evaluation (e.g., "good," "useful," "ugly," "right"). Primary properties are inherent in the stimuli, while secondary "properties" are not really properties of the stimuli at all but are found in the interaction between the person and the stimuli and are the result of language.

Ordinarily, the difference between these two types of properties is obscured. Clients usually come to therapy with a whole host of evaluations about themselves, their world, and the people in their lives. They treat these evaluations as if they were primary, inherent properties of themselves or others. For example, a client might have evaluations such as "I'm bad," "I'm worthless," or "I'm evil." Held literally, these would indeed be very difficult to accept. The acceptance agenda would be difficult to adopt if these evaluations were actually a description of the client's essence. Change would be virtually a necessity. The only way to change the primary properties of a stimulus is literally to break it down and reconstitute it into something else; for example, if we did not like the red rose, we could burn it and turn it into ashes. However, if a distinction can be made between description and evaluation, then that which evokes evaluation does not necessarily need to be changed to be acceptable because the properties aren't in the thing itself, but only in thought. Various exercises that help illustrate the difference between evaluation and description are described in further detail in chapter 5.

Another ACT strategy involves creating contexts in which language can be experienced more directly and with its literal symbolic functions weakened. In these exercises, therapists are not attempting to eliminate the derived functions of words (e.g., the meaning) in any permanent way. Rather, they are trying to bring other, possibly more flexible, functions to the fore, such as those based on the direct stimulus properties of the word (e.g., the way the word looks or sounds, or the effort it takes to create it). Bringing forward the direct stimulus functions of languaging can help make it easier to observe the process of language without fusing as much with its products. In the Milk, Milk, Milk exercise example used earlier, you hear the word "milk" as a word rather than as the substance to which it refers. You can also try other techniques to create this effect. Saying a thought in a Daffy Duck voice, singing out thoughts, speaking them as a fight announcer would, or having contests with clients to see who can come up with the worst evaluation are some techniques (Hayes & Smith, 2005). The point of these exercises is not to ridicule thoughts, but to expand the functions of these thoughts beyond those typically experienced and to develop flexibility with these thoughts so they need not always be experienced in their old, habitual, literal ways, which often lead to yet more struggle and inflexible behavior.

A sample exercise with a client further illustrates how clients can learn to approach thoughts with less attachment to their literal meaning. Consider the following session exchange with a client who suffers from panic disorder.

*Therapist:* I'd like us to do an exercise. Let me tell you what the exercise is, and then you can tell me whether you are willing to do it. I've generated some sentences, and the exercise is to practice saying them. We'll each take turns simply saying all the sentences. I'll go first. The job of the person saying the sentences is to read them out loud, without any attachment to their content. This is about practicing dispassionate observation of thoughts. We will be practicing experiencing the words as words, not as what they say they mean. Got it?

Client:     Sure.

Therapist:  The job of the person listening is to judge whether the other person successfully completed the task; in other words, whether the person was attached or not. Just go with your gut on whether I did it or not. No need to get "mindy" with it or take a long time to decide. Are you willing to do this? I'll go first and then it will be your turn.

Client:     Sure.

Therapist:  [Therapist takes turns with the client reading the following sentences: "I can't seem to find myself." "I'm going to go crazy if I can't get out of here." "A horse, a horse, my kingdom for a horse." "How many times do I have to tell you to stop pressuring me?" "I can't stand it anymore." "Saddle up, cowboy." Each judges the other as pass or fail, depending upon whether the reader seemed attached.] Now, the point of this exercise is not to help these thoughts be easier for you, but rather to practice being in this more detached, observing place with these thoughts. It's also to notice how difficult it is to not get caught by these thoughts, to not process their meaning. Here we were working to just see them for what they also are—just strings of words. What did you notice as you did the exercise?

Other examples of exercises include asking the client to walk around the room while repeatedly saying, "I can't walk around the room" or to do something that might be silly, such as hopping on one foot, and noticing it is possible to feel embarrassed and still engage in the behavior.

## Undermine Larger Sets of Verbal Relations

Most of the strategies just discussed are aimed at undermining literal attachment to smaller sets of mind chatter. Different strategies are required to work on more complex forms of mind behavior. The mind holds extended and interconnected forms of verbal behavior, such as clients' stories about who they are, how they came to be the way they are, and reasons for doing what they do. These stories and reasons provide the verbal glue that creates the incredible stability of many unworkable patterns of behavior.

As humans, we are taught that we must have explanations for our behaviors, and furthermore that these explanations must be coherent. In the realm of behavior that doesn't work, we *all the more so* are expected to have good explanations. The social community demands a person with depression have a really good reason for not getting out of bed or to account for not having worked in three months, and so on. For example, for some people, having a "chemical imbalance" is a good reason for depressed behavior. Data exist that show people who think they have good reasons for their depression tend to be more depressed and less responsive to therapy (Addis & Jacobson, 1996).

Unfortunately, through attachment to these stories, these verbal networks come to control our behavior. Our past becomes our future, with the potential for very negative outcomes. If a client has a story that he or she can't have good relationships because of being abused as a child, then that client is really stuck because no other childhood can be had. If the client is unable to see this story as one of many possible stories, but rather fuses with it and sees it literally as "the truth," then we can easily see how he or she might not engage in finding a relationship. It becomes particularly difficult if clients also buy that they are right about their stories. They can get stuck in very difficult and unworkable patterns of behavior. Fortunately, defusion seems to modify attachment to the validity of reasons to an even greater degree than does cognitive disputation of them (Zettle & Hayes, 1986).

Consider Jessica. A few years ago, she was diagnosed with bipolar disorder following an episode of manic behavior. She since has engaged in extensive reading about what people diagnosed with bipolar disorder are like and how it is a genetic problem resulting in a chemical imbalance in the brain. She feels that because this is biological, she is doomed to repeat endless cycles of excruciating lows and out-of-control highs for the rest of her life, and that there's not much she can do about it. Although her acknowledgment of the diagnosis of bipolar disorder might be potentially helpful in some ways, her story suggests she cannot recover and thus has no reason to try.

As with most clients in such a situation, Jessica has good evidence for her story in the form of research and personal anecdotes of medications helping her. She has been following this story for several years, with the outcome that she takes her medications, but doesn't take many other active steps to improve her life. From an ACT perspective, the question is not whether this story is literally true, but whether it is helpful. Does it lead Jessica toward the kind of life she wants?

The basic strategy ACT uses to undermine attachment to unhelpful stories is to help clients make experiential contact with their constructed nature so their focus can turn from the literal truth of the story to its workability. These strategies are aimed at helping clients develop a healthy skepticism about the mind's ability to evaluate and explain aspects of personal history in a useful way. The following transcript provides an example of how a therapist can introduce this idea.

*Therapist:* We're constantly telling ourselves a story about our lives. In the background, there's a voice that is always narrating about things—telling us about who we are, what we like, how things are going, and so on. It's constantly going, and it's narrating a story to you. The question is, is that story necessarily true? From where did it come? For instance, if I ask you what happened three days after your eleventh birthday, and I want to know in detail about that day, would you be able to tell me?

*Client:* Hmm. No.

*Therapist:* [playfully] How about four days after or five days after? [pause] We could try even one hundred days, and you might catch one or two details. We know very little about what went on in our lives. We remember just a few snippets, and we string these little pieces together into a story. Do you see this? We have these little snippets of things we remember, and massive portions of what happened are missing. We then try to string it all together and create stories to make sense of the pieces we still remember. We tell these stories to ourselves frequently. We conclude things about ourselves—what we are capable of, who we are—and then we live out of that.

*Client:* I see.

*Therapist:* Interestingly, these stories build. Our minds just keep taking in new stuff. And this isn't something that just happened way in our past; it's happening right now. Let's do an exercise about new content being added all the time … and about how we usually don't even recognize it. I'm going to tell you about an imaginary creature called a Gub-Gub (Hayes & Smith, 2005). If you remember what the Gub-Gub says, then we have a million dollars set aside to give to you. Are you ready? Here it is. Gub-Gubs go "Wooo." Can you say it?

*Client:* Wooo.

*Therapist:* Now, don't forget it. Because if I ask you tomorrow and you get those million bucks, it's worth it. What do Gub-Gubs say?

*Client:* Wooo.

*Therapist:* Okay, so now I have to let you know that there's no million dollars. So you can just forget it. What do Gub-Gubs say?

*Client:* [laughs] Wooo.

*Therapist:* Suppose I came back in a month. Would you know what Gub-Gubs say?

*Client:* Sure.

*Therapist:* How about two months? A year? What do Gub-Gubs say?

*Client:* [chuckles]

*Therapist:* If we spent a bit more time talking about Gub-Gubs, it might be that I could visit you at your deathbed and say, "What do Gub-Gubs say?" Might you remember? Now think about what this means. We spend a few minutes on something, and you carry it around in your head for the rest of your life. You have things like this that reach way back across your history. You may not be sure where it came from, but this is the stuff that's your story. These are the thoughts you have about yourself. For example, "The worst thing about me is …" [pauses and directs the client to answer]

*Client:* I'm weak.

*Therapist:* The best thing about me is … [pause]

*Client:* I'm kind.

*Therapist:* The reason I am so weak is …

*Client:* I never learned to be able to stand up for myself.

*Therapist:* Good. That's a beautiful one. Magical. See how fun this is? [sarcastically] Your mind generates explanations, stories, reasons for everything. We could go on, right? There's a story for everything.

Other ACT techniques can point to this same issue and also serve to disrupt problematic in-session storytelling. Most clinicians have had the experience of a client who talks for hours about what has happened to him or her, eating up the session with complaints, explanations, and descriptions. One way to disrupt this process is to focus on the functional utility of the client's talk. Therapist statements such as, "And what is this story in the service of?" or "Let's say God came down and said you were 100 percent correct. How would this help you?" (Hayes et al., 1999, p. 164) bring the focus back to the immediate implications of the client's talk and away from attempting to figure out, be correct, or analyze the situation.

Another example, called the *autobiographical rewrite*, has clients explore the largely arbitrary connections between events in their life stories (Hayes & Smith, 2005, pp. 91–93). In this exercise, participants are given the homework to write their life story on a couple of pages. Following this, clients are asked to rewrite the story, keeping all the events exactly unchanged, but shifting the meaning and outcome of the story. The story is not challenged directly, but hopefully seen as one of many possible life stories that are available.

The ACT therapist is sometimes challenged on the grounds of the literal truth of reasons. Arguing back is almost always unhelpful. Instead, reasons are acknowledged as possibly helpful verbal formulations, and the question turns to, "What does your experience say … how helpful is this?" A client may also be asked, "Well, that sounds right. But which would you rather be: right or living a vital life?"

# WORKING WITH ONGOING DEFUSION IN SESSION

The preceding sections largely consist of the presentation of a range of specific defusion metaphors and exercises. In order for these techniques to be used powerfully, they need to be integrated into the ongoing flow of the session. A common mistake for ACT therapists is to use the metaphors and exercises in a piecemeal fashion, whereby a defused space is created during the exercises, but client talk is responded to literally during other parts of the session. Rather, the focus on the functional utility of thinking and attention to languaging as an ongoing behavior process must occur throughout therapy, even with regard to whatever the therapist might say. In any given situation, the primary focus is on whether buying a thought would move the client (or therapist) toward a more vital, values-based life.

This section introduces some specific techniques for practicing defusion in the ongoing flow of the session, addressing ongoing episodes of highly fused behavior on the part of the client, and holding a defused space in the room.

## Verbal Conventions

ACT therapists sometimes ask their clients to adopt simple verbal conventions that can be called on to help the client step out of some of the traps of literal language and create some distance between the client and the content of his or her mind. For example, the therapist can ask clients to state things as experiences they are currently having, rather than as something they actually are:

✓ "I am having the thought that I am worthless" versus "I am worthless"

✓ "I am having the feeling of anxiety" versus "I feel anxious"

Although this exercise often feels awkward at first, it can be very helpful if practiced for a period of time, perhaps thirty minutes of a session. This exercise helps create a healthy sense of separation between the client and the content of his or her thoughts.

The therapist might also ask the client to replace the word "but" with the word "and" (Hayes et al., 1999, pp. 166–168). The word "but" literally means to "be out" the thing that came before. So if a client says, "I love my husband, but he makes me angry," anger functions to be out love. Substituting "and" can remind clients that both things are true: the client loves her husband *and* he makes her angry. Multiple meanings are present and the "be out" doesn't have to negate what came before.

## Metaphor Reminding

The power of metaphor and story is that they can bring new functions to bear on a situation in a rapid manner, without an excess of description. Referring back to familiar metaphors can catalyze defusion. Compare these two sentences: "Hold that thought lightly, as you might hold a butterfly that has just landed on your finger" versus "You should respond to your thinking in a defused way—with detachment and acceptance; and willingly, with openness, fascination, and curiosity; and not with violence, struggle, battle, possession, being right about it, argument, or trying to figure out if it is true and criticizing it if it isn't." Notice how the brief analogy can get across many of the qualities of defusion, without the need for an exact description.

Once a defusion exercise has been conducted or a metaphor related, a therapist can rapidly bring defusion into the room by referring back to earlier defusion exercises or metaphors. Take, for example, the following transcript, in which the concept of "buying a thought" versus "having a thought" had been introduced in an earlier session. The goal of this distinction is to help clients respond to their thoughts based on the functional utility of those thoughts, rather than on their literal truth.

Client: I just don't know what to do. I just can't connect with people. I get in social situations and I just can't do it. I just have nothing to say.

Therapist: Let's take a look at this. You've just shaken this person's hand, and your salesman mind shows up and sells you the thought, "I can't connect with people." It looks as if you've been buying that so far. Maybe the important question here for us is whether that's a thought you want to continue to buy. Let me ask it this way: when you follow that thought, where does it lead you in terms of your values in this area?

Client: I just stay at home. Or when I'm at a party, I don't talk much to people.

Therapist: And I'm guessing there's a story connected to the idea that you can't connect with people?

Client: Yeah, it's true, I don't connect with people.

Therapist: So then your mind sells you "It's true." When you buy that, where does it lead you?

Client: Again, not toward where I want to go.

Therapist: So, we've talked before about how you have a value that you want to connect with people. Right?

Client: Yeah.

Therapist: And now your mind is selling you the thought that you can't do it. And it can even marshal evidence. Now, let me ask you another question. Suppose you were to go out tomorrow and actually be able to connect with people; suppose there were people out there who really could "get" you, and you were able to just really get with them, really open up to them, and let them know you. Let's say you did that tomorrow. Who would be made wrong by that?

Client: Huh? I'm not sure ... [ten-second pause] I guess *I* would.

Therapist: Yeah, you'd have to give up this story that you can't connect with people. You'd be wrong about that story. Your choice here seems to be either to defend your story or get your life back. What do you think would come up for you that would be painful if you were to do this?

Client: It would mean I could have done it all along ...

Therapist: Yeah, let's stay with that. When you say that, I notice some sadness coming up. Can we make room for you to have that right now?

Client: [quietly] Okay.

Therapist: If having this sadness, this sense of loss, could make it possible for you to really connect with people, to be able to really be there for your sister in a way you've never been able to before, would it be worth it? [At that point, the therapist can guide the client into an exercise in which he would be present with his sadness and could practice willingly holding it.]

Asking clients, "Who would be made wrong by that?" if carefully timed, can be a powerful intervention to help clients whose story about who they are, or how their life works, is in conflict with a valued direction they wish to take. Asking this question often results in a pause before clients respond, and sometimes their reaction is confused because the question seems to have come out of nowhere. It also has the potential to sound accusatory if poorly timed, or if the client and therapist have not already created a compassionate, accepting relationship, built around agreement about the client's values. This statement is not meant to blame the client for his or her difficulties, but rather to help the client see how being correct, logical, or coherent (being right) can actually stand in the way of living a vital life. Done skillfully, the confrontation is between the client's mind and the client's experience or values, not between the client and the therapist.

## Teach Clients to Recognize Fused Qualities of Mind

Another useful technique is to help clients to be able to identify—or to use technical language, to discriminate—when they are getting caught up in the fused world of verbal relations in their minds. We can learn to recognize patterns in our environment that weren't previously apparent, and once we do, we tend to not "unsee" it in the future. This process works similarly to the optical illusion in figure 3.1. What do you see in this drawing? If you haven't seen it before, probably you will see only a random bunch of dots. Look again and see if you can see a Dalmatian on a sidewalk. Once you've gotten it, try to *not* see the Dalmatian. It's quite hard to do without literally distorting the image. If you've seen this optical illusion before and you've seen the Dalmatian in previous demonstrations, you'll see it still, even though it may have been years. Once a discrimination is well learned, it is available to operate on behavior forever.

If a therapist can teach clients to recognize when they are caught up in highly verbal, old, entrenched ways of thinking, this can serve as a long-lasting cue to take a step back and apply any of the defusion strategies the clients have learned. Clients can be taught to recognize when they are caught up in their minds by identifying characteristics of their thinking such as (Wilson, 2003):

**Figure 3.1**

✓ Presence of comparison and evaluation

✓ Complex/busy

✓ Confused (*and* trying hard to clarify)

✓ Adversarial (has two sides or conflict)

✓ Warnings about consequences (yes, *but*)

✓ Strong future or past orientation to the conversation (must, should, can't, shouldn't)

✓ Strong orientation as to what something *means* about you or others

✓ Strong problem-solving orientation

✓ Familiar ("old," "has the smell of age")

# FLEXIBILITY IN APPLYING DEFUSION

As a therapist, it is important to keep in mind that defusion as a process does not refer to any particular form of behavior. Considered in isolation, there are no defusion techniques, metaphors, or exercises in and of themselves, any more than a piece of candy on the table is a reinforcer, or the word "good" is praise. Defusion is a functional concept that requires attention to tact, timing, pacing, and context. Key among these is therapists' awareness of clients' behaviors that indicate when defusion is needed.

Working with clients can be a bit like traveling through a dense thicket. It is easy to lose direction, get caught on a bramble, or get stuck. When a session becomes thick with reasons, justifications, and stories, therapists can sometimes find some "air" by asking themselves, their clients, or both, questions that focus on the functional utility of talk through questions such as (Hayes et al., 1999):

✓ "And what is that story in the service of?"

✓ "Is this helpful, or is this what your mind does to you?"

✓ "Have you said these kinds of things to yourself or to others before? Is this old?"

✓ "Okay, let's all have a vote and vote that you are correct. Now what?" (p. 164)

Another way to cut through literality is to help clients contrast what their minds say *will* work with what their experience says about what *has* worked. This can often serve as a way of cutting through excessive literal thinking. An ACT therapist might say, "I don't want you to see this as a matter of belief, but to examine it against your experience," or "What does your experience say?" The goal of these types of questions is to move clients out of literal, evaluative thinking and into a stance that is more oriented to the opportunities afforded by their environment and directed by the practical considerations of their values.

Another way is to acknowledge the situation directly. "Hmm. Have you noticed it's getting awfully 'mindy' in here?" or "I notice I'm fighting here, trying to figure it out and persuade you. Is it okay if we just take a deep breath and notice we're still both just here in this moment, each with our chattering minds?" or "I have no idea what to do or say next. My mind is being pretty harsh on me for saying this—I guess therapists are 'supposed' to know. It's the truth, though. Do you have thoughts about how to proceed?"

---

## EXERCISE: DEFUSION, PART 2

Go back to the three thoughts you listed at the beginning of this chapter. Now that you have read about the defusion techniques, consider one technique you could use for each of the thoughts you recorded before. Describe these below.

Thought 1:

Thought 2:

Thought 3:

You might want to try these techniques in session with this client.

# CORE COMPETENCY PRACTICE

This section is intended to provide practice in using defusion techniques in response to sample transcripts based on ACT sessions. Listed here are the ten ACT core competencies for defusion. For each core competency, you are presented with a description of a clinical situation and a section of a transcript. The transcript ends after a client statement, and you are asked to provide a sample response that reflects that competency. The model responses at the end of the chapter are not the only right responses; they are just examples of ACT-consistent responses. If you disagree with the responses or want to double-check your response or talk more about it, you can post a question to the bulletin board at www.learningact .com/forum/. Again, try to generate your own responses before you look at the samples at the end of the chapter.

# CORE COMPETENCY EXERCISES

## COMPETENCY 1: The therapist identifies the client's emotional, cognitive, behavioral, or physical barriers to willingness.

### EXERCISE 3.1

The client is a thirty-four-year-old female who has panic attacks, particularly in social situations. She wants to go back to school, but feels she's "too anxious." This transcript occurs in the third session, following a discussion in which she has related how hard it is for her to participate in class, particularly in terms of raising her hand in class.

*Therapist:* What stands in the way of your raising your hand in class?

*Client:* I just can't do it. When I even think about it, I get scared.

*Therapist:* Okay, you have the thought "I can't do it" and the feeling of being scared. What else stands in the way of your raising your hand?

*Client:* I'm afraid I'll panic.

*Therapist:* Anything else?

*Client:* No. Isn't that enough?

Write here what your response would be (remember you are using competency 1):




What are your thoughts in saying this? What are you responding to and what are you hoping to accomplish?

## COMPETENCY 2: The therapist suggests that attachment to the literal meaning of these experiences makes willingness difficult to sustain (helps clients to see private experiences for what they are, rather than what they advertise themselves to be).

### EXERCISE 3.2

*This transcript continues with the same client as in competency 1.*

*Therapist:*  [gives the response found in Sample 3.1b, in the model response section at the end of this chapter]

*Client:*  I guess, but I just can't do it. I'd be too scared. I'd just end up embarrassed.

Write here what your response would be (using competency 2):

What are your thoughts in saying this? What are you responding to and what are you hoping to accomplish?

## COMPETENCY 3: The therapist actively contrasts what the client's mind says will work with what the client's experience says is working.

### EXERCISE 3.3

*This transcript continues with the same client as in competency 2.*

*Therapist:*  [gives the response found in Sample 3.3b in the model response section]

*Client:*  But I can't do it. I know that if I raise my hand, and I haven't been able to get my breathing under control, I won't be able to say anything when he calls on me. If I could just get my breathing under control, I could probably do it without panicking.

*Therapist:*  So, let's check this out. Your mind says, "I need to get my breathing under control." Right? That's a thought. Is that a familiar one?

*Client:*  Yeah.

*Therapist:*  Now, let's look at what your experience has to say about this. How long have you been following what that thought has to say?

*Client:*  A long time ...

Write here what your response would be (using competency 3):

What are your thoughts in saying this? What are you responding to and what are you hoping to accomplish?

**COMPETENCY 4:** The therapist uses language tools (e.g., get off your "buts"); metaphors (e.g., Bubble on the Head, Passengers on the Bus); and experiential exercises (e.g., Thoughts on Cards) to create a separation between the client and the client's conceptualized experience.

## EXERCISE 3.4

A forty-four-year-old male client is struggling with alcohol addiction. One of his biggest triggers of alcohol use is when he is alone at home. He was on disability for a long time and spent a fair amount of his life simply sitting at home, drinking and watching TV. He has been sober for the past two months and just started a new job for the first time in several years. He's beginning to question his commitment and wondering if the job is really worth the stress. The therapist and the client discussed the bus metaphor in a previous session; this transcript is from the sixth session.

Client: It's just that I go to work and they don't pay me enough, so it's stressful. I feel like I screw up and don't work fast enough. I'm not sure it's really worth it. I get home at the end of the day, and there's no one there. I want to do better, but I just want a drink ... so badly.

Write here what your response would be (using competency 4):

What are your thoughts in saying this? What are you responding to and what are you hoping to accomplish?

**COMPETENCY 5:** The therapist works to get the client to experiment with "having" difficult private experiences, using willingness as a stance.

## EXERCISE 3.5

*This transcript continues with the same client as in competency 4.*

Therapist: [gives the response found in Sample 3.4b in the model response section]

Client: I feel lonely. I feel anxious, like I need to do something.

Therapist: So lonely shows up. Anxious shows up. If those passengers could speak to you, what would they tell you to do?

Client: They would tell me to just have a drink. Just take the edge off.

Therapist: So these are old passengers, ones who are very familiar. You know them well. What do they say they will do if you just do what they're asking you?

Client: They say they will go away, they'll shut up for a while. And they do.

Write here what your response would be (using competency 5):

What are your thoughts in saying this? What are you responding to and what are you hoping to accomplish?

## EXERCISE 3.6 (continuing with competency 5)

*This transcript continues with the same client.*

*Therapist:*   [gives the response found in Sample 3.5b in the model response section]

*Client:*   I don't know if I could do that.

Write here what your response would be (using competency 5):

What are your thoughts in saying this? What are you responding to and what are you hoping to accomplish?

---

**COMPETENCY 6: The therapist uses various exercises, metaphors, and behavioral tasks to reveal the hidden properties of language.**

## EXERCISE 3.7

The client is a depressed forty-year-old male who constantly compares himself with others in social situations and often sees himself as worth less than others. A common pattern for him is being in a conversation with someone and simultaneously thinking, "This person seems to have it pretty together. If he knew how much of a loser I am, he wouldn't want to be friends with me. He can't really be as together as he seems. I'm sure there's some way in which he has problems. I don't know what it is, but I'm sure I'll find it eventually." The client is talking about this situation in the fourth session.

*Client:*   I'm just so sick of comparing myself with others, feeling bad, and then tearing them down.

*Therapist:*   What's the thought that is most troublesome? That you're bad?

*Client:*   Hmm. I guess it's that I think, "He's better than me."

*Therapist:*   He's better than me. And that makes you …

*Client:*   Bad. Worse.

*Therapist:*   Which one feels more at the heart of it?

*Client:*   Hmm. Bad.

*Therapist:*   So, are you willing to do a little exercise with me around this thought that shows up for you, "I'm bad"?

*Client:*   Sure.

*Therapist:*   So, what I'd like us to do is play around with this thought a little. Let's try something out. How about we sing a song? I'll go first. "I'm bad, I'm bad, you know it." Your turn.

*Client:*       [in a high, funny voice] Uh, "I'm bad, I'm bad. I'm the worst there is."

*Therapist:*   And, let's do a duet of it ... [sings a few more rounds with the client] So, tell me, what was your experience of that?

*Client:*       Well, at first it was pretty weird. I didn't like making fun of something that felt so personal. But then it just got a little lighter; it wasn't such a big deal.

Write here what your response would be (using competency 6):

What are your thoughts in saying this? What are you responding to and what are you hoping to accomplish?

---

## COMPETENCY 7: The therapist helps the client elucidate the client's story and helps the client make contact with the evaluative and reason-giving properties of the story.

### EXERCISE 3.8

*This transcript continues with the same client as in competency 6.*

*Therapist:*   [gives the response found in Sample 3.7a in the model response section]

*Client:*       Yeah, but it seems really solid when I'm there. It's like I think that's really true about me. I feel like I really am bad in some ways. It's like believing something else would be a lie.

Write here what your response would be (using competency 7):

What are your thoughts in saying this? What are you responding to and what are you hoping to accomplish?

### EXERCISE 3.9 (continuing with competency 7)

*This transcript continues with the same client.*

*Therapist:*   [gives the response found in Sample 3.8b in the model response section]

*Client:*       I guess. But, I'm not sure how.

*Therapist:*   I want to have us take a little look at something I think is part of what holds all this together. I propose that we all have a story about how we are the way we are. Right? I have mine, you have yours. We all have this narrative we piece together from the memories of all the events in our lives that we can remember. I'd like us to spend a moment getting in contact with your story about this depression. What happened in your past—when you were a kid or an adult, whenever—that resulted in your being depressed?

Client: Well, I think it started with my parents. I felt they never cared about me. Maybe it's genetic, too, like I have a chemical imbalance.

Therapist: You have some memories and thoughts about being neglected by your parents, and then more thoughts about causes: maybe it's genetic, a chemical imbalance.

Client: Right.

Therapist: So, can I set aside the chemical imbalance part just for a second and focus on the part about your parents not caring about you as what might be causing you to be depressed?

Client: Sure.

Therapist: So, you had an evaluation first: you were mistreated by your parents. And then you also had the thought that this caused you to be depressed. Is that fair to say?

Client: Yeah, I guess. But I think that's really what happened, not that I had a thought.

Therapist: So, let's say I agree you were neglected by your parents. It can be true, or not true in a literal sense—that's not in dispute. I'm not arguing with you. And that treatment was associated with a lot of pain. Your pain. Now, kids do the best they can, so I'm absolutely not blaming you. Still, I would like to ask you this: As an adult now looking back, could you have reacted differently in any way to what they did or didn't do? And even now, in this moment, do you have any choice in how you respond to this painful memory?

Client: Sure, I guess. I could have been angry. I actually am angry sometimes. I guess I could have said, "Screw them," and found someone who cared about me. I actually did try to do that, but it didn't seem to help.

Therapist: You've actually had a whole host of reactions to it. Let me propose two things that might be there: one is your reaction to what they did, and the other is your feelings of depression. Now, if they actually neglected you, is there anything you can do about what happened in the past?

Client: No, of course not.

Therapist: So get this. If the reason you are depressed is that your parents neglected you, then you're stuck. The only way you can be is depressed. Do you see this? Your mind gives you this as the reason you are depressed. If it is literally true that this is the reason, can you change the past?

Client: No.

Therapist: So, if it's the case that this literally is what caused you to be depressed, then we might as well throw in the towel. You're going to be depressed the rest of your life.

Client: Okay, I think I see where you're going. You seem to be saying it's actually my fault I'm the way I am.

Write here what your response would be (using competency 7):

What are your thoughts in saying this? What are you responding to and what are you hoping to accomplish?

## COMPETENCY 8: The therapist helps the client make contact with the arbitrary nature of causal relationships within the story.

### EXERCISE 3.10

*This transcript continues with the same client as in competency 7.*

Therapist: [gives the response found in Sample 3.9b in the model response section]

Client: Well ... I guess I don't have to feel so bad about being depressed. It's not my fault.

Therapist: Right, so it helps you to feel a little better. You don't need to feel so guilty about lying in bed all day or dropping out of school ... [sarcastically] It really helps, right? You feel great! [laughs with the client] And how does it cost you?

Client: Well, I've got to stay depressed.

Therapist: And you can't ...

Client: I can't be happy, I can't connect with people. I can't hold down a job.

Therapist: Let me ask it another way. If you were to suddenly get better and no longer be depressed, who would be made wrong by that?

Client: Huh? [Clients are often confused by this question.]

Therapist: If you were to suddenly just go out and no longer live a depressed life, who would be made wrong by that?

Client: I guess me?

Therapist: [compassionately] Yeah, you. Here you have a story that says your parents caused you to be depressed. You'd have to let go of that. In order to do that, you'd have to stop being right about it. The question I have for you is this: Would you rather be right about how your parents' neglect made you depressed or would you rather have your life back? In order to get your life back, you'd have to let go of this story.

Client: I want my life back, but they weren't there for me, and I can't change that. And I have been depressed ever since then.

Therapist: Right. Absolutely. You can't change what they did. And being depressed is descriptive of how you've lived your life. Let me ask you this: Do you have to stay depressed to still think you are right that they shouldn't have done this? Would it be possible to have that story, as a story—not right, not wrong—and move on with your life, reclaim your life? Do you need to change the story for you to move forward with your life or can you just let it be there, as a story, as a thought, and move forward? Notice how now it serves as a reason for your acting depressed.

Client: Okay, I see what you are getting at, but I just can't seem to get beyond it.

Write here what your response would be (using competency 8):

What are your thoughts in saying this? What are you responding to and what are you hoping to accomplish?

**COMPETENCY 9: The therapist detects mindiness (fusion) in session and teaches the client to detect it, as well.**

## EXERCISE 3.11

The client is a fairly intellectual female in her forties who is considering leaving a distant relationship with her spouse, Rebecca, whom she describes as alternating between withdrawing and being verbally overbearing and critical. The client has read dozens of self-help books, spent years in counseling with other therapists, and displays a lot of insight into her own and her partner's problems. Nevertheless, she continues to be very passive in her relationship and avoidant of conflict. This transcript picks up fairly close to the beginning of the seventh session, after the client has been talking for several minutes about what her partner did that week to intimidate and bully her. The therapist has noted that the conversation feels very lifeless, old, and stale.

Client:   I just don't know what to do. I've been thinking about leaving, and yet I know if I leave, it also means I'll lose the kids. I just feel so stuck. What do you think I should do?

Write here what your response would be (using competency 9):

What are your thoughts in saying this? What are you responding to and what are you hoping to accomplish?

**COMPETENCY 10: The therapist uses various interventions to reveal both the flow of private experience and that such experience is not toxic.**

## EXERCISE 3.12

*This transcript continues with the same client as in competency 9.*

Therapist:   [gives the response found in Sample 3.11b in the model response section]

Client:   Old, familiar. I've thought about this a million times.

Therapist:   And your mind is here, yet again, suggesting ways to figure this out. Can you notice your mind right now? What's it saying right now?

Client:   It's saying, "Okay, so what do I do, then?"

Therapist:   And what's next?

Client:   Um, I'm not sure.

Therapist:   Next your mind gave you a thought with the words "I'm not sure." Did you notice that was a thought?

Client:   Um, no, I guess not.

Therapist:   So what's next? What thought comes up next?

Client:   I don't like this.

Therapist:   And ... did you notice that's a thought?

| | |
|---|---|
| *Client:* | Yeah. |
| *Therapist:* | And what shows up next? See if you can simply notice each thought as it comes up—not get stuck with what it says it is, but simply notice it as a thought. See if you can let each one simply be there as a thought, just let each one pass in and pass out again. [ten-second pause] Okay, so what thought's next? |
| *Client:* | I'm having the thought that I don't know where this is going. |
| *Therapist:* | Good. Another thought that looks like "I don't know where this is going." That's a really good one. Isn't the mind a great machine? [pause] Do you notice how automatic this verbal machine is? You don't even need to do anything, and it keeps producing these words, these sentences, that then structure your world. So, what we've been practicing here is simply noting when you move in and out of seeing the world as structured by thought, versus being able to see thoughts as thoughts. The important thing is to be able to tell when you're observing thoughts as opposed to when you are looking out at the world as structured by them. One skill we want to practice is being able to catch yourself when you're caught up in this world of thought, with all its judgment, planning, evaluation—for example, "If I only did this, then that would happen"—and to simply come back to the moment and observe what's there. |
| *Client:* | Yeah, but I still don't know what to do about Rebecca. |
| *Therapist:* | Yeah, that thought is still there. So, you've gone around and around about what to do here, and yet you find yourself stuck. I'd like us to step outside of this a bit and look at the bigger picture. You've told me before that a value you have is respecting yourself. And another value you have is connecting with your partner. Have those values changed? [The therapist did work earlier to evaluate the risk of violence, and all signs suggest it is minimal.] |
| *Client:* | No. |
| *Therapist:* | Okay, so it hasn't. Yet with what happens with your partner, do you respect yourself in how you respond to her? |
| *Client:* | No, not really. I let her walk all over me. |
| *Therapist:* | Right, it seems as if something stands in the way of your respecting yourself when she's talking to you. What stands in your way? |
| *Client:* | Well … I feel so small. And I think about saying something, but I'm so scared. I know she'll blow up and just walk away and sulk or something if I don't let her have her way. |
| *Therapist:* | And when that happens, you feel…? |
| *Client:* | I'm scared that I just made things worse. And I just walk around on eggshells for a couple days, waiting for her to blow up on me again or leave me. |
| *Therapist:* | And how is that for you? |
| *Client:* | It's just terrible. I feel like … like … I can barely stand it. |

Write here what your response would be (using competency 10):




What are your thoughts in saying this? What are you responding to and what are you hoping to accomplish?

# Core Competency Model Responses

## COMPETENCY 1

**Sample 3.1a**

*Therapist:*  We want to be open to anything that is there, and sometimes things float around that are not noticed. So, in addition to the "I just can't do it" thought, the fearful feelings, and the "I'll panic" thought, let me just ask you about some other dimensions that might be part of not raising your hand. What do you feel in your body?

*Client:*  [answers]

*Therapist:*  Good, and does this remind you of anything in the past?

*Client:*  [answers]

*Therapist:*  Cool. And what kind of judgments and evaluations show up?

*Client:*  [answers]

*Therapist:*  And when you have all of that what do you want to do?

*Client:*  [answers]

**Explanation:** This response amplifies the client's observations of experience, and treats each observation in a defused way. Linking these observations to action tendencies categorizes them as possible barriers to moving forward in a valued direction. The goal is to communicate that all of these barriers are acceptable; none are to be avoided or taken literally.

**Sample 3.1b**

*Therapist:*  Sure, what's important is your actual experience. So, you're going along, and this thought shows up: "I just can't do it." And a feeling shows up: fear. It's also saying its buddy is coming along for the ride: "I'll panic." Notice, panic isn't here yet. At the moment, what you are having is the thought "I'll panic." So, let me ask you this: could you have that thought, "I just can't do it," and the other thought, "I'll panic," as thoughts, and still raise your hand?

**Explanation:** This response outlines how these emotions and thoughts present themselves as barriers to moving forward in a valued direction. The goal is to orient the client to the way that these barriers function and to help her step back from them as being simply reality and start to notice how they function for her. The context of nonliterality is assumed in the answer because the thoughts are treated more as objects that can be had, rather than as something to be believed literally.

## COMPETENCY 2

**Sample 3.2a**

*Therapist:*  Hmm. Let me just ask you this: How old is that? You've been buying that thought for a long time, yes? And meanwhile the clock is ticking, life is going on, and you are stuck in the same situation. And not just that, do you even know where "I'd be too scared" comes from, or why avoiding embarrassment is something worth harming your life over? What if these are just bits of programming—your history showing up in the present—and in taking them literally, you are amplifying them into events to run your life. Gub-Gubs go …

Client:     Wooo.

Therapist:  Yeah. And I can't raise my hand because I'm too.... So who is in charge here, you or your mind?

**Explanation:** By focusing the client on the historical fact that thoughts bought regulate negative actions, the cost of fusion is made more evident. Appeals to history make it clear that we can expect these thoughts to continue as they have for some time. The issue, however, is their role in overt behavior. Highlighting the client's ignorance of the source of these thoughts and drawing an analogy with a current trivial source of a thought can help the client see the thought as an ongoing, historically produced process, not as a literal event that must be complied with, argued with, resisted, or avoided.

### Sample 3.2b

Therapist:  The thought "I can't do it," held literally, does indeed make it hard to be willing. So, for example, when you feel anxious and "I can't do it" shows up, if that's literally true, you're stuck. On the other hand, if it's a thought, you might be able to react to it in a different way. What if thoughts are kind of like a tool, like a hammer or something? We don't spend time trying to figure out if a hammer is a true hammer; we just use it, or we don't. Now, in this situation, would picking up the thought "I can't do it" and using it lead you toward or away from your values?

**Explanation:** The therapist suggests that buying the thought, or holding it literally, is going to make it hard to do anything with respect to this client's value. The therapist compares the thought to an object in order to help the client possibly relate to it in a more pragmatic way, based on its usefulness rather than what it literally says it is. The therapist then asks the client to evaluate whether this thought is useful in relation to the client's values.

## COMPETENCY 3

### Sample 3.3a

Therapist:  So, now we've heard from your mind. What does your experience have to say? Has it turned out the way your mind said it would—that if you just keep trying, eventually you'll get your breathing under control and you'll be able to speak in class and participate in the way you want? Has it worked out that way in your experience?

**Explanation:** The therapist examines whether the verbal rule implied by the thought "If you just try to get your breathing under control, you eventually will, and then you'll be able to raise your hand" actually turns out as the rule specifies (i.e., breathing slows and the client gets to raise her hand).

### Sample 3.3b

Therapist:  [gently] So, let's just notice that. Your mind is trying to protect you, and yet as you do what it says, look at what happens. If you had an investment banker with such a record, you would have fired him long ago. So which are you going to believe: your mind or your experience?

**Explanation:** Same as for sample 3.3a, only the therapist is using a slightly different style.

## COMPETENCY 4

**Sample 3.4a**

*Therapist:*  It's worth noticing that word "but." You know, the word "but" long ago came from a contraction of two words: "be" and "out." "But" is a fighting word. You are saying that the fact you want a drink somehow invalidates wanting to do better, and wanting to do better should somehow remove the urge to drink. Yet check and see if this isn't so—what you experienced was not that. I'm guessing what you experienced was two things: the thought that you want to do better *and* a feeling that you want to drink. Is there anything I said there that you cannot have? "I want to do better *and* I want a drink." Both things are so. Now, what are you going to do with your feet?

**Explanation:** The therapist is trying to draw out the hidden fight and help the client see there is really nothing about which to fight.

**Sample 3.4b**

*Therapist:*  Would you be willing to do an exercise with me?

*Client:*  Sure.

*Therapist:*  I'd like you to shut your eyes, and I'll bring you back to that moment.

*Client:*  [shuts eyes and follows instructions]

*Therapist:*  Think of the last time you were at home, sitting there after work, exhausted, feeling lonely. Do you remember the bus metaphor about which we talked?

*Client:*  Yeah.

*Therapist:*  What passengers show up there and start pushing you around? See if you can see what feelings show up.

**Explanation:** The therapist is trying to make the work as experiential as possible. To do this, one wants to get the actual avoided content into the room. The therapist does a short experiential exercise that helps the client make contact with the avoided content. The therapist then refers back to an earlier metaphor in which thoughts and feelings were compared to bullies that push the person around. The goal is to bring the passengers into the present, but in an altered context in which the avoided private experiences can be met with more willingness and with some healthy distance.

## COMPETENCY 5

**Sample 3.5a**

*Therapist:*  Well, they will sit down, sure. As you say, for a while. When they come back, are they bigger or smaller, weaker or stronger? Bigger and stronger, right? So it has a cost. So here is my question: what do you have to be willing to experience in order to let them be there and not sit down?

**Explanation:** The therapist is asking the client to consider the possibility of having these experiences by being more willing to have whatever will show up when that step is taken.

**Sample 3.5b**

*Therapist:* Right, they sure do. So, one way to work with them is to do things so they'll agree to sit down. Let's check this out, though. If you do that, what happens with respect to your values? Do you head toward or away from your values?

*Client:* Away. But even then, they're just as powerful.

*Therapist:* Yeah, powerful. And old. And familiar. And you've been fighting with these passengers for a long time ... How has it worked to fight them? Or turn the direction of your life over to their demands? Has it been working?

*Client:* No.

*Therapist:* So maybe we'd want to do something different with them. How about this? Just let them be there as thoughts, as feelings. Don't do anything with them, except notice them.

**Explanation:** The therapist is asking the client to examine the workability of the client's solution and to consider willingness as an alternative.

**Sample 3.6**

*Therapist:* Right, so your mind gives you the thought "I don't know if I could do that." As if you got to decide somehow whether it works. Are you willing to check it out in your experience? What does your experience tell you about whether struggling with them has worked?

*Client:* It hasn't.

*Therapist:* [smiles, speaks jokingly] Have you had enough pain to try something else? Or do you want to wait for more?

**Explanation:** The therapist identifies the client's presented barrier as another thought, and then proceeds to ask the client whether he would be willing to try a new behavior, the behavior of willingness. The therapist refers back to the client's experience of struggle and asks whether that has worked. If the client agrees to try something else, this would probably lead to willingness and exposure work.

## COMPETENCY 6

**Sample 3.7a**

*Therapist:* And even if it didn't feel especially lighter, there is a point in here. At one level, this is also just language. Mary had a little ...

*Client:* Lamb.

*Therapist:* And Gub-Gubs go ...

*Client:* Wooo.

*Therapist:* And he is better than ...

*Client:* Me.

*Therapist:* These words are worth restricting your life over?

**Explanation:** The therapist highlights the automaticity of thought and the difference between literal meaning and pragmatic meaning.

**Sample 3.7b**

*Therapist:*   What happened to the meaning of it?

*Client:*   It didn't mean much after a little while, beyond seeming a little funny.

*Therapist:*   So, when you say that to yourself, "I'm bad," in addition to the meaning your mind gives to those words, isn't it also true those words are just words? In some way, they're kind of like smoke—there's nothing solid there.

**Explanation:** The therapist highlights the aspect of words being other things, in addition to simply what they mean.

## COMPETENCY 7

**Sample 3.8a**

*Therapist:*   Yeah, minds don't like us just letting go of the story: it has to be true or proven false. If you just let it go, it's like a lie, like you aren't genuine. The etymology of the word "genuine" is interesting. It comes from a word meaning a close relative. But what do you want closer to you: your values or your story? Do you want defended reasons or effective actions? Suppose you can only pick one. Which do you choose?

**Explanation:** The client is trying to move the issue to the literal truth of the story. The therapist is drawing that out and moving it back to the functional truth.

**Sample 3.8b**

*Therapist:*   I'm not asking you to believe something else. In fact, I'd recommend you don't try to believe something else. That would be just more of the same thing. You've already tried that, right? Telling yourself you are basically a good person—has that worked to the point to which you now don't worry about being a bad person? Could you just have that thought, as a thought, and still do what matters to you?

**Explanation:** The client seems to be hearing the therapist saying that he shouldn't believe these things. This isn't an ACT-consistent message because it is within the context of literality. The therapist says something that steps outside of literal understanding, and includes the dimension of belief versus nonbelief by saying, "I'd recommend you don't try to believe something else." Then the therapist refers back to the issue of workability and the client's experience, and finally suggests a way of relating to the thought.

**Sample 3.9a**

*Therapist:*   Is that where you think I'm going? No, you aren't at fault. *And* maybe there is something you can actually *do*, now, right here. If so, that won't change the history. If we create a miracle here—and you just step forward in your life from here, with your history—what will your parents think?

*Client:*   They did great as parents.

*Therapist:*   Exactly. It is as if a fishhook went through you first, and then you stuck them on the end to keep them accountable. Inside the story, you can only get off the hook if you can keep them on it. But if we create a miracle, and you get off it, they have to slide right off, too. What a pisser! Short of ripping it through your body, there is no other way off. So, which would you rather have? Would you rather have them on the hook or would you rather be free to live your life?

**Explanation:** Fusion with the story will show up in the form of being right. Being right is great fun, except it is destroying the client's life.

### Sample 3.9b

*Therapist:* Well, not exactly. As I said, I come from the assumption that you came by this naturally, that you have done the best you can, given your circumstances and what you knew at the time. This isn't about blame. But if there is anything you can actually do right now, your mind will treat that almost as if it were blame. What if it's the case that you are response-able [said as two words]; in other words, able to respond here? That is a joyful idea: there are things we can do. And it is scary: your mind will claim this means you are to blame. What if the biggest danger about your past here is that it's about to become your future? Let me ask you this: Does this story that you are depressed because of something that happened in your past serve you? How does buying this reason for being depressed serve you?

**Explanation:** Having the client confront the effect that buying this story has had on him is not about blaming the client, but rather about empowering him to be response-able about his own behavior. The therapist then returns to the question of workability. Does this story work for the client?

## COMPETENCY 8

### Sample 3.10

*Therapist:* That's okay, you don't need to get beyond it. What we need to do is practice having it, but from a little different vantage point, so perhaps it's a bit less sticky, a bit more flexible. That way, your story is something you can have a bit more like an object, rather than a cold, hard fact. I'd like to propose an exercise that might help you develop a little flexibility with the story. Are you willing to do that?

*Client:* Sure.

*Therapist:* So, here's the exercise. We've done a little bit of work on your story about why you are depressed. I'd like to suggest a homework that relates to this. Again, I'm not trying to contradict the truth of this story or change what happened. I'd just like us to develop a little flexibility with it. You're free to stay right about your story. This is the way the exercise works. I'd like you to write an autobiography, about a page or two in length, describing the major events in your life that are part of why you are the way you are—the most influential events in your life. After you do that, we're going to take those events and rewrite them into a new narrative in which we have the same events, but in which the events affect you in a different way or lead to a different outcome. It doesn't matter whether the outcome is better or worse, just that it is different. I want us to have a look at how the mind seems to have this never-ending ability to generate stories, to link things together in an attempt to make sense of them, even if this sense-making isn't useful. Are you willing to do this?

**Explanation:** The therapist suggests a particular homework—the autobiographical rewrite—and checks to see if the client is willing to do it. Notice the therapist suggests that this is not about changing history or saying what happened did not happen. That approach could seem invalidating to the client and also engage literality. Instead, the therapist is engaging the client in an experiential process, which hopefully will get across the point that particular events need not determine a person's life and that many interpretations are possible for any given event. In fact, the interpretation of the event is, in a sense, what happened in the event, and this interpretation is dependent on context.

## COMPETENCY 9

**Sample 3.11a**

*Therapist:* Have you said to yourself before that you need help? Does this feel old?

*Client:* Yeah.

*Therapist:* Let's say I gave you a definitive answer. Let's say I said, "You need to stay and work this out." Would that help?

**Explanation:** The therapist highlights one of the characteristics of fused thinking: it feels old, tired, repetitive. The therapist then adds to this by utilizing a defusion response focused on the functional utility of thinking.

**Sample 3.11b**

*Therapist:* Let me ask you something about this conversation you're having right now with yourself. Does this feel alive, new, different, or does it feel old, lifeless, familiar?

**Explanation:** The therapist is trying to highlight some of the qualities of mindy conversations; in this case, particularly their tendency to go on for a long time and feel lifeless. The therapist contrasts this with vital conversations.

## COMPETENCY 10

**Sample 3.12**

*Therapist:* And so you do what it takes to make that feeling go away. You shrink, you get small, you give in, you distract yourself, you walk on eggshells. But something's weird here: your mind says you can barely stand it, yet you've been standing it for years. And you go on standing it, struggling with it, for years. I'm wondering, would you be willing to have the thought "I can barely stand it" as a thought, and make some more room for these scary feelings next time they show up? Your job would be to feel thoroughly terrible, to do a really good job at feeling that, rather than trying to feel differently. Then you will find out whether they can hurt you, whether you come out injured and beat up, or if the getting beat up comes from your struggle with them. You can pick how long. Would you be willing, even for five minutes, to just notice what thoughts show up, what feelings show up, and to just feel your feelings, watch your thoughts without doing anything about them? Afterward, you can always go back to doing what you were doing before. Are you willing?

*Client:* Five minutes? That's too long. I'll try one minute.

*Therapist:* Great. Cool. One minute. And then you can come back and tell me whether you were able to stand it or whether it really injured you.

[Alternately, the therapist could introduce a Tin Can Monster exercise (Hayes et al., 1999, pp. 171–174) to expose the fears of being respectful of herself with her partner. Or the therapist could do a role play with the client in which the client practices getting in contact with these feelings.]

**Explanation:** The therapist has guided the client to acknowledge a value in relation to her partner and that she has avoided mental content. This can serve as the focus of an experiential exercise or between-session practice in which the client is coached to contact the avoided material in an opening, accepting, compassionate posture.

---

## EXPERIENTIAL EXERCISE: DEFUSION

What was the most difficult thought about your practice or your learning that you had while working with this chapter?

Now pick one of the principles of defusion that seems most relevant to this thought.

What exercise or activity can you do to apply this principle to your own difficult thought? Describe a plan and then try it out, noticing especially what it does to your entanglement with the thought.

---

## FOR MORE INFORMATION

For more about defusion, including exercises and metaphors, see *Acceptance and Commitment Therapy: An Experiential Approach to Behavior Change*, by Hayes et al. (1999), chapter 6 (pp. 148–179).

For more exercises and worksheets about defusion to use for yourself and clients, see *Get Out of Your Mind and Into Your Life*, by Hayes and Smith (2005), chapters 5 through 7 (pp. 53–104).

# CHAPTER 4

# GETTING IN CONTACT WITH THE PRESENT MOMENT

*Our true home is in the present moment.*

—Thich Nhat Hanh (1992, p. 1)

Key targets for contact with the present moment:

✓ Help clients to discover that life is happening right now, and to return to now from the conceptualized past or future.

✓ Help clients to make contact with the life that is happening now, whether it be filled with sorrow or happiness.

✓ Help clients to notice what is happening in relationships in the moment.

Life is always lived right here and right now: there is nothing else that can be directly experienced but the present moment. All else is a conceptual rendering, a sketch, a picture drawn, a thought, a plan, a memory. Although all these refer to an imagined future or past, all can be experienced only in the now. The abilities to consider the past and plan for the future are essential for humans and extremely helpful most of the time. However, problems arise because people tend to get excessively and rigidly engrossed in the future or past and thus lose contact with the present. Because of cognitive fusion, people tend to interact with these conceptualized futures and pasts as if those conceptualizations were really happening, and end up spending little time in the now. ACT suggests that the problem isn't that we need to eliminate future or past thinking, but rather that we need to help people be more flexible—to be in the present when a present focus works best, to be in the future when planning works best, and to be in the past when remembering works best. A focus on the present is particularly important because that is where new learning occurs and where the opportunities afforded by the environment are discovered.

One of the key targets of ACT is to help clients let go of the struggle with personal histories, feelings, thoughts, and sensations and to show up to the life that is being lived in this moment. Contact with the present moment refers to the process of helping clients repeatedly step out of the world as restructured by thought and to more directly, fully, and mindfully contact the here and now, including both sensory contact with the external world and contact with the ongoing processes of thinking, feeling, and remembering.

# WHAT IS CONTACT WITH THE PRESENT MOMENT?

Showing up to the present moment involves bringing our awareness to internal and external experiences as they occur in the moment. A here-and-now focus is created by observing or noticing what arises in awareness on a moment-by-moment basis. When attending to your external and internal experience, for instance, you might first hear the sound of a bird, followed by the sight of a yellow color in the petal of a flower, followed by the feel of your foot touching the ground, followed by the sensation of an itch at your nose, followed by a thought ("this is nice"), and so on. Each one of these experiences is noticed as it occurs. No effort is needed and we do not cling to the experience; it arises and then falls away, and our observation is turned to the next experience as it arises and falls away, too.

Contacting the present moment is both easy and difficult at the same time. It is easy to turn our attention to an experience. However, it is difficult to continue to keep our attention on ongoing experience. Our minds quickly wisp away from the moment, leading us into thought. It takes practice to stay present. In ACT, we have clients practice numerous defusion, acceptance, and mindfulness exercises to help grow their "staying present" capability. It should be noted that not even the best of those who practice can stay present at all times. The goal is to establish observation and awareness skills, and to continue practicing them so they are honed, but also to recognize it is nearly impossible to stay present all the time. We work to establish the ability to be focused and present not because we want clients to always be in the present moment, but so they are able to do this when it works to do so (e.g., in the presence of an aversive experience that constricts behavior). Ultimately, present moment awareness is put in the service of a client's values through its contribution to psychological flexibility.

# WHY CONTACT WITH THE PRESENT MOMENT?

Much suffering results from fusion with thinking. Through fusion, we get "caught up" and dragged around by negatively evaluated states. We get invested in exploring our past so we can understand it and figure it out, largely with the goal of eliminating those negatively evaluated experiences that cause us discomfort. We also spend large amounts of time in our future—thinking about what is coming next or worrying about what will happen. When we are caught up in the world as conceptualized by our minds, we tend to miss some of the opportunities that are present in the current situation. Coming back to the present moment, and mindfully and nonjudgmentally observing and describing our current experience, can put us back in contact with the environment and help us to be present and able to act on our values.

Contact with the here and now also undermines avoidance and struggle. If we are connected to the moment, then we usually have nothing against which to fight; we have only what is present. Much of what is present is, in and of itself, not threatening: feelings, thoughts, sensations, and so on. When we lose the present, we can lose awareness and end up entangled with evaluations, judgments, and assessments about the feelings and thoughts and sensations, creating needless suffering. Thus, contact with the now undermines fusion, including attachment to a conceptualized self.

Presence also has a vital, creative, and connected quality. If we are in the moment rather than in the past or future, we are able to receive or take in what occurs in life, while letting go of the desire to make it come or go. We know through experience that any difficult emotion that may be present in the moment can be felt and is not destructive. It is when we fight against a feeling, wishing it were not so, that harm can occur. At one extreme, this destructiveness can take the form of suicide spurred by a seemingly bleak and hopeless future, or it can take a more subtle form, such as withdrawing from a relationship in order to avoid hurt. When experiencing emotion from the point of view of "I am having this experience *now*," we are freed from being controlled by our own pain and history. We're able to choose based on values rather than on the notion that something must first be different in our lives before we can choose.

"There is as much living in a moment of pain as in a moment of joy" (Strosahl et al., 2004, p. 43). Clients often take the stance that their lives will begin when they finally feel better. What this position fails to recognize is that life is occurring right now. Each moment is here to be lived. Whatever historical events have happened, have happened and there is no going back and undoing those events. History is unidirectional. It occurs from one moment to the next, and we cannot go back and have some other history. Time is best spent on what is happening in the present moment, and it is from this perspective that you can help your clients bring their values to life.

Equally important, whatever events may happen in the future, they have not yet happened. We cannot accurately predict the future, and we are often surprised by what the future brings. It is rarely what we hoped for, rarely what we expected. We can, however, take specific actions toward creating a fuller, deeper, richer life. In the moment, action that is engaged and values consistent can help create the life for which we are hoping. This is not to say things will turn out just as we imagine. However, suppose you could choose either a year of living your values, even if it had pain, or a year of struggling with pain. Which would you choose? This is easy to answer, and it is easy for clients to answer. If time is spent in the now, trying not to feel or think something, then that is what we will have: time spent trying to be something other than what we are. However, if time is spent in awareness and with intention to live values, then that is what we have: a life valued.

Finally, it is in the present that flexible and fluid self-knowledge is developed (Hayes et al., 1999). Because much of private experience can be painful, we often avoid awareness of our own thoughts, feelings, and responses. This has significant costs in terms of living well and responding flexibly. Through attending to the present, we learn more about ourselves, what our reactions are, and how to respond to and regulate our own behavior in a skillful manner.

# WHAT SHOULD TRIGGER THIS PROCESS?

ACT therapists spend a significant amount of time helping clients develop a stronger ability to return to the present moment through structured exercises, such as mindfulness meditation. In addition, this process can also be used as a response to client behaviors that indicate a need for present moment awareness. Focusing on present moment awareness is likely to be especially useful when the client:

✓ Seems out of touch with feelings or thoughts

✓ Is unable to describe what is contacted, indicating chronic avoidance or fusion

✓ Becomes too heady in therapy—for example, about values

✓ Fails to track the ebb and flow of issues in the therapeutic relationship

✓ Is immersed in a fused, well-practiced behavior pattern; for example, is bound up with a conceptualized self

✓ Fails to notice opportunities for choice and valued living in the current situation

Therapists can also use their own reactions in session as indicators that more of a present moment focus may be warranted. One possible indicator is the clinician's attention wandering—either when the client feels distant; when therapy seems predictable or wordy; or when therapy becomes a discussion about other times and places, as if to distract from the present. These clinician reactions can be due to the therapist's own history, not to anything related to the client. However, clinician reactions often indicate something about the client, and thus it is wise to use yourself as a barometer to help guide treatment.

# WHAT IS THE METHOD?

A therapist can introduce the idea of getting in contact with the present moment in this way:

*Therapist:* Part of what happens is that we interact with our own problems, and with much of our life, as if we were a math problem to be solved. However, it's not always useful to treat everything in life as if it were a math problem. A lot of things are more like sunsets. It doesn't work well to treat sunsets like math problems. If we do, what do we get? We get chatter in our head that goes something like this: "Hmm, that red isn't as nice as the red I saw the other day on that painting. It would be nice if it were just a little lighter. And if that cloud were just up a little bit, that would be better." That way of relating to a sunset doesn't work too well. What a sunset needs is simply for us to show up, be present, and witness it.

What if a lot of the things with which you struggle in life don't need your attention in a math problem sort of way, and instead just need you to show up, as you would with a sunset? If that's the case, then part of what you want to do in therapy is slow … down… look … feel … and see what actually shows up in your experience, and learn from that—rather than simply going based on what your mind has to say. You may have to slow down, show up, and look thousands of times before doing this becomes more natural.

Following such an introduction, the therapist can suggest participation in one of the experiential exercises described in the next section.

## Using Structured Exercises to Develop Present Moment Awareness

Clients have a difficult time connecting with a sense of self that is not about the content of thought (e.g., "I am sad," "I am Ralph," "I am tall"). As we discuss in chapter 5, the persistence and ubiquity of our private verbal commentary obscures the distinction between self as knower and self as known. Contact with the present moment helps clients develop a more ever-changing, flowing, and therefore flexible sense of self. This sense of *self as process* refers to a nonjudgmental, present, ongoing description of thoughts, feelings, and other private events (Hayes et al., 2001).

One of the easiest ways to help clients find this sense of self as process is through *structured mindfulness* exercises. In mindfulness exercises, the client is asked to gently observe without judgment a specific event, or an ongoing set of events, that occurs inside the skin. Let's take an example. One helpful eyes-closed exercise is Leaves on a Stream. In this exercise, clients are asked to picture themselves sitting next to a stream of water. They are then asked to imagine that leaves are floating down the stream and to place each thought gently on one of the leaves as it passes by. If a client notices he or she is getting hooked by a thought and dragged into a place where he or she is no longer observing the thoughts, the client is asked to note what just happened and to gently return to placing the thoughts on the leaves and allowing them to go down the stream. The therapist, at well-paced moments, can make comments to this effect, such as, "Notice if your mind has drifted onto other things, notice if it got caught by a thought. If so, gently bring it back, place the thought that got you caught onto a leaf, and send it down the stream, too."

This exercise can be done using a variety of images, including having thoughts attached to signs carried by a marching band or vehicles passing by on the road. One client imagined a futuristic city that contained roads that ran on electricity, and the roads were floating in the sky and running all over the place. In such a case, going with the client's image can work, too. Another image that can be used is clouds floating by in the sky. This transcript shows a short example of this kind of exercise led by the therapist.

*Therapist:* I would like you to take in a deep breath, and when you exhale, allow your eyes to close. Take a couple more deep breaths and then gently settle into your normal breathing and just rest there for a moment. [pause] Now I would like you to imagine that you are lying in a field—a field of your choice. It could be one with grass or flowers. Just picture yourself lying there and imagine you can see the blue sky above you. In this sky, clouds of all shapes and sizes are gently floating by. [allows a few moments for the client to create and connect to this image]

Now I would like you to imagine that every thought you experience is magically attached to a cloud. It can rest in the cloud as a word or image, or the cloud itself can take on the image of your thought. The key here is to take each thought as it occurs and attach it to a cloud and allow it to gently float by. If you find you lose the image, that's fine. When you notice this has happened, then without judgment just gently bring yourself back to lying on your back, watching each cloud float by, and attach the thought that took you away. I'm going to be quiet for a few minutes and let you practice this, just noticing each thought as it passes and placing it in or on a floating cloud. [lets the client quietly observe this process for a few minutes]

Remember, if you get lost in thought and are no longer viewing your thoughts, just gently come back. [allows another few minutes]

Now I would like you to gently leave this field in which you have been lying, and mindfully paying attention to the transition, come back to the room.

You can take time to process with the client the ongoing nature of thinking and point out how thoughts change, how they seem to be in motion—coming and going, sometimes chaotic and all over the place, sometimes more linear, sometimes as images, sometimes difficult to view. You can also discuss with the client how he or she went from looking at the thoughts (on the clouds) to looking from the thoughts (lost in the thoughts).

A second mindfulness exercise expands awareness of ongoing experience beyond the constant flow of thought to include the constant flow of all experience. In the "free experiencing" exercise (Walser & Westrup, 2007), the client is asked to pay attention to moment-by-moment experience:

*Therapist:* Let's prepare for an exercise that points to the sense of self as an ongoing experiencer. First, I would like you to get comfortable in your chair, and when you are ready, close your eyes. As your eyes close, notice that your ears tend to open. Take a moment and listen to what you hear. [pauses for about ten seconds] Now gently turn your attention to your breathing and simply follow your breathing as you inhale and exhale. Allow yourself to "be" your breathing for just a few moments. [ten-second pause] Now I would like you to follow—just as you followed your breathing—any sensation, thought, or emotion that arises. Be aware of each new sensation or thought or emotion and just simply observe it come and go. For instance, in one moment you may be aware of an itch, the next of a feeling of anxiety, the next of a thought, the next of a muscle pain or discomfort, and the next of a sound.

Your job in this exercise is to simply observe each new experience as it arises, as it comes into your awareness. For the next several minutes, I would like you to just notice the *you* that is an ongoing experiencing being—the you that senses, feels, and thinks in an ongoing fashion. Just let each new experience be there, observe, and then be aware of the next. [lets the client engage in this process for perhaps five to ten minutes]

Now I would like you to gently return to your breathing; spend the next few moments focusing on the rise and fall of the breath. And now open your eyes and return your attention to the room.

The key practice here is to help clients sustain a pattern of ongoing attention to, awareness of, presence with, and contact with their immediate, ongoing, changing experience, without having to retreat from it or get pulled up into conceptual thought. Clients can also practice this skill through mindful awareness of simple, daily activities, such as eating, washing the dishes, driving, and waiting in line. As an in-session activity, the client might practice eating a raisin mindfully (Kabat-Zinn, 1994). Not only does this help the client develop an ongoing awareness of sensations, but as the exercise continues, the client can notice how experience continues to occur, even as the content of experience shifts over time. For example, at first the client does not have a raisin, then he or she does, then it is tasted and chewed and swallowed, and finally the client does not have a raisin anymore. Time moves forward, and with each passing moment, a new awareness arises.

Structured mindfulness practice outside of session can contribute to cultivating present moment awareness in everyday life. Possible exercises include focusing on the breath; walking meditations; simply noticing while doing a daily activity; sitting meditations; journaling reactions to daily events; and paying particular attention to feelings, sensations, and thoughts. Often, clients initially benefit from practice with basic awareness exercises and meditation, and eventually progress to more exposure-like mindfulness exercises in which they are asked to invite in distressing content (e.g., anxious thoughts). We provide a resource guide for meditations at the end of the chapter.

## Discovering the Moment

The point of mindfulness exercises is not so much to develop mindfulness during the periods of the exercises themselves, but to raise present moment awareness more generally, so it is available when needed or helpful. As such, ACT therapists also work to weave mindfulness into the fabric of the sessions in an ongoing manner. One common way to bring more present moment focus into sessions is to begin sessions with a brief mindfulness exercise (for an excellent example see Eifert & Forsyth, 2005, pp. 125–126). This can be particularly appropriate for clients—and for therapists, if you do it with the client—who are more in their heads because it helps them to get present and to psychologically show up to the session, ready to work. We recommend doing mindfulness exercises along with the client, if possible, because this often results in more fluid and better-timed exercises, helps the therapist be mindful and present, and can help equalize the therapeutic relationship.

Contact with the present moment is an essential skill for fostering acceptance, defusion, and values in session. Experiential work with all of these processes requires clients to bring experiences into the room in order to work with them. One way to do this is to have clients slow down, stop, and check in with their own present experience during moments that suggest something is showing up that the client is avoiding or with which the client is fused (either consciously or unconsciously).

Cues that indicate it may be helpful to have a client stop and attend to what is showing up include shifts in client vocal tone; sudden changes in the direction of the conversation; the appearance of bodily tension or hoarseness in the client's voice; repetitiveness in thinking or speaking (e.g., worry, obsessiveness, or rumination); or anything that suggests restriction, tension, or inflexibility. When these behaviors are noted, you can gently ask the client to slow down, get present, and notice what he or she is feeling, sensing, or thinking. It can be useful during these moments to intentionally direct the client's attention to various domains of experience (e.g., emotions, thoughts, bodily sensations, urges to act, associated memories) and directly ask him or her to notice what is being felt in each domain. Sometimes it can be helpful to have a client slowly and carefully repeat a particularly poignant phrase in order to further heighten what is present and make it easier to identify. Here is an example from a session.

*Therapist:* You have been talking a lot about your difficulties at work, yet you don't seem too bothered. It must be frustrating.

*Client:* It is frustrating. It makes me really mad.

*Therapist:* It seems as if it might be painful, too. This is the third job you've had this year, and it is unfolding just like the last two.

*Client:* [turns red] Well, they are just so stupid. I mean, I'm doing what they tell me to do. If they would just leave me alone and let me do my job, things would be better.

*Therapist:* It seems you wish for that quite a bit, and yet it never seems to happen.

*Client:* [pause] Oh, yeah, I just remembered. I wanted to let you know I went to see the psychiatrist. She thinks I should get some more testing done.

*Therapist:* Did you see what just happened? We started to talk about pain, and you changed the topic.

*Client:* Yeah, I see … But I don't want to cry. I look silly when I cry. I feel stupid.

*Therapist:* [pauses to slow down the process] I wonder if you could notice those thoughts … silly, stupid … and let yourself show up to what is happening right now, to your feelings?

*Client:* [gets tearful]

*Therapist:* All I want you to do is just notice this experience as it is unfolding right now. [pause] What do you feel in your body? Take a slow moment to look. Look and see exactly where you feel it.

*Client:* [answers]

*Therapist:* And what kind of judgments and evaluations show up? Just pause, and even before you answer, take a careful, calm look.

*Client:* [answers]

*Therapist:* Good. And does this experience remind you of any situations from the past?

*Client:*     [answers]

*Therapist:*   And when you have all of that, what do you notice yourself wanting to do?

*Client:*     [answers]

Therapists can use a number of other ways to work with clients to help them discover the moment in therapy (Strosahl et al., 2004, p. 44). These include asking clients to simply be aware of thoughts, feelings, and memories as they arise; to identify when being present is needed; to pay attention to the shift between being present and getting pulled into the future or the past; and to do an experiential seeking exercise in which they notice the sights, sounds, and sensations that are present in the room. If clients are not very effective in noticing what is present, it is a good idea to start with simple, structured bodily sensations. A client can be asked, for example, to say out loud what sitting in a chair feels like or what it feels like to hold a breath, extend an arm, or rub his or her face with a cloth.

## Relating in the Moment

Because most clients' problems are, in part, problems with their relationships with others, it is particularly important to develop clients' abilities to be present, open, and nonjudgmental when in relationship with others. The constant process of evaluation, classification, and comparison in which we all engage is applied to everything—whether it be objects, other people, or ourselves. As a result, we tend to interact with the people around us not as rich, historical, complex individuals, but rather in terms of our ideas about them. Yet the words for what is in our experience are never the same as our experience. If we only interact with people as filtered through our ideas about them, we place a very basic barrier between ourselves and others.

In the therapy room, the client's most immediate relationship is with the therapist. Thus, the therapy relationship can be a powerful opportunity to work on the ability to be present, to help the client show up more directly with the people in his or her life. Metaphorically, the goal is to live with real people, rather than with cartoons. One way to do this is by bringing present moment awareness into the context of the therapy relationship (see chapter 9). The therapist helps the client to notice and be aware of what is happening within, moment by moment, in relation to the other person in the room. For example, a therapist might ask, "Are you willing to notice what is happening right now, within you and between us?" Focusing on this type of process gives the client the opportunity to experience connectedness and presence. It is a valuable way to show up in relationship and can be an action directly taken to support a personal value. In the transcript that follows, the therapist helps the client to notice his present moment reactions with the therapist that parallel difficult reactions he has with his wife.

*Client:*     It is lurking in the background all the time. It's like I'm tiptoeing.

*Therapist:*   You're feeling defensive?

*Client:*     Yeah. My wife just seems to criticize everything I do. I can never get it right.

*Therapist:*   [pause] Do you feel like that in here sometimes?

*Client:*     Like I'm tiptoeing around you?

*Therapist:*   Hm-hmm.

*Client:*     [pauses, and moves in his chair as if uncomfortable] I don't know.

*Therapist:*   And what are you feeling right here, right now?

| | |
|---|---|
| *Client:* | Should I feel something? |
| *Therapist:* | Just look. Take your time. |
| *Client:* | To be honest, I'm feeling defensive. I don't know why. I know you aren't doing anything … but I feel like I'm being criticized. |
| *Therapist:* | Where do you feel that? Let's start with your body. |
| *Client:* | [silence] I feel tense in my stomach … almost as if I'm tensing to be hit there. |
| *Therapist:* | Good, okay, any other sensations? |

## Using Present Moment Awareness to Build Self as Context

Contact with the present moment is intimately connected with the development of *self as context* (see chapter 5). This is because being aware of the content of experience in an ongoing, fluid way undermines attachment to a static, conceptualized self and requires a more fluid sense of consciousness. For this reason, coming into the present can be fostered by noting a conscious sense of self-observation. During mindfulness exercises, the therapist can say things such as, "And as you notice that, also notice there is a part of you noticing all these things," or "Just for a moment, I'd like you to connect with the sense that you are here now, noticing what you feel in your body and what emotions you are having."

Some clients have a difficult time doing mindfulness exercises because they have a difficult time locating a sense of self as observer. In this circumstance, the therapist may wish to work in smaller and more immediate ways on a sense of perspective as part of work on the present moment. For instance, the therapist can ask at appropriate times, "Who is saying this right now?" or "And as I ask you again, can you tell that someone is there listening, having the experience of listening, and in a moment is going to have the experience of speaking as you answer the question?" (Walser & Westrup, 2007). This kind of questioning can begin to help the client connect with the *observer self* that is encountering an experience in each new moment.

The therapist can model both of these processes (i.e., contact with the present and a transcendent sense of self), as well. For example, the therapist can say, "And even as you say that, I notice my heart rate pick up a bit, and my thoughts begin to get more evaluative. That gives me a sense that if I were in your shoes looking out at this set of difficulties, I'd be feeling more anxious and be pulled to be judgmental." The latter part of that statement is deictic and thus fosters an observing sense, as we discuss in chapter 5.

## CORE COMPETENCY PRACTICE

This section is intended to provide practice in using techniques designed to amplify contact with the present. As in previous chapters, we present a description of a clinical situation and a section of a transcript. At some point, the transcript ends after a client statement, and you are asked to provide a sample response that reflects the core competency at issue. Remember, the model responses are not the only right responses. If you disagree with the responses or want to double-check your response or talk more about it, you can post a question to the bulletin board at www.learningact.com/forum/. Try to generate your own responses before you look at the samples at the end of the chapter.

# CORE COMPETENCY EXERCISES

**COMPETENCY 1:** The therapist can defuse from client content and direct attention to the moment.

## EXERCISE 4.1

The client is a fifty-seven-year-old veteran of the Vietnam War who is presenting to therapy to work on issues of PTSD. He has been in and out of therapy for about twenty years. He has complaints about the government and its response following the war. He feels his life has been permanently changed by his experience.

*Client:*      I have a lot of resentment about the government. I mean, they should have done something. It has been how many years? I still have all this anger.

*Therapist:*    It seems like the past has taken over your life?

*Client:*      It has, every day. I mean, every damn day this is with me.

Write here what your response would be (remember you are using competency 1):

What are your thoughts in saying this? What are you responding to and what are you hoping to accomplish?

**COMPETENCY 2:** The therapist brings his or her own thoughts or feelings in the moment into the therapeutic relationship.

## EXERCISE 4.2

*This transcript continues with the same client as in competency 1.*

*Therapist:*    [gives the response found in Sample 4.1b in the model response section]

*Client:*      It's just that I've been working on this for so long, I have forgotten what it is like to be normal, to be without a problem. I know I said this, but all I think about is the government and how they screwed me. They really did a number on me.

*Therapist:*    It is hard for me to imagine the level of frustration you must have felt across the years.

*Client:*      You can't even begin to know. There is a strong part of me that wants to get back at them. This grudge is really strong.

*Therapist:*    It really does linger, and even in here it has lingered. We have spent quite a bit of time talking about it ... It even has a grip in here.

*Client:*      Yeah ... [sighs]

Write here what your response would be (using competency 2):

What are your thoughts in saying this? What are you responding to and what are you hoping to accomplish?

---

## COMPETENCY 3: The therapist uses exercises to expand the client's sense of experience as an ongoing process.

## EXERCISE 4.3

*This transcript continues with the same client as in competency 2, but a little later in the session.*

*Therapist:*   It seems part of the struggle is related to how much this issue has consumed your life.

*Client:*       Yeah, I hate it. This is all I think about.

Write here what your response would be (using competency 3):

What are your thoughts in saying this? What are you responding to and what are you hoping to accomplish?

---

## COMPETENCY 4: The therapist detects the client drifting into past or future orientation and teaches him or her how to come back to now.

## EXERCISE 4.4

*This transcript continues with the same client as in competency 3, but in a later session.*

*Therapist:*   What could you do today to take one specific action with respect to your value about your wife? Is there something you could do to let her know you love her?

*Client:*       She's been asking me to fix the door handle to the closet for months now. I guess I could do that.

*Therapist:*   Great. I can see how that might bring appreciation into the relationship.

*Client:*       I don't know. She asks me to do stuff, and I wait so long to do it that I'm not even sure she knows I've done it. She doesn't comment on it, anyway. She just kind of leaves me alone ... except to ask me to do stuff. I think I've been a "leave me alone" kind of guy for so long that she just keeps her distance. Ever since I got out of the service, things have been different. If the government only would have recognized what a lousy deal it was to be in Vietnam ...

Write here what your response would be (using competency 4):

What are your thoughts in saying this? What are you responding to and what are you hoping to accomplish?

## COMPETENCY 5: The therapist tracks content at multiple levels and emphasizes the present when it is useful.

### EXERCISE 4.5

The client is a thirty-three-year-old female who is complaining about wanting to hurt herself. She feels depressed and anxious and has come to this session angry at her boyfriend. She is extremely emotionally avoidant, not showing any pain since the beginning of therapy five weeks earlier.

Client:     [matter-of-factly] On top of all of my other problems, I'm now having problems with my boyfriend. I hate to say this, but he is just getting under my skin. Don't get me wrong, I love him. But, man, I don't think I can take this anymore.

Write here what your response would be (using competency 5):

What are your thoughts in saying this? What are you responding to and what are you hoping to accomplish?

## COMPETENCY 6: The therapist practices and models getting out of his or her own mind and coming back to the present moment in session.

### EXERCISE 4.6

This transcript continues with the same client as in competency 5.

Therapist:   [gives the response found in Sample 4.5b in the model response section]

Client:      Yeah, I can see that, but you don't know how upset he's making me. I really think I'm going to go over the edge if he doesn't stop. This week alone, he asked me for more than a hundred dollars. I don't have that kind of money. He's draining me dry. I have to pay bills, I have to get my car paid off. He just doesn't get it. I think I'm going to snap.

Write here what your response would be (using competency 6):

What are your thoughts in saying this? What are you responding to and what are you hoping to accomplish?

---

# Core Competency Model Responses

## COMPETENCY 1

**Sample 4.1a**

*Therapist:* The pull is to try to figure this out. But you've been doing that for years, and you told me it did little to move things forward. Let's shift from the past for a moment, and tell me: What are you aware of right now? What do you notice this moment?

**Explanation:** As the therapist, it can be easy to get caught up in client content. Many clients have compelling stories that can lead the therapist down a path that may be helping the client to avoid. This is not to say we shouldn't listen to what our clients have to say. However, ACT is a very active therapy and is not a therapy in which the therapist provides supportive listening most of the time. Supportive listening is valuable, but plays a smaller role in ACT than it does in many other types of therapy.

This kind of response, if engaged by the client, immediately pulls the client out of the past and into the now. If the client is able to stay with being aware of what he is currently feeling, the therapist can point to how the client is not in the past but is here, feeling this feeling, being aware of what is present. Even if the feeling is anger, the therapist can work with that to explore how anger is affecting the client's life and can see if there is something underneath the anger, such as sadness. These strategies are much more focused on the now than staying with the story of what happened because of the government in the past.

**Sample 4.1b**

*Therapist:* So, one of the things we could do in here is focus on how the government messed up so many years ago. Do you think that would be helpful?

*Client:* Not really.

*Therapist:* Is it possible that focus is problematic, and what we need to do is focus on what you can do now … work on finding out what is available to you in this moment, today?

**Explanation:** Here, the therapist suggests the strategy of focusing on the past is not going to be helpful. Many clients are aware this is true. Helping the client to show up to today and to what can be done from this moment forward is a useful step for a client who has been stuck in the past for a long period of time.

## COMPETENCY 2

**Sample 4.2a**

*Therapist:* So, I'm feeling this sense of frustration. [pause] I really want you to be able to move forward, but we keep landing back here. I don't want you to rescue me here. I just want to share what feeling is showing up for me. It feels hopeless. What shows up for you as I say that?

**Explanation:** This is a more risky move, wherein the therapist directly models showing up to personal experience and is willing to state this experience. This is an honest, in-the-moment response to the client being stuck. The goal would be to model willingness to experience in the moment, while also pointing to the feelings of hopelessness that arise when trying to undo history. It also points directly to how the therapist needs to be willing, exactly as he or she is asking the client to do.

### Sample 4.2b

*Therapist:* Right now, I'm having the experience of finding myself wanting to tell you to move on and let go. My mind is really working on me. I wonder if this is what happens to other people in your life … they tell you to move on or let go?

**Explanation:** The therapist reports on the honest content of his or her mind. This in-the-moment reaction and report not only model being present to content, but can serve to elucidate a larger problem: what it is like for other people in the client's life. If the client is always focused on how the government has ruined his life and is holding a grudge, then probably it is affecting most of his relationships. The therapist can link this back to values and see if this is what the client intended to happen with his relationships.

## COMPETENCY 3

### Sample 4.3a

*Therapist:* I wonder if we could work to find the cracks in this idea that this is all you think about. A while ago, you told me something about your wife and your children. So your thinking, and I suspect your feeling, changed across time. It is just when you're stuck in this piece about the government that it feels like nothing changes. Would you be willing to do an exercise with me?

*Client:* Yes.

*Therapist:* [The therapist guides the client through an exercise in which the client has a pen and paper, draws a line down the center of the page, and writes "thoughts" on the top left and "feelings" on the top right; suggests the client observe his thoughts moment by moment and write them in the left-hand column and also observe his feelings and write them alongside in the right-hand column. Alternately, any other present moment awareness exercise can be used here, such as the Continuous You exercise.]

**Explanation:** The therapist is working with the client to help him see he is more than his single experience with the government. In fact, he has had experiences without number. He has been stuck on this single experience, and his efforts to fix it have made it grow rather than diminish. The experiential exercise directly helps the client contact a sense of ongoing experiencing self that has numerous experiences, not only one.

### Sample 4.3b

*Therapist:* Would you be willing to explore with me the possibility that you are larger than this experience … that it is not everything?

*Client:* Sure.

*Therapist:* I'd like you to close your eyes.

Client:     [closes eyes]

Therapist:  Tell me what you become aware of when you do that; notice what is happening in the moment.

Client:     I hear the sound of your voice.

Therapist:  Good. Now focus your attention, and I'm going to sit quietly for a minute. Stay in the moment and tell me what you notice with each moment that passes.

Client:     I hear a car outside ... I feel uncomfortable with my eyes closed ... I notice my leg feels stiff and I want to stretch it. [continues to report]

Therapist:  [lets this continue for a minute or so; alternately, the therapist may need to be more directive and repeatedly ask, "What do you notice now?"]

**Explanation:** The therapist is working with the client in the moment to help him discover he is an ongoing experiencing being. This helps loosen the grip of "I'm a mad person, I hate the government," so the client can see he has much more experience than that. Pointing to moment-by-moment experiencing and the sense of ongoing process can help the client discover this larger sense of being.

## COMPETENCY 4

### Sample 4.4a

Therapist:  [interrupts the client] Notice what just happened. We were talking about ways you could bring your value about your wife alive today, and you drifted right back into the past. Did you see it happening? What feelings might show up for you if we shifted back to working on the value?

**Explanation:** Here, the therapist has detected the shift into the past and makes the client aware of that shift. It is helpful to work with clients on discovering these shifts. Sometimes they happen so quickly and naturally that the client is barely aware of what is going on. The mind is great at dragging people around. After the therapist helps the client notice the shift, the client can be helped to shift back to the present by noticing the current experience of making another shift and then refocusing on working on the value. It can also be important for the therapist to explore what emotion shows up about focusing on the value. The shift back to the past may have been an attempt to avoid the emotional pain associated with years of not living the value. This, too, can be felt, observed, and experienced, while making the choice to fix the door to the closet.

### Sample 4.4b

Therapist:  Do you recognize where you are going now?

Client:     Yeah.

Therapist:  Is that a place you want to go?

Client:     No.

Therapist:  Where would you like to be now?

Client:     Anywhere but there.

*Therapist:* Just prior to this, we were talking about how you might show your love for your wife. Would you prefer to talk about this?

**Explanation:** Again, the therapist is drawing the client back to the here and now. The therapist helps the client notice what the latter is doing because shifting into past-focused thinking is something the client could benefit from catching in flight. The therapist then reorients the client to the room.

## COMPETENCY 5

### Sample 4.5a

*Therapist:* Yeah, you feel right on the edge, like there's nowhere else to go ... Can I ask you a question?

*Client:* Sure.

*Therapist:* What are you noticing in your body right now?

*Client:* Nothing.

*Therapist:* Take a second, let yourself slow down and look inside. What's showing up? If you need to, you can close your eyes. And as you do this, see if you can let go of any resistance you feel to letting this stuff show up. See if there's not some sense of something important in sticking with whatever you feel right now. What does your mind say would happen if you were to simply sit, holding these reactions, without doing anything to make them go away?

*Client:* I can't.

*Therapist:* Good. And can you notice that thought, as a thought, and stay here, stay present?

**Explanation:** The therapist could engage this at a content level by talking to the client about the problems in the relationship. However, the therapist suspects the client is contacting some feelings not being expressed in the session. The therapist uses this opportunity to help this emotionally distant client contact a reaction at some other level than the purely cognitive, and to do so by noting something very concrete— her bodily reactions. Then, when the emotion is present, the therapist suggests taking an acceptance stance, while also being mindful of the mind because the mind might pull the client back into a struggle.

### Sample 4.5b

*Therapist:* So, multiple things are happening in here. You're struggling with your problems and thoughts about your problems, and you're feeling angry at your boyfriend. Plus, you're letting me know this story and perhaps wishing for something to be different. And right at the end there, you say, "I don't think I can take this anymore." And then this thing happens ... you take it some more. I want to be careful and make a distinction about what you're taking. I'm not saying you should live with bad behavior, but right here, in this moment, you are taking it. You're having your thoughts and feelings, and you're able to experience them. And ... you continue to experience them. You don't fall to pieces, even though your mind says you will.

**Explanation:** The therapist is tracking emotional content, thought content, and relationship content. In this moment, the client has bought what her mind offered: "I don't think I can take this anymore." This is a good time to gently point to all the content and then help the client show up to the moment, noticing that even though her mind handed her what seemed like a literal truth ("I can't take it anymore"), the experience of the moment shows she can and does take it.

COMPETENCY 6

### Sample 4.6a

*Therapist:* I can sense the frustration, and I find myself wanting to problem solve. But in this moment, I feel helpless to fix it. I wonder if your mind telling you that you're going to snap is about that same helplessness?

*Client:* Yeah, I feel it, too.

*Therapist:* Let's take this moment to notice helplessness, to show up to what it feels like when it seems there is no answer. [pauses to allow silence]

*Client:* [becomes very quiet, approaching tears]

*Therapist:* And also notice that you don't snap.

**Explanation:** Perhaps the most obvious thing to do under this circumstance is to help the client problem solve. This could include teaching her to be assertive. However, doing so would miss the opportunity to experience the feeling of helplessness and to learn experientially that she won't snap. Bringing the process back to the moment helps the client defuse from the content of her mind. From this place, the therapist can work with her on the cost of being unwilling to feel helpless (e.g., losing financially, wanting to be distant from her boyfriend) and focus on what will work for her, given her values with respect to her boyfriend. This could include problem solving, but that wouldn't be the first road taken.

### Sample 4.6b

*Therapist:* I notice my brow furrowing … a tension in my neck … and I have a feeling of helplessness as I reflect on all the frustration you must be feeling, both with your boyfriend, and right now, with me for not understanding. I wonder if you could take a second and notice what you are feeling right now, in this moment. [proceeds to have the client note feelings, sensations, and thoughts noticed in the moment, in the therapeutic relationship]

**Explanation:** The therapist begins by noting out loud the therapist's own process of observing personal sensations and feelings, as a model for the client. The therapist also acknowledges the client's expression of tension in the therapeutic relationship when she said, "You don't know how upset he's making me." The therapist then explicitly focuses the client on experience in the moment, and steps out of the stream of thoughts in which the client is caught and moves into a more present-oriented, relational, and direct mode of experiencing.

## EXPERIENTIAL EXERCISE: FREE CHOICE MEDITATION

This exercise takes about ten minutes. Sit in a quiet place. Make sure you have no distractions or interruptions. Make yourself comfortable, sitting straight but not rigid.

When you have found a comfortable position, gently close your eyes. Notice that your ears tend to open and become more alert when you do this. Be aware of sound for a few moments, and then gently turn your attention to your breathing. Spend a few moments just paying attention to your breath. You can be aware of your breath at the tip of your nose and nostrils or in the rise and fall of your chest.

If you find your mind begins to wander, as minds tend to do, gently say to yourself, "Wandering," and without judgment, refocus your attention on your breath. After following your breathing for a period of one to two minutes, gently release your attention from breathing and begin to attend to whatever arises in your awareness next. This may be a sound or a sensation. It may be a thought or a feeling. Your job is to simply notice it and let it go, moving on to the experience of the next moment. For instance, you may notice the sound of the air-conditioning, and then an itch on your nose, then your breath, then a twitch, then a thought—don't let it capture you; just notice it and let it go—then a sensation, then a sound, then a taste, and so on. Simply follow whatever comes into your awareness from moment to moment. Don't cling to any experience; gently observe each. Notice how they come and go.

After about six minutes, return your attention to your breath, and as before, follow your breathing for a period of about two minutes. Then gently open your eyes, completing your meditation. Remember, your mind will hook you over and over again, taking you out of the meditation. When this happens, bring yourself back to just noticing. If it happens a hundred times, bring yourself back a hundred times. This is part of the process.

Good luck with your free choice meditation.

## FOR MORE INFORMATION

Many mindfulness exercises created for use in ACT sessions can be found in Eifert and Forsyth (2005); Hayes and Smith (2005); and Hayes et al. (1999). Audio recordings of some ACT exercises can be found at www.contextualpsychology.org and www.learningact.com.

*Meditation for Dummies* (Bodian, 2006) and *Zen-Master: Practical Zen by an American for Americans* (Hardy, 2001) are good, accessible introductions to mindfulness meditation practice.

Jon Kabat-Zinn has produced a number of excellent audio CDs that cover guided imagery, breathing, and body scan mindfulness exercises (www.mindfulnesstapes.com).

# CHAPTER 5

# DISTINGUISHING THE CONCEPTUALIZED SELF FROM SELF AS CONTEXT

*You can see a lot just by observing.*

—Yogi Berra

Key targets for distinguishing conceptualized self from self as context:

✓ Help clients to make contact with a sense of self that is continuous, safe, and consistent, and from which they can observe and accept all changing experiences.

✓ Help clients differentiate this consistent sense of self as the context, arena, or location in which all experience happens, from the content of that experience (e.g., emotions, thoughts, sensations, memories).

Who are you? This seems like a simple question, yet issues such as "What is the self?" and "Who are we at our most basic level?" have troubled scientists, philosophers, theologians, and other thinkers for hundreds of years. In this chapter, we seek to answer this question by describing two ways of coming to understand the self (a third important sense of self is described in chapter 4). ACT holds that each of these ways of understanding the self has broad implications for human potential and functioning. The two senses of self addressed in this chapter are the *self as conceptualized*, which is useful to human survival in numerous ways but can also lead to great suffering and limitation, and *self as context*, which is liberating and an avenue to decreasing suffering. Our goal in this chapter is to define each of these senses of self and focus on how they function from an ACT perspective.

# THE CONCEPTUALIZED SELF

When children are first learning to talk and verbally understand the world, in addition to imitating their parents' words, they are peppered with questions about themselves: "What do you like?" "What do you want?" "Where do you want to go?" "What do you want to eat?" "How old are you?" "Why did you do that?" and so on. Adults generally expect answers to these questions in return. At first, children do not know how to answer these sorts of questions, and often answer with responses such as "I don't know" or "Just because." Through a largely unintentional training process, however, as they grow and learn, children come to give more acceptable and coherent stories about why they do what they do, who they are, and how their emotions and life histories cause and justify their actions. Eventually, children—we, as adults—develop elaborate repertoires of verbal behavior that are used to describe, evaluate, judge, explain, assess, and question. We talk to ourselves and others, and our minds are alive and at work. Because we come to understand and know so much about ourselves and the world through the lens of the mind, we begin to believe and live by our own stories about ourselves and who we are—stories we ourselves made up.

The result of this societal training process is the development of a conceptualized self, or *self as content*—all the many ways we say "I am" that declare the beliefs we have developed about who we are and the concepts we have created that seem to describe our being. For instance, we might say, "I am a professional" or "I am someone who suffers" or "I am a victim" or "I am intelligent (or dumb)." Associated with this self content are all kinds of images, thoughts, and behaviors that seem to indicate these senses of self are true. Altogether, this mental content is the stuff we call our *identity*. There is nothing inherently wrong with building, categorizing, and discovering this identity—or, rather, identities because we often have several. Doing so helps us communicate and interact with the world in ways that are healthy, expected, and useful. For instance, our professional identities and all of the verbal information that goes along with them can be helpful in getting us to go to our jobs, even on days when we don't feel like it. We might say, for example, "I am a good worker," "I don't want to disappoint the boss," or "I need the money." From the perspective of the social community, fusion with the conceptualized self is largely positive because it allows others to better understand our behavior and therefore to be able to predict and perhaps influence our behavior. Unfortunately, the same positive outcome that can work for the social community can be troublesome for the individual. Those same verbal processes that help us build our identities, evaluate and control situations, assess, and problem solve can lead to unworkable and destructive behaviors, trapping us into patterns of living that are problematic. Through the mind's tendency to want to be consistent, to justify and explain, to evaluate and assess, we can end up in a kind of verbal straightjacket that limits our lives.

For example, one of us (RW) had a client who fully embraced a conceptualized self that was defined as being a "proud man." His proud man self-concept included the idea that he was a person who deserved respect no matter what. He felt his family should listen to him at all times and do so without disagreement; as a proud man, he thought he should never have to admit he was wrong. In the process of clinging to this conceptualized self, he began to lose relationships with his family. His self-made identity was costing him intimacy and closeness in relationships. He was so glued to his self-perception that he became angry and even more prideful, insisting others needed to change and see his way in order for the relationships to work. He did this instead of working on what he most desired: close family relationships. The proud man concept specified that he could not change; indeed, he would no longer "be a man" if he were to let go of his attachment. In the end, only two of six children would even speak to him, and most of his grandchildren chose not to be around him at all. He traded his family for attachment to a story and a label.

Whole lives can become dictated by a particular conceptualized self. Think of the child who was abused and has become a lifelong victim or "damaged goods," the Vietnam era veteran who has become "the Vietnam vet," the hardworking person who has become "the professional," the self-sacrificing mother who has become "the martyr." Each of these self-made concepts can lead to pain and struggle, especially if other things the person cares about and values are lost as a result.

The verbal knowledge in the conceptualized self is limited. We do not truly know all the history and context that have served and serve to affect our behavior. Rather, in our imperfect understanding of our lives, we are left with stories, justifications, and descriptions that, although they make reference to many facts and provide descriptions of patterns of behavior, can be quite limited in their ability to be helpful in living.

# SELF AS CONTEXT

Relational Frame Theory (RFT; Hayes et al., 2001) explains how the same social training process that leads to a sense of self as content also typically leads to another sense of self: a self that is continuous and stable, and yet hard to define. When, as children, we are asked questions such as "What did you see?" "Are you worried?" and "What would you like to eat?" we learn to provide responses such as "I saw a doggie," "I feel scared," and "I want a cookie." The content of the answers continuously varies (e.g., "I see," "I feel," "I want"), but the word "I" taps into a constant, the conscious place from which events are known. According to RFT, "I/you" is a basic relational frame that, along with frames such as "here/there" and "now/then," is deictic, meaning it needs to be learned by demonstration with reference to a speaker. This is different from "I" as conceptualized. Self as context is a perspective from which one perceives, speaks, acts, and lives. In other words, I/here/now becomes the context for the content of experience.

The sense of self that emerges is transcendent and inherently social. It is transcendent because the limits of this conscious context cannot be consciously noted. Everywhere you go, there you are, and it is not possible to be conscious of unconsciousness. Said in another way, this experience is not thing-like and does not seem from the inside out to have spaciotemporal limits; thus, it provides a naturalistic basis for experiences of transcendence or spirituality (Hayes, 1984). This sense of self is social because it is not possible to have relational frames that are not bidirectional. In order to understand "here," you must understand "there." In order to understand "now," you must understand "then." And in the same way, to contact a sense of "I," you must be able to contact a sense of "you." To see that you see through your eyes, you have to see that others see through theirs. This is why empathy and a transcendent sense of self are so closely linked. The same relational framing processes that give rise to the sense of self give rise to a sense of what it must be like for others to feel.

Once this sense of self as context begins to emerge in the preschool years (McHugh et al., 2004), it becomes part of everything we consciously experience. For instance, if you were asked what you ate for dinner last night, where you went on vacation last year, and what high school you attended, you would be able to answer all those questions by seeing through the eyes of the one who ate the dinner, the one who went on vacation, and the one who attended a certain high school. You would be able to view each of these events from a stable sense of self that stretches back in time. From this perspective, you observe the content of your life, including thoughts, feelings, memories, and sensations. The self to which we are referring is a larger, timeless, interconnected sense of you, a context that holds all of your experiences, and yet is not any one of them. It is, in a profound sense, not a thing—or we could say it is "nothing" or it is "everything"—simply because this locus, or arena, in which all the content of experience unfolds is hard to define; it is not a concept or belief.

# WHY DISTINGUISH SELF AS CONTEXT FROM SELF AS CONTENT?

The purpose of this kind of work is not to create a new sense of attachment. We are not arguing that people "really" are one sense of self or another. Rather, by helping the person contact a sense of "being here," we can facilitate three key ACT processes: 1) decreasing an attachment to a conceptualized self, 2) creating a context in which acceptance and defusion work is not threatening, and 3) fostering greater flexibility. Making the experiential distinction between the knower and the known empowers the client to observe experience more freely and get on with the business of living, rather than struggling to eliminate negatively evaluated experiences before any valued direction can be taken (e.g., living according to the thought "When my anxiety goes away, I will live my life").

Let's take an example that illustrates how self as context can moderate our usual way of knowing. A client might say, "I hate myself. I can't stand feeling like this a moment longer," and then in the process of attending to and believing what the "mind has just said" about the feeling, the client may choose to drink alcohol as a means to escape the experience. In this example, the content of the mind is being held literally and is being applied to the self as a conceptualized object. The content includes an evaluation about the self and a predictive outcome ("I can't stand this"). If a literal verbal sense of knowing dominates, it seems that immediate action must be taken or some awful event will follow. Behavior is quickly organized around fixing or controlling the mind's content, but that very work can be problematic; for example, if a client numbs out to forget bad memories, uses cocaine to feel better, or avoids intimacy to avoid fears of being unlovable.

If the client simply attends to the moment and observes his or her thoughts, another avenue is possible. For example, the client might watch the thought "I can't stand feeling like this a moment longer" arise and then notice what happens. Immediately thereafter, another thought will arise and … the stream of experience will continue to flow. Coming to know this ongoing flow of experience—that is, experiential knowledge—will tell the client that he or she won't perish; in fact, another moment will pass and another experience will come along. If the client can be present to directly experience the moment, he or she will have an opportunity to learn how thoughts and emotions are not destructive and will also have the opportunity to expand his or her sense of self, coming to recognize that the client is an experiencer or observer, rather than the experience itself.

# WHAT SHOULD TRIGGER THIS PROCESS?

In ACT, therapists work with clients on an ongoing basis to explore the problem of being too attached to the conceptualized self and to explore self as context. However, therapists will want to increase their focus on these issues at two key times. The first is when a client's attachment to a particular conceptualized self interferes with the ability to make needed changes in his or her life. For instance, a client might be overly identified with being a victim. In believing the content of this conceptualized self, the client mistrusts others and refuses to engage in intimate relationships, even though intimacy may be held as part of the client's relationship values. When fully engaged in this conceptualized self, the client's life as victim can be largely constraining. The therapist's job is to help the client make contact with self as context and engage a larger and more encompassing sense of self that is separate from the content of the mind. In other words, the client is able to contact a sense of self that is separate from the victim self. The goal is to increase flexibility and support the client in engaging in new behavior.

The second time involves helping clients find a secure and safe place from which to contact and confront feared emotions, memories, thoughts, and sensations. Feared experiences often threaten a person's very sense of self. Making contact with the transcendent "I" can help clients see there is a place—in fact, *they* are a place—that is unchanging and stable and does not need to be threatened by the experiences of their mind or felt emotions. This can facilitate the work of defusion and willingness, which necessarily entail contacting painful and distressing experiences. Self-as-context work can also aid in values work, especially because it undermines attempts to please others or avoid guilt or shame in the guise of values.

Clinicians can watch out for certain signs in themselves, as well, that suggest the utility of this ACT process. These include a sense of personal disconnection, lack of empathy, boredom, arguments with the client, or the pull to protect the client's self-image.

# WHAT IS THE METHOD?

The main goal of this process is to help the client establish or reconnect with the continuous sense of self that is involved in noticing or observing the moment-by-moment flow of thought and emotion as ongoing experience, rather than as believed or disbelieved instances of thinking or feeling to which the client must respond. When the client can observe experience with a sense of perspective and the equanimity that provides, new and more flexible ways of responding can develop. Some strategies used in this process include:

Recognizing a sense of "you" exists that is aware of thoughts and emotions.

Teaching and requesting the practice of mindfulness and awareness (see chapter 4).

Actively practicing noticing a transcendent and compassionate, socially expansive sense of self in and out of session.

Focusing on experience instead of logic.

Defusing from the content of thinking (see chapter 3).

More specifically, contact with an observer self (Hayes et al., 1999) is created through a series of metaphors, interventions, and experiential exercises that help the client come into contact with self as context, rather than self as content. Typically, this is accomplished through a variety of exercises aimed at helping the client attend to various aspects of the present moment, and then notice an "I" exists that is noticing these aspects of experience.

## Metaphors

As with many ACT interventions, it helps to have organizing metaphors. Several metaphors exist to describe self as context; one example compares the self as context to a house, and the self as content to the furniture in the house (see figure 5-1). Metaphors used in other parts of the work, such as the bus metaphor (Hayes et al., 1999, pp. 157–158), can easily be expanded to provide an organizing metaphor for self as context. For example, if the therapist is using the metaphor of a bus full of unruly passengers in work on defusion, acceptance, and values, it is easy to talk about the driver as the part of the person that is aware of all of these experiences.

The chessboard is a central ACT metaphor (Hayes et al., 1999, pp. 190–192). In this metaphor, the self (i.e., the arena or context in which experience takes place) is likened to a chessboard. The chess pieces are said to correspond to the client's thoughts, feelings, sensations, and so on. After this metaphor is established, it can be elaborated in many ways; for example, by discussing how chess is a war game and the board ("I") has no real investment in how the war turns out. The therapist can also note that, although the various pieces are threatening to each other, they are not threatening to the board, which simply touches and supports them. The therapist can use an actual chessboard to help make the metaphor more concrete. Using physical props, such as a chessboard, is especially helpful for clients with limited abstraction abilities. The following transcript illustrates how this metaphor, once laid out, can be made more experiential by integrating it into the flow of the session.

**Figure 5.1**

*Client:* [immediately after the chessboard metaphor was described and an actual chessboard with pieces was used] So, I'm the board and my thoughts and feelings are the pieces? But what about my thoughts about who I am?

*Therapist:* [picks up more chess pieces and sets them on the board] More pieces to be added to the board.

*Client:* But when I feel things, it's real, it's overwhelming.

*Therapist:* [picks up another chess piece] Yes, it is definitely an experience you are having. [sets chess piece on the board, representing the feeling] And that thought you just had, the one that said, "But when I feel things, it's real, it's overwhelming," is another piece, too, another experience. [sets another chess piece on the board]

*Client:* So everything I say will become another piece?

*Therapist:* Yes, each experience you have, whether it be a feeling or a thought, is another piece on the board. And, as the board, notice that you are in touch with the pieces, you are in contact with them [slides pieces around on the board to demonstrate contact], yet the pieces are not the board.

*Client:* Well, I think I would just like to dump the board over.

*Therapist:* And that thought, too, is another piece on the board. [sets another piece on the board] See how this works?

*Client:* I know, but I don't want those bad pieces.

*Therapist:* [compassionately] I can understand why. But, again, check your experience and see. Have you ever been able to kick the pieces that you didn't want off the board? Have those bad memories and feelings disappeared?

*Client:* No.

Therapist: So even "I don't want those bad pieces" goes on the board. [puts another piece on the board] Remember, though, the board is not the pieces. The board—you, the experiencer—is larger than any single piece. You are in contact with your thoughts and feelings. You are aware of having them, and yet you are not them. You experience them, and you are continually adding to your board … and the pieces are not the board. The board can hold the pieces and remain intact and whole, even if a piece says, "This is overwhelming."

Here, the therapist is demonstrating self as context by pointing to the board as the holder of experience (the pieces) and the observer of experience, while also demonstrating that experience is ongoing and additive. Experience flows from one moment to the next, and each new experience is to be observed, just as another piece is added to the board. It is worth noting that we, as therapists, and our clients are not always in contact with this sense of self. It is difficult to remain in the observing perspective. It takes practice to be aware of this sense of self. Regardless, it is a freeing position. If the client is not the experience, then he or she is free to choose, while holding the pieces. No effort is needed to change the piece before effective action can be taken.

## Brief Interventions

In addition to metaphors, a number of interventions can help the client make contact with the conceptualized self and self as context. These are generally done to better facilitate the ability to take the perspective of an observer and also to help clients recognize when they are entangled with self as content. For instance, clients usually come to therapy unaware that their stories about themselves are different from what they have actually experienced. Instead, they see their lives as their stories, and they see their self-evaluations as an issue of being. Initial work can focus on helping clients to be aware of the fact that they have a concept of themselves, to see what some of that content might be, and to understand how it functions in their lives.

One way to illustrate to clients how to identify the functions of their self as concept is through a short, humorous story that draws an analogy between our conceptualized self and a suit we wear. A man walks into a tailor's shop to pick up his new suit. As he tries it on, he realizes the suit fits terribly. It sticks out near the elbow, one shoulder is too high, and the waist is lopsided. In surprise, the man turns to the tailor and says, "Hey, I'm not paying for this. The suit doesn't fit."

"Not to worry, sir," says the tailor. "Just hunch your shoulder like this, twist your body like this, lean a bit to the left. You've got it."

When the man follows these instructions, the suit falls perfectly into place. He walks out of the shop, and as he walks down the street, he passes two women. The first woman whispers to the other, "Look at that poor crippled man."

And the second says, "Yes, but isn't his suit fantastic?"

This metaphor is usually delivered to clients who are struggling with self-identities that are "ill-suited" to the valued directions they would choose for their lives. Through discussion, clients can understand that we do not simply live our lives, but we distort ourselves and our lives to fit our interpretation of reality. We twist ourselves to fit the suit. In thinking about the woman who likes the man's suit, clients can also see how the social community provides support for us to live within our narrowly defined self-concepts, and that some people are disappointed or upset if we change to live outside their ideas of who we are. Following this metaphor, the therapist might have a discussion with the client and ask questions such as, "What suits have you been wearing that don't fit you?" "Who made the suits you wear?" "Did you choose to wear them or is it just out of habit?" "What would it be like to take off the suit?" and "Who might you have to disappoint, upset, or make wrong if you were to be a different person in your life?" Throughout this process, the therapist helps the client to see "You are not the suit."

Another intervention is called Pick an Identity (Hayes et al., 1999, p. 196). In it, clients try on various self-concepts to see the arbitrary nature of the concepts and how they affect the totality of the clients' memories, perceptions, thoughts, feelings, and predispositions. In this exercise, the therapist makes up slips of paper, with various statements on them describing particular identities, some of which reflect things the client has said about himself or herself, and some of which are novel. For example, the therapist might have slips of paper that say, "I am a ballerina" or "I am bad" or "I am funny" or "I am powerful." The client is then asked to try to "be" these identity statements in the session. The therapist helps the client explore what it would be like to be this identity and helps the client notice the impact that identifying with these identities has on his or her thoughts, feelings, predispositions, and so on. This exercise can also help the client connect with the observing self. For example, when the therapist is fairly certain the client has tried on an identity, the therapist can ask questions such as, "Can you notice there is a person here who is noticing the various thoughts and feelings you are having?"

The transcendent sense of self about which we are speaking is impossible to look at because it *is* the sense of perspective involved in consciously looking. Looking for this sense of self is rather like trying to jump from behind one's eyes in order to watch them watching. In order to see anything that might result, metaphorically the eyes must follow. But it is possible to catch oneself for brief instants. In the "find a free thought" exercise, clients are asked to close their eyes and try to find a thought that is totally free and not connected in any way with anything else in their history. Usually the setup for the exercise seemingly suggests this is possible, but the actual client experience is different. As the following transcript illustrates, the therapist then asks a surprising question.

Therapist:  So, just go on watching the thoughts that come up and see if you can find one that is not programmed, that is free and unconditioned and has nothing to do with anything else in your life. [pause] Just let me know what comes up.

Client:  [pause] I'm having lots of thoughts, but all seem familiar.

Therapist:  Well, keep trying. [pause] And let me know what pops up.

Client:  Okay. Well, I thought of a beach scene. I've never been there, and I thought, "This is a new one." But then I realized this beach scene was like a commercial I saw.

Therapist:  Okay.

Client:  Plus, when I started to consider whether it was new, I realized I felt just like I did in third grade when my teacher asked me a hard question. So even that isn't new.

Therapist:  Cool. Keep looking. Keep searching. And while you do that, I have a question to ask. Raise your finger when you are clicked into "search mode."

Client:  [raises finger]

Therapist:  As you notice your mental conditioning, notice this also: Who is watching? [silence]

Client:  I am.

Therapist:  Don't try to grab this sense and look at it because it will just slip away, but let me ask you one more thing: when you caught that you were looking, did *that* part of you seem programmed and conditioned?

*Client:* No. It just is.

It is important not to reify this experience during debriefing. The point is not to grab transcendence by the throat and create yet another conceptualized self. The point is to experientially touch no-thingness (Hayes, 1984), and from that contact to act with faith in our inherent wholeness at that level.

There is an ACT saying that points to what needs to be done in relation to the self as concept: "Kill yourself every day" (Hayes et al., 1999, p. 200). Contacting a contextual self is about letting go of the conceptualized self and the struggle that comes along with it. The idea is to create flexibility. If we don't have to cling to pride or victim or martyr or any other conceptualized self, then we are freer to make choices that are about values, not about what we think a particular conceptualized self deserves or needs or insists on having. Behavior can be flexible and aligned with values.

## Experiential Exercises

A number of experiential exercises can be used to help clients let go of their conceptualized self. One of the central ACT exercises is the observer self exercise (Hayes et al., 1999, pp. 192–196), which helps the client quickly contact a sense of "I" that is larger than any single experience. This exercise is generally done as an eyes-closed exercise, often taking thirty or more minutes. Hayes et al. should be consulted for the full process, but the core is first to notice the continuity in consciousness itself, as illustrated in this transcript:

*Therapist:* If you're willing, I suggest we do a short exercise to discover that place in which you are a context for all that you experience, a place in which you are an observer of your experience. [gets permission to move forward]

I'd like you to close your eyes and follow along. Take a moment to get centered by focusing on your breathing and getting comfortable in your chair. [allows a few moments for the client to settle in] Now I'd like you to take a moment and think back to a memory of something you did this morning, such as eating breakfast or getting ready for work. Take a look around that memory; notice what you were doing and who was there, if anyone. See if you can remember the sights and sounds of this memory. [allows the client time to reflect on the memory]

Now, as you notice this memory, as you observe it, also notice who is noticing. Now release this memory and travel back in time to find another—from perhaps a month or a year ago. Once you have found this memory, also take a look around this one. What are the sights and sounds of this memory? [pause] And, again, as you notice this memory, notice who is noticing. Notice there is a "you" there who is observing that you have this memory.

The strategy is then to contrast that sense of continuity with dimensions of experience, such as roles, sensations, emotions, thoughts, and behavioral urges. In each case, the therapist asks the client to note how the specific dimension ebbs and flows and is constantly changing, yet the sense of consciousness itself does not change. The bottom line is that the experiences with which we struggle are not really "us" anyway.

Many other exercises in the ACT literature can be used to help clients build self as context. These include the Card Labeling exercise (Walser & Pistorello, 2004) and Letting Go of the Conceptualized Self exercise (Walser & Westrup, 2007).

# Fusion with Self-Evaluations

As noted earlier, evaluation is very useful for some things. It can help keep us from danger, guide our decisions, and help us to know culturally defined rights and wrongs. However, although the ability to evaluate can be helpful in some contexts, it can be quite damaging in others, particularly when directed at oneself. Most clients we see are engaged in stating—privately, publicly, or both—and wholeheartedly buying negative evaluations of themselves. It is also often the case that these evaluations have been around for as long as the clients have been conscious beings, continuously plaguing them or showing up when problems arise. Therapists can feel the harm done by fusion with these evaluations just by reviewing the ones clients bring to session: "I'm worthless," "I'm evil," "I'm pitiful," "I'm ugly," "I'm undeserving," "I'm a failure," "I'm a lost soul," "I'm a creature, not even human," "I'm damaged goods," and so on. Finding an effective way to work with self-evaluations can be difficult because this is a natural and well-rehearsed part of human language.

Often, clients come to therapy with the idea that their self-evaluations need to change; that they need to have better, more positive self-evaluations (e.g., a higher self-esteem) in order to live a better life. This is a battle clients are unlikely to win because, ironically, the battle to eliminate negative self-evaluations holds the seeds of the problem. Clients' evaluations are part of themselves and their histories, and so in order to change or eliminate these evaluations, clients have to go to battle with themselves. The result is a self-attacking, self-critical stance, a stance that is at the heart of the problem in the first place. In contrast, rather than help clients change the content of these evaluations, ACT therapists help clients to see them for what they are—evaluations—while also guiding clients to dispassionately observe them. The idea is to help clients see that these evaluations are part of their programming, and that when certain buttons get pushed, this programming shows up on the screen. To use the chessboard metaphor, these are more pieces on the board, not part of the board. The client is a whole human being *with* the evaluations, and as in the case of reasons, evaluations do not need to determine the client's choices or quality of life.

A number of exercises are useful to help clients notice evaluations, rather than hold them to be true. First, the therapist can make the distinction between description and evaluation. For instance, in session, the therapist might hold up a pen and describe it, as shown in the following transcript.

*Therapist:* This pen is white, with black letters and a black cap. The tip is metal and has black ink. Agreed?

*Client:* Yes.

*Therapist:* Now, suppose I say this is the best pen in the world, there is no better pen. Agreed?

*Client:* Well, I don't know. I own a pretty darn good pen.

*Therapist:* Right, you can see how the description is different than the evaluation. "Best pen in the world" isn't *in* the pen. It is something I'm saying about the pen. It's an evaluation I have about it ... It doesn't exist in the pen. [pause] And "worthless" is an evaluation that doesn't exist in you. It's just something you say about yourself. It has nothing to do with whether you are whole or not.

This type of interaction with the client can also be demonstrated with the milk deliteralization exercise found in chapter 3. Even though the client can imagine milk, see it in the mind's eye, and perhaps even "feel" the cold glass or "taste" the milk, the milk isn't there. Saying "milk" and describing milk do not suddenly make milk literally present. Saying "I am bad" and feeling "I am bad" do not make bad exist in the person. It is just something the person is saying about himself or herself. Again, the client is the context for the content of "I am bad," nothing more.

## Self as Context and Living Well

Developing contact with self as context facilitates the development of a sense of choice by the client. Choice becomes important because it is the behavior that allows clients to select actions consistent with their stated values. Often, clients who are stuck report they are in that state because they don't have a choice. Some thought or feeling is interfering with their ability to move forward. Often, reasons and stories are offered to explain why they remain stuck. These reasons can range in nature from traumatic childhoods to anger to unforgivingness to feelings of worthlessness. The therapist's job is to help the client defuse from these stories and recognize that choice is still possible.

If the client can operate from self as context, it is easier to notice thoughts and feelings without avoidance or fusion. For instance, the client can have the thought "I can't do this," and then do it. The key is to observe the thought and then take action with respect to what is there to be done. The therapist can help clients build this repertoire in a number of ways. Helping them connect with their experiential sense of knowing is one way, as shown in the following transcript.

*Therapist:*  Have you ever said to yourself that you can't stand it for another moment?

*Client:*  Yes.

*Therapist:*  What happened?

*Client:*  Well … [chuckles]

*Therapist:*  Another moment passed, didn't it?

*Client:*  Yes.

*Therapist:*  And then another and another. Those moments just kept on coming, and here you are now. You stood it, even though your mind told you that you couldn't.

*Client:*  Yes, but it still felt very bad.

*Therapist:*  Agreed. I do believe it felt bad. But imagine for just a moment that your thoughts actually controlled all your behavior, that every thought you had caused you to do something. What if thoughts actually caused everyone's behavior? What would the world look like?

*Client:*  It would be a mess. It would be obliterated.

*Therapist:*  Yeah, things would really be bad. Thank goodness our thoughts don't cause our behavior. Our reasons, our stories, don't force us to do things. But they do like to look big and scary sometimes, as if they could force us to do things. But all they can do is *look* big and scary. Your mind tells you, "I can't stand this another moment," and then your experience tells you that you can. My question is: who is aware of all these thoughts in the first place?

*Client:*  I am.

*Therapist:*  And is that sense of awareness dependent on only certain thoughts being there? Can you notice thoughts you like and thoughts you don't?

*Client:*     Sure.

*Therapist:*   It is from that place that choice is possible. Whose life is this, anyway? Your thoughts? Can you make choices while observing your thoughts? While being with your thoughts, while noticing them, can you take actions that fit with the life you want to live?

The therapist can give a number of homework assignments that are specific to the client and that help the client practice making choices *with* his or her thoughts and emotions rather than *for* those thoughts and emotions, while being fully aware as a conscious person. This effectively links self as context to the other ACT processes of contact with the present moment, defusion, and valued living, for example.

# CORE COMPETENCY PRACTICE

The rest of this chapter focuses primarily on the core competencies of a therapist working on helping clients distinguish self as context from the content of self that is conceptualized. Four ACT core competencies are involved in distinguishing self as context. Each core competency is described, followed by sample transcripts and practice opportunities.

# CORE COMPETENCY EXERCISES

**COMPETENCY 1: The therapist uses metaphors to help the client distinguish between the content and products of consciousness, and consciousness itself.**

## EXERCISE 5.1

A sixty-one-year-old client presents to therapy following a divorce from her husband. She has never been in therapy and has often used avoidance strategies to deal with difficult emotions. She would like to discover how to live her new life, given that she has not been alone in more than forty years. She is fearful about trying new things and wants the fear to go away. She has tried multiple types of avoidance to escape the fear, including isolating at home, drinking alcohol while alone, and avoiding new situations and activities.

*Client:*     [directly following the chessboard metaphor] But isn't there any way to win this war? I would really like this fear to go away. Can't I just push the pieces over on the board?

Write here what your response would be (remember you are using competency 1):

What are your thoughts in saying this? What are you responding to and what are you hoping to accomplish?

## COMPETENCY 2: The therapist utilizes exercises to help the client make contact with self as context and distinguish this from the self as conceptualized.

### EXERCISE 5.2

*Transcript continues with the same client as in competency 1, but in a later session.*

*Therapist:* It seems you have been in this relationship for so long that you have come to see yourself as "the housewife."

*Client:* It's the way I've always been. I'm the one who does the dishes, cleans the house, stays at home, takes care of other people. I just can't do anything else.

Write here what your response would be (using competency 2):

What are your thoughts in saying this? What are you responding to and what are you hoping to accomplish?

## COMPETENCY 3: The therapist utilizes behavioral tasks to help the client notice the workings of the mind and the experience of emotion while also contacting a self who chooses and behaves with these experiences, rather than for the experiences.

### EXERCISE 5.3

The client is a twenty-eight-year-old female who is having difficulty with colleagues at work. She feels intimidated and wants to quit her job, but feels she can't due to financial pressures. She wishes her feelings would not get hurt by these interactions. She reports keeping a "stiff upper lip," but struggles silently at work and cries at home about the work interactions. She is angry at herself for feeling this way.

*Therapist:* [toward the end of session] How is this stiff upper lip thing working?

*Client:* Not very well. I'm really trying, but it's getting harder and harder. I feel like I'm going to break down in tears all the time, but I've been able to fight them off so far.

*Therapist:* What kinds of things do you say to yourself about breaking down in tears?

*Client:* That I'm weak and that I shouldn't let these petty things bother me.

Write here what your response would be (using competency 3):

What are your thoughts in saying this? What are you responding to and what are you hoping to accomplish?

**COMPETENCY 4: The therapist helps the client recognize the distinction between the self who evaluates and the evaluation itself.**

## EXERCISE 5.4

*Transcript continues with the same client as in competency 3, but in the next session.*

*Client:* These interactions make me feel so awful. I feel like I'm worthless to them and I'm starting to believe that I *am* worthless, that something is wrong with me or it wouldn't be this way.

Write here what your response would be (using competency 4):


What are your thoughts in saying this? What are you responding to and what are you hoping to accomplish?


# Core Competency Model Responses

## COMPETENCY 1

**Sample 5.1a**

*Therapist:* Notice that you've been in this war and you've been trying to win it. Your battle has included staying at home to eliminate the fear piece, and drinking alcohol to try and squash the fear piece. The result is you've limited your life in this battle, this war, to try to push the fear piece down. Meanwhile, let me just ask you this: Are you still "you"? Are you still aware of all of this? In what sense do you have a huge stake in this war if you've been you through all this struggle?

**Explanation:** The therapist is helping the client connect to experience, then points to the distinction between the content of struggle and the conscious context of this struggle.

**Sample 5.1b**

*Therapist:* Let's suppose you engage the battle to win the war and you're able to push the pieces all over the board. Remember, you can't push them off because this board stretches in all directions. [takes chessboard and pushes piece over] Here's my problem with that. You went from who you are to who you aren't, and now large aspects of "you" are your own enemy. Of what threat to the board are all of these pieces?

*Client:* None.

*Therapist:*   Right. But of what threat to the pieces are the other pieces? It's huge, right? So how can you possibly stop fighting? You can't. You won't. So, my question is just this: if you make that move, when could the suffering possibly end?

**Explanation:** Here the therapist highlights some of the costs of attachment to particular forms of self as content (e.g., large parts of yourself and your history become your enemy) and then points to contact with a transcendent sense of self (i.e., self as context) as a possible way out of the war.

## COMPETENCY 2

### Sample 5.2a

*Therapist:*   So, it really seems as if no other sense of "you" exists; there's only the housewife you. But you also told me you have a sister and you've been a daughter. You let me know that you volunteered at one point. So we could describe each of these senses of you, too, and they would look different from the housewife you, I would guess.

*Client:*   [thinks] Yes.

*Therapist:*   But also notice there is a "you" who's aware that you were a housewife, that you are a sister, and that you were a volunteer. And you're here right now. Who's aware of all of these aspects?

**Explanation:** The therapist is, again, helping the client connect with the board-level sense of self—self as context—by pointing to all of the conceptualized selves about which the client has talked or could formulate, and is helping her notice that she's aware of these and more than these. It is from this place that the client can be encouraged to take actions that are not about continuing to cling to the conceptualized self as a housewife.

### Sample 5.2b

*Therapist:*   I'm wondering if you'd be willing to do a little exercise with me?

*Client:*   Sure.

*Therapist:*   [adapted from Walser & Westrup, 2007] I'd like you to close your eyes and imagine yourself in your home as the housewife. When you have that image in your head, raise your right finger.

*Client:*   [raises finger]

*Therapist:*   Okay, now silently to yourself describe her appearance. What does she look like? [pause] Now notice how she feels. What emotions does this self—self as housewife—experience? [pause] What does this housewife say about the world and the way it operates? [pause] How does she define herself? [pause] Now, as you have the full image of this you in your mind, with all of her thoughts and feelings and ways of being, what would it mean if you had to let her go? [pause] What emotion shows up for you as you think about letting go of her? [pause] And if you find any resistance there, see if you can notice that she is not you anyway. She is just a role you play. Now imagine you could hold her lightly, like you might hold a butterfly in the palm of your hand, and choose to live those values you would like to bring to life.

**Explanation:** The therapist engages an experiential exercise to help the client disentangle from the conceptualized self. This provides a small window through which the client may be able to free herself from the housewife role and make alternate choices about how she will live her future.

## COMPETENCY 3

**Sample 5.3a**

*Therapist:* I'm wondering if you'd be willing to have the thoughts that you are weak and that petty things shouldn't bother you and to let yourself cry. Let yourself have this experience.

*Client:* I'm afraid I'd fall apart.

*Therapist:* Okay, then that one, too. Would you be willing to have the thought that you're weak and you'd fall apart, and let yourself contact that emotion? Is it possible to sit and open yourself up to this emotion, even to cry?

*Client:* I could give it a try.

*Therapist:* Okay, here is what I think might be helpful. Go home, and tonight go through the observer exercise we did using this tape. And when you're finished and are more deeply in contact with this transcendent self of "you," spend at least fifteen minutes deliberately remembering some of those painful experiences. Cry if that comes up. But all the while, see if you can also hold those experiences lightly, as a whole conscious person, not as a person defined by your emotions.

**Explanation:** The therapist is encouraging the client to actively turn toward her avoided emotion, while also experiencing the thoughts that she is weak and may fall apart, but to do so from the stance of the observer self. If the client is able to do this, her experience will tell her that she may cry, but that she will not literally fall apart and that she is far more than her emotions.

**Sample 5.3b**

*Therapist:* I wonder if you'd be able to do something at work that is consistent with your values, while holding and observing these thoughts and emotions? What value would you like to bring to life at work? [explores with the client a work-related value and assigns a specific task that is consistent with that value (e.g., saying hello when she doesn't feel like it); asks the client to complete the homework between sessions]

**Explanation:** The goal is to help the client contact the self that can observe thought and emotion, while also choosing to do things on a regular basis that bring personal values to life. She may not get what she expects (i.e., others saying hello back), but she is still choosing to live her value.

## COMPETENCY 4

**Sample 5.4a**

*Therapist:* It makes sense to me that you'd feel sad about what's happening. I'm curious, though, about your reaction to your own experience. I wonder if there's a more compassionate stance you could take with respect to these feelings. If you were to observe someone feeling awful, would you believe that person was worthless?

*Client:*     No, I'd try to comfort the person.

*Therapist:*  So I wonder if there's a way to take this stance toward yourself? Is there a way to have a comforting, compassionate stance in this moment of experiencing the thought that you are worthless?

*Client:*     Well, I could work on "seeing" the thought.

*Therapist:*  Yeah, we're not talking about convincing yourself otherwise or talking yourself out of it—just standing with yourself, being present as you observe this thought... And you could take actions in your life that are consistent with compassion and comfort for the self; for instance, not isolating or hiding, but talking with others. What other things can you think of?

**Explanation:** The therapist is working with the client not to eliminate or debate the thoughts she has, but instead to simply observe them nonjudgmentally. A deictic relation is used to contact a transcendent sense of self by shifting from "I" to "you" and then recontacting the difficult content from this perspective. This is a far more compassionate and loving stance than buying and believing something is wrong with her because she experiences these emotions. Notice that no effort is made on the part of the therapist to make the thoughts be different; the focus is on viewing the thoughts as content being experienced, rather than content she literally is.

## Sample 5.4b

*Therapist:*  Look at me, right in the eyes. [pause] Suppose I am you. Look right in these eyes and notice "you," now from the outside looking back. I want you to see a person is here who is having these evaluations and being aware of them. What would you say to "you" if you wanted to speak to this more conscious part and not just with the part all entangled in evaluations?

**Explanation:** This statement by the therapist uses deictic frames to appeal to a sense of empathy grounded in a contextual self.

## Sample 5.4c

*Therapist:*  Notice that you're evaluating your experience. You say you feel awful, and then you evaluate it as something bad or wrong. But notice that this thought—"something is wrong with me"—is another piece on your board. It's an experience you're having in this moment. I'd like to help you connect to the place in which you are larger than the experience. One quick and easy way to do this is to say things such as, "I'm having the thought that something is wrong with me" instead of saying, "Something is wrong with me." And as you do that, see if you can notice this: who is noticing the thought?

**Explanation:** This response points directly to the self that is having an experience categorized as an evaluation. Pointing to this distinction is helpful when clients are buying their evaluations, when they see themselves as the chess pieces instead of as holding the chess pieces.

## EXPERIENTIAL EXERCISE: DISTINGUISHING SELF AS CONTENT FROM SELF AS CONTEXT

Describe two conceptualized selves (e.g., professional self, self as parent, self as victim). Write a description of these selves: what they feel, how they think, and how they appear. After you have completed these descriptions, go back to each and add several sentences that describe a behavior that is directly the opposite of what you would expect this conceptualized self to do. Be creative, wild, or extreme in writing down these opposites.

Once you have completed the writing, get into a comfortable position, close your eyes, and imagine each of these described conceptualized selves. You don't have to imagine it as yourself, although you can if you want. But, rather, give it whatever form seems to represent the way it is for you. Then, in your imagination, picture it engaging in the behavior you described as the opposite. Notice what happens in each case and write down a few notes when you have finished.

## CONCEPTUALIZED SELF 1: _____

Description:

Opposite behavior:

Notes:

## CONCEPTUALIZED SELF 2: _____

Description:

Opposite behavior:

Notes:

# FOR MORE INFORMATION

This chapter has been written from a clinical perspective, but there is a growing behavior analytic science of self and deictic frames. For an orientation to the basic literature, see Barnes-Holmes, Hayes, and Dymond (2001).

For contemporary basic research in this area, see McHugh et al. (2004) and Rehfeldt et al. (2007).

More exercises and metaphors can be found in chapter 7 (pp. 180–203) of *Acceptance and Commitment Therapy: An Experiential Approach to Behavior Change*, by Hayes et al. (1999).

# CHAPTER 6

# DEFINING VALUED DIRECTIONS

*When I dare to be powerful, to use my strength in the service of my vision, then it becomes less important whether I am afraid.*

—Audre Lorde (1997, p. 13)

Key targets for defining valued directions:

✓ Help clients contact and clarify the values that give their life meaning.

✓ Help clients link behavior change to chosen values, while making room for their automatic reactions and experiences.

What are your values as a therapist? How high do you aim in your work? This chapter starts with an exercise to help you clarify and focus on your values as a therapist and also to help you develop an experiential sense of the process of defining valued directions.

## EXPERIENTIAL EXERCISE: DEFINING VALUED DIRECTIONS

Move through this exercise slowly, giving yourself time to fully engage with each question. Complete each element before you move on, and the text will cue you when you have finished.

Take a few moments to connect with what you hold as most important in your role as a mental health professional. What do you want to stand for or be about in your work? Write your answer here:

Consider the following categories of therapists for a few moments:

☐ An okay therapist  ☐ A good therapist  ☐ A very good therapist  ☐ An extraordinary therapist

What do you notice as you think about each of these categories? Do you find yourself checking to see where you fit on this list, perhaps judging your skills as a therapist? Do you feel uncomfortable or hesitant to place yourself in a category?

Make a few notes here about what you noticed and felt:

Now, assume that choosing among these four alternatives is as simple as choosing an item from a restaurant menu. With menu in hand, what if you chose to be an extraordinary therapist? What implications would that have for the way in which you interact with your clients? Write down one or two implications here:

Bring a current client to mind; any client is fine. If you were going to be an extraordinary therapist for that person, what would it mean for how you would interact with him or her? Is there anything you are not doing that you would do—or anything you are doing that you would not—if you were shooting for being extraordinary? If you were going to be extraordinary with this client, what are one or two things that would change? Write these below:

Given your usual way of doing things, what is the most likely internal barrier that would stand in the way of your choosing to make these changes?

Is there any way in which buying into these barriers has cost you and your clients in the past? Be honest with yourself.

Now review the implications you noted and the changes you would need to make if you were to be an extraordinary therapist. Suppose you had an opportunity to commit to an action that would support these changes and bring the implications to life. Would you accept the opportunity and be willing to notice the barriers without giving them veto power over your behavior? Write down at least one concrete action you could do as a commitment related to the changes you wrote about.

*I commit to* [behavior]

*as an expression of* [value]

You have just completed a values exercise similar to one in which a client in ACT [...] You were presented with a choice about a particular domain (being a therapist) and ask [...] some options. You were led to consider the implications of that value for your behavi[...] would have to address, and the costs of not doing so. You were offered an opportunit[...] value and its behavioral implications. This short exercise covered all the major aspec[...] discuss in this and the following chapter.

Values are the very heart of meaning and purpose for humans. They guide and define our lives. For nonverbal animals, discrete consequences are fairly adequate for defining purpose. A pigeon pecks a key "in order to get" a food pellet; a rat presses a bar to get a drink of water. For verbally capable humans, the situation is not so simple. Reinforcers, in this context, only go so far. Money can be a reinforcer, but given the choice between ten thousand dollars and a rich, loving relationship with a child, many people would leave the money behind.

The ACT approach to values is not about teaching clients any particular set of morals or the correct values or virtues. Rather, it is about teaching clients a process of valuing that can guide them in making life choices long after the therapist is gone. This process is intended to help clients select directions for their lives that resonate with their deepest longings and establish goals that are ultimately more workable than goals uninformed by intentional valuing.

ACT therapists working on this process focus on the central question "In a world where you could choose to have your life be about something, what would you choose?" (Wilson & Murrell, 2004, p. 135). This question is explored with the client in a number of ways, including conversation; writing; and eyes-closed and experiential exercises. Versions of this basic question are asked again and again, calling clients' attention to the question of purpose in their lives, what really matters to them, and what a well-lived life would look like for them.

# WHAT ARE VALUES?

The job of the ACT therapist is to help clients be more aware, mindful, and intentional in their pursuit of their life goals and values. *Values* have been defined in ACT as verbally constructed, global, desired, and chosen life directions (Dahl, Wilson, Luciano, & Hayes, 2005). The metaphor of a direction is a way of speaking about the intentionality that is potentially embodied in every purposive act.

Valuing does not exist separate from human action; it is a continuous quality of what we do. Values are like deliberately chosen combinations of verbs and adverbs. They are embraced as qualities of ongoing action across time. To relate to others lovingly is a value. To raise one's children kindly and attentively is a value.

To some degree, we engage in an act of valuing each time we do something that is purposive or instrumental. We value various qualities of outcomes; we value ways of living; we value ideals; we value what kind of friend, lover, partner, parent, child, worker we are. These implicit purposive qualities of any instrumental act are elevated to a value by the action of choosing that very quality.

In one sense of the term, values must be a free choice, rather than a reasoned judgment, because values provide the metric, or meaning, of aspects of our lives. If you try to justify a value, you must appeal to some other metric; but then this metric needs to be justified, and so on forever. If any action is to be taken, at some point you need to just take a stand and say, "I hold this to be important." Verbal reasons still may be present in the form of thoughts and opinions about "why I choose this," but the action is not defended by these reasons (or else you are back into the justification loop). Ultimately, a vital, committed life means choosing and then living, with reasons coming along for the ride.

This does not mean values choices are not deeply considered; in fact, we recommend they be very deeply considered. Scientifically speaking, it also does not mean values choices have nothing to do with our history or context. Choices are historically and currently situated, as is any human action, but they are not specifically linked to and defended by verbal rules in the form of reasons and justifications.

# WHY VALUES?

Values are important in the ACT model for several reasons.

**Constructive direction:** Values work is about helping clients define what their lives are about when escape, avoidance, and fusion are no longer controlling their behavior. Avoidance and escape are fundamentally about getting rid of and keeping away some experience. They are not about going toward or constructing anything in particular. Values-oriented behavior is constructive; it is about moving in a particular direction or having a particular quality in the client's life. One client said it this way: "It's as if I have spent my life on the open ocean, swimming away from this one island that I don't want to be on. Ultimately, it doesn't lead anywhere … What I want to do is starting swimming toward something, not away from it."

**Response flexibility and motivation:** Values are inherently linked to choice. From a functional contextual point of view, free choice in the realm of valuing is "true" because it is useful to speak in that manner, not because it is literally true. Scientifically, we would guess that values are largely culturally conditioned. However, from the perspective of the individual human, it is more empowering and life affirming to see our own behavior as a choice because it loosens the largely artificial link between actions and verbal storytelling. This loosening, in turn, leads to greater behavioral flexibility and to the possibility of contacting desired and chosen life directions that have an intensely vitalizing, motivational quality. Research supports the idea that values that are decided based on experiential avoidance, social compliance, or cognitive fusion (e.g., "I should value X" or "A good person would value Y" or "My mother wants me to value Z") tend not to be related to positive outcomes. Life directions chosen based on intrinsic properties of action are the ones that work (Sheldon & Elliot, 1999).

**Support for ACT processes:** Practicing acceptance and defusion often means wading into swamps of anxiety, loss, sadness, and confusion. Values provide the context that explains why these difficult experiences are being contacted. From an ACT perspective, values are what make willingness and acceptance more than simple wallowing or an attempt to reduce unpleasant experiences through exposure. Similarly, clarity about our chosen values provides a guide for workable action when not responding literally to our thoughts (i.e., defusion).

**Consistent direction:** Defining a valued direction produces a more consistent compass heading to direct action during the storms of life, when waves of emotion crash and the screaming winds of the mind blast. Anyone who has engaged in mindfulness meditation for any period of time is aware of how fickle and changeable emotions and thoughts can be. However, values tend not to change so rapidly over time. If the therapist can help clients describe their most basic values for their life, clients can contact a source of stability in an often-chaotic landscape of changing thoughts and feelings. Once clarified, stated, and committed to, values can be like a lighthouse, providing direction during dark psychological nights and stormy situations.

**Effective and pragmatic goal setting:** Values work also provides a way to establish goals that are flexible, pragmatic, and likely to lead to effective action across time. Many therapies work to help clients develop goals for themselves. ACT goes deeper in the exploration of values because values are what underlie the selection of concrete goals in the first place. Values are like the direction, and valuing is similar to walking in that direction. Values are present from the first moment of taking a direction and they do not have an end, whereas goals are something that can be completed, accomplished, or finished. In ACT, goals are selected to conform with the valued direction, not the other way around. Thus, if working toward a particular goal does not effectively further values, it is time to change the goal. Work on values in ACT helps clients focus on the process of living, whereas a focus on goals tends to encourage evaluation of the discrepancy between present and possible outcomes.

**Contextual purpose:** Values work is important in ACT for a deep philosophical reason. In a contextual approach, what is true is what works to achieve our chosen ends. That is empty, however, unless we can define what "works" means (Hayes, 1993). Values do precisely that; and without values, ACT is impossible. It is the criterion of workability that makes sense of the concept of defusion, for example, because in defusion, functional truth is replacing literal truth. But in the same way that literal truth is linked to conventional meaning within a language community, functional truth is linked to values.

# WHAT IS IN THIS CHAPTER?

This chapter focuses on helping you as a therapist develop fluency with the core competencies of defining valued directions with your clients. We do not attempt to review the full body of available techniques or methods for doing this work, but rather focus on some of the most central therapeutic skills and common roadblocks to helping clients define valued directions. Table 6.1 lists some of the more important exercises, metaphors, stories, worksheets, and procedures available in other resources.

## TABLE 6.1

| Exercise | Explanation | Reference |
|---|---|---|
| Choice vs. decision | Helps clients distinguish choices from reasoned judgments | Hayes et al., 1999, pp. 212–214, 218–219 |
| Process vs. outcome, direction vs. goals | Values as a process of living, not outcomes to be achieved | Hayes et al., 1999, pp. 219–222 |
| Using Values Compass as assessment method | Moderate length, detailed procedure for values assessment (~1 session) | Eifert & Forsyth, 2005, pp. 186–187; Dahl et al., 2005, pp. 91–111 |
| Using Valued Living Questionnaire | A brief form for structuring values assessment | Wilson & Murrell, 2004, pp. 120–151 |
| Values, actions, goals, barriers process | Outlines an extended, multi-session procedure for values assessment | Hayes et al., 1999, pp. 221–229 |
| Eulogy exercise | Client imagines people giving eulogies he or she would most want to hear | Hayes et al., 1999, pp. 215–218 |
| Tombstone metaphor | Client writes what he or she wants for an epitaph | Hayes et al., 1999, pp. 217–218; Eifert & Forsyth, 2005, pp. 154–155 |

# WHAT SHOULD TRIGGER THIS PROCESS?

Valuing is typically worked on throughout therapy; however, there are a few times when an additional focus on defining valued directions is warranted. Both values and committed action have a constructive aspect to them that is not as present in the other four core ACT processes (i.e., defusion, acceptance, self as context, and being present), which are more oriented toward ameliorating or responding to clients' problematic behaviors.

The primary indicators of a need to engage this process is when clients are out of contact with the cost of avoidance in their lives or when they are numb, distant, intellectual, or uninvolved. Clients who are not experiencing much acute pain often do not have the "push to change" that can come from the drive to escape pain. In their cases, motivation to change can come from the "pull" that bringing values present into the session can exert on behavior. Discussing clients' hopes, dreams, and desires for their lives can bring them psychologically into contact with the discrepancy between their current paths and the paths they would choose. Contacting this discrepancy often evokes internal reactions or barriers that, when brought into the room, can be worked on through other processes.

# QUALITIES OF EFFECTIVE VALUES CONVERSATIONS

Defining valued directions almost always begins with a conversation about values. The overall goal is for the client to construct a vision of the life he or she could live with integrity, depth, and vitality. Values conversations that are effective have certain qualities that can guide the clinician who has learned to detect them; namely, vitality, choice, a present orientation, and willing vulnerability. Clinicians also encounter several common barriers to developing these qualities when helping clients clarify valued directions. In the following section, we describe these qualities in more detail and outline some common problems and ways of working with them.

## Vitality

Making psychological contact with that which they most value in life tends to evoke a certain qualitative reaction people often describe as vital, alive, or meaningful. A client, and often the therapist empathically, can sense the value in the room, even though no action has actually been taken in that direction. Just as a dog begins to lick its chops when its guardian gets out its food bowl, similarly, people begin to psychologically taste the outcome of valuing when it is present. They light up or wake up.

An essential role of the therapist is to monitor the vitality of the values conversation. The therapist's job is to draw out the client's hopes and dreams, and to help the client detect the life directions he or she would choose freely, not select in order to avoid guilt, anxiety, shame, or the negative opinions of others. At times, when working on values, the therapist will experience the conversation becoming small, lifeless, grinding, intellectual, rote, old, constricted, or tired. Usually, the client and therapist are stuck in a pattern of experiential avoidance and fusion. The session has become *about* values, rather than an active process of contacting and choosing values in the moment. Discussions, analysis, and interpretations *about* values are often dry and boring; experientially contacting actual valuing in the moment is not. The therapist's job is to bring values into the present moment, and that requires clinical creativity. Here we offer examples, but no prescriptive methods are likely to be successful.

Recalling past experiences that relate to the client's values can help set the emotional tone for therapy and bring forward some of the functions of valuing in the present. For example, the therapist can help the client locate experiences in the past in which he or she felt intense vitality, contact, presence, or purpose. Eyes-closed exercises in which the client re-creates the event in imagination and then considers its meaning can give guidance about how to live life now. What is recalled should be important and specific. For example, the therapist could say, "Tell me about the day you met your wife" or "Tell me about the day you left home" or "Tell me about the most moving event in your life. What did that feel like inside? Help me to see it the way you saw it, feel it the way you felt it. I want to understand." This can set the stage for a more meaningful values discussion.

Listening together to meaningful music at the start of a therapy session can augment contact with values, as can poetry, moments of silence, or mindfulness exercises. The client can be asked whom he or she admires or finds noble. The therapist can ask, "Who inspires you?" After this person has been identified, and what the client considers admirable has been specified, the therapist can ask, "If this person knew you really well, what would he or she want for you in your life?" If the client is unable to identify someone to whom they look up, a favorite movie or favorite fictional character can be used to elicit the same types of response.

The following transcript illustrates this process. The client is a high school student dealing with issues about procrastination at school. She has been struggling in school and is at risk for dropping out. This session occurs at the point when she is having trouble starting work on a term paper.

*Therapist:* If you think of all the people you've known and looked up to, does anyone particularly stand out?

*Client:* My third grade teacher, Ms. Schweibert.

*Therapist:* And what was Ms. Schweibert about? What did you admire about her?

*Client:* She was always upbeat, always having fun. We always knew she cared about us kids.

*Therapist:* So, what would Ms. Schweibert want for you now?

*Client:* She'd want me to learn something, to graduate at the head of the class.

*Therapist:* Yeah, head of the class. She'd want that for you. I have a sense that is something you deeply respect about her—the way she was toward people and learning. [pause] Is there anything else she'd want for you, in addition to being head of the class?

*Client:* She'd want me to be happy. She'd want me to do this because *I* enjoy it, because *I* want to, not because I had to or because she told me to.

*Therapist:* Is there a way you could make writing your paper live up to that—for yourself, I mean?

*Client:* Yeah, something a little bigger than writing a paper. Not so much what I have to do, but why I would want to do it.

*Therapist:* Yeah, what are you here for? What do you want on your tombstone? I want you to consider how what you're doing now lines up with that. I have a sense that what you've been working for is others' regard for you, but it sounds like what they want for you is for you to be yourself. I want you to look for something that's yours. It will probably be bigger than you, but it comes from you. And "I don't know" is not an answer. As a kind of homework, would you be willing to write about this on your own this week and bring it in next time?

*Client:* Yeah, sure.

*Therapist:* What you might want to write about is something that would make you think, "I would be inspired by a person who could do this." [writes this on a piece of paper so the client has a copy of what to write about] What could you do that would be inspiring to you? Okay?

In this dialogue, the therapist is helping the client link up schoolwork to the larger context of her life: her values and life direction. There is a reason the client respects this particular teacher. By helping the client contact the admired qualities of this teacher, the client is also brought into closer contact with the qualities she wants in her own life. The hope is that the client will see how a small issue is related to a much more important and life-transforming issue.

## Choice

By choice, we are speaking of the experience of values being selected freely and without avoidance, rigid rules, or social manipulation. ACT works to break up a sense of "have to's," "musts," and "only ways," and to create a sense of open possibility. Clients can feel coerced by others or by their own histories, their own feelings and thoughts, and even their own values. In ACT, it is important for therapists to keep their therapeutic antennae out for this sense of coercion and its alternative (i.e., choice) in the room. For example, it is common for clients to say they "have to" value certain things. Almost always, this is a verbal trap. Values are not a stick with which to beat anyone's head and ears; they are a chosen connection to qualities of action.

Sometimes clients provide vague or noncommittal answers because they do not have histories that taught them how to effectively identify or describe their needs, wants, or desires for their lives. For clients with this problem, the therapist may need to begin by building the client's ability to make choices through focusing on micro-level, moment-to-moment, situation-to-situation wants and desires, rather than on broader values. One place to start with this is in the moment, in session. The therapist can ask, "In this session, right now, if anything could happen here—aim high—what would you want?" Often the client will state a process goal of some sort, such as, "I'd want to feel better" or "I would want to understand this problem better." In order to get to the value, the therapist needs to look for the way of living that is blocked because the client's verbal system says a particular goal must be accomplished first. Possible responses to such client statements include "And if that were to happen here, then what would you do?" and "If that were to happen, then what do you imagine life would be like?" Questions such as these can lead the client to describe the kind of life he or she wants to live, rather than the more common response of what the client would like to feel, be right about, or know.

Most human values have a social component, and the therapeutic relationship provides one of the most immediate areas for exploration. Strategies to help clients make valued choices, for instance, can be intensified by focusing in session, where the therapist can model, instigate, and reinforce positive ACT processes in a way that is immediate, vital, and vulnerable. In the preceding example, the therapist could have said, "If our therapeutic relationship, right now, had the qualities you most want, what would they be?"

Another barrier to choice is that clients can feel coerced by their own chosen values. For example, values-based choices sometimes lead to pain, as in the case of an abused client who knows an abusive relative will be at her sister's wedding. The client might take the stance of "I have to be willing," and thus think that having values means she has to fight her way through the suffering. This takes the heart out of the values work. It is important not to allow this to be regarded as an ACT-consistent approach merely because it involves values. In this case, a therapeutic goal would be to help the client bring a sense of choice into this situation. For example, the therapist might say the following:

*Therapist:* Well, you don't *have* to go to the wedding, do you? You could choose not to go. It's a matter of what you hold as important. Let's say I could offer you a choice. Let's say, on one hand, you could send a perfect robot replica of yourself to the wedding so no one would ever know you hadn't been there. Your sister would be happy and so would your relatives. You wouldn't have to face your uncle, nor would you feel at all bad that you did this. Of course, you'd completely miss out on this important event in your sister's life. On the other hand, if you go to the wedding, you get to be right there next to your sister when she says, "I do." However, if you make this choice, in order to fully be there for the wedding, you also will have all the discomfort and anxiety of facing your uncle. Consider this for a moment before answering: if this were the choice, which would you choose?

## Present Oriented

Although conversations about values extend into the future, they are also about the immediate present. Something that is valued is valued *now*. Values work brings the extended moment into the present moment in the service of building larger and larger patterns of action linked to valued life directions. This present focus provides a powerful prophylactic to avoidance. Normally, immediate consequences are much more important in controlling behavior than are delayed consequences. Part of what makes experiential avoidance so powerful is that often its impact is immediate. Retreating from anxiety in a social situation is immediately reinforcing because it results in a reduction of anxiety, for example. The consequences of lack of intimacy and of loneliness are only felt later, often as a result of the pattern of social avoidance extended over time. Values work pulls extended appetitive consequences forward in time. For example, choosing to go to a wedding in order to be with a sister is a value not just when the wedding occurs, but also *now*.

## Willing Vulnerability

One of the best guides to effective values conversations is their bittersweet qualities. When a client opens up to values, the single most common emotional reaction is crying. These are not the resisted tears of unwelcome pain, but the embraced tears of caring and vulnerability. They occur in the context of past pain, but honor present values. We can only be hurt in areas about which we care. If valuing has been put aside to avoid hurt, a much greater hurt is created through the life not being lived. When a client once again turns in a valued direction, the emotional vulnerability of that turn will be present. And yet it will be pain carried for a purpose. Inside pain, we find our values, and inside values we find our pain. Like a person once hurt who chooses to love again, vulnerability is a guide to what we hold dear. In session, a sense of willing vulnerability is a beacon to be followed.

## Values? What Values?

One final barrier worth mentioning is the fact that it is not uncommon for clients to deny they have any values at all. Often, this is because of the pain associated with having that conversation. Clients who respond like this may be hopeless about the possibility of expressing their values or may find it too painful to contact what they care about most. In these situations, clients are focused on how their situations will turn out and are afraid to step out of the safety zone of "I don't know" or "it doesn't matter." Undermining this type of avoidance means taking the client into the pain of caring. Helpful responses by the therapist include "What did you value before this cloud descended on you?" and "Is this how you dreamed as a small child that your life would turn out? What did you dream it would look like?" The clinician can ask the client to temporarily set the barrier aside, for instance by saying, "Pretend you were someone who knew what you wanted. What would you want?"

Here is a case that illustrates such an approach. Julie is a thirty-five-year-old female who has an extensive history of sexual trauma, both as a child and as an adult. She works as an exotic dancer and print designer, and is constantly chasing the next dollar to make ends meet. She perceives herself as living on the edge of financial disaster. She has no close friends, and most of her time outside of work is taken up by smoking marijuana, exercise, and masturbation. The few relationships she has are filled with conflict, and she finds herself being chronically angry. She says that, years ago, she gave up hope her life could be better, and now she just wants to know how to get by without getting victimized again. This transcript is from her fourth session.

Therapist: I want you to consider a question I think might be really difficult for you. It's a central question for this therapy, if you're willing to consider it. What I'd like to know is, what do you want to do in your life that you are not doing now?

Client: What? There's no point in thinking about that. I don't care about anything anymore. I just get disappointed whenever I hope for something.

Therapist: I can see it is painful to hope for something. You've had many experiences of things not working out. I'm just asking, if you could have it be some other way, what would that be? What would you rather be doing with your life that you aren't now?

Client: I don't know. I don't care anymore. Nothing.

Therapist: You could follow this path out for the next five years, ten years, fifteen years. You could continue the way you've been going. Take a second to picture what that would be like. [long pause] Are you okay with that?

Client: [pause] It's awful.

Therapist: I can see you feel so hopeless about anything turning out the way you want. Your mind wants to protect you by saying it's easier not to care. That's what you just saw in those five, ten, and fifteen years, yes? And apparently it doesn't look good ... Are you willing to play with me for a minute around this? Let's pretend, if you were someone who cared, what would you care about? What would you want?

Client: It's hard to think about. [sighs] I guess, uh ... I'd want to have someone in my life whom I could trust. I've never had that. [starts to cry]

Therapist: I can see how much you want that, and how much it feels like that is missing from your life. I want to help you have that in your life.

The client is hesitant to speak about what she might want, not because she hasn't had ideas about the future, but because it's painful for her to consider this. Due to chronic avoidance, the client has no idea about what she feels or wants. In such situations, the rest of the ACT model is very much needed to support clients learning to contact their values.

# WHAT IS THE METHOD?

The idea of values is usually introduced early in therapy, either in a more limited fashion (as discussed in chapter 2) or perhaps in a more extended manner, depending on the client case conceptualization (chapter 8). Clients are often so focused on their problems that turning their attention to the larger context of their dreams, hopes, and aspirations for their lives can be unexpected. Thus, a bit of introduction can be helpful to orient them to this aspect of therapy. For example, the therapist could say the following:

*Therapist:* You've told me now a bit about your problems, and I feel like I have a good beginning sense of what those are. Your problems are important, and we'll certainly respond to them in here, but your life is also more than your problems. I'd like us to spend some time focusing on the larger context of your life, which includes your dreams, your hopes, your aspirations for your life. These are a large part of what makes life worth living, and they are the context in which you experience your problems. What I'm suggesting we talk about is, "What do you really want in life? What do you want your life to be about? What do you want to do? Who do you want to be?" Would it be okay if we spent some time focusing on that?

The breadth, depth, and focus of the initial values work can vary greatly, depending upon the needs of the client and the clinical situation. Sometimes the focus can be as narrow as helping the client specify what he or she values in a given life situation, as might happen in a brief clinical encounter. Or it can be as broad as helping the client specify valued directions across all major life domains, as might happen in more extended therapy.

A more extended values assessment process (see Hayes et al., 1999) can take multiple sessions and include between-session work in which the client writes out descriptions of valued directions and goals in several life domains (e.g., family, couples, parenting, friends/social, work, education, recreation, spirituality, community, self-care), along with discussion focused on clarifying, specifying, and succinctly recording in writing the stated value in each life domain, followed by ratings of consistency and importance. Finally, actions would be initiated based on goals developed within each domain (as described in chapter 7). A briefer, relatively unstructured values clarification process can be instigated using the Valued Living Questionnaire (VLQ; Wilson & Murrell, 2004). Based on their work with anxious clients, Eifert and Forsyth (2005, pp. 171–177) described the use of a similarly brief values assessment process. They also discussed a process called the Life Compass (pp. 186–189), which was originally developed by Dahl et al. (2005, pp. 91–111). Several other measures and aids have been developed and are available at the con textualpsychology.org website. Although more or less extensive, each of these processes has in common a number of steps that are important in helping clients define a valued life direction. These common elements are described here.

## Guide Clients to Contact Their Values and State Them Explicitly

Other ACT processes are essential to overcome the barriers that stand in the way of clients fully contacting and taking a stand for what matters most in their lives. Because valuing inherently contains vulnerability, acceptance is critical. Because values are a choice, defusion is critical. Conscious, present-focused, and active valuing is linked to all of the other ACT processes and cannot be fully contacted without them.

Values conversations take values out of the abstract and make them clear and explicit. For example, clients can be encouraged to distill their values in various domains down to what is most essential in that domain. These distillations are usually in the form of statements, and are often recorded on a form or handout that clients can keep with them. However, the statement is not the value; it is an explicit guide to the qualities the client intends to bring to the moments that make up his or her life.

## Coach Clients to Take a Stand for Their Values

Often, publicly stating a value is the first step down a new valued path. Opportunities are structured in ACT for clients to make an explicit commitment to bringing their values more fully into their lives. Clients can be encouraged to make commitments to the therapist, or to other people whom they know, about what they intend to do in regard to their values. The next chapter outlines how to help clients develop concrete actions and goals that, if taken, indicate they have progressed further in their valued directions.

A prerequisite for clients freely choosing their own values is the absence of any sense of coercion from the therapist. However, sometimes therapists may find themselves unwilling to support a client in a particular value. If a therapist doing ACT finds his or her values conflict with a client's value in a fundamental way, then it is incumbent upon the therapist to consider whether it is possible to fully support the client in the pursuit of that value despite the conflict. If the therapist is unable to be fully behind the client, it is the therapist's duty to consider other resources for that client.

For example, if the therapist is a conservative Christian and feels unable to support a gay client in living his or her value of intimate same-sex relationships, the therapist has a responsibility to find a referral to someone who can. Similarly, if the therapist cannot support a gay Mormon who values living a straight lifestyle, even if that means being celibate while experiencing same-sex attractions, then the therapist has a responsibility to find another resource. Many of these situations can be addressed through following normal ethical practice, but because ACT is more overt about values than are many other therapies, it provides a space for these value conflicts to be more openly acknowledged and addressed.

We can imagine situations in which a referral would not be appropriate, and ACT neophytes or critics regularly raise imagined situations of this kind. For example, we are asked what a therapist would do with a Nazi who wanted help in accepting discomfort while trying to kill minorities, or with a pedophile who wanted help in accepting guilt so he could molest children. A therapist does not have an obligation to refer if that very act is illegal and unethical. Although such situations could exist, they often disappear under the light of the ACT model. For example, pedophiles may want support for their actions, but that usually occurs within the extreme experiential avoidance pattern needed to keep from feeling what it is like to be a molested child. When that issue has been addressed, the underlying value may not, in fact, be to molest children. Thus, even though we admit that some value conflicts may be irresolvable, we prefer to try to find common ground and see if a healthy therapeutic contract is possible.

## Help Clients Examine Current Life Directions in Relation to Values

A life lived outside our most closely held values generates a great deal of suffering. The current behavior of many clients is inconsistent with what they value. Thus, an essential part of values work is to help clients discriminate how closely their current behavior lines up with their intended direction for their lives. Doing so requires looking at the ways in which they are not living in line with their values.

This can be shame inducing, which is usually counterproductive, so it is important for clients not to fuse with thoughts such as "I'm bad" in the process of looking at the pain that comes from a life not being lived as truly intended. When helping clients experience this discrepancy, it is important for the therapist to take the stance that whatever the client has been doing is understandable given his or her history, while at the same time helping the client courageously examine whether his or her current behavior lines up with where he or she wants to head. The focus is on helping the client contact the pain of a life not lived as intended.

This concept is illustrated by an interaction with a lonely but thoroughly defended and overly intellectual client who had worked on a between-session assignment in which she was asked to write two epitaphs: one that summarized what her life had stood for were she to die today, and one that would be on her tombstone were she to die in twenty years, if it could say anything she wanted.

*Therapist:* So, how did the writing go? What did you come up with?

*Client:* Uh, I didn't like doing the one about what it would say if I died today. But I did come up with something. What I wrote was "She spent a lot of time trying to figure out what would make her happy." And what I wanted on the tombstone if it could say anything is "She was happy."

*Therapist:* Do you mind if we focus on the first one for a minute?

*Client:* Okay.

*Therapist:* So, you would say the best summary of what your life has been about so far is that you spent a lot of time trying to figure out what would make you happy. And how has it turned out?

*Client:* It hasn't. I haven't figured it out.

*Therapist:* And so maybe the tombstone would say something like, "Here lies Elisha, she spent her whole life trying to be happy, and never made it." How do you like that tombstone?

*Client:* Ah, I don't. It sucks. I don't want to be a failure.

*Therapist:* I'd like you to sit for a minute with that. Are you willing to do that?

*Client:* Okay.

*Therapist:* Just shut your eyes and notice for a moment what it's like to have that be on your tombstone. [speaks slowly and deliberately] "Here lies Elisha, she spent her whole life trying to be happy, and never made it." Notice what feelings come up … What your body feels like … what you feel in your stomach … your arms … your shoulders … What thoughts come up? Notice if there are any memories associated with this. [pause]
Okay, you can open your eyes.

*Client:* It sucks. I feel terrible. I don't want to think about it.

*Therapist:* Go into it a little further.

*Client:* It seems so impossible. And I can't imagine what it would be for anyway. The world's all going to end some day. Ultimately, it won't matter anyway.

*Therapist:* You are building a wall of words. What do you want? Your pain is your biggest ally here. Go into it. What are you defending yourself against? Look there … What do you really, really want?

*Client:* [crying] People. I want people in my life.

# Teach Relevant Discriminations

It can be helpful to teach clients three distinctions relevant to values. The first is the distinction between values as directions and goals, as we have already mentioned. The second is the distinction between process and outcome (Hayes et al., 1999, pp. 219–221). Finally, ACT teaches the distinction between values as qualities of actions rather than feelings (pp. 209–212).

## DISTINGUISHING BETWEEN VALUES AND GOALS

When a therapist asks a client what he or she wants in life, often the therapist will get in response a mixture of goals and values. Usually, many of the goals are process goals; in other words, things the client thinks are necessary to acquire or achieve in order to have the wished-for values. These goals often take the form of feeling better (e.g., less anxiety, less pain, less loneliness, higher self-esteem).

ACT helps clients distinguish between values, which are characterized as the direction of an ongoing pattern of behavior, and goals, which are concrete achievements or events that can be accomplished and finished. As part of the process of defining valued directions, when a client presents a goal as a value, the job of the therapist is to dig and abstract the ongoing value that underlies or is connected to the goal as presented.

Take a minute now and practice classifying some client statements according to whether they are more goal-like or more value-like. Remember, values are chosen qualities of action. As such, they can be made into verbs and adverbs. They are more like directions, whereas goals are something that can be completed. Goals are outcomes that happen as a result of movement in a valued direction. If you can accomplish something and finish it, then it's a goal. Doing this exercise can help you increase your ability to detect statements of client values, as opposed to client goals.

---

## EXERCISE: VALUES AND GOALS

In the following transcript, circle the parts you think are values and underline the parts you think are goals. Do this before you look at the model responses that follow.

*Therapist:* So, tell me, if this anxiety were to just magically go away and your life were to be how you want it, what would your life be like then?

*Client:* Hmm. I'd be happier. I'd have at least two or three friends with whom I really share things. I'd go out and do things I like, such as going to the movies or riding my bike. I might be in a community theater, or at least go to plays. I'd stay more in touch with art. It helps me appreciate beauty. I'd have a good relationship with my boyfriend. There'd be a lot less fighting and crying. I'd probably have a better relationship with my mom; I'd try to be there more for her. And I'd be making more money.

Now let's walk through the clients response, sentence by sentence, trying to decide if they refer to goals or values.

*Client:* Hmm. I'd be happier.

You might think being happier is a value, and if you define it as eudemonia, or the happiness that comes from living in a way that is consistent with your values, it is the very essence of values. But if you define happiness as an emotional reaction in the ACT way of thinking about it, happiness is a goal, not a value. Looked at that way, happiness is an event that comes and goes as a result of action, not a chosen quality of action. Emotionally, it is not possible simply to choose happiness.

*Client:*      I'd have at least two or three friends with whom I really share things.

"Having two or three friends" is a goal because it can be completed, but this sentence includes the explicit value of sharing in relationships.

*Client:*      I'd go out and do things I like, such as going to the movies or riding my bike.

This is primarily a values statement. The statement "things I like" could use some clarification. If we consider it to be only an emotional result, it is not a value. But in our normal way of speaking, we use this wording to refer to things that engage us in the joy of living, in which case it is a value.

*Client:*      I might be in a community theater, or at least go to plays. I'd stay more in touch with art. It helps me appreciate beauty.

Appreciating beauty by participating in art is a value.

*Client:*      I'd have a good relationship with my boyfriend.

"Good relationship" is not yet a value because we do not know what qualities of relationship are being held as important.

*Client:*      There'd be a lot less fighting and crying.

This is a goal.

*Client:*      I'd probably have a better relationship with my mom. I'd try to be there more for her.

"Better relationship" is not yet a value because we do not know what qualities of relationship are being held as important. Being there for her mother is a value; it could do with a bit of clarification, however, because it's a bit vague.

*Client:*      And I'd be making more money.

This is a goal, not a value.

Often when a client reports a goal, one or more values underlie that goal. As the therapist, it is important to abstract the important valued directions that underlie the goal, and to make these explicit. You can practice this in the following exercise.

If you were responding to the client who made this statement, what sorts of questions could you ask to get to the values that underlie the goals the client presented? Write two questions you could ask, and then look at the model responses that follow.

Response 1:


Response 2:

Here are some examples of questions that might be helpful.

What would a good relationship with your boyfriend look like? Draw me a picture.

What is "not fighting or crying" about? Why is that important?

Imagine you had more money. What would you be doing with it?

## DISTINGUISHING BETWEEN PROCESS AND OUTCOME

The main purpose of teaching clients to distinguish between values and goals is to help them become more focused on the process of living and less attached to the outcomes of their actions. Many people become attached to the idea of achieving goals as the way to a happy life (Hayes et al., 1999). In ACT, goals are used pragmatically in the sense that they can provide a proximal marker for effective action, but they can only do that if they also are held lightly, as a guide for valued action, not as an end in themselves.

On the one hand, the problem with having too strong of an attachment to goals is that it tends to draw attention away from the present moment. We are never at the goal because as soon as a goal is achieved, another goal needs to be established, and we are again short of the goal. On the other hand, values draw our focus to the process of living and the process of valuing in the given situation life has handed to us. The opportunity for valuing is always here and now, in our behavior. There is nowhere we need to go before we can value, and nothing for which we need to wait to begin valuing. From the ACT perspective, therefore, we can say that what is important is a meaningful process of living. Connection to what matters is possible in every moment and in every situation in which we live, not in the future or after we have achieved a particular goal or end state.

We can control our choices and what we do with our hands and feet and things like that in our lives, but we can't always control how life turns out. For example, a daughter may value a relationship with her mother, but her mother may refuse all contact. That doesn't mean the value is not present and manifest in small ways—whether it be through a thought, a card, or a conversation with a sibling. Consider water held back by a dam. The force of the water on the dam is like the value. Unable to move, the water can't express what is latent. But given an opening, the force of water (i.e., the value) will be fully revealed. Similarly, just because behavior is constrained by a situation does not mean the value cannot still be held.

## VALUING AS AN ACTION AS OPPOSED TO A FEELING

Finally, ACT teaches the distinction between values as qualities of actions and as feelings (Hayes et al., 1999, pp. 209–212). Clients often think values are how they feel about a given situation; in other words, their wants or desires. Values, however, are chosen life directions. Values can be thought of as like a compass heading that we are following. The direction keeps us oriented as we move forward. Although our feelings and thoughts in the moment can have some bearing on what we do, and can result in twists and turns in the path, ultimately the value is revealed through the overall direction.

# Directly State Your Therapy-Relevant Values

Therapists practicing ACT implicitly value clients' valuing. They value redirecting clients' efforts away from futile and ultimately costly goals (e.g., reducing unwanted feelings and thoughts) and toward living a life defined by what they most want to "be about." By making this therapeutic value explicit and committing to it with the client, the therapist both models and instigates valuing and commitment, just

as he or she is asking the client to do. When doing this, it is important to create an opportunity for the client to take advantage of, rather than creating something the client must do.

In early sessions, before the specific form of client values is clear, this commitment can take the form of the therapist saying, "I want this therapy to be connected to what you most want your life to be about. I want you to know I'm committed to working with you during our sessions to help you discover what you most want in life and I will dedicate our work to that."

Therapists can also make more specific commitments, depending upon what they know about a client's values and life situation. Often, the therapist makes a commitment after the client has taken a public stand for a value. Consider the following transcript from a session in which the client has just engaged in an exercise in which he attended his own funeral in his imagination.

*Therapist:*  So, you don't think your daughter would say those kinds of things about you now?

*Client:*  Nope.

*Therapist:*  Because of how you haven't been there in the past … You haven't always been there for her. You've spent time in prison, you abandoned her and her mom, drugs got in the way. What was it like for her to say those nice things about you in this exercise?

*Client:*  That's exactly what I'd want her to say about me. It felt good, but I also felt fake because that's not how it really is.

*Therapist:*  Yeah, that's how you want it to be.

*Client:*  Right, but she won't let me.

*Therapist:*  She can make it hard sometimes to love her. You call, and the first thing she does is ask for money. She doesn't trust you. It's tough to be loving when she's like that. By the way, you know that whether or not people will say things like that about you at your funeral depends on how you live your life now. I can't guarantee how it's going to turn out, but I can guarantee that if you are a loving dad—there for her when she calls; supportive, as you said—it will increase the chances she might some day feel that way about you and even say something like that. But not if you keep on withdrawing from her. Let me ask you this: Are you willing to stand up here, look me in the eye, and tell me the kind of father you'd like to be with your daughter? Even though she makes it difficult, even though you feel crappy a lot of the time when she calls and all she seems to want is money—what is it you want?

*Client:*  I want to be loving and supportive when she calls, regardless. That doesn't mean I'm going to just give her money, necessarily. But I'm going to be there for her as a dad.

*Therapist:*  Are you willing to stand up and say that is what you're going to be about in relation to your daughter, even knowing there will be times that she makes it hard, that you feel used, that you feel disappointed, that you feel angry? Will you stand up and commit to that, even knowing it will be extremely difficult at times?

*Client:*  Yeah, I want to be that kind of father.

*Therapist:*  Okay, then stand up and tell me what kind of father you want to be.

*Client:*  [stands up, looks the therapist in the eye] I want to be a loving, supportive father, even when she makes it difficult.

*Therapist:*  Awesome! I'm inspired by that. I want our work to be about that. I'm committed to making that possible for you.

Therapists conducting ACT benefit from working to identify their own values in relation to their clients. However, this often goes unexamined by therapists. Consider yourself. For example, how many times during your professional training did you have a conversation with a supervisor or mentor about what kind of therapist you most wanted to be, or what you held as most important when it came to your work with your clients? This topic is not often talked about in graduate school. If you had more than a conversation or two, your experience was unusual. If you aren't clear about your values in your work with clients, you will probably have problems making commitments to your clients that are consistent with an ACT framework. The following exercise can help you identify your values as a therapist.

## EXPERIENTIAL EXERCISE: IDENTIFYING YOUR VALUES AS A THERAPIST

When you are at your best during sessions, what are you like?

If you could give your clients anything as a result of your work with them, what would you give them (e.g., particular skills, change, knowledge, relationship, an experience)?

To use a more experiential mode of approaching this question, we recommend you do a brief eyes-closed exercise in which you imagine you are at your retirement party. Begin by closing your eyes and taking some time to get centered. Next, imagine you are at the party and take time to picture what it would look like, who might show up. Finally, imagine three of your favorite clients are at this retirement party, and each of them gives a short speech about what you meant to him or her (we know this probably wouldn't happen, but this is your imagination, so you get to choose). Give them a chance to say what you meant to them, what was most memorable about your sessions together, and/or what was most important about how you were with them. Then write a short summary here of what they said.

Now that you have thought about this domain from all these angles, see if you can summarize the essence of what you value as a therapist. What kind of therapist do you want to be? What do you want to do? Write a preliminary statement here.

*As a therapist, I most want to be*

How important is this to you? _____ (0 = not at all important, 10 = very important)

How consistent has your action been over the past two weeks with respect to this value? _____ (0 = not at all consistent, 10 = very consistent)

What is one thing you could do this week to be the therapist you most want to be?

Do you commit to do it? ❑ Yes ❑ No

We want you to practice how you might make a commitment to two of your current clients. Bring two of your current clients to mind. When you consider them, think about what you are working on together, what these clients most value, and what you value. Then ask yourself, if you were going to make a commitment to each client that expresses a value you have in terms of your work with him or her, what would you say? For example, "I want you to know that I am committed to ..."

Client 1:

Client 2:

Finally, consider whether you are going to actually tell your clients these commitments.

Will you tell Client 1? ❑ Yes ❑ No

Will you tell Client 2? ❑ Yes ❑ No

# CORE COMPETENCY PRACTICE

The rest of this chapter focuses primarily on moment-to-moment interactions taken from conversations between therapists and clients about values. It provides examples and practice opportunities to evoke the qualities of powerful values conversations. We are not repeating here the structure of values assessments that can be found in other volumes (see table 6.1); rather, we focus on the skills needed to deliver such interventions. Each section describes a core competency, followed by sample transcripts and exercises. Your job is to generate your own responses before consulting the model responses provided.

# CORE COMPETENCY EXERCISES

## COMPETENCY 1: The therapist helps the client clarify valued life directions.

For this competency, we present a series of brief transcripts that reflect nonvital conversations about values that occurred between clients and therapists. Each dialogue is from a session with a different client.

### EXERCISE 6.1

The following client is a fifty-eight-year-old female with severe social anxiety.

*Therapist:* What do you want in your life that you feel you don't have today?

*Client:* I want to have less of this anxiety. I just want to be able to go out of my house and be like a normal person.

*Therapist:* And why do you want to be able to get out of your house?

*Client:* Because the life I live is not much of a life.

Write here what your response would be (remember you are using competency 1):

What are your thoughts in saying this? What are you responding to and what are you hoping to accomplish?

## EXERCISE 6.2 (CONTINUING WITH COMPETENCY 1)

The client is a forty-six-year-old, chronically low-functioning male.

*Therapist:* What dreams do you have for your life?

*Client:* I don't know.

Write here what your response would be (using competency 1):

What are your thoughts in saying this? What are you responding to and what are you hoping to accomplish?

## EXERCISE 6.3 (CONTINUING WITH COMPETENCY 1)

The client is a seventeen-year-old female who is highly emotionally avoidant and has few life goals.

*Therapist:* What is it you want? What do you really, really want?

*Client:* Happiness. That's what I want more than anything.

Write here what your response would be (using competency 1):

What are your thoughts in saying this? What are you responding to and what are you hoping to accomplish?

## EXERCISE 6.4 (CONTINUING WITH COMPETENCY 1)

*Therapist:* When was the last time you had dreams for your life? How far back do we need to go?

*Client:* It's been so long, I don't want to think about it.

Write here what your response would be (using competency 1):

What are your thoughts in saying this? What are you responding to and what are you hoping to accomplish?

The last two transcripts for this competency reflect somewhat trickier barriers to identifying or contacting values. Your job is to generate a response that will help the client temporarily set aside the barrier and perhaps get more in contact with what is important to him or her.

## EXERCISE 6.5 (CONTINUING WITH COMPETENCY 1)

The client is a forty-five-year-old homeless male.

*Therapist:* What would you most want your life to be about?

*Client:* Becoming president of the United States.

Write here what your response would be (using competency 1):

What are your thoughts in saying this? What are you responding to and what are you hoping to accomplish?

## EXERCISE 6.6 (CONTINUING WITH COMPETENCY 1)

The client is a twenty-eight-year-old depressed female.

*Therapist:* What dreams do you have for your life?

*Client:* I guess I'd dream of pleasing my parents.

Write here what your response would be (using competency 1):

What are your thoughts in saying this? What are you responding to and what are you hoping to accomplish?

---

COMPETENCY 2: **The therapist helps the client commit to what he or she wants his or her life to stand for, and focuses the therapy on that.**

## EXERCISE 6.7

Moving the client toward commitment is a distinguishable ACT skill in the values aspect of the work. In this next exercise consider how you might move a client in that direction.

The client is a forty-three-year-old male with lifelong dysthymia and difficulty in initiating and maintaining intimate relationships. The therapist and client have already identified high-priority values for the client and recently identified an important value in the area of couple relationships that is being neglected. In this transcript, the therapist is working toward helping the client move toward committing to what he wants his life to stand for.

*Therapist:* You've identified that it is important in your life to be in a relationship that is supportive, close, and fun. Yet you find yourself still without a partner, and not even headed in that direction. Is this what you want for your life?

*Client:* Of course not. But I really don't see anyone who would want to be with me. Reaching out is hard. I think I'll be rejected.

*Therapist:* And so I have some important questions for you. First, I want you to take a moment and connect with the intention toward which you want to work: a supportive, close, fun relationship. The questions are this: What are you going to be about in your life? Are you going to be about keeping away rejection and preventing failure in relationships? Or are you going to be about being in a supportive, close, fun relationship? Are you willing to take a stand for this value in your life? What would you be doing if you weren't busy avoiding rejection?

*Client:* But I'm not sure if I can do it.

Write here what your response would be (using competency 2):

What are your thoughts in saying this? What are you responding to and what are you hoping to accomplish?

---

COMPETENCY 3: **The therapist teaches the client to distinguish between values and goals.**

## EXERCISE 6.8

Earlier in this chapter, you practiced distinguishing values from goals. Take time now to apply this same kind of practice to some of the clients with whom you have worked for a while. Pick two clients and list a value you believe each client has. Considering the client, list goals that would be supportive of that value:

**Client 1**

Value:

Goals:

**Client 2**

Value:

Goals:

---

## COMPETENCY 4: The therapist distinguishes between outcomes achieved and involvement in the process of living.

### EXERCISE 6.9

A twenty-six-year-old male client is about to begin dating for the first time in several years. The previous week, he described a value of wanting to be "someone who was reaching out, loving, involved, and real in relationships." He committed to sending out at least one e-mail every day in response to an online personal ad, as a way of moving in this direction. He returned to the session, having sent out an e-mail every day, but disappointed that no one had responded to his e-mails yet.

Client:     Yeah, I did it. But no one has responded. It didn't work.

Therapist:     Okay, hold on a minute. Let's go back to the point of this exercise. Why were you sending these e-mails? What is it about?

Client:     Getting a new girlfriend. And it didn't work out. I'm not getting any responses. At this rate, this is a total waste of time.

Write here what your response would be (using competency 4):

What are your thoughts in saying this? What are you responding to and what are you hoping to accomplish?

**COMPETENCY 5:** The therapist states his or her own therapy-relevant values and models their importance.

*EXERCISE 6.10*

Write three sentences that describe your therapy-relevant values. State them as if you were talking to a client.

# Core Competency Model Responses

## COMPETENCY 1

**Sample 6.1**

*Therapist:*   And what feels as though it's missing from your life? What did you wish for in your life that you don't have now? When you're sitting at home, afraid to go out, what are you wishing you could have or be about in your life? Take a moment and consider it. Sometimes your pain itself is a guide.

**Explanation:** Getting out of the house is a goal, not a value. The therapist needs to get the issue focused on what the client wants, but the client is giving defended answers. So the therapist needs to move closer to the moment and closer to the pain.

**Sample 6.2**

*Therapist:*   When you were a child, did you imagine your life would turn out like this? Is this what you imagined for yourself?

**Explanation:** The client's answer is defended. But connecting the client with childlike dreams and hopes can make the defense begin to look self-invalidating. Many clients will stop the avoidance and defense at this point.

**Sample 6.3**

*Therapist:*   And if you were happy, what would you be doing now? Take a look more closely. Is happiness something you can do? Let's try something right now. I'd like you to just make yourself feel really happy right now. [pause] Were you able to do it?

*Client:*   No, it doesn't work like that.

*Therapist:* Right. So, what I'm wondering is what you'd want to be about, how you'd want to live—not exactly how you'd want to feel. For example, if you could intend to do anything with your hands, your feet, your mouth, what would those actions be about?

**Explanation:** Happiness is a goal, something that can happen to the client, rather than a direction in which the client can head, or a value. So the therapist sidesteps this comment. The therapist does a short exercise with the client to illustrate the problem with emotion as the outcome. It isn't something under the client's direct control. Values are more about what we directly approach or aim toward as a quality of our action.

## Sample 6.4

*Therapist:* Yeah, it's painful to think about how your life is so far from what you wanted for yourself. I get that.

*Client:* [begins to sob]

*Therapist:* You've given up on so many dreams and hopes for your life. I really want to hear about the dreams you've given up on. Are you willing to talk about those dreams?

**Explanation:** The therapist thinks the client is not willing to contact his or her values because of the loss and the pain associated with caring. So the therapist makes an empathic comment that helps the client contact the pain of a life not lived in the moment.

## Sample 6.5

*Therapist:* What would being president allow you to do?

*Client:* Take care of people ... people like me.

*Therapist:* And if you were helping in that way, whether or not you were president, would that still be something you'd value?

**Explanation:** Even if goals are grandiose, they nevertheless often contain values. One great advantage of discussing values is that the therapist usually does not have to talk clients out of believing in grandiose goals. Digging down to the values level is likely to reveal immediate implications for action, and addressing workability will more gently rein in any excesses (even psychotic ones), without shaming the client or making him or her appear wrong.

## Sample 6.6

*Therapist:* Imagine your parents have passed away and no one in your life remembers what they wanted you to do. What would you most want to change in your life?

*Client:* Nothing really. I want to have a family and to raise my children in a loving way. I think that is what would please my parents, but it is what I want to do, too.

**Explanation:** ACT is often targeted at undermining pliance; that is, following rules to achieve the arbitrary approval of others. In this statement, the therapist assessed for pliance by asking the client to imagine conditions in which social approval would be less of a direct issue. But the therapist did it in a way that did not assume any social goal is necessarily pliance. We are social creatures. The issue is freedom of choice and personal connection, but we tend to care about the same things our community or family cares about.

## COMPETENCY 2

### Sample 6.7

*Therapist:* I'm not asking you if you can do it. The result will turn out one way or the other—you don't have complete control over that. And you will have your scary feelings and worrisome thoughts. What I'm asking is, what are you going to stand for in your life? What I'm presenting here is an opportunity to make a commitment to a new direction in your life, not knowing how it's going to turn out. I want you to consider whether this is a commitment you are willing to make. And if so, then tell me, what do you want to be about?

*Client:* Yeah, I want to make this commitment. I'm going to do it. [takes a deep breath] I want to be about having a supportive, close relationship. I want to give myself a chance to have a relationship with passion!

*Therapist:* Yes! I want that for you, too. I want our work to be about that.

**Explanation:** The therapist has to use some defusion and acceptance skills to keep the client focused. The therapist is not asking for a commitment to an outcome, but for a commitment to a direction, a process of living. The client presents common barriers, such as fear of rejection, failure, and inability. The therapist sidesteps this obstacle and continues to present an opportunity for the client to commit to a new direction.

## COMPETENCY 3

### Sample 6.8

*Therapist:* I want to remind you about what you wrote as your intention in this domain. You wrote that you wanted to be someone who was reaching out, loving, involved, and real in relationships. What we're working on is the process of moving in that direction. Sometimes it will work out, and you'll enjoy how it has turned out. Other times it'll work out in ways you don't like. But what we've been working on is what you've been standing for. It seems as though you got off track here for a little while and got attached to the goal of having a girlfriend. While that would be nice, we're not working on that. Right?

*Client:* Okay, I think I get you. I forgot for a minute.

*Therapist:* So, by sending out these e-mails, did you move further in your direction of reaching out, being loving, involved, and real in relationships?

*Client:* Yeah, actually, I did. Just by sending out the e-mails, I was being real because I normally pretend I don't really want relationships. But I went even further than that. I normally work really hard to be witty, impressive in my e-mails. You know, I worry that if I don't play that game, they won't like the real me. What was cool was that I was more real. I said what I thought, and responded more genuinely to what they wrote and said what interested me about it.

*Therapist:* Cool. I think it's really great you made that commitment last week and fulfilled it during the past week, even with all those barriers that came up. Let's keep our eye on the ball of how you are living, and we'll let the outcomes fall how they may.

**Explanation:** The client seems to be overly focused on the outcome instead of on the process of living his value. He has become attached to a particular goal. As a result, he is evaluating all his behaviors in relation to his perceived distance from his goal, rather than in relation to whether he has kept moving in the direction of that goal. The therapist reminds the client that his value is not about the outcome, but about how he is living his life. The therapist checks in with the client to see if the client understands.

---

## FOR MORE INFORMATION

More information about values, including exercises and metaphors, can be found in *Acceptance and Commitment Therapy*, by Hayes et al. (1999), chapter 8 (pp. 204–234).

Other resources of interest include writings by Dahl et al. (2005, pp. 91–111), Eifert and Forsyth (2005, pp. 154–155, 186–187), and Wilson and Murrell (2004).

For more exercises and worksheets on values to use for yourself and your clients, see *Get Out of Your Mind and Into Your Life*, by Hayes and Smith (2005), chapter 12 (pp. 165–176).

# CHAPTER 7

# BUILDING PATTERNS OF COMMITTED ACTION

*It takes a deep commitment to change and an even deeper commitment to grow.*

—Ralph Ellison (1914–1994)

Key targets for building patterns of committed action:

✓     Work with clients for behavior change in the service of chosen values, while making room for all their automatic reactions and experiences.

✓     Help the client take responsibility for patterns of action, building them into larger and larger units that support effective values-based living.

A core problem for many clients who present for therapy is that they have dropped out of important activities, relationships, or pursuits in their lives or only engage in these in a limited way. Consider Leonard, a client with depression, who has friends but cannot seem to really connect with them, or only calls them when feeling desperate and alone. Or Kirsten, who no longer goes to her son's football games or drives alone in the car for fear of panic. Or Jose, who now spends most of his time alone in his living room, watching TV, and fears that if he goes out, it will trigger his voices again. Given the option, Leonard would choose to be more connected with friends, Kirsten would choose to go to her son's football games and have her independence back, and Jose would choose to spend more time in the world outside his living room. All of these people have visions of a whole life they wish to inhabit, but find themselves stuck living lives that often feel visited upon them, not their own, or not of their own choosing.

# WHAT IS COMMITTED ACTION?

Committed action is a step-by-step process of acting to create a whole life, a life of integrity, true to one's deepest wishes and longings. Commitment involves both persistence and change—whichever is called for in living one's value (Hayes et al., 2004). Commitment also includes engaging in a range of behaviors. This is important because sometimes sustaining a valued direction means being flexible, rather than being rigidly committed to and persevering in unworkable actions.

Committed action is inherently responsible, in the sense that it is based on the view that there is always an *ability to respond*. This is not idealistic. The ability to respond about which we are speaking is the ability to link action to values in any situation. For example, a person in a prison may have a limited ability to show an overt commitment to family. However, being helpful in prison so that parole becomes more likely or being prepared for family visits can reveal this commitment. In fact, commitments can be revealed through all kinds of chosen behaviors. The specific form of committed action needed in a given situation depends on what that situation affords and what action would be most effective.

Committed action is the core process through which a therapist can best incorporate traditional behavioral methods into the ACT model. Exposure can be used for anxiety problems, skills training for social problems, behavioral activation for depression, scheduled smoking for smoking cessation, and so on. Because behavioral methods are so diverse, we can only deal with them in this section in the broadest sense. However, these behavioral methods are an essential part of ACT and should be included whenever called for in therapy. Research on ACT has occasionally excluded traditional behavioral approaches in order to make a scientific point. For example, in one study, obsessive-compulsive disorder (OCD) was treated successfully without any in-session exposure (Twohig, Hayes, & Masuda, 2006) merely because positive results would otherwise be dismissed as nothing more than the well known effect of exposure. However, ACT is based in clinical behavior analysis, and behavioral technologies are a key feature of ACT. In-session exposure, for example, would normally be part of an ACT approach for OCD. In clinical practice, there is no reason to limit the full implementation of the model.

# WHY COMMITTED ACTION?

If defining valued life directions provides the compass for the route, then committed action describes the steps of the journey. A well-lived life is ultimately the goal of all the other ACT processes (developing acceptance and present moment awareness, defusing from entangling thoughts, developing a transcendent sense of self, and clarifying one's chosen direction). These processes help clients develop psychological flexibility and help clients persist in or change behavior, as needed in the service of their valued directions. Committed action encompasses the behaviors and therapy targets that are specifically aimed at helping the client move from inaction to action in the realm of overt behavior and to maintain the consistency of new, more flexible behavior over time.

# THE LINK BETWEEN WILLINGNESS AND COMMITTED ACTION

Willingness and commitment are so deeply intertwined that one could argue that commitment depends 100 percent on willingness. This is so because values are often linked to difficult internal experiences, and conversely, difficult internal experiences are usually linked to values. Any committed action can evoke a whole host of private experiences, at least some of which will be evaluated as negative (Hayes et al., 1999). If a person is wholly committed to not experiencing any unpleasant or difficult thoughts, feelings, sensations, or images, then that person will be unable to commit to and maintain a course of action because every course will eventually evoke something that is unpleasant. With valuing love comes the experience of loss, with valuing community comes the possibility of rejection, with valuing creativity comes a negative evaluation of one's abilities. Metaphorically, it's as if you were on a journey called "living well" and you ran into a swamp that stretched as far as the eye could see. Swamps are no fun. They're smelly, they're icky, they're scary, and yet swamps are part of the journey. Life asks, "Will you wade into the swamp or will you abandon your journey?" In order to choose to act on our values, willingness to experience difficult events is necessary.

This action of willingness has the quality of a leap of faith. The job of the therapist is to create situations in which clients engage in a leap of faith into a future that is unknown and—to the best they can tell—in the direction of their values. A leap of faith implies the willingness to have whatever happens when one makes that leap, to touch down wherever one lands. We are looking for this quality in client commitments.

In a scene from the third *Indiana Jones* movie, Indiana is at the final stage of his quest to find the mythical Holy Grail. He finds himself just short of his goal, with a seemingly bottomless chasm between himself and his goal, and no way across. He is presented with the choice of either giving up his goal and turning back or facing his fear and making a leap of faith to step into the chasm. With trepidation, he steps into space, seemingly to fall to his death. Unbeknownst to him, a bridge is there, which has been painted to blend perfectly with the chasm below. He is supported by this bridge and makes it safely across to his destination. Committed action is like that. His willingness to face his own fear allows him to move toward his goal, and his commitment makes sense of his willingness.

Committed action also provides the opportunity to practice and build the capacity to choose to be willing again and again, over time. Clients should not be coerced in any way to make a commitment in ACT. Rather, therapists want to build opportunities for clients to choose to commit to actions in their lives because these actions are opportunities for pursuing the kinds of lives their clients want to live, rather than something they have to do. Ideally, commitments are made with 100 percent willingness. In the *Indiana Jones* movie, the character's leap of faith was seemingly into a chasm that could end his life. Some private events appear threatening at the same level. Clients avoid these events just as they would avoid actual death. Committed action, however, allows clients to experience that thoughts, feelings, and sensations cannot literally harm them, but are only harmful if allowed control over how the clients act in their lives.

# WHAT SHOULD TRIGGER THIS PROCESS?

Engaging in committed action typically follows work on defining valued directions. This can range from quickly exploring one valued area of living for a client seen in a primary care setting, to multiple sessions spent helping a client define valued directions in a more conventional therapy setting. What's important is that the client and therapist begin committed action work with a shared sense of what the client values.

Working on committed action can be useful when therapy becomes lifeless or dull, or when the client is talking about values rather than acting on them. If the client is not in contact with the barriers to valued action, beginning to work on this process will be sure to evoke those barriers. In a sense, committed action is a process that can provide the emotional and cognitive barriers to be addressed through the other ACT processes. For example, if a client is talking about the importance of intimacy and openness, but the therapist senses a lifelessness in the room, shifting to actual actions to which the client is willing to commit can sweep away the cobwebs. If even that is not enough, moving directly to the therapeutic relationship will almost certainly do the trick; for example, the therapist might say, "Could you apply that value to this moment? What is a difficult and more open thing you could say right now about our relationship?"

# WHAT IS THE METHOD?

Once the therapist and client have a shared sense of what is important, then committed action can be broken down into four steps:

1.  Pick one or two high-priority valued domains and develop an action plan for behavior change, based on a functional analysis, the best available evidence, or both.

2.  Help the client commit to actions that are linked to values—to be accomplished between sessions—being mindful of the larger behavioral patterns that are being assembled.

3.  Attend to and overcome barriers to action with acceptance, defusion, and mindfulness skills.

4.  Return to step 1 and generalize to larger patterns of action, to other domains of living, to feared or avoided private experience, or to other areas of psychological inflexibility, until the client has sufficient practice to be able to maintain a pattern of flexible and wise committed action without the therapist's support.

This process is the core of translating abstract values, such as being healthy or engaging in a spiritual practice, into concrete actions that express and instantiate these values in the world.

## Identify Valued Life Goals and Link to an Action Plan

Typically, in collaboration, the therapist and client identify one or two high-priority areas as the initial focus for committed action. Usually it is helpful to focus on areas of living in which the client feels a loss of engagement, choice, or vitality, and in which this constriction appears to result in ongoing suffering (Wilson & Murrell, 2004). Ideally, the therapist will suggest areas of high importance to the client. The actions or goals to be selected should include ones that are likely to occasion private experiences that are feared and avoided by the client, in order to maximize the opportunity for developing psychological flexibility. After the initial focus has been decided, the therapist and client work together to develop specific plans for places and times to implement the chosen actions or goals.

Workable goals and action plans can be characterized by the six qualities or elements described in the following paragraphs.

First, they should be *specific and measurable*. Goals need to be specific and concrete so that both the therapist and client can determine whether a commitment has been kept. A common error is to develop vague goals, which makes it difficult to assess whether they have been accomplished. Examples of vague goals include "engaging more with friends" and "calling my brother more" and "being more accepting." Although such activities might be values consistent, it would be difficult to pinpoint the manner in which the goals were engaged or to know what qualities the client brought to the situation. It is more effective to have clear goals, such as "call my friend Jake and ask him to go to a movie, and go to coffee with Rebecca" and "call my brother two times this week" and "get my daughter a card and write in it how much I love her." In addition, goals can be further clarified by specifying when, where, and how the actions will be done. The therapist often needs to help clarify goals because clients find this difficult to do on their own.

Second, goals also need to be *practical* and *within the client's ability to accomplish*. Small steps done with intention and consistency are more doable than are heroic leaps attempted in a more sporadic fashion; however, the latter are sometimes necessary. Be careful not to pick goals that are beyond the ability of the client. If a client does not have the skill to accomplish a particular goal, work with that client to develop the skill as an intermediary values-consistent step. An example of what the therapist can say is shown in the following transcript.

*Therapist:* The size of the goal here isn't important. What *is* important is that you are taking steps in the direction of what matters, that you're moving forward in a way that counts. How fast isn't important. So, let's find an action you can commit to that you will be able to do between this and the next session.

Third, *avoid dead man goals* (Lindsley, 1968). Dead man goals are goals that a dead person could do better. For example, a dead person would almost always do better than a client who is trying to "withdraw less from my mom" or "be less lazy," or who wants to "argue less with my spouse." Put another way, dead man goals are like giving directions to your office by only telling someone which streets *not* to go down (Heffner & Eifert, 2004). That is, dead man goals specify what the client is trying to avoid. In contrast, the therapist is trying to build the ability to approach a chosen goal. Reformulating the dead man goals mentioned in the previous examples could result in statements such as "spending time connecting with my mom," "being productive at work," and "being supportive." Even more specific and measurable goals are "having dinner with my mom this week and telling her how much I miss her," "spending at least two hours every day working on computer code," and "helping my husband during this stressful week by mowing the lawn."

Fourth, as research has shown, when people make *public* commitments, they are more likely to accomplish them (Hayes et al., 1985). Thus, ideally, the client commits to specific goals in the presence of the therapist, and these goals are recorded in a fashion that allows them to be checked later. For example, the goal could be written down on a card, diary sheet, or a goals document. The physical reminder can also be used to prompt the client so he or she remembers the commitment. Without a physical reminder, clients often get confused about the exact nature of the committed action. Forms on which clients can track their goals and achievements over time are useful to reinforce progress. Sample forms can be found in Hayes and Smith (2005, pp. 177–186) and Eifert and Forsyth (2005, pp. 218, 244).

Fifth, any goals or actions committed to by a client need to be *on target* and linked to the client's values. As they move toward their goals, clients need to attend to how well aligned their actions are with their valued directions (Dahl et al., 2005). Typically when we move in a valued direction, natural feedback occurs in the form of a sense of vitality, freedom, and flexibility. Clients can begin to develop a sense of this vitality and use it to guide them so they know whether they are hitting the bull's-eye or are off target.

Finally, goals need to be *linked to the evidence and to the functional needs of the client*. A vast literature has developed describing forms of action that are psychologically helpful, based on a functional analysis and the linkage of client action to basic principles of behavior. ACT expands considerably on the breadth of this process by linking case conceptualization to the principles of relational framing drawn from

RFT (Moran & Bach, in press; Ramnerö & Törneke, in press). Because RFT is entirely consistent with behavioral principles, it enables a more coherent expansion of traditional functional analysis into processes involving human cognition. The literature on functional analysis and behavioral methods for specific problems is so vast it is impossible to cover it all here, even in a cursory way. It suffices to say that no ACT practitioner can be wholly ignorant of behavior therapy and behavior analysis and be effective because ACT is part of these traditions and uses their empirically supported methods.

These six qualities are relevant to every ACT case. Suppose a client values intimate and supportive friendships. For a client with that value but with no friends, a long-term goal might be having two good friends. Various actions and steps would be part of this longer term goal. For example, the client could join a sports league. Even smaller substeps could include finding information about what leagues are available, then calling the office and enrolling. Smaller, more precise skills may need to be targeted. For example, an isolated client may need to practice how to make such a phone call or how to interact with fellow players in a way that could lead to friendship.

It's important to keep in mind that committed action is not simply about achieving goals, but more accurately about the process of living a life worth having. Goals serve as signposts that let clients know they are headed in the right direction and are keeping on track. A second, therapeutic purpose of the action plan is to help clients engage in a process of valued living while simultaneously developing greater psychological flexibility. The focus is on the quality of clients' pursuit of their goals (e.g., whether they are living in the present, using defusion skills, being willing, watching the workability of each step) as they approach their goals, rather than on goal attainment disconnected from such concerns.

A common problem is that clients are unwilling to generate goals because they feel nothing new is possible for them. This is less likely to occur if work on defusion, acceptance, and values has already happened. However, if unwillingness does occur during this stage, defusion and acceptance techniques are often helpful in overcoming it. The following transcript provides an example of a therapist using defusion as a way to overcome verbal barriers to commitment in session through focusing on the functional utility of the client's thinking.

Client: Why should I write down goals? I never follow through on them anyway. It just seems like a waste of time.

Therapist: If you were to listen to the advice of that thought—that you never follow through on your goals—would that lead you toward or away from this value of making a difference with your life?

Client: Hmm. Away.

Therapist: And if this value of making a difference were to give you advice, what would it say with respect to setting goals?

Client: It would say, "Go ahead and set the goals, and then accomplish them."

Therapist: So, if you could choose between those, which one would you choose?

Client: I'd choose to set goals and accomplish them.

Therapist: Okay, so then let's start with the first step: setting goals. If you were living your life to make a difference, what would be one thing you would be doing that would be about that?

Another common problem is that the client is unable to move beyond the generic value and needs help being more concrete in setting goals. In response to this, the therapist can help the client learn how to divide larger goals or values into more manageable steps. An example of working with this situation is presented in the following transcript.

Client:       Yeah, I know I want a job that is more rewarding, that requires more from me than the one I have now, but I don't know what to do to get there.

Therapist:    Okay, so let's break this down a bit. You don't need to leap all the way to the goal of having a new job in one step. Can you think of one action that, if you completed it, would put you one step further in the direction of that new job? Maybe something you've been thinking about doing, but are afraid of doing?

## Keeping Commitments in the Presence of Emotional Barriers

When therapists work with clients on goals and on building patterns of commitment, this work usually involves contact with thoughts and feelings the clients were previously avoiding. ACT assumes that what keeps clients from living their values is, at least in part, their unpleasant and difficult private reactions and their avoidance of those reactions. When clients engage in committed action, they are engaging in exposure to feared and avoided stimuli. This gives them opportunities to practice other ACT skills and to develop greater psychological flexibility.

The focus is on helping clients learn to act on their values, while also "leaning in" toward their own experience, whether their experience consists of anxiety, sadness, depression, boredom, negative thoughts, unpleasant memories, or something else. Through this process of choosing and taking action, clients both build new patterns of perseverance in the face of difficulty and also have the chance to build breadth and flexibility of responding by interacting more richly with avoided experiences. As they pursue a valued direction, life provides the material for practicing acceptance and defusion.

In one sense, ACT is an exposure-based method. But there are differences. First, the model of extinction that is embraced in ACT is not as much about response elimination and emotion reduction as it is about response flexibility and breadth of repertoire. Thus, exposure would never be presented to an ACT client as a method of reducing arousal; rather, it is a situation in which willingness and action can be practiced. Because ACT is based on a response-flexibility model of exposure, ACT therapists deliberately create variable responses during exposure. The goal is to undermine fusion and experiential avoidance, while watching for subtle forms of avoidance.

The following transcript is an example from an exposure session with a client who has panic disorder and who is visiting a mall for the first time in many years.

Therapist:    So, are you ready to go in? The only commitment is that you will stay physically present for five minutes. Anything else is gravy.

Client:       I don't want to go.

Therapist:    Okay. [gently] Be aware of that thought. What else are you feeling?

Client:       My heart is pounding really fast.

Therapist:    Okay ... Go there for a second and see if you can let go of any struggle with that experience. Your beating heart is not your enemy. Just watch it beat for a few seconds ... And I want to ask you one more thing. Why are we here, anyway? Why the mall? What is a mall good for?

Client:       I used to buy a lot of cool things here for my family.

Therapist:    Yeah, so let's allow this little trip to be about visiting a place where cool things can be bought for your family. Are you on board? Are you willing to be present for five minutes?

| Client: | Okay. [enters mall] |
|---|---|
| Therapist: | What are you feeling? |
| Client: | Sick. |
| Therapist: | Where exactly? |
| Client: | In my stomach … there is a kind of tightness. [closes eyes] |
| Therapist: | Open your eyes, Frank. Look at me. Come on out. Out into the environment. Good. Now go back to your stomach *and* … look at me, Frank, come out here into the world. Now … staying out here, add in exactly where your stomach gets tight. Noting its edges. Notice what it feels like. |
| Client: | Okay. [breathes a bit more slowly] |
| Therapist: | [pause] How are you feeling? |
| Client: | Really anxious. |
| Therapist: | On a scale of one to ten? |
| Client: | Eight. Eight at least. |
| Therapist: | Good. Stay with it. Notice how your body feels… Notice your thoughts … Notice what you feel a pull to do … Stay present. If you find any sense of struggle—if a tug-of-war is going on anywhere within your experiences—see if you can go there and just gently drop the rope … [refers to a metaphor used earlier with the client of being in a tug-of-war with anxiety] Your experiences are not your own enemy. |
| Client: | [breathes a bit more regularly] I'm here. |
| Therapist: | Good. Now I just want to add one more thing. This is not to subtract anything from your experience. Stay mindful of your body, your thoughts, your emotions, and your urges to do things as you feel your anxiety rise and fall. Now, let's *add* in one more thing. Look around you and find the ugliest hairdo you see in the mall. |
| Client: | [giggles for a second] That one. Whoa! What was she thinking? |

The last part of this transcript shows how ACT exposure seeks to create response flexibility in the context of values-based action, acceptance, defusion, and mindfulness. Looking for the ugliest hairdo is not designed as dis-traction; it is a form of attraction. That is, we are *adding* new response forms. People-watching is fun to do in a mall. In a session such as this, response forms can turn quickly from silly things, such as the hairdo example, to values-based actions, such as looking for items to buy for others. The client's repertoire is thus gradually expanded.

Second, defusion and acceptance enable a kind of exposure that otherwise would be impossible because these core processes permit exposure to the process of thinking and feeling, not just to the products of thinking and feeling. For example, a person thinking "I'm bad" does not need to expose himself or herself to being bad; rather, defusion and acceptance allow the person to expose himself or herself to the process of thinking "I'm bad." The work on interoceptive exposure (i.e., exposure to feared bodily sensations) is ACT consistent, but ACT takes it a sizable step further.

Third, exposure is values linked. For example, a between-session commitment for a client with a germ phobia could be to go to a restaurant with a friend and work toward being present with the friend, engaged, and sharing of himself or herself. Some form of deliberate exposure could be arranged as part of this event; for example, limiting hand washing to once before the meal and once again before leaving the restaurant. This exposure would not be toward the goal of reducing arousal per se, but toward the goal of increasing behavioral flexibility linked to the value of being present with the friend, engaged, and sharing of self. This value necessarily involves not spending excessive time engaging in compulsive rituals aimed at eliminating thoughts about contamination; thus, exposure has a values-based purpose.

As with any good exposure procedure, it can be useful to prepare clients for the presence of experiential barriers as they engage in committed actions. Without the awareness of probable experiential barriers, clients who choose to engage in committed actions are not likely to also choose to have these barriers willingly. Helping a client to see what is likely to happen enhances the sense of choice. The following transcript provides an example with a socially anxious client.

*Therapist:* One thing I can pretty much guarantee is that, as soon as you head in this direction you value, some pretty uncomfortable thoughts and feelings will start to show up. For example, as soon as you start to make moves to develop friendships with people, your passengers [from the Passengers on the Bus metaphor, Hayes et al., 1999] who say it's not worth it, people are disappointing, and you will be hurt are almost certainly going to show up. The question life is asking you in these moments is, "Will you have those feelings, thoughts, images, sensations—will you say yes to those passengers when they show up?" Now, I'm not at all asking whether you *want* them there. I'm asking if you're willing to have them there. It's a bit as if you just got out of bed at home, feeling really depressed, and your friend Craig, whom you haven't seen in several years, knocked on your door and asked if he could come in. Now, you might not *want* him there, but might you be *willing* to let him in? Similarly, with this action of asking this guy you met in your English class to go play racquetball: would you be willing to do that, knowing it also means you will need to make room for those passengers who say, "It's not worth it," "He's going to disappoint you anyway," and "You're eventually going to be hurt"? The question I have is this: are you 100 percent willing to have these passengers show up *and* to ask this guy to play racquetball?

*Client:* Yeah, but I've done this before, and people don't want to be friends with me. Why should I be willing when it's not likely to work out?

*Therapist:* What's not likely to work out?

*Client:* He's probably not going to say yes.

*Therapist:* Well, certainly there's no guarantee of a particular outcome. What I'm asking you is if you're going take a stand in your life for what is important to you. You told me before you wanted more friends in your life. The outcome will be what it will. If you don't ask, you definitely know how that will turn out: no possibility of making a new friend. Asking creates the possibility, doesn't it? From there, it will either work out or it won't. What I'm asking is, "What are you going to stand for?" If you ask this person to do something, is it about working toward making friends?

*Client:* Yeah, I guess so ... Yeah, it is.

*Therapist:* Then, not knowing whether it will work out and knowing that it's possible you will feel rejected—and certainly that you will feel anxious and worried—are you 100 percent willing to feel and think all these things and take steps in the direction of making more friends ... by asking this guy to play racquetball?

*Client:* Yeah, I'm going to do it *and* I'm willing to feel whatever I need to feel.

As you can see from this dialogue, the therapist helped the client to be aware of his barriers to committed action. Internal barriers, such as difficult emotions, traumatic memories, fear of failure, and being right, can be differentiated from external barriers, such as lack of financial resources, lack of connections, an unsupportive spouse, and lack of effective skills. In this context, by "external barriers" we mean any situation in which a change of overt behavior is what is needed to address the problem. Internal barriers generally call for acceptance, mindfulness, and defusion, while external barriers are usually steps—or preliminary goals that might become steps—in a valued direction.

External barriers require hard work and practice in one way or another. First-order change strategies, including skills training, psychoeducation, problem solving, behavioral homework, and exposure, are appropriate here, as long as they are targeted at overt behavior. For example, a client may value social relationships, but lack the social skills to engage effectively in these. Thus, a subgoal could be to have the client engage in social skills training in order to develop these goals.

Some internal and external barriers can be hard to differentiate. For example, on the one hand, "I don't know" can function as an internal barrier that keeps the client from moving ahead, such as when "not knowing" serves as a way of not engaging in a difficult social situation. On the other hand, "I don't know" can indicate a problem about knowledge; in this case, the problem might be solved by taking preliminary steps such as gathering more information about the subject at hand. Sometimes having a client go out and get more information and see if that moves the process along will clarify whether "I don't know" is really a knowledge barrier. Clarity can also be reached by examining whether the quality of pursuing this additional knowledge is vital and growing or seems limiting.

Occasionally, the barrier to committed action is that the therapist and client have set a goal that is not connected to a valued end, but is the result of social pressure (e.g., from parents or the therapist) or of avoidance, trying to be right, or trying to make others happy. Without connection to a value, clients have little motivation to engage in the hard work of therapy and the process of contacting feared states. If the therapist thinks this may have happened, the therapist's job is to return to the process of defining valued directions and again search for values that are chosen, vital, and present oriented.

## Appreciating the Qualities of Committed Action

Clients do not have speedometers glued to their foreheads. What matters most is maintaining forward movement and growth, not the amount or the rate of movement. By drawing attention to this process, therapists can help clients learn to discriminate a sense of expansion from a sense of constriction or loss of choice or possibility that comes from being hemmed in by avoidance or fusion. ACT uses various metaphors about journeying, sports, or growth to orient clients toward recognizing the qualities of vitality and growth in their behavior. If clients are able to discriminate these qualities, they can use them as guides for effective action. The following transcript demonstrates a metaphor that can be used for this purpose.

Client:      I feel as if I've been playing it safe for so long, as if I'm always scared.

Therapist:   I'd like to share a metaphor and see if you feel it fits the experience you are talking about here. The metaphor is of a basketball game. There are two basic groups of people at a basketball game: the people in the stands and the people on the court. People in the stands have certain sorts of conversations. They sit there and talk, analyzing the game, trying to figure out what's happening, cheering sometimes, eating, whatever. They do lots of talking. But, ultimately, how much impact does this have on how the game turns out? Very little, right? Let's contrast that with the people on the court. The kinds of conversations the people on the court have are all about advancing the game. They aren't doing a lot of judging and predicting how it's going to turn out. In order to play well, they are working on being present, fully invested, and moving the game along. The kinds of conversations they have affect the game strongly and make a big difference. And, ultimately, they are the ones taking the risks. How the game turns out matters most to them. Where do you find yourself in your own life: Are you sitting in the stands, watching, evaluating? Or are you on the court, working, having conversations that will advance the game?

*Client:*  In the stands.

*Therapist:*  Where do you want to be?

*Client:*  Of course I want to be on the court.

*Therapist:*  If you were going to be on the court this week, what would that look like? What is one thing you could do that would let you know you were on the court?

Here's another metaphor that can be helpful on this same point:

*Therapist:*  [draws image in figure 7-1] Now, the dominant metaphor of the good life in this society is that life is always supposed to be going up, getting better over time, until the moment you die, preferably in your sleep or some such. I want to suggest that you've been following this metaphor without knowing it for a long time, always trying to get better, achieve the next goal, have better self-esteem, reduce your anxiety, rack up the next accomplishment. Whatever.

**Figure 7.1**

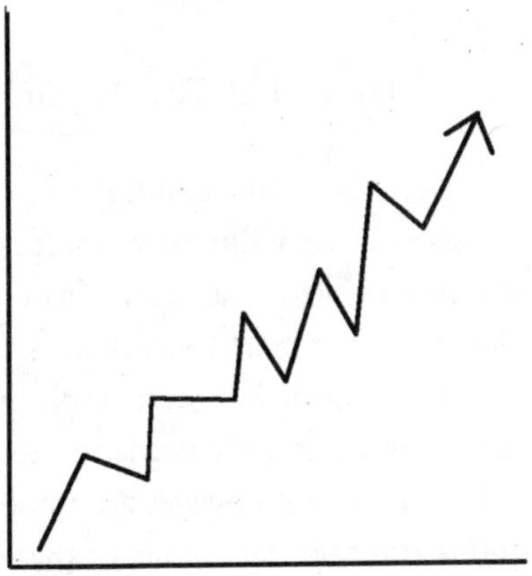

*Client:*  Okay, that seems about right.

*Therapist:*  In therapy here, we've been working on a bit of a different metaphor for what it means to live a good life. This metaphor is more like an expanding circle. It isn't about things getting better in life, but about how much space you have to live your life in, how much room you have to move around, having freedom. [draws image in figure 7-2]

**Figure 7.2**

The way this metaphor works is that you are always either expanding or contracting in your life, growing or regressing. And on the outer edge of this circle there is always some experience. A good deal of the time, it's something difficult. Let's say, for you, it often takes the form of fearing you will panic or go crazy. So, here's the thought "I'll go crazy," and here's the feeling "anxiety." In a particular moment in your life, your bubble happens to bump up against these. The question life is asking you at this moment is, "Are you willing to have this—are you going to say yes to this experience and have it inside you, as part of you?" Or will you say no, which means your bubble will draw back a little and start

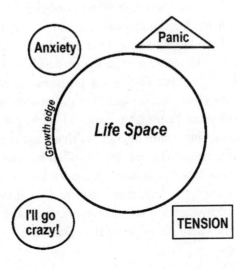

to distort. You say no enough times, and your bubble starts to get small, and you don't have much room to live in at all. Now, in this metaphor, some things are always on the outside, always asking yes or no, and life is waiting for you to answer. The question we are working on here is, "Are you going to say yes or no to life?"

ACT therapists also help clients discriminate between these qualities in their own behavior during sessions. A therapist might notice a shift in session between behavior about avoidance, fusion, or reason giving into behavior that is a form of committed action (e.g., making a choice to do something life affirming or exploring a possibility) or that involves opening up to a fear or judgmental thought. The role of the therapist in this moment is to draw out the difference between the client's subjective experiences of these respective forms of behavior so the client is able to better discriminate between them in the future. For example, a therapist could let a client talk for a minute or so about why he or she is stuck in a current pattern of behavior. This could be followed by saying, "You've spent the last couple minutes talking about all the reasons you are stuck. As you did this, did you feel freer and more open, as if your life were expanding, or did you feel more and more stuck, as if the life were draining out of the room? Just slow down for a second and check out your experience at this moment before you answer the question."

## Build Patterns of Action over Time

The goal in building patterns of action over time is to start small and help the client to act with consistency as willingness increases. Consider how one learns to drive a car with a manual transmission. When first learning, every little action is awkward and requires attention: how hard to push down the clutch, which gear to shift into, how to coordinate the release of the clutch while pressing down on the gas, and so on. However, with practice and time, these small patterns of behavior become almost automatic, and one only needs to attend to the larger pattern. Similarly, small patterns of committed action in which the client engages are important because small behaviors, practiced regularly, can eventually become automatic and part of larger patterns.

Focusing on larger patterns over time also refers to the process of helping the client see where present behavior falls into the larger direction of the client's life. The goal is to verbally tie current actions to larger patterns of meaning for the client's life (i.e., his or her values) and to bring active, intentional valuing into as many moments of the client's life as possible. For example, part of what leads to drug addiction is that short-term consequences weigh more heavily as a determinant of behavior than do long-term consequences. A therapist working with addiction tries to bring long-term consequences into the moment by helping the client see the larger pattern of behavior to which drug use is linked and how this behavior relates to the client's larger life goals and values. Linking behavior in the moment to larger patterns brings the influence of the latter to bear on current behavior, weakening the influence of short-term consequences.

Consider a situation in which a client with a weight problem is beginning a new program of diet and exercise. Part of the program involves eliminating sugary snacks in between meals. After two days, the client has a candy bar in between meals. Building larger patterns of committed action requires this moment be integrated into a healthy pattern. The client may be tempted to quit because "after all, I can't keep my commitments." In that case, the pattern is to make a commitment, keep it for two days, break it, say you can't do it, and abandon it. A more effective pattern would be to make a commitment, keep it for two days, break it, say you can't do it, notice that thought, renew the commitment, and keep the commitment for at least three or more days. If the client is mindful of the process and chooses the second option, then when the second commitment is broken—say, after a week—the whole cycle can continue instead of the client abandoning the commitment.

# Slips and Relapses

Fusion, avoidance, dominance of the conceptualized future or past, and attachment to the conceptualized self are all processes that are heavily supported by the culture at large and are highly practiced by clients, resulting in their constant recurrence. In addition, research has shown that old patterns of behavior, both verbal and nonverbal, are likely to reappear when new patterns of behavior are frustrated (Wilson & Hayes, 1996). These reasons, among others, make it likely clients will relapse to old patterns of behaving. The job of the ACT therapist is to help clients learn how to integrate relapses into the larger patterns of effective action they are trying to build into their lives.

One way to respond to setbacks is to teach the client to expect them as a part of being human. Relapse often occurs in the form of a return to an old control agenda in the face of negative self-evaluations, unpleasant emotions, or painful memories. The role of the ACT therapist is to function as a support for the client's deepest wishes and dreams, especially during times when the client is out of contact with them. The therapist aligns with the client's desires, even when the client's mind is not being supportive, and encourages the client to reengage in valued action, while working with thoughts, feelings, and other private events with acceptance, mindfulness, and compassion.

The ACT therapist has a number of concrete tools to use to help clients prepare for setbacks. After clients have gone through most of the ACT processes, it can be useful to teach them two core acronyms (Hayes et al., 1999). The first is

**A**ccept

**C**hoose

**T**ake Action

This acronym describes the basic ACT process in a shorthand clients can use as an aid to deal with difficult situations. It can be helpful to write this acronym on a business card that clients can carry in their pockets as a reminder.

A second acronym can be useful to clients when they find themselves stuck and don't know what to do.

**F**usion

**E**valuation

**A**voidance

**R**eason Giving

This acronym helps clients identify major barriers that may be functioning to keep them stuck. This, too, can be given to the client in a pocket-sized form.

The ACT therapist can also use journeying metaphors to emphasize that life is not a perfectly straight road toward continuous improvement, but rather a meandering path that can take one in a certain direction despite its many twists and turns (see Hayes et al., 1999, pp. 222, 248). Detours that occur can be seen either as times the client got off the road or as turns in the path that was chosen by the client. In this metaphor, the client can at times even be facing in the opposite direction from the intended destination, but still be on the path. This metaphor can help clients give themselves a break when they make mistakes.

When clients return to old behaviors (e.g., depressive behavior, anxious avoidance, judgmental and distant interpersonal behavior, or addiction), they can find themselves dispirited and confused about what they want in the moment. Such clients are again fused with current evaluations or worries about the future, consumed in past mistakes or regrets, or living out a story about how their life "should" or "must" be. Clients who have slipped back into old behavior patterns often think their values have changed simply because they are valuing something else through their actions in the moment. However, although values may change with time, values do not go away simply because we fail to live by them consistently (Eifert & Forsyth, 2005). A therapist in this situation could speak to the client as illustrated in the following transcript.

*Therapist:* Given all that has happened, it's not surprising you feel hopeless and helpless. You feel you are unsure about what you want and unsure about what to do. Given this, I have one question for you: have your values changed? What I mean is, a few weeks ago, you told me that what is really important to you is having a good relationship with your wife. Has that changed? Is she still important to you, or has going back to drinking resulted in your not valuing that anymore? And if she is still important to you, what stands between you and getting back on track right here and today?

The therapist may also want to use a metaphor about what to do when getting into a skid while driving. If we find ourselves in a skid and headed toward a telephone pole, the natural thing to do is to turn and look at the object as it comes toward us. But the thing we need to do instead is to keep our eyes focused in the direction we want to head and turn the wheel in that direction. The therapist could ask the client, "What would keeping your eyes on the road look like for you in this situation? How would you know you were looking at the telephone pole?"

Finally, therapists can work with clients to prepare for setbacks by identifying high-risk situations and developing ACT-consistent plans for dealing with these situations. These plans can be recorded on paper so the client has them when a situation arises. Most of these plans involve applying particular ACT techniques or strategies that were developed in an intentional way during therapy.

The purpose of therapy is the empowerment of a human life. And that can ultimately be tested only in the world of behavior. Behavior is the bottom line.

# CORE COMPETENCY PRACTICE

This section is intended to provide practice in the competencies of using committed action with your clients. Directions on how to complete the exercise for each competency are provided. Remember, the sample responses are not meant to illustrate perfect responses, but rather to serve as models to consider in applying the competency. Try to generate your own responses before you look at the models at the end of the section.

# CORE COMPETENCY EXERCISES

## COMPETENCY 1: The therapist helps the client identify valued life goals and build an action plan linked to them.

Consider each of the following goals in terms of the six desirable properties of behavioral goals within the ACT model (i.e., specific and measurable, practical, active, public, on target with client values, and linked to the empirical evidence and the functional needs of the client). You might want to review the desirable properties of behavioral goals, as described in detail earlier in this chapter.

In the following three exercises, describe all the problems you can see in terms of the six properties. You may find as many as six.

## EXERCISE 7.1

A client with anxiety disorder wants to begin to face anxiety-provoking situations by worrying about them less.

## EXERCISE 7.2 (CONTINUING WITH COMPETENCY 1)

A socially withdrawn client has the goal of calling thirty women each week to ask on dates.

## EXERCISE 7.3 (CONTINUING WITH COMPETENCY 1)

A father states that he is going to make a commitment to "be less critical of my daughter this week."

---

COMPETENCY 2: **The therapist encourages the client to make and keep commitments in the presence of perceived barriers (e.g., fear of failure, traumatic memories, sadness, being right) and to expect additional barriers as a consequence of engaging in committed actions.**

## EXERCISE 7.4

The client is a thirty-four-year-old woman with a lifelong history of panic disorder. The therapist has already worked on the other five core ACT processes with the client and developed a plan during the last session to go with the client to the mall for five minutes to practice the willingness to be present with anxiety. The therapist and client have just arrived at the mall when the following dialogue occurs.

*Therapist:* So, are you ready to go in? The only commitment is that you will stay physically present for five minutes. Anything else is gravy.

*Client:* I don't want to go.

*Therapist:* Okay. So notice that thought. What else are you feeling?

*Client:* My heart is pounding really fast. Can I go home? I really want to leave.

Write here what your response would be (using competency 2):

What are your thoughts in saying this? What are you responding to and what are you hoping to accomplish?

## EXERCISE 7.5 (CONTINUING WITH COMPETENCY 2)

*Transcript continues with the same client.*

*Therapist:* What are you feeling now?

*Client:* Sick.

*Therapist:* Where exactly?

*Client:* In my stomach ... there is a kind of tightness. [closes eyes] Jeez. I'm losing it completely. I can't even think. I'm losing my mind!

Write here what your response would be (using competency 2):

What are your thoughts in saying this? What are you responding to and what are you hoping to accomplish?

## EXERCISE 7.6 (CONTINUING WITH COMPETENCY 2)

*Transcript continues with the same client.*

*Therapist:* What are you afraid will happen?

*Client:* I'll just fall down. I can't go on. I'm going to make a complete fool of myself.

Write here what your response would be (using competency 2):

What are your thoughts in saying this? What are you responding to and what are you hoping to accomplish?

---

**COMPETENCY 3: The therapist helps the client appreciate the qualities of committed action (e.g., vitality, sense of growth) and to take small steps while maintaining contact with those qualities.**

## EXERCISE 7.7

A fifty-six-year-old client reports his PTSD is causing a lot of anger and preventing him from interacting with his children. He fears his children have come to hate him and reports they don't understand what he is dealing with when he flies into a rage. He has identified his values in relation to his children and the therapist is now working on helping him identify goals on which he might act that are in line with his values.

Client:     I'm not going to let my anger push me around anymore. I'm going to make a phone call to my youngest daughter and tell her how I feel about her and that I'm not going to yell at her anymore.

The client has said this several times before in session and hasn't followed through. As the therapist, you think this is because it is too big of a step for his current level of willingness and want to help him break down the goal into smaller steps in an ACT-consistent way.

Write here what your response would be (using competency 3):

What are your thoughts in saying this? What are you responding to and what are you hoping to accomplish?

## EXERCISE 7.8 (CONTINUING WITH COMPETENCY 3)

What are two smaller, concrete actions the client could take that would lead him in the direction of his values regarding his daughter and also prepare him for the eventual conversation with his daughter?

Action 1:

Action 2:

**COMPETENCY 4: The therapist keeps the client focused on larger and larger patterns of action to help the client act on goals with consistency over time.**

## EXERCISE 7.9

In the previous session, a forty-seven-year-old single man contacted a value of wanting to be understood by and have a deep and rich relationship with a woman. His three previous significant relationships were marginal and unsatisfying, with women whom he felt little connection and attraction, but with whom he stayed "because I don't want to be alone." About a month ago, he found himself alone, after again "fading out" of a relationship with a girlfriend of four years. His pattern of overfocusing on issues about money, work, and financial security draws him away from relationships. In the previous session, he made a commitment to write a personal, open, heartfelt ad in preparation for participating in a professional dating service. When he returned to the next session, the following exchange occurred.

*Therapist:* So, how did it go with the ad?

*Client:* [speaks quickly] I wasn't able to do it. Things blew up at work. All I've been doing is working to keep from being overwhelmed.

*Therapist:* Let me slow you down for a moment. How do you feel as you tell me this?

*Client:* I, uh, okay. I mean, I would have done it if I had time, but I didn't.

*Therapist:* That thought—that you don't have time—is that a familiar one? An old one?

*Client:* Yeah, that happens all the time.

*Therapist:* And when you follow that thought—that you don't have time—where does it lead you?

*Client:* Away from what I value. But I really didn't have time.

*Therapist:* [jokingly] Ooh, there it is again! The passenger is back! And where does that lead you?

*Client:* Away ... But I don't know what else to do.

Write here what your response would be (hint: help the client focus on the pattern of action he is creating in his life):

What are your thoughts in saying this? What are you responding to and what are you hoping to accomplish?

---

COMPETENCY 5: **The therapist nonjudgmentally integrates slips or relapses into the process of keeping commitments and building larger patterns of effective action.**

### EXERCISE 7.10

A thirty-four-year-old single male, who has been abusing alcohol since the age of fifteen, is in his seventeenth session. He has had several periods of sobriety lasting a few years, but none in the past decade since his wife divorced him. For the last five years, he has had no friends and has been living with his parents. His only income comes from disability payments related to a diagnosis of schizophrenia he received at the age of twenty-three. He reports that his family are "jerks"; they appear to take advantage of him frequently, such as by borrowing money and not paying him back. He is not on any medication and does not currently show any symptoms of psychosis. Over the past few months, he has begun volunteering at the local humane society and has developed a friendship with James, with whom he has gone out three times. He has been able to successfully make room for his social anxiety and intense fears of humiliation for the past four weeks without drinking.

*Client:* I, uh, uh, I didn't do well this week.

*Therapist:* Mm-hmm. Didn't do well?

| Client: | Yeah, uh, James ... he turned out to be a jerk. |
|---|---|
| Therapist: | A jerk? [pause] What happened? |
| Client: | Well, I was supposed to go to the baseball game with him on Saturday, and he never showed. So I went home and got hammered. It always turns out like this. I should just stay home ... I'm an idiot. |
| Therapist: | And then what happened? |
| Client: | Well, I kept drinking and didn't stop until this morning because I was supposed to come in here. |
| Therapist: | And how were you able to do that? |
| Client: | I just did. It's important for me to keep these appointments. |
| Therapist: | So, where do you go from here with your value of having friends? |
| Client: | I'm done. I give up. It always turns out like this. |
| Therapist: | Yeah, it's hard to meet people with whom you connect. It's going to be painful. Lots of them will reject you. But if you keep trying, you can find some who won't. It seems as if your mind is saying James is one of those who's rejecting you? |
| Client: | Yeah, well, he ditched me. I'm tired of trying. I should just go back home and stay there. It's just not that important. It's not worth it. |

Write here what your response would be (using competency 5):

What are your thoughts in saying this? What are you responding to and what are you hoping to accomplish?

## Core Competency Model Responses

### COMPETENCY 1

**Sample 7.1**

**Explanation:** This goal has strong problems in the area of specificity and measurability. It is not an active goal, and the link to client values is unclear. This is not an empirically supported approach, and the link to the functional needs of the client is unclear.

**Sample 7.2**

**Explanation:** The goal is active but impractical. It is hard to imagine making the calls at that rate, and even harder to imagine the number of dates implied if the calls begin to be successful. It needs to be broken into smaller steps.

**Sample 7.3**

**Explanation:** This is a dead man goal—a dead person could be even less critical than the client. Something like this is also not likely to be on target or feel vital. Contrast this with the probably more vital-seeming goal of scheduling a father-daughter dinner at which he makes it a point to tell his daughter how much he loves her and what he appreciates about her as a daughter. Finally, the goal is not specific or measurable. It is possible that it would be hard to tell a week later whether the goal had been accomplished.

## COMPETENCY 2

### Sample 7.4a

*Therapist:* And you can leave. But before you choose to do that, would you be willing to watch your mind scream "I want to leave"? Just listen to it. How familiar is this place? How old is this?

*Client:* Very old. Very familiar.

*Therapist:* Good. Let's take advantage of this moment. Here we get a chance to see something that has been troublesome for you up close and personal. What shows up in your body as you hear the words "I want to leave"?

**Explanation:** Never try to stop a client from leaving, especially not physically. It has to be the client's choice. *And* the therapist should try to take the client into what he or she has been avoiding. Every minute that the client stays and goes into the experience a little more deeply is a minute of progress. It is a great opportunity; it is in no way a failure.

### Sample 7.4b

*Therapist:* We came here to find something. We came to find exactly what is coming up right now … so we could learn ways to do something truly different with it. It's not bad that fear is here now. So let's just reconnect with why we're here. Are we here to not be anxious?

*Client:* No. But I wish I could be.

*Therapist:* Right. And attachment to that is the core of the whole system. How much suffering is enough? Have you had enough?

*Client:* More than enough.

*Therapist:* Cool. Let's take a turn right here, right now, in a new direction. Are you willing?

**Explanation:** The barriers appear as problems, but they are not problems. They are opportunities. Taking the client into them is something new, and the client has a chance for growth.

## Sample 7.5a

*Therapist:* "Help, I've fallen and I can't get up!" So, would you be willing to lose your mind for a few minutes? Just a few. I will be here to rescue you if need be. How would you go about losing your mind?

**Explanation:** Humor is a powerful ally if well-timed. In this response, the therapist uses some humor, but then gets right back into the avoidance.

## Sample 7.5b

*Therapist:* So, just open your eyes. Look around for a moment. If you're going to lose your mind, let's at least see where you are when you lose it. Where are you?

Client: At the mall.

Therapist: Right. And as you notice that, notice who is aware of that. Who's at the mall?

Client: I am.

Therapist: Right. And notice you are not the mall. Now go back into those thoughts and feelings deliberately. Notice a tightness. And deliberately think, "I'm losing it completely ... I can't even think ... I'm losing my mind." And, once again, notice who is aware of that.

Client: Okay. I'm here. I'm just having thoughts. And feelings.

Therapist: And they are not your enemy.

**Explanation:** In this response, the therapist uses acceptance, defusion, a transcendent sense of self, and contact with the present moment to situate the frightening feelings and thoughts in a different context, one in which they operate differently and need not undermine commitments.

## Sample 7.6a

*Therapist:* Would you be willing to lie down with me here? Maybe we could both make total fools of ourselves. What would we do to do that?

**Explanation:** This is an advanced move, but if the therapist is willing to do it and it is well-timed—and if the therapist can manage the client's waves of emotion—using a reverse compass can be powerful. Wherever Mr. Mind says not to go, that is exactly where you want to go.

## Sample 7.6b

*Therapist:* Super. There goes Mr. Mind again. Elegant. And before we spend more time making fools of ourselves, what else is there to do here at the mall?

Client: Other than have a lot of anxiety?

Therapist: [chuckles] Right. And other than just watching Mr. Mind scare us.

Client: I could do some shopping.

Therapist: Super. So, let me ask you a question, but don't answer this right away. Would you be willing to have the thought "I'll just fall down. I can't go on. I'm going to make a complete fool of myself" *and* go buy things, if that meant you were now free to shop? Don't answer. Just sit with the question. And would it be okay if we went and bought something while you considered the answer?

**Explanation:** This is a move in which acceptance and defusion lead quickly to yet another commitment—a small one, but one that is very likely linked to values. The request to have a question without an answer is a defusion exercise.

## COMPETENCY 3

### Sample 7.7a

*Therapist:* I know you are frustrated right now and want to jump to make big changes. But we're not here to win a race. What's more important is making small, consistent steps in that direction, rather than huge heroic leaps. Those don't tend to last. What I'd suggest is that we develop some goals that may seem a bit easier and also would take you in the direction of eventually making a call like that to your daughter. Do you have any ideas for some steps? If not, I could suggest a couple.

**Explanation:** Without blaming or shaming the client or questioning the importance of the value to the client, the therapist simply backs off the size of the commitment and keeps it connected to the client's values. The size of the step is not important; rather, the focus is on getting the pattern started.

### Sample 7.7b

*Therapist:* I can hear the urgency in your voice, indicating how badly you want to change how you've been with your daughter. You really want to leap into this, with guns blazing! I think maybe we can use that energy to our advantage, but also we need to keep in mind the long-term picture here. My sense is that if you really want to make some changes here, it's going to take time. Yes?

*Client:* Yeah.

*Therapist:* So we can be pretty sure that your daughter isn't going to respond the way you would like right away, and that the relationship is only going to change if you're consistent in acting on your value over a good bit of time. To do this, it's probably going to be important to keep your eye on how *you* want to be with your daughter and let go of how you think *she* should respond, at least for now. In coming up with a longer term strategy, we'll need to consider a number of goals you might want to have, in addition to phoning her and making this commitment to her. Some of these goals may even seem easier than phoning her. That seems like a pretty big step right now. I wonder, would you be willing to brainstorm about other actions you could take that would lead you in the direction of having a better relationship with your daughter?

**Explanation:** The client seems to be a bit constricted in his selection of possible actions and goals to take him further in his valued direction. Opening him up to multiple possible goals could increase his flexibility and give him more of a sense of choice in the matter. Additionally, the therapist orients the client toward the process of living his value while simultaneously letting go of the outcome.

### Sample 7.8

**Action 1:** Ask the client to make a list of five feelings he has with respect to his daughter. Ask him to practice stating these out loud, with his wife, before making the call to his daughter: "I love you." "I feel happy to be around you." "I feel sad when I get angry and push you away," and so on.

Ask the client to do this practice while being mindful of the additional thoughts and feelings that come up, and to make room for them.

**Action 2:** Ask the client to write one paragraph about how he thinks his anger toward his daughter has affected him and her. Ask him to try to let go of any defense and to let go of any self-judgments that show up. Ask him to bring the paragraph to session the following week, so you can review it together.

**Explanation:** These actions, or subgoals, have the qualities of effective goals/actions outlined in this chapter. They are likely to be helpful in the sense that they give the client a chance to practice approaching avoided thoughts and feelings, but hopefully in a context that does not surpass his current level of willingness.

## COMPETENCY 4

**Sample 7.9a**

Therapist: Well, this is a bit tricky because, in some ways, you do know what to do. We've been spending time talking about it. The thought "Time is in my way, I am too busy" appears to keep getting in the way. So, would it be fair to say it is not knowledge about what to do that stands in your way?

Client: Yeah, that would be fair.

Therapist: So, here we are, reaching an important point in your therapy, asking what sorts of patterns you're going to build into your life by your action. What I'm wondering about is what pattern you're going to build here, with this commitment, in this very moment. Over this last week, you've strengthened an old pattern slightly—make commitment, have thoughts, break commitment. Now you have a choice. What kind of pattern do you want to build?

Client: I want to remake the commitment.

Therapist: Okay, I want us to spend some time getting back in contact with what this is about for you. Are you willing to do that?

Client: Uh-huh.

Therapist: What are you working for here?

Client: I want to learn how to have love in my life.

Therapist: Okay. But what kind of pattern gets in the way of that?

Client: I start focusing on all the things I have to do, and gradually my relationships fade away.

Therapist: Similar in some ways to this week, yes?

Client: [softly] Yeah. I don't want to continue that. I know where it leads.

Therapist: So, what are you going to do this week?

Client: I'm going to write out that ad.

Therapist: And if something comes up?

Client: I'm going to feel however I feel about it, and then write the ad.

*Therapist:*   I've got your back.

**Explanation:** The therapist sees that if the client does not recommit to this valued action, he is building a pattern of "make commitment, break commitment, give up on commitment," which is a dangerous pattern to build if one is trying to build a life in which one can keep commitments in the face of difficulty. The therapist thus points out this pattern to the client and suggests he choose to make a new pattern that includes recommitting after a broken commitment. After all, values are a choice and a direction and inherently mean recommitting to an action many, many times. Building a pattern of recommitting after a slip is a necessary pattern to have as part of our lives because we all get off track.

### Sample 7.9b

*Therapist:*   The patterns we're trying to build are big, but they are built from tiny moments. Like this one, right now. And old patterns are hard to change. But if we can get them down to the moment, we have a chance. So, what are you pulled to do right now?

*Client:*   [pause] Explain myself.

*Therapist:*   Good. That's not new. Right?

*Client:*   [pause] Right.

*Therapist:*   So that's not it. What else are you pulled to do? Right now. Take your time. Try to look for more subtle things, as well.

*Client:*   Give up. Get angry. Go to work. [pause] Cry.

*Therapist:*   Perfect. Those come easily, so they can't be it either. I'm not sure about that last one. What's inside that?

*Client:*   I want to have love in my life. I just don't think anyone really will love me. They all will reject me. It will hurt too badly.

*Therapist:*   It may hurt. And this doesn't? Which would you rather: the pain of love and loss or the pain of closing yourself off from what you most deeply desire? Slow down before you answer. You're building a pattern right now—right now in this very moment.

**Explanation:** Pattern acknowledgment, responsibility, and construction sound dry and intellectual. However, this process is anything but. It is an active, often emotional process that occurs moment by moment in the present and requires every aspect of the ACT model to enhance it.

## COMPETENCY 5

### Sample 7.10a

*Therapist:*   Yeah, this feeling of it being really disappointing is a familiar one. These thoughts are familiar too, right? "It's not worth it." "It's not that important. I was rejected again." It seems as if they're trying to protect you from something, right? It's almost as if they were saying, "Hey, buddy, we'll keep you safe, just hang out with us. Those guys are all jerks anyway." But let's check your experience. When you follow where these thoughts tell you to go, where does it lead you?

*Client:*   I don't know. To being alone.

*Therapist:* Yeah. It's not bad to think "It's not worth it." This is an old thought, yes?

*Client:* Very old.

*Therapist:* And that is great because it gives us a chance to break an old pattern, to do something new, really new.

**Explanation:** The therapist does not take the statement "It's not worth it" as a literal example of what the client would choose, given a variety of options. Rather, first the client is helped to distance a little from this thought by objectifying it, and then the therapist moves back to the original commitment.

**Sample 7.10b**

*Therapist:* Let me ask one thing: as a result of your slip, which of your chosen values has changed?

*Client:* I don't understand the question.

*Therapist:* Which of your values has changed? Which one is fundamentally different today than it was two weeks ago?

*Client:* None of them has changed.

*Therapist:* But notice that your mind is telling you that you have to stop caring about what you care about, that you can't move in the direction of what you care about. All very old stuff, yes? So, let me ask a second question: what would you have to have or what would you have to let go of in order to turn in the direction of what you value?

*Client:* I'd have to have the pain of being let down.

**Explanation:** The logical, problem-solving mind cannot help but be oriented toward avoidance. But it carries a cost: the client has to pretend he doesn't care about what he in fact cares about. A slip means he can't be sober. A rejection means he can't have relationships. The therapist is very quickly cutting through this thicket with questions that focus on the heart of the matter, as is called for by this competency.

## EXPERIENTIAL EXERCISE: COMMITTED ACTION

Please write your responses to the following questions. Give yourself time to be thoughtful and seriously consider your answers.

What would be a bold move for you to make in your life (e.g., be creative, think big, take a risk)? Choose one you are currently not doing.

What are the barriers to making that move?

Imagine what your life would look like if you were to make that move, and describe it.

Name one thing you could do today that would be about making this bold move.

See if you can do it, and describe your reactions.

## FOR MORE INFORMATION

For more information about committed action, including exercises and metaphors, see *Acceptance and Commitment Therapy*, by Hayes et al. (1999), chapter 9 (pp. 235–264).

For more exercises and worksheets on committed action to use for yourself and clients, see *Get Out of Your Mind and Into Your Life*, by Hayes and Smith (2005), chapter 13 (pp. 177–194).

# CHAPTER 8

# CONCEPTUALIZING CASES USING ACT

*There is nothing so practical as a good theory.*

—Kurt Lewin (1951, p. 151)

A recent trend, particularly among cognitive and behavior therapies, is the use of treatment manuals linked to specific diagnoses from the *Diagnostic and Statistical Manual of Mental Disorders* (DSM). Although, for research purposes, some ACT treatment manuals are specific to certain syndromes, in practice ACT favors the use of general principles of behavior, such as the six core ACT processes described in this book, to understand and explain a large variety of client presenting problems, complaints, and histories. These principles of behavior, which are linked to interventions, have been increasingly supported by research evidence.

*Case conceptualization* refers to applying these principles to a client's behavior (by "behavior" we mean everything the person does, including thinking, feeling, and overt action) and then using the understanding gleaned to guide the selection and evaluation of treatment interventions. An ACT case conceptualization leads the therapist to focus on a unique set of functional processes (i.e., the six core ACT processes and their corresponding pathologies described in chapter 1) that ACT and RFT research and theory suggest either hinder or foster psychological flexibility. ACT theory argues that when psychological flexibility is present, life experiences (i.e., what behavior theorists call *contingencies*) tend to lead to effective behavior and a life filled with value, meaning, and vitality. If that is correct, it is the job of the ACT therapist to examine the learning history and current life context of the client and think through how these are related to the functional processes that support or reduce psychological flexibility. Thus, an ACT approach to case conceptualization seeks to answer the following question: what unique factors in this client's life have given rise to his or her particular problems and led to this client's particular version of psychological inflexibility and life constriction?

In contrast with the topographically defined approach typified by the DSM, ACT's functionally based case conceptualization allows for the possibility that different interventions can be effective for sets of client problems that look similar but are actually quite different. Different interventions may be appropriate depending on a client's history and on the initiating and maintaining factors associated with that client's behaviors. Thus, the ACT approach to conceptualizing cases and selecting treatment interventions focuses on the function of client behavior, rather than on its form. Less technically stated, understanding the function of behavior means understanding where the behavior *comes from* and what that behavior is *for*, rather than what it *looks like*.

For example, a growing body of evidence (Hayes et al., 2006) suggests that most anxiety disorders are maintained, at least in part, by the same functional process: experiential avoidance. In PTSD, the client is avoiding thoughts and feelings related to a trauma; in panic disorder, the client is avoiding the experience of panic (i.e., the thoughts, feelings, and sensations that arise during a panic attack); and in OCD, the client is avoiding obsessive thoughts. Although the form of what is avoided and how it is avoided can vary a great deal from client to client, the common functional processes is experiential avoidance. In these examples, behaviors that appear different share the same function, but it is also true—as we just noted—that clients can perform behaviors that appear the same but are functionally different. For example, one client might throw a barbeque for friends to show off and avoid feelings of inferiority, while another client might throw a barbeque to express appreciation for friends and to act on the value of connection and community. Although both sets of behavior appear similar in terms of their form, one is probably an example of experiential avoidance while the other is probably maintained by positive contact with valued ends.

In the ACT approach to case conceptualization, the job of the therapist is to look beyond the particular form of what the client does and to make intelligent guesses, which are then tested in therapy, about the function of that behavior, given the client's unique life history and context. The therapist works to understand the history that gave rise to the client's behavior, why it occurs in this particular context, and what continues to maintain it. This is *functional analysis*. The functional analysis is then used to guide the therapist's interventions, rather than to provide clients with insight into the meaning of their behaviors.

# WHY CASE CONCEPTUALIZATION?

Practicing case conceptualization is useful in at least two clear ways. First, it can help you, as the therapist, to learn ACT theory in a deeper and more nuanced manner. Having a thorough understanding of the theory underlying ACT is essential for its fluid and flexible practice. Practice with ACT case conceptualization can help you see a client's behavior through a functional lens, and help you develop your theoretical understanding, which in turn helps you modify, select, and time techniques to the needs of your client.

Second, solid case conceptualization leads to a more focused, consistent, and thorough intervention. This is particularly important for complex, difficult, or multiproblem clients. These clients often push therapists to the limits of their abilities and frustrate the easy application of any exercise, metaphor, or other technique. Without a good case conceptualization linked to a practical theory, therapists tend to be erratic and unfocused in their selection of interventions. Interventions selected in this way can work at times, but if they fail, the therapist has learned little about what to try next. Case conceptualization can give you ideas about what to do when a technique falls flat. If you can assess which functional processes are most important for a particular client, you can be creative, persistent, and flexible in selecting a variety of exercises and techniques to use with that client.

Case conceptualization in this chapter is guided by what might be called a *middle-level* theory, in which we use relatively less technical language compared with what would characterize a more rigorous behavior analytic account of client behavior. This middle-level theory focuses on understanding the client's behavior in terms of the processes described in chapter 1 that either detract from (e.g., fusion, experiential avoidance) or promote (e.g., committed action, acceptance) psychological flexibility. To apply these concepts at several levels of analysis simultaneously and dynamically is the goal. The *micro-level* theory of case conceptualization, on the other hand, is directed at understanding client behavior using operant and classical learning principles or relational framing. Research on this micro level of analysis is well underway in the ACT/RFT community. Fortunately, for our purposes in this book, middle-level theory is enough, and we emphasize it here because of its relative accessibility.

The case conceptualization process described in this book is not intended to take the place of more general assessment considerations, such as assessment of mental status, physical health, family functioning, developmental history, and the like. You may find clients for whom ACT processes are not central. For example, a child with problems stemming primarily from a deficit in reading skills that do not involve experiential avoidance or cognitive fusion would be more appropriately treated with an intervention that directly addresses those deficits.

When conducting a case conceptualization, in addition to formally recording the specifics determined by assessment, your job is to generate a number of hypotheses. We recommend holding these lightly so you can be open to having them disproved as you work with the client. It is important to be open to letting go of hypotheses that do not hold up.

The remainder of this chapter is aimed at helping you think about your cases in ACT terms. We guide you through a process of analyzing client behavior using the ACT theory of human suffering, and using this analysis to develop tailored interventions based on the six core ACT processes outlined in chapters 1 through 7. We also guide you to consider other interventions that can fit into an ACT framework even though they lie outside the six ACT processes.

# OUTLINE OF ACT CASE CONCEPTUALIZATION PROCESS

This section provides an outline of a concrete process you can follow to conduct an ACT case conceptualization. Although fairly time consuming initially, we encourage you to stick with it and complete the practice exercises in this chapter. Repeated, intentional case conceptualization will help you deepen and expand your understanding of ACT theory and increase the flexibility and fluidity of your interventions. With practice, you will find it easier and quicker to see the applicability of ACT and the functions of client behavior. At first, it can take up to a couple hours to conduct a case conceptualization using this outline, but eventually it should take a half hour or less to go through the whole process.

We outline a ten-component process for conducting an ACT case conceptualization. This outline was significantly influenced by the chapter on case conceptualization by Hayes, Strosahl, Luoma, Varray, & Wilson (2005), and you may find it useful to reference that chapter for additional guidance. We also provide brief introductions to the therapeutic interventions related to the components assessed.

## 1. Begin Your Assessment with the Presenting Problem, as Understood by the Client

Explore the client's conceptualization of the problem that brings him or her into therapy. How does the client see his or her problem at the present time? What does the client think he or she needs to do to make things better? What are the client's goals for therapy and for life?

One assumption that guides early work in ACT is how what the client has been doing to solve the problem is typically part of the problem. The therapist's job here is to draw out the verbal system that has the client stuck in the presenting problem. When collecting this data, do your best to take an open, non-judgmental stance and to avoid buying into or challenging the initial formulation presented by the client. The key to this step is being able to understand the client's formulation of the problem and then being able to reformulate it in ACT-consistent terms.

Clients usually describe a range of goals for therapy, some of which can be considered outcome goals and some of which can be considered process goals. In an ACT formulation, outcome goals refer to desired end states linked to the client's values and can include having a better relationship with a partner, engaging work, being a supportive and loving parent, living with integrity, developing close and fun friendships, and developing spiritually. Process goals are goals that are linked to outcome goals, in the sense that the client thinks attaining the process goals will make it possible to achieve the outcome goals. Process goals often include reducing anxiety (e.g., "I need to be less anxious so I can meet new people"); being less critical (e.g., "In order for me to be close to people, I need to stop comparing myself to them"); having less pain (e.g., "I can't do the things I used to because it's too painful"); and feeling less depressed (e.g., "I don't really care about anything anymore"). ACT assumes that much of the client's problem lies in the linkage between the process goals and the outcome goals. ACT therapists often challenge this linkage during therapy.

The final part of this step is to reformulate the client's version of the presenting problem in an ACT-consistent way, if necessary. ACT formulations usually focus on helping clients live better and *feel* better (i.e., get better at *feeling*), while reducing the emphasis on feeling *good*. At a deeper level, this reformulation needs to be consistent with the client's most cherished life goals and values (the outcome goals) and be detailed enough to create a treatment contract focused on the initial goals and methods of treatment. Clients typically identify negative feelings, thoughts, memories, or sensations (e.g., depression) as the problem. Often, this problem is fundamentally reformulated during therapy. For example, a client may come into therapy complaining, "I just don't care about anything anymore. I can't stand feeling so lifeless. It's hopeless." Eventually, this statement might be reformulated as "undermines close relationships and work commitments in order to avoid feelings of rejection and failure." Another client may come with the presenting complaint of "I want help feeling better about myself. I need to have higher self-esteem." An ACT case conceptualization in this case might be "fusing with negative evaluations of self, and in the process missing out on opportunities that life offers" (i.e., the problem is the struggle itself). Additional information relevant to this step of the conceptualization can be found in chapter 4.

## 2. Discover the Most Central Thoughts, Feelings, Memories, Sensations, and Situations the Client Is Fused With or Is Avoiding

The most central and difficult private experiences are often identified by clients as part of the presenting problem. In some cases, the therapist has to dig to discover them. This often can be accomplished by getting descriptions of the presenting complaint in fairly concrete terms. For example, the therapist might ask, "What do you mean when you say you are anxious?" or "Can you give me some examples?" General, open-ended questions can invite additional information; for instance, "If I were on the inside of your head, what would I be hearing in that situation?" It can help to ask about specific dimensions, such as, "Do these issues show up in your bodily sensations at all?"

Fusion with thoughts often can be seen in clients' evaluations of themselves, their experiences, or their situations. This form of fusion can be a bit tricky to detect in the sense that the fused evaluation is generally not presented as a thought, but rather as an implicit characteristic of the event being described (e.g., "I have really bad anxiety"). If the client externalizes or chronically avoids, the psychologically active features of the situation may be vague. For example, a client who has avoided calling a friend to ask that person to do something because the friend saying no would mean the client is a "loser" may initially present the issue as if the problem were the avoidance of calling. Thus, if a client avoids particular physical situations, the therapist should attempt to discover the particular feelings, thoughts, or other experiences that show up during the event and that may be difficult for the client. Usually, this is what the client is avoiding, not the situation itself.

The purpose of recording the content of the avoided thoughts and feelings is not to change or modify them, but rather to make them available for use later in treatment as the target of experiential exercises focusing on acceptance and defusion.

## 3. Consider Behaviors That Function as Experiential Avoidance of the Events Described in the Previous Step

Usually, both the therapist and client need to develop a better ability to track the particular patterns of behaviors the client uses to avoid difficult internal experiences, such as thoughts, feelings, memories, and sensations. Experiential avoidance can take many forms, including overt behavior, internal verbal behavior, or combinations of the two. Sometimes the therapist can see these patterns directly, and at other times has to rely on the client's report.

Three types of avoidance, and examples of each, that you may see are:

*Internal avoidance behaviors:* distraction, excessive worry, dissociation, telling oneself to think differently, daydreaming

*Overt emotional control behaviors:* drinking, drugs, self-injury, thrill-seeking, gambling, overeating, avoiding physical situations or physical reminders

*In-session avoidance behaviors:* topic changes, argumentativeness, aggressiveness, dropping out of therapy, coming late to sessions, always having an acute crisis that demands attention, laughing, focusing exclusively on the positive

Sometimes these behaviors are not apparent at the start of therapy. Nevertheless, it can be helpful to guess about their function so they can be addressed in a proactive way in therapy. For example, imagine you discovered that a client has the tendency to flee relationships when beginning to feel threatened by intimacy. In order to avert dropout risk, you could have a conversation at the start of therapy in which you predicted the appeal of dropout as an experiential avoidance process, and talk about what the client could do instead of leaving therapy, should this arise.

Finally, assess how pervasive experiential avoidance is in the client's life. Is it a major controlling variable for behavior across most domains of the client's life or only restricted to some? Or is the client's life consumed by experiential avoidance, so that almost everything the client does is tied to it?

## 4. Consider Domains in Which Behavior Is Excessively Narrowed or Constricted, or in Which Living Is Avoided Altogether

The key goal of ACT is much broader than simply helping clients respond more effectively to unpleasant emotional or cognitive states. ACT is fundamentally about helping clients create full, meaningful, vital lives. Thus, in the case conceptualization, the therapist wants to investigate a broad range of domains in the client's life (e.g., family, health, relationships, spirituality, and work) to get an overview of the client's functioning in these important domains.

When people respond with avoidance and fusion, behavior tends to become excessively rigid and narrow, resulting in a lack of flexibility. Behavior that is not working can continue to persist; conversely, in areas in which persistence is needed, behavior can change impulsively. It is common for clients to adjust to these patterns of living so thoroughly they no longer notice them clearly; in this case, the therapist may have to work to see them. At one extreme, clients completely drop out of some or all valued life domains. Alternatively, engagement is excessively narrowed, inflexible, or inconsistent. Engagement with a domain in a defended manner can result in limited expression, effectiveness, or vitality. These actions exist on a continuum, so it is important not to miss subtle forms of the same processes. For example, both of the following examples could be maintained by avoidance of vulnerability: one client cuts off any sort of interaction with potential romantic partners, whereas another client engages with her partner in a superficial or limited manner.

Focus on the most important areas of a client's life, particularly those areas from which the client has dropped out or in which he or she experiences a lack of engagement, choice, or vitality. On the case conceptualization form, begin by writing about the two or three domains in which the client's behavior is most narrow and inflexible and in which this constriction appears to result in ongoing suffering. As a therapist, you are most likely to have leverage for client behavior change in these domains. Consider such domains as family, couple, parenting, friend and social relationships; work; education; recreation; spirituality; community; and physical self-care. Describe how behavior is limited or constricted in each domain, if applicable.

One way to assess these domains is to ask clients about what they would be engaging in if their problems were solved. If appropriate (e.g., when working with clients whose issues are relatively less chronic), ask what life was like before the problem appeared. What was the client doing with his or her time? What were the qualities of the client's relationships, work, play, or other relevant domains? The therapist can ask, "If a miracle happened and all your problems were solved, what would your life be like?"

## 5. Consider Other Core ACT Processes That Contribute to Psychological Inflexibility and Their Treatment Implications

Behavior patterns that occur at a particularly high rate, are invariant, are consistent across situations, or that have all these qualities, often involve psychological inflexibility. You have already spent significant time analyzing the process of experiential avoidance in the previous sections. Here we guide you through reviewing a client's behavior in the five other pathological processes (cognitive fusion; dominance of the conceptualized past and future, and limited self-knowledge; attachment to the conceptualized self; lack of values clarity/contact; and inaction, impulsivity, or avoidant persistence) and guide your emphasis and sequencing of the six ACT processes as a whole.

To complete this section, review each of the five processes described and consider whether the client exhibits notably rigid and inflexible patterns of behavior relating to that process. Although every client probably exhibits some behaviors relevant to each of these processes, the therapist's job is to recognize behavior patterns that are particularly strong for the client and that can have important implications for treatment planning. A client may exhibit only one particularly strong pattern or rigid and inflexible behavior, but that behavior can result from several of the processes. On the assessment form, record the client patterns that are particularly strong as well as their treatment implications.

This section has the potential of coming across as a cookbook approach linking behavioral patterns with interventions. We do not intend this material to be used as a cookbook; rather, we wish to provide some concrete guidelines to help those who are relatively new to ACT move toward more functional ways of thinking. Ultimately, the functional analysis of clients, based on a solid understanding of theory, is the foundation of case conceptualization.

## COGNITIVE FUSION

Cognitive fusion refers to the tendency of us as human beings to get caught up in the content of what we are thinking. Cognitive fusion tends to support experiential avoidance. We don't just avoid uncomfortable thoughts, emotions, sensations, and memories—we constantly talk to ourselves about this process. We create stories about why this is necessary (reason giving) and explain, justify, and link our actions to these reasons. Sometimes we develop plans and goals that incorporate experiential avoidance as a focus. We can get so caught up in this world as conceptualized that we miss our experience as lived right now and miss the opportunities the present situation affords. This is the essence of cognitive fusion.

Cognitive fusion can be seen in clients who come to therapy with *a strong belief that unworkable control strategies will eventually work* or who *continue to engage in unworkable strategies even while aware they are not working*. If you see this, it is usually important to address it early in therapy through creative hopelessness interventions targeted at undermining the client's strong belief or conviction in the ultimate workability of these strategies. When doing creative hopelessness work, it is important to avoid arguing directly with the belief, but rather repeatedly help clients examine what their experience has to say about the workability of their current behavior versus what their mind has to say. Behavioral experiments designed to examine the workability of psychological struggle and control can be useful in this regard.

Another highly fused pattern occurs when clients are attached to *highly logical or rigid thinking patterns*. For some clients, this can take the form of a strong attachment to being right, even at significant personal cost. Other versions include clients who engage in a great deal of reason giving for their behaviors or who overfocus on understanding or insight. Some clients tend toward overconfidence in their evaluation of themselves, others, or situations. They may hold rigid expectations of themselves and others, despite the unworkability of these expectations. The primary interventions for this pattern of behavior include a strong focus on confronting reason giving through defusion strategies, and helping clients examine the cost to their vitality and life direction when they are focused on being right. Work on self-as-context and mindfulness exercises can also help to reduce attachment to thoughts and the conceptualized self.

## DOMINANCE OF CONCEPTUALIZED PAST AND FUTURE; LIMITED SELF-KNOWLEDGE

Fusion, avoidance, and attachment to self as content tend to pull us out of the moment and away from our direct experience. This can result in a lack of fluid self-knowledge or self-awareness or a limited ability to notice and to describe the present or what we are thinking, feeling, remembering, and sensing in the moment. Instead, the conceptualized past or future tends to dominate over the present. Two types of patterns exemplify these issues and are described in the following paragraphs.

Clients can *poorly track their ongoing, moment-to-moment experience*. Clients can be generally unaware of what they are thinking, feeling, or sensing in the moment and lack the ability to put words to these experiences. This can take the form of an alexithymic client who expresses not having feelings, or a client who responds to all questions about what he or she is feeling by saying, "I'm stressed." Clients can find it difficult to accurately describe their current experience and may provide socially acceptable but hollow answers unrelated to current experience or current events in therapy. This can also show up in therapy when therapists believe they have observed an emotional reaction from the client, but when the client is queried, he or she is unable to describe feeling anything. Such clients also tend to stay at a rather conceptual level in therapy and rarely use emotional terms, particularly in response to current experience.

Another way this kind of process presents itself is in a narrowness of focus, which results in inattention to the range of events in the environment. Clients who do this may not notice if the therapist has a new hair color or if the office has changed, or they may ask the therapist to repeat things frequently. Exercises targeted at contact with the present moment, including simply observing and describing current experiences in a relatively safe context, are particularly important for these clients. When a client cannot quickly describe an emotional reaction he or she seems to be having, you can ask for permission to take a closer look at his or her present experience through a gestalt-type exercise. In this type of exercise, you ask the client to shut his or her eyes for a few moments and then guide the client through a process of exploring and describing bodily sensations, emotions, and thoughts from a posture of acceptance and willingness. You can also use exercises designed to increase regular contact with the present moment (e.g., daily mindfulness practice). Exercises to increase mindfulness during situations in which the client is trying something new or experiencing a difficulty can also be useful; these include diaries or worksheets to track private experiences and struggle in the moment, as well as in-session experiments in which difficult private events are brought into the room while the client watches how he or she reacts to them.

Clients can be *excessively caught up in the conceptualized past or future*. This pattern is often seen in clients who have pervasive worry, anticipatory fear, resentments, or regret that functions to block constructive behavior. In session, this can be exhibited in a tendency toward lifeless storytelling or seemingly endless repetition of ruminative thinking. For clients with this pattern of behavior, extensive work is needed to practice contact with the present moment, in and out of session. The therapist may need to frequently interrupt the client (after a discussion about why this is important) and bring him or her back to what is happening in the moment. Brief mindfulness exercises that help clients be more aware of their present moment experience can be useful both at the start of and throughout sessions. Also important is the development of a sense of self as an ever-present observer (i.e., self as context) so that temporal thoughts can be observed without belief or disagreement. Consider identifying feared, evocative content at the end of the "worry chain," or identifying uncomfortable past memories linked to regret, and then conduct imaginal or in vivo exposure or willingness exercises, using these scenes or related stimuli in combination with a focus on values.

## ATTACHMENT TO THE CONCEPTUALIZED SELF

The conceptualized self consists of our autobiographical stories and evaluations of ourselves, which we use to justify and explain our behavior. As humans, we generally try to live up to our own and others' view of ourselves, even to our own detriment. As a result of fusion, we can even be drawn into defending our conceptualized self as if it were our physical self. This can lead to rigidity in behavior and trap us into patterns of living that are limiting and unworkable. In this section, the therapist's job is to consider whether the client is strongly attached to any stories or self-evaluations that, if not addressed, can interfere with the client's flexibility in bringing personal values to life.

Attachment to the conceptualized self can be seen in clients who are *strongly identified with a particular way of viewing themselves*. For example, a client can be very attached to a description such as "I'm cheerful … peppy. I bounce back." Although seemingly a positive self-assessment, this conceptualization can be a problem if the client distorts or interprets events so they are consistent with this conceptualization, rather than openly acknowledging and directly addressing situations in which the client did not act cheerful or bounce back. Alternatively, a client can be wedded to a self-concept of "broken, defective, and weak" and can defend this conceptualization and the story that supports it, despite its superficially negative form. A considerable amount of self-as-context and defusion work may be needed to address this type of attachment to the conceptualized self. In particular, the therapist needs to work on differentiating primary, directly observed qualities of events (descriptions) from secondary, verbally derived qualities of events (evaluations). The client can be asked to take on or act out different roles or self-concepts for periods of time to gain flexibility in trying on different types of self-evaluation and to experience their effects on behavior.

Clients with chronic, long-standing, pervasive problems and clients with extensive trauma histories often come to therapy with a *strong belief that they cannot change, or that a better life is not possible for them, combined with a strong attachment to a life story that supports this belief.* This can be combined with an identity that is defined in simplistic or black-and-white terms (e.g., "I'm weak" or "I'm evil" or "I'm broken"). It can also appear as a victim stance that manifests in frequently blaming others for the client's actions. Particularly important for such clients is defusion and self-as-context work targeted at undermining attachment to the client's life story. Although not directly challenging the story's content, the therapist can help the client examine the cost of following the story (e.g., in terms of the chance to live fully) and determine if he or she wants to continue this pattern. Often it is useful to focus on the cost of "not trying" in terms of life goals and valued directions. Consider autobiographical rewrite exercises (Strosahl et al., 2004). Also, conduct behavioral experiments to see whether even small changes could occur. The therapist may want to consider introducing issues related to forgiveness and victimization later in therapy (Hayes et al., 1999, pp. 257–258).

## LACK OF VALUES CLARITY/CONTACT

Experiential avoidance, reason giving, and fusion can increasingly dominate a client's behavior so that short-term goals, such as feeling good, being right, and defending a conceptualized self, dominate over behavior oriented toward long-term desired qualities of life (i.e., values). Clients' time and energy can become increasingly oriented toward relief from psychological pain, resulting in a loss of contact with what they want in life (if they had developed this capacity in the first place). As an ACT therapist might say, "You trade control of your life for control of your feelings."

Clients can be *unable to describe wants, goals, or values that are not heavily socially determined or influenced by the presence of the therapist or other major figures in their lives.* In ACT terms, the client's behavior is dominated by *pliance*; in other words, by following social rules because of a history of being reinforced for rule following. These clients often present as motivated to be a good girl or good boy. Behavior is oriented largely toward shoulds and "looking good," and clients tend to look for the right answer to the therapist's questions. Clients with this pattern can exhibit "problems with self" in the sense that they feel their behaviors (and even perceptions) are heavily influenced by the presence of others. What they want can also be drastically influenced by the person to whom they are currently responding. In conducting values clarification with these clients, therapists usually need to closely track their own behaviors and do their best to remove cues that could tell the client what is the right thing to do or the best value to have. It may be necessary to help the client gradually build the ability to contact and describe his or her own needs, wants, and desires.

The client's behavior is *so dominated by escape and avoidance that he or she is unable to articulate goals and values for his or her life that are heartfelt or meaningful.* Alternately, the client can describe *tightly held but unexamined goals (e.g., being popular or making money) as if they were values.* These two patterns are often seen in clients with chronic pain, chronic suicidal tendencies, or substance abuse. To the extent that a client's behavior is tied up in experiential avoidance, the client will have a hard time saying what he or she really wants in life because to do so produces a sense of vulnerability. Additional work and attention may be needed to develop values that are solid and strongly felt by the client. Here, it is important to do considerable work on values clarification and contrast the client's current life direction with valued life directions and goals. You can help the client examine life losses due to engaging in behaviors that are only rewarding in the short term. The key issue is to bring values forward in time so they can be more present for the client in avoidance situations and so that longer term desired qualities can exert greater control over the client's behavior. Creative hopelessness exercises should focus on what experiential control attempts have cost the client in terms of long-term life direction and vitality.

## INACTION, IMPULSIVITY, OR AVOIDANT PERSISTENCE

Because of experiential avoidance and its amplification through these other processes, clients develop larger and larger patterns of action that are detached from their long-term goals and life desires. Behavior is oriented toward getting through, getting by, or surviving the moment (i.e., avoidant persistence), rather than toward building a life that would be more rewarding, satisfying, meaningful, or workable in the long run. Clients' behavioral repertoires narrow and become less sensitive to learning opportunities and to the possibility of putting their values into action in the here and now.

The client may *live a life that is relatively free of the acute experience of pain, but also relatively narrow and unsatisfying.* This pattern is often seen in clients who feel stuck in unsatisfying jobs or relationships for fear of the unknown or of the consequences of change, and in clients who have chronic physical pain. It is important to educate clients with this pattern about the qualities of committed action, such as holding goals lightly, and to focus on the process of living rather than on the outcome of actions. It can also be important to focus on the idea of willingness as a whole action. Teaching clients the distinction between choice and decision can help free them up to make new choices rather than continuing to live out old stories. When clients are engaged in novel actions, therapists can help them focus on developing a mindful, nonjudgmental, compassionate, and accepting stance toward themselves in those situations.

The client may *engage in impulsive or self-defeating behavior.* Avoidance behaviors result in powerful short-term reinforcement that overshadows behavior that is ultimately more workable, but also more painful in the short run. This can show up as chronic self-control problems, such as impulsivity, substance use, aggression, or risky or self-injurious behavior. Clients can have problems with the ability to delay gratification or an extremely low tolerance of difficult emotional experiences. Impulsive clients tend to lack practice engaging in "plan-full," step-by-step patterns of action, as seen in procrastination, underperformance, poor health behaviors, and difficulty completing homework in therapy, for example. In addition to other ACT strategies, when the client begins engaging in committed action, the therapist can start small and reinforce the client for being willing to commit to something and for following through, no matter how small those actions may seem. At times when the client is engaging in valued behaviors, impulsive behaviors, or inflexible behaviors, the therapist should focus on contact with the present moment, acceptance, and defusion; this can help the client develop greater flexibility to persist or to change, as required by the situation.

# 6. Consider Factors That Can Limit Motivation for Change

As you examine the various processes discussed so far in this chapter, you need to consider your clients' motivation to change. For example, a client can be out of contact with the cost of experiential avoidance, especially if values are unclear, but experiential contact with the cost of avoidance is essential before doing acceptance or exposure work that requires significant motivation. In this situation, it can be helpful to begin therapy with a heavier than usual focus on values clarification and then to examine the discrepancy between current behavior and hoped-for directions and life goals. It also can be helpful to link work that requires significant motivation to valued goals and relationships; for example, by asking, "If feeling anxious could make it possible for you to be the kind of teacher you really want to be, would you be willing to feel anxious?"

Research has shown that the therapeutic relationship is a powerful motivator to change. In the ACT model, relationships are built using ACT processes (see chapter 9). In assessing the quality of the therapist-client relationship, you should look for signs that the client is present, caring, and engaged. Signs that the client feels coerced or misunderstood are also important. If problems exist, check the integrity of the therapeutic contract. Are you and the client working toward agreed-upon goals or is there a mismatch between your goals and the client's goals? Consider your level of commitment to the client. Are you lacking investment or are you distracted with this client? Also examine whether the client is triggering emotions or thoughts that are difficult for you—for example, if you are engaging in avoidance and undermining the relationship yourself. Decide on an action plan that addresses your own reactions (e.g., consultation).

Another kind of motivational problem occurs when clients are strongly attached to fears about the consequences of confronting feared events. This can suggest the need for a greater focus on defusion and self as context prior to any work that involves significant contact with feared events. Be sure to titrate exposure or willingness exercises to a level the client is willing to experience fully and without defense. Small steps with 100 percent willingness are much better than "white knuckling" through larger steps.

In general, the greatest factor limiting motivation to change is the lack of direct contact with present values. People learn not to be motivated as a form of defense: it hurts to care. Thus, in a sense, the entire ACT model is relevant to this one limiting factor.

## 7. Consider the Client's Social and Physical Environment and Its Influence on the Client's Ability to Change

Clients do not live in a vacuum, and you need to know whether some of the same ACT-relevant processes that apply to the individual level can be played out at the social level or even physical level. Reinforcement for engaging in behaviors that promote the status quo can occur at financial, social, familial, and institutional levels. For example, a client can be motivated to stay stuck in order to keep disability payments, a spouse can be unsupportive because the client's change is difficult or challenging to him or her, or an addicted client can be without any sober friends. A spouse can be so terrified of real intimacy that the client is encouraged to pretend everything is fine, even if it means not knowing his or her own feelings. Thus, you need to consider how the social and physical environment bears on the case. If possible, consider direct interventions that could change the environment (e.g., couples therapy with an unsupportive or fearful spouse, referral to support or therapy groups). Also consider early values clarification to examine the cost of not changing in terms of the client's larger life goals.

## 8. Examine Client Strengths That Could Be Harnessed to Build Psychological Flexibility

The therapist can examine how a client might have engaged with life difficulties in the past in ACT-consistent ways. Sometimes these experiences can be used to catalyze rapid change in therapy. Past experiences of acceptance, mindfulness, and committed action can serve as metaphors for how the client could behave in the current situation. By drawing parallels between the current struggle and a struggle the client previously overcame, useful action tendencies and perspectives from the past event can be transferred to the new one. If a client has had experience with mindfulness, 12-step, spirituality, or human potential concepts that appear positive from an ACT perspective, you can explicitly link new experiences to these former ones. For example, if the client practiced letting go of struggle with uncontrollable thoughts, memories, or feelings in the past and had positive results, or if the client was able to have a healthy sense of humor or irony regarding a life difficulty, you can bring these past experiences to bear on the current situation in a helpful way.

Sometimes past behavior can serve as a template for currently needed change, and effective behavior in one domain can serve as a template for effective behavior in a domain in which the current behavior is not as effective. For example, a client can have facility with acceptance or mindfulness, or with setting step-by-step goals and following through on them in one domain of living (e.g., work) but not in another (e.g., relationships). The area in which this skill is strong can serve as a template for action in the domain in which movement is lacking. Or a client can have a prior experience in which he or she set out in one direction and then changed toward another more rewarding direction. Such experiences can be used as models for acceptance, flexibility, and persistence in a valued direction. The client can be asked to recall how the initial change inspired fear and uncertainty and how, with time and practice, he or she developed competency in the new direction.

# 9. Describe a Comprehensive Treatment Plan

After completing steps 1 through 8, you should have the information you need to develop an ACT-consistent treatment plan. Although most treatment plans include all six ACT processes in some fashion, the level of emphasis on each process can vary according to your case conceptualization. As you complete this section, we recommend reviewing steps 1 through 8 of the case conceptualization, and in particular the treatment implications you generated. With this information in mind, consider how much the treatment should focus on each of the following:

- ✓ Confronting the system and creative hopelessness (e.g., if the client continues to persevere in the unworkable change agenda)

- ✓ Developing knowledge and direct experience with emotional control as the problem, and practicing willingness (e.g., if the client does not experientially understand the paradoxical effects of control; if the client's life goals are blocked by experiential avoidance)

- ✓ Developing and practicing cognitive defusion (e.g., if the client is fused with the content of his or her own thought, caught up in evaluation, or trapped by reason giving; if the client needs experience with private events as nondestructive)

- ✓ Generating experiences of self as context (e.g., if the client is unable to separate self from thoughts, feelings, memories, sensations, stories, and self as conceptualized; if the client needs a safe place from which to engage in exposure)

- ✓ Making contact with the present moment, mindfulness (e.g., if the client lives in the conceptualized future; if the client is not learning from contingencies present in his or her environment)

- ✓ Exploring values (e.g., if the client is unable to articulate a set of stated values or has little guidance for behavior outside of fusion and avoidance; if the client has little motivation to engage in exposure)

- ✓ Engaging in committed action based on chosen values (e.g., if the client needs help developing consistent patterns of behaving in line with his or her chosen values)

As part of your treatment plan, you may want to include all or some of the following types of resources:

- ✓ Find and adapt a specific, relevant treatment manual that has been shown to be effective with this type of client (see www.contextualpsychology.org/treatment_protocols or various ACT books).

- ✓ Obtain ACT process and outcome measures and determine which are relevant (see www .contextualpsychology.org/act-specific_measures).

- ✓ Identify social (e.g., family therapy, couples therapy, spiritual guides/ministers, mentors/ advisors, support groups); financial; and vocational (e.g., training or educational) resources available for use during treatment.

- ✓ Refer to other compatible techniques and theories that may be relevant but not be obviously theorized about in ACT (e.g., contingency management, cue exposure, education).

- ✓ Determine if the client has life skill deficits; if so, consider direct, first-order change or education efforts (e.g., social skills, time management skills, study skills, assertiveness skills, parenting skills, problem-solving skills training).

## 10. Reevaluate the Conceptualization Throughout Treatment; Revise Functional Analysis, Targets, and Interventions

Case conceptualization is not a process that ends after the formal assessment has been completed. Rather, ongoing assessment and reevaluation of treatment targets and conceptualization need to occur throughout treatment, and at times must occur moment to moment. Thus, we include a tenth step: constantly reevaluate.

# SAMPLE CASE CONCEPTUALIZATION

In this section, we present some introductory information about a client; a section from the transcript of the first session, with comments by the therapist; and a model case conceptualization based on this information. We have intentionally chosen a relatively complex case in order to illustrate some of the subtleties in the ACT model.

## Sample Case: Alfonso

Alfonso is a twenty-six-year-old divorced Latino male on disability related to back pain and chronic depression resulting from an injury that occurred at his construction job three years ago. Alfonso was referred by the therapist from a chronic pain group who said Alfonso had a hard time connecting with other group members, frequently appeared angry in group, and often stated that others were misunderstanding him. The therapist referral stated that Alfonso seemed quite rigid and inflexible in his thinking and unwilling to entertain others' ideas or opinions. When he arrived to session, his left arm was noticeably emaciated and hung limply at his side. The following dialogue occurred in the first session.

# TRANSCRIPT 8.1

**Commentary**

*Therapist:* So, what brings you in to see me today?

*Client:* I'm depressed. I was told you might be able to help. [stares at the therapist]

*Therapist:* I hope so, but first can you tell me a little more about your depression—like how long you've been depressed and why you think you are depressed?

*Client:* Well, I've been having a hard time of it ever since I hurt my back on the job three years ago. I think I'm just down because I can't work anymore. I was really good at what I did, and now I'm useless because of my damn arm and the pain in my back.

The client's statement "I'm useless" suggests fusion to self as content in his work identity.

*Therapist:* Your arm and your back? Did that happen because of the injury?

*Client:* No ... Only my back was injured. I've had about four surgeries to try to fix it. I've spent maybe ... ten months of the past three years in the hospital. The first three surgeries worked pretty well, but I was still having some problems. So they did one more. It was supposed to be the last one, but the damn doctor screwed it up and damaged the nerve that goes to my arm. Now I can barely use it.

One might begin to wonder if the client is ruminating about how the surgeon "screwed up" his arm, and if this fusion is keeping him from moving forward. Issues of right and wrong may be present and feeding fusion.

*Therapist:* How much use do you have?

*Client:* Well, I can lift it up about a foot. [demonstrates] They told me it was hopeless and I'd never get any movement back, but I knew I could. I've been working out in the pool almost every day, and I've gotten to the point where I can close my hand and lift my arm to my shoulder when I'm in the pool. It's taken a lot of work, but I made it happen. I'm the kind of person who, when I set my mind to doing something, I get it done. [grins] Like with the pain from this injury—I don't use any drugs. I control it with self-hypnosis ... Works pretty good to keep the pain manageable. But it doesn't matter, anyway, because I can't do anything because of my back and arm ... Now I'm like a piece of crap, I'm just worthless. I don't know why I even try.

His ability to exercise regularly suggests strength in being able to make and keep commitments, which could be useful in therapy.

"I get it done" suggests possible fusion with self as someone who doesn't fail, but could also be a strength.

He's using hypnosis as a control method; will need to assess the workability of this solution, although it seems relatively innocuous at this point.

"I'm a piece of crap" and "I'm worthless"— fusion probably is occurring with these evaluations.

*Therapist:* When I hear you say you can't do much of anything, what I hear you saying is that you can't do anything important. If you're not doing anything important, what are you doing with your time?

The therapist is stepping around some fusion and drawing the client's attention to the valuing process ongoing in the client's behavior.

*Client:* Well, I have a schedule I follow pretty much every day. I've always been really disciplined. I get up, I do my self-hypnosis, I eat breakfast, I watch a little TV. I get ready and go to the pool and work out. By the time that's done, I'm tired and I come back home, take a nap, fix some dinner, watch some TV, and go to bed. A lot of nights, I also talk to my son. That's about it. I'm a loser, huh?

*Therapist:* That thought, "I'm a loser," has been around for a while, huh?

*Client:* Yeah.

*Therapist:* Is that one of the things you say to yourself when you're feeling down?

*Client:* Yeah.

*Therapist:* What other things do you say to yourself?

*Client:* Hmm. That my life is ruined ... That the bastard doctor did it. I think a lot about how he screwed up that surgery ... I think about my son.

*Therapist:* You think about your son?

*Client:* Yeah, Casey is six. He's the greatest. He stays with my parents a few hours away. They take care of him because I can't anymore. I need my time to take care of my arm, and I can't take care of him anyway in the physical shape I'm in. I used to be able to help him put his shirt on in the morning, but I can't even do that right anymore. With my arm and all ... If I can't do that, how can I do what I need to be a father?

*Therapist:* How do you feel about not taking care of him?

*Client:* [sighs] I'm okay with it. I wish I could take care of him, but I just can't. He's better off with my parents. Ever since Casey's mother and I broke up, it's been just him and me. His mom's an addict and took off when we separated. I haven't talked to her in a year.

*Therapist:* Do you get to visit him much?

*Client:* No, he lives too far away. But I talk to him most nights on the phone. That helps ... I'm not so sure about my parents taking care of him, but I don't have much of a choice. I can't do it the way I should.

Here we see a possible valued domain (son) that needs to be investigated.

He says he is a "loser," not "I have the thought I'm a loser" or "I sometimes think I'm a loser." This suggests fusion with evaluation and concern over the evaluation of others, and perhaps is a test of the therapist in this area.

The therapist does a defusion move with the thought "I'm a loser." Also, the therapist could use some light humor to model acceptance in the therapeutic relationship.

The client has a significant amount of time out of contact with the present and in thoughts about the physician and his son, who are not present.

The therapist is investigating a valued domain.

The client indicates avoidance in what is probably a valued domain—not taking care of his son.

Fusion is evident in "I can't take care of him anyway"; saying he can't take care of his son because he is unable to help him get dressed is a somewhat rigid, seemingly illogical statement.

The therapist is probing for the experience of pain from avoidance on a daily basis.

The client seems not to be in contact with the cost of avoidance in this domain. This could suggest a chronic pattern of avoidance.

The therapist is probing for the client's functioning in the domain of his relationship with his son; contact seems fairly limited and constricted.

Probably more fusion in his saying "I can't do it the way I should."

*Therapist:* You're not sure about your parents?

*Client:* Uh, they, uh ... they were pretty physically and mentally abusive of me as a kid. A lot of hitting, yelling ... When I was younger, I used to spend a lot of time thinking about that. I got pretty out of control around that. I was even suicidal until I figured out how to get it under control. I don't think about it much anymore ... Anyway, they've mellowed as they've gotten older and they don't hit him.

*Therapist:* You've got the memories of the abuse under control?

*Client:* Yeah, I used to think about it all the time and have nightmares and stuff. But I learned to block it all out ... We're not going to have to talk about that, are we? I don't want to. If I remember that stuff, I'll get out of control again and maybe hurt someone or myself.

*Therapist:* We don't have to talk about anything you're not willing to talk about. My intention here is to never make you do anything you're not willing to do, and if I ever do think that is something we should talk about, I will ask permission first to see if you're willing. I want this therapy to be about what you want most in your life. And so, if remembering those memories is part of that, then I'd want us to take a look at that. If they don't need to be remembered, then your experience will show you that. Either way, we'll see what your experience has to say.

*Client:* Okay, I'm okay with that. So we'll see, then?

*Therapist:* Yeah.

*Client:* So then, what do we talk about?

*Therapist:* Hmm ... It sounds as though you spend a lot of time alone. What are your friendships like?

*Client:* I don't really have any friends. Not for the last couple years. I used to hang out with some guys at work, but ever since I left, no one wants to be around me.

*Therapist:* Sounds pretty lonely.

*Client:* Yeah.

*Therapist:* What do you think about when you are home all day?

The client's statement suggests that interacting with his abusive parents (an external barrier to change) could be challenging or the parents could resist change.

The client says he experienced some success with control of painful memories in the past. The therapist needs to examine how this works: it could be okay or a problem (e.g., part of a larger pattern of avoidance).

The therapist is probing for the client's assessment of the success of this control move.

The client sees the short-term effects of this strategy as quite positive, but is clearly still experientially avoidant of abuse memories. He seems unaware of the cost to flexibility (e.g., even in these first few moments, he has to warn the therapist away). The therapist should pay attention to the other valued domains in which these memories might block action.

The therapist sets a context of acceptance and client choice in the therapeutic relationship.

The therapist sets client values as the purpose of the therapeutic relationship.

The therapist begins to define the client's values as the ultimate goal of therapy and as a higher guide than immediate comfort, and begins to link values to willingness and appeal to experience.

Good sign. Values trump avoidance, at least at the content of the talk level.

The therapist is probing for functioning in another important life domain, and situates the struggle in values, not in avoidance.

The client reports very restricted behavior in the domain of friendships. These processes need to be tracked at the social level.

The therapist probes for cost experienced on a daily basis.

*Client:* I wish my son was there … I don't know. I think a lot about my surgery and my arm. I think about getting back at that surgeon who screwed up. I think about how I can win the court case. I just can't let it go. I think about how I could just get them to do one more surgery to fix my arm. But they keep saying there's nothing they can do.

*Therapist:* Anything else you think about?

*Client:* I think about how worthless my life is now that I can't work. I try to figure out how this happened, where I went wrong. I just can't see a way out. I used to be good at what I did. That was who I was. Now I can't do it anymore. I don't do anything anymore. I don't know who I am without my work.

*Therapist:* And you feel as if the pain you are in from your back and arm is what stands between you and working? You feel it needs to change, yet you say you don't use any medication?

*Client:* Yeah, after the surgeries, I used morphine for a while, but then I got it under control with self-hypnosis a doctor taught me. I sometimes take a pill after I work out if the pain is too bad, but that's about all. I don't like to take pills at all because that would mean I can't handle it.

*Therapist:* Can't handle it?

*Client:* Yeah, you know, I'm weak. Can't take the pain.

*Therapist:* I see. And if you had to rate your usual pain level without hypnosis on a scale from one to ten?

*Client:* Seven.

*Therapist:* And with it?

*Client:* Most of the time, like a four. It's not too bad.

*Therapist:* Okay, thanks. So, let me ask you something: What do you think you need to do to have things get better? How do you imagine therapy helping you?

*Client:* I need to feel better and not so negative all the time. I'd be more motivated to work on getting my arm back in shape. I didn't used to be like this. I think if I won my court case against the doctor who screwed me, that would help.

The client expresses some cost, mainly in terms of his son.

The client describes time spent in the conceptualized past and needing to be right, not wrong.

Possible fusion is evident in the story that they need to fix his arm; the client shows attachment to physical solutions and indicates possible avoidance.

Fusion dominates. Indications of fusion include heavy evaluation, spending lots of time in the past, and mental problem solving.

The client shows more fusion with self as content, particularly in terms of his work identity.

The therapist is probing for whether the client sees pain control as a goal that needs to be accomplished before he can live. The therapist begins to draw out the system of experiential control.

The client's pill taking is contingent on his level of pain. The therapist should be careful of that control strategy because it will probably increase over time.

Conceptualized self: pain = weakness.

The client fears he is weak and "can't handle it" and could be fused with this self-concept or the opposite (i.e., that he is strong). This could create rigidity.

The therapist is trying to get a sense of the success of the client's pain control strategies.

The therapist is beginning to draw out the system the client is in, the client's goals for therapy and life, and how these are linked to valued outcomes.

The client seems fairly caught up in the experiential avoidance agenda. He again shows more right versus wrong thinking and is more in the future instead of the present.

| | |
|---|---|
| *Therapist:* Let me ask you another question. It's kind of a silly question. If you were to wake up tomorrow and a miracle could have happened—like your fairy godmother came down and granted all your wishes—what would your life look like then? | The therapist is trying to get to statements about values in addition to avoidance goals. |
| *Client:* Ah ... I don't want to think about that. I've lost too much ... [quietly] It can't happen. | The client is exhibiting in session avoidance of the pain of talking about what he wants in his life. |
| *Therapist:* Would you be willing to play with me for a minute? Just imagine. If a miracle happened, what would your life be like? | The therapist persists and tries to sidestep avoidance and not confront it directly, which probably will increase avoidance. |
| *Client:* Okay ... I wouldn't be depressed, I'd have my arm working again, and I'd be working as a carpenter again and taking care of my son ... I'd have more money ... But that can't happen. Why should I think about this? | The client expresses some mixture of process goals (not depressed, arm working, more money) and outcome goals (taking care of son, working again) with some fusion (attachment to self as carpenter). |
| *Therapist:* Yeah, it's painful to think about what you want and feel you can't have. If thinking about it in here could make it possible for you to find some new, meaningful work and have your son back, would you be willing to do it? | The therapist again ties willingness to the client's living his values in his life, and compares the value of avoidance to the value of his relationship with his son, in order to increase the salience of his values. |
| *Client:* Of course, but I don't see how it would help. | |
| *Therapist:* I don't want you to believe me. I'm not trying to make a guarantee here. I want us to see how much pain, how much hard work would be worth it, if it meant you could be living life again, not just surviving as you do now. | The therapist makes a little defusion and relationship equalizing move: "I don't want you to believe me." Then the therapist draws the client's attention back to the issue of willingness and its link to values. |

## Completed Case Conceptualization Form for Alfonso

This form is provided as a model for a comprehensive case conceptualization for Alfonso. As you read it over, you may want to refer back to the ten steps for case conceptualization outlined previously.

## 1. Presenting problem(s) in client's own words

*Client says he is depressed and needs to have his depression get better.*

Client's initial goals (What does he or she want from therapy?)

*Feel better, have more motivation to work on getting movement in his arm back*

ACT reformulation of presenting problem

*Although more assessment is needed, client is probably struggling with avoidance of sadness and fear, hopeless thoughts, self-critical thoughts, fear of more pain in the future, and continuing loss. This struggle consumes almost all of his time, to the point that few valued activities are engaged in or are even actively avoided, such as giving his son to his parents.*

## 2. What thoughts, emotions, memories, sensations, or situations is the client fused with or unwilling to experience?

Thoughts

*I'm a piece of crap, I'm worthless. I'm a loser. No one wants to be around me. I can't handle it.*

Emotions

*Possibly sadness, loss, embarrassment/shame, fear (particularly of intimacy)*

Memories

*Client has a history of extensive abuse as a child. These memories are probably avoided in some way, but this was not assessed in this session. He may avoid thinking about his son.*

Other

*Avoids, to some extent, physical pain from injury, rejection from others, work-related activities and the failure and difficulty that might go with that. At times, showed concern about therapist evaluations. Being wrong or wronged is a fear.*

## 3. What does client do to avoid these experiences?

Internal emotional control strategies (e.g., distraction, excessive rumination/worry)

*Distraction, hypnosis, rigid positive self-statements, TV watching to "zone out," oversleeping*

External emotional control strategies (e.g., drugs, self-harm, avoided situations)

*Client avoids care of his child. He avoids intimacy or friendship with just about anyone. He does not work or engage in activities headed toward working. Client avoids tasks he could only perform at reduced physical ability. Takes occasional opioid medications. Highly routinized schedule.*

In-session avoidance or emotional control patterns

*Probable dropout risk related to feeling misunderstood and angry. May also fear getting close to people. Client has shown a history of anger in group therapy and often feels others are not understanding him. Consider cultural factors that could be promoting avoidance of emotion.*

Pervasiveness of experiential avoidance:    Limited 1 2 3 ④ 5 Very extensive

## 4. Describe domains and ways in which client's behavior is narrowed and inflexible (e.g., family, couples, parenting, friends/social, work, education, recreation, spirituality, community, self-care)

*Client has dropped out of parenting, for the most part. He makes daily phone calls to his son, but is no longer caring for him. He finds this extremely painful and is fused with the idea he can't be a good father due to his disability. Client has no friends or social support and is not working to develop any. He is rigidly attached to self-concept as a carpenter and not considering other work options.*

## 5. Consider other types of psychological inflexibility and their implications (e.g., cognitive fusion; dominance of conceptualized past and future, limited self-knowledge; attachment to conceptualized self; lack of values clarity; inaction, impulsivity, or avoidant persistence)

| Core Process | Pattern | Treatment Implications |
|---|---|---|
| Cognitive fusion | Overly logical, rigid thinking; perfectionistic, self-critical (cuts out tasks can't do perfectly); attached to being right; has found control fairly effective for pain, but over-extended to other areas of life | Need stronger focus on workability of control versus what the mind has to say will happen, particularly in area of emotional control vs. pain control; more focus on defusion undermining being right |
| Dominance of c onceptualized past/future, limited self-knowledge | Attached to self as carpenter, harsh, rigid self-evaluation. | Calls for more contact with present moment work; good to use brief centering exercises, developing self as context; perhaps mindfulness meditation as practice |
| Attachment to conceptualized self | Attached to self as carpenter, harsh, rigid self-evaluation; fears evaluation of others. | Focus on self-as-context work; teach evaluation vs. description |
| Lack of values clarity | Excessively caught up in past and future; future seems certain and bleak. | Suggests early focus on values clarification and on contrast with current direction in life; particularly in domains of work and personal relationships as broadly defined |

## 6. Motivational factors (e.g., what is the cost of this behavior in terms of daily living, client's experience of unworkability, clarity of values, therapeutic relationship)

| Motivational Factors | Treatment Implications |
|---|---|
| Client is fairly out of contact with a sense of a larger life direction; overly attached to specific goals (helping his son dress, being a carpenter) that may be now unattainable/unworkable. | Need early values clarification with focus on process versus outcome and holding specific goals lightly. Getting in contact with values may allow for more flexibility in setting goals that are less rigid and more attainable. Contact with values could be a motivator for positive behavior change. |
| Client fears being overwhelmed by memories of abuse and fears he would "lose control" and hurt someone or himself. | If abuse memories are discovered to be a barrier at some point, a heavy dose of defusion and self-as-context work would probably be needed before step-by-step, careful willingness/exposure exercises. |

## 7. Environmental barriers to change (e.g., unsupportive home/social environment, unchangeable circumstances, financial circumstances, costs of changing, social losses)

Client may be reinforced for sick role by keeping disability benefits. Parents were primary abusers when he was a child, so ongoing interaction with them is likely to be particularly difficult. Client has no social support. Consider how cultural variables might influence experiential avoidance as a coping mechanism.

## 8. Client strengths (and how you might use them in treatment)

Client has shown the ability to problem solve and carry out plans of action in the midst of chronic pain. He regularly exercises his injured areas, even with pain, and makes room for this discomfort in order to do something he knows probably will be helpful in the long run. This could become a metaphor for what he could do with some other areas of his life. Likeable in session; reactions of the therapist (felt connected and caring) suggest client could draw people into relationship with him.

# 9. Initial ACT treatment plan

*Consider using* Acceptance and Action Questionnaire (AAQ) *and* Automatic Thoughts Questionnaire-Believability (ATQ-B) *for measures of believability and acceptance.*

*Client may have deficits in problem-solving skills and could benefit from practice with problem solving in more interpersonal and job-related areas. Client could benefit from vocational referral if he commits to progress in the area of work.*

*Begin with undermining control, particularly focusing on attempted control of emotions and thoughts related to depression, loss of job, self-criticism, and son, because experiential avoidance does not appear to be working in these areas. Creative hopelessness is probably important because of client's extensive history of the usefulness of control with respect to pain. Differentiating the success of pain control from lack of success in other areas will be important.*

*Client's rigid thinking suggests a strong focus on the functional utility of thoughts through defusion. If he could step back from his thoughts about himself and his situation and see thoughts as thoughts, he could expand his abilities to problem solve and to plan courses of action, as he has done with respect to physical health, to other domains of his life.*

*Conduct values clarification to help guide the selection of goals and reduce attachment to current goals.*

*Client could benefit from specific, planned, mindful, and willing exposure to tasks he did not do as well in the past in order to undermine fusion with perfectionism.*

*Client fears change and lacks a sense of direction. A focus on values clarification and step-by-step plans to change would be helpful to increase motivation to change. Make practice of willingness manageable in small doses. Focusing on process versus outcome and on holding goals lightly could help decrease attachment to his current goals of working as a carpenter and caring for son, which he does in rigid ways that are probably unworkable.*

*A focus on self as context and a distinction between evaluation and description are needed to decrease attachment to rigid self-evaluation, particularly if exposure to abuse memories is to occur. Use therapeutic relationship to model ACT processes and undermine attachment to conceptualized self.*

*Client probably could benefit from brief centering exercises during session. In between sessions he could practice getting present, perhaps in the form of mindfulness exercises.*

# CASE CONCEPTUALIZATION PRACTICE

Now you have a chance to practice case conceptualization with a sample case. We provide model responses so you can compare your responses with ours. Then you have an opportunity to practice conceptualizing your own cases.

## Practice Case: Sandra

Sandra is a thirty-eight-year-old married female who was referred for therapy after having not previously benefited from traditional CBT treatment or from several other courses of counseling. She describes herself as having been a "worrier my whole life," and says, "They called me a nervous Nellie as a child. I've always been this way. I'm oversensitive." She exhibits intense emotionality, becoming easily overwhelmed with the problems in her life. She meets the criteria for a diagnosis of generalized anxiety disorder and exhibits nearly constant worry about a variety of concerns, including never having a loving relationship, becoming financially destitute, and having a stroke. She is concerned her friends and family will become ill and that her friends will reject her. Her sleep is disrupted when lying in bed by her constant worry about the future. She often notes sensations in her body, such as tightness in her chest or tingling in her hands, and wonders if she is having a heart attack. When she feels she is getting too anxious at work or in social situations, she retreats from the room "until I've calmed down a bit."

Sandra's presenting concern is that she wants help "being less oversensitive." She says, "I push people away. I also want to do something about my worry. It's incapacitating at times." When asked to describe what she hopes would come out of therapy, she states she wants "to deal better with my life so I'm not so anxious all the time, so I can do better at work." With more discussion, she also acknowledges she would like help figuring out what to do about her relationships.

Her most central current concern is being fired from her job as a secretary at a law firm, which she has had for the past six months. She feels she is performing poorly "because I'm so anxious." She was previously fired from several jobs and has a history of taking jobs below her level of training. Her current job consists of mostly secretarial duties, even though she has a master's degree in design. She is currently in a fifteen-year marriage she finds distant and unsatisfying. Her husband does not work and she is the sole source of income for her family. She has no children and does report multiple solid friendships. She denies drinking alcohol at all and exercises at least one hour almost every day. She is very creative and is always doing different drawing and writing projects.

In session, Sandra frequently appears anxious and, unless the therapist interrupts her, talks endlessly about her worries, her current strategies to deal with them, or how she got to be the way she is. She cries easily and often appears anxious and distraught. Apart from her nearly constant storytelling, she is very friendly and frequently apologizes for "taking up too much session time." When doing exercises in session or between sessions, she frequently expresses worry she is "doing it wrong" or "messing it up."

---

## EXERCISE 8.1

Make a copy of the blank case conceptualization form in this chapter and fill it out as best you can, using the case information about Sandra. When you are finished, compare your answers with the model case conceptualization presented here. Do your homework first and then examine what we have done.

When comparing your conceptualization with the model, particularly note where your answers diverge from those in the model. Consider the ways in which your responses are either ACT consistent or inconsistent; if they are different, but still clearly ACT consistent, that is not an issue. If you have a question about the model or your responses, remember you can post a query to the relevant forum on www.learningact.com. As you compare your responses with the model, consider the following questions: Are there any places you do not understand what is being said in the model? Do you disagree in any way with the model? If so, attempt to understand why this is so in terms of an ACT approach. Your background might suggest approaches that are different from the ACT approach, but try to conceptualize the case from an ACT perspective.

## Completed Case Conceptualization Form for Sandra

### 1. Presenting problem(s) in client's own words

*Being a worrier and nervous Nellie; being overly sensitive*

Client's initial goals (What does he or she want from therapy?)

*She would like to be able to "deal better with life"; to not be anxious all the time; to do better at work and not be so sensitive.*

ACT reformulation of presenting problem

*Client seems to avoid thoughts, feelings, and images relating to several feared outcomes (e.g., destitute, rejection, health problems) through constant worrying (i.e., a form of fusion with ineffective problem solving), which serves to keep her life focused on these worries and not on living her values in her life.*

### 2. What thoughts, emotions, memories, sensations, or situations is the client fused with or unwilling to experience?

Thoughts

*I'm oversensitive; perhaps I push people away; I'm a failure; I'm inadequate*

Emotions

*Rejection, fear, uncertainty*

Memories

*Need more information about this domain; perhaps client has upsetting memories related to losing jobs, relationships, or failing due to being too anxious or overwhelmed*

Other

*Avoids setting high expectations for self or allowing expectations to be placed on her (e.g., a job with more responsibility, social situations, marriage conversations)*

## 3. What does client do to avoid these experiences?

Internal emotional control strategies (e.g., distraction, excessive rumination/worry)

*Worrying, telling herself to stop being so sensitive, distraction*

External emotional control strategies (e.g., drugs, self-harm, avoided situations)

*Avoids challenging work and social situations, and seeks reassurance from others by always talking about her problems*

In-session avoidance or emotional control patterns

*Talkativeness, storytelling, reassurance seeking, trying to "do it right"*

Pervasiveness of experiential avoidance:    Limited 1 2 3 4 5 Very extensive

## 4. Describe domains and ways in which client's behavior is narrowed and inflexible (e.g., family, couples, parenting, friends/social, work, education, recreation, spirituality, community, self-care)

*Seems complacent in unsatisfying marriage and job; probe for whether there is avoidance in the realm of being a parent; fear of rejection could be constricting valued action in friendships*

## 5. Consider other types of psychological inflexibility and their implications (e.g., cognitive fusion; dominance of conceptualized past and future, limited self-knowledge; attachment to conceptualized self; lack of values clarity; inaction, impulsivity, or avoidant persistence)

| Core Process | Pattern | Treatment Implications |
|---|---|---|
| Cognitive fusion | Continues to use unworkable control strategies (i.e., calm down, relax, not be so sensitive) | Consider strong focus on experienced workability and creative hopelessness. |
| Dominance of conceptualized past/future, limited self-knowledge | Extreme worry and anticipatory fear | Client probably needs frequent interruption from storytelling, reorientation to present moment, and awareness of current experiences (body, thoughts, feelings); develop sense of self as observer through practicing mindfulness in and out of session; identify feared images at the end of the worry chain and conduct willingness exercises or exposure to them. |
| Attachment to conceptualized self | Rigidly holds onto identity as worrier; oversensitive; is someone with problems | Do self-as-context and defusion work, description versus evaluation, taking on different roles. |

## 6. Motivational factors (e.g., what is the cost of this behavior in terms of daily living, client's experience of unworkability, clarity of values, therapeutic relationship)

| Motivational Factors | Treatment Implications |
|---|---|
| Attached to fears of consequences | Need extensive defusion and self-as-context work prior to confronting fears in any extensive exposure or willingness work; be careful in titrating exposure to willingness. |

**7. Environmental barriers to change** (e.g., unsupportive home/social environment, unchangeable circumstances, financial circumstances, costs of changing, social losses)

*More assessment is probably needed; client's husband may be unsupportive of change, and couples therapy could be useful in this regard.*

**8. Client strengths** (and how you might use them in treatment)

*Client has shown she is capable of establishing and maintaining solid friendships, and these might be enlisted as support for change strategies; she also has the experience of demonstrating committed action in the form of regular exercise, which could be used as a model for other forms of committed action/practice.*

**9. Initial ACT treatment plan**

*Consider using the book entitled ACT for Anxiety as a treatment manual; consider Acceptance and Action Questionnaire, Anxiety Sensitivity Index, and Penn State Worry Questionnaire as outcome/process measures.*

*Probably useful to begin with undermining control focused on workability of worry versus what the mind has to say about the strategy of trying to prepare for and solve every problem the mind identifies.*

*Help client clarify values to help with willingness to confront feared images/feelings/sensations.*

*Include considerable focus on defusion and self as context prior to conducting exposure and willingness work.*

*Eventually include imaginal exposure to fear images or situations at the end of the worry chain; perhaps consider interoceptive exposure to feared sensations.*

*During commitment portion, consider calling on support from friends to assist with commitments or bringing in husband for couples work if he is serving as a barrier.*

---

*EXERCISE 8.2*

The final practice exercise in this chapter involves conceptualizing one or more of your own cases using the ACT case conceptualization process, as described in this chapter. Make a copy of the case conceptualization form and fill it out for one of your clients. We recommend using a client with whom you are willing to do some ACT intervention because this will make the conceptualization more relevant. If you are new to ACT, holes may be revealed in your assessment process while conducting the case conceptualization. Perhaps you'll notice you need to do more assessment for ACT-related variables, or you may have a lack of understanding about your client's patterns of experiential avoidance or fusion. If this is so, consider how you can assess this more thoroughly. The first conceptualization will probably take an hour or more. Stick with it, and you will speed up with practice.

---

# ACT CASE CONCEPTUALIZATION FORM

You may want to photocopy the case conceptualization form to fill out with one or more of your own cases.

**1. Presenting problem(s) in client's own words:**

Client's initial goals (What does he/she want from therapy?):

ACT reformulation of presenting problem:

**2. What thoughts, emotions, memories, sensations, situations is the client fused with or avoiding?**

Thoughts

Emotions

Memories

Other

**3. What does client do to avoid these experiences?**

■    Internal emotional control strategies (e.g., distraction, excessive rumination/worry, dissociation, numbing, daydreaming)

■    External emotional control strategies (e.g., drugs, self-harm, avoided situations)

■    In-session avoidance or emotional control patterns (e.g., topic changes, argumentativeness, dropout risk)

Pervasiveness of experiential avoidance:    Limited  1    2    3    4    5  Very extensive

**4. Describe the domains and ways in which the client's behavior is narrowed and inflexible** (e.g., family, couples, parenting, friends/social, work, education, recreation, spirituality, community, self care)

**5. Consider other domain of psychological inflexibility and their implications** (e.g., fusion; dominance of conceptualized past and future, limited self-knowledge; attachment to conceptualized self; lack of values clarity; inaction, impulsivity, or avoidant persistence)

| Domain | Pattern | Treatment Implications |
|---|---|---|
|  |  |  |

**6. Motivational factors** (e.g., what is the cost of this behavior in terms of daily living, client's experience of unworkability, values clarity, therapeutic relationship)

| Motivational Pattern | Treatment Implications |
|---|---|
|  |  |

**7. Environmental barriers to change** (e.g., unsupportive home/social environment, unchangeable circumstances, financial circumstances, costs of changing)

**8. Client strengths** (and how you might use them in treatment)

**9. Initial ACT treatment plan**

# FUNCTIONAL ANALYSIS AS AN ONGOING PROCESS

For an ACT therapist, case conceptualization is not solely a formal process, such as that outlined in this chapter, but also occurs on an ongoing basis throughout therapy. Attention to the function of behavior in an ongoing manner with the client requires attention to three broad areas.

**The content level:** Assess the content of avoided and fused private experiences and of the forms of avoidance behavior so these can be accurately identified and targeted in an intervention. This level can be further divided into four channels or tracks.

1.  *Overt:* This is the level of client complaints, taken literally. For example, if a client says he or she is anxious, you can deal with this as a literal report of anxiety.

2.  *Social:* Because all therapy interactions are also social interactions, you need to consider the possibility that whatever a client says is how he or she handles the social world outside therapy. For example, a client complaining of anxiety may be showing you how he or she regulates the behavior of others through the use of emotional terms.

3.  *Therapeutic relationship:* Because all therapy interactions are also personal interactions between two people, you need to consider the possibility that whatever a client says is relevant to your relationship. For example, a person complaining of anxiety may be telling you to back off or may be appealing to you to take an authority role in the moment.

4.  *Hidden functional process:* Finally, content complaints can reveal deeper functional themes. For example, a complaint of anxiety may be put forth to avoid talk about sexuality or death.

**The process level:** Analyze the behavior for factors that promote or reduce psychological flexibility.

**The intervention level:** Consider the sequencing of intervention components that flow from the content and process analysis.

## Multiple Tracking

ACT case conceptualization asks the clinician to actively practice the skill of multiple tracking: listening to overt, social, therapeutic relationship, and hidden functional content tracks all at once. For example, suppose a client who is usually excessively quiet and compliant says during a session, "Gee, it's cold in here." You need to consider it simultaneously in terms of overt content (the temperature of the room may be low); as a sample of social behavior (perhaps this is a social step forward for the client with respect to learning to ask for things); as a move in the therapeutic relationship (perhaps the client is asking, "Are you noticing my needs?" or is stating, "I'm feeling more equal to you," or is asking, "Are you a cold person?"); and as part of the hidden functional track (the client could have changed the topic to avoid something, or the temperature is functioning as a metaphor for emotion or sexuality).

Each client behavior considered in each track can be attended to in terms of the ACT psychopathologies (e.g., avoidance, fusion, lack of contact with the present) and each therapist behavior can be described in terms of how it fits into the larger scheme of directions and skills the therapist is trying to foster. Particularly important is the therapist's attention to the process of experiential avoidance and fusion in the room. The ongoing observation of these two processes occurring in a client's behavior can provide very important information to guide the therapist's interventions. Ask yourself, "Is this client engaging in experiential avoidance right now?" If so, think how you can interrupt the process in a way that will work for the client. Similarly, ask, "Is the client fused right now with his or her ongoing verbal behavior?" If so, consider helping the client practice simply observing his or her responses or noticing other qualities of his or her current verbalizing, rather than simply its literal meaning.

## Looking Through a Functional Lens

Looking through a functional lens means repeatedly asking yourself during session, "What is the client's current behavior in the service of?" In addition, if you are seeing the client's behavior through a functional lens, you should be able to quickly describe the purpose of what *you* are doing from an ACT perspective and state how this matches your conceptualization of the client. A useful practice for beginning ACT therapists is to stop in session and ask themselves, "Why am I doing what I am doing right now?" or "What process am I targeting?" or "What about what the client is doing tells me this is a good intervention to be conducting at this time?" A good case conceptualization will guide you to much more nuanced and fluid answers to these sorts of questions. If you aren't able to answer such a question rapidly, you probably need to consider more deeply how your choice of intervention relates to the conceptualization of the client's problems.

---

# HOW DOES AN ACT CASE CONCEPTUALIZATION DIFFER FROM TRADITIONAL CBT?

ACT case conceptualization can be both similar to and different from traditional CBT and behavior therapy (BT). We discuss this in the hope of helping therapists to see important differences and also to better integrate ACT with the skills they already have in these two therapies.

## ACT and Traditional BT

ACT is a model of how to do BT, so it is not surprising that pretty much any traditional BT technique can be used (with some adaptation) as part of ACT. Stimulus control strategies aimed at controlling external triggers, contingency management, problem-solving skills, behavioral parenting skills, psychoeducation, exposure, and social skills training all can be used. The difference is that ACT uses traditional behavioral change strategies in the service of the client's most dearly held values and in a context of acceptance and defusion.

A few BT procedures are commonly thought to conflict with an ACT model. The most common example is relaxation training, which seems oriented toward direct emotional change as a method of dealing with anxiety. But relaxation training was originally presented as training in learning to let go—in which case, no conflict exists besides the needless conflict created by a relaxation rationale that casts it as a tool in an emotional war.

We can think of no instance in which ACT is incompatible with empirically validated BT methods, but at times an ACT model may add only a little to existing approaches.

Skills training provides an example of how an ACT model fits with BT. Skills training is called for when a client simply does not know how to do something and needs to learn. An ACT therapist who sees poor functioning that could be due to a skills deficit (e.g., lack of social engagement or lack of assertive behavior) can examine two possible etiologies. One scenario would be that the person has the basic skill, but it is at least in part suppressed by such factors as avoidance of fear or of other unpleasant emotional reactions assertive behavior can occasion. In this case, the problem is linked to experiential avoidance, and the ACT work would involve identifying internal barriers to action and engaging in defusion, acceptance, and committed action. In a second scenario, the client's behavior is unskillful due to a lack of learning or practice. Despite the straightforward etiology, when the client begins to practice, difficult emotions and thoughts may arise because the deficit will lead to socially awkward behavior. In this case, once again, the ACT model is relevant. If the behavioral deficit is due to a lack of skill and no barriers impede its acquisition, an ACT model will not add anything to straightforward skills training, but probably will not interfere either.

## ACT and Traditional CBT

ACT shares a number of attributes with traditional CBT, such as emphasis on learning processes in the development of problems, focus on a goal-directed active therapy style, use of traditional behavioral strategies, emphasis on developing a collaborative therapy relationship, respect for empiricism, and considerable emphasis on the role of human cognition in psychopathology and on its alleviation (Herbert & Forman, 2005). The difference is in the model of cognition itself. As a result, ACT is not compatible with traditional CBT techniques that attempt to "modify dysfunctional beliefs and faulty information processing" (Beck, 1993, p. 194), especially through cognitive restructuring techniques such as disputation.

A therapist who is attempting to integrate ACT with CBT needs to be careful of messages (consistent with CBT but not with ACT) that imply a need to modify, control, or reduce particular thoughts, feelings, memories, or sensations. Any message implying that a client needs to think more rationally or adaptively in order to live well is going to be inconsistent with ACT. Messages such as these can be confusing to clients and also reduce the effectiveness of both approaches.

The second major area of difference between CBT and ACT pertains to the goals of treatment and the definition of a good outcome. CBT tends to be oriented toward helping clients feel better and think more clearly, with the assumption that they will live better if this can be achieved. In contrast, ACT is directly aimed at helping clients to live better, fuller, deeper lives, which sometimes results in better feelings and sometimes does not. Empirically, so far, ACT has done as well as or better than CBT, even in terms of clients feeling better, although that is not its goal. A life well lived is the primary outcome of interest and is defined in the context of the client's chosen values and is based on evidence that the client is acting on those values in his or her life.

---

## EXPERIENTIAL EXERCISE: SELF CASE CONCEPTUALIZATION

Imagine you are a client going to see an ACT therapist. Take the case conceptualization outline and complete it as if you were the client. What would be your treatment plan for yourself?

After you have completed this treatment plan, consider how you could engage in this process in your life. If you are willing, make a commitment to follow through with the plan.

---

## EXPERIENTIAL EXERCISE: SELF CASE CONCEPTUALIZATION IN THE MOMENT

Take a difficult or upsetting experience you have had over the past week. Read the following directions and complete the exercise.

Close your eyes and imagine the scenario. Note what comes up in different domains of experience (e.g., thoughts, feelings, memories, sensations) and note your stance toward these experiences.

At the time, what did you see as the problem?

What was avoided in the situation? (e.g., thoughts, feelings, memories, sensations)

Did you buy into or fuse with any thoughts? Especially look for evaluations that seem to be just descriptions of the situation, yourself, or others.

What did you do with the thoughts, feelings, and reactions you experienced?

Can you come up with a more ACT-consistent reformulation of what happened in the situation? For example, was there something you needed to accept, something with which you were fused, or a value on which you needed to act?

## FOR MORE INFORMATION

For more about ACT case conceptualization, see *A Practical Guide to Acceptance and Commitment Therapy*, edited by Hayes and Strosahl (2005), chapter 3, "ACT Case Formulation." See also Moran and Bach (in press).

For more information (written for clinicians) about basic behavior analytic concepts, such as rule-governed behavior or classical and operant conditioning, see Ramnerö and Törneke (in press).

For more information about similarities and differences between ACT and traditional CBT, see Herbert and Forman (2005).

# CHAPTER 9

# THE ACT THERAPEUTIC STANCE: USING ACT TO DO ACT

*When you begin to touch your heart or let your heart be touched, you begin to discover that it's bottomless, that it doesn't have any resolution, that this heart is huge, vast, and limitless. You begin to discover how much warmth and gentleness is there, as well as how much space.*

—Pema Chödrön (1994, p. 128)

Decades of research examining virtually all types of psychotherapy have found that the therapeutic relationship is consistently correlated with clinical outcome (Martin, Garske, & Davis, 2000). It is not clear that this empirical fact has resulted in more effective therapies or therapists, however. Knowing this fact might help training programs select warm and caring people to become therapists, but does not tell us much about how to train therapists to create effective therapeutic relationships. Moreover, attempts to train therapists to build effective alliances have so far generally produced insignificant improvements (Crits-Christoph et al., 2006). In other words, *knowing* that the therapeutic relationship is important does not tell us *how to produce* good therapeutic relationships.

The ACT model provides clear suggestions about how to improve therapeutic relationships. Although some specific supportive data exists (Gifford et al., under review), at this point the model relies primarily on the strength of the theory underlying ACT. In this chapter, we first outline the basic competencies of the ACT therapeutic stance that have been identified by a consensus of ACT trainers (Strosahl et al., 2004), and then we present a theoretical analysis of the therapeutic relationship.

# CORE COMPETENCIES OF THE ACT THERAPEUTIC STANCE

Ideally, the function of the therapeutic relationship in ACT is to increase the client's psychological flexibility by responding effectively to client expressions of psychological flexibility or inflexibility that occur in immediate interaction with the therapist. This can occur through the therapist's modeling of psychological flexibility (e.g., "I'm noticing that I'm thinking, 'I don't know what to say.' You don't need to rescue me, I just thought I'd share that") or through supporting psychological flexibility on the part of the client; for example, by asking, "And could you notice that anxiety and still call your dad?" It can also occur through targeting psychological flexibility in relation to what is occurring in the moment of therapy; for example, by asking, "And instead of pushing away the tears, could you open up to them a little more right now?"

Achieving such flexibility is a very difficult task for therapists because we all bring our own histories, quirks, and interpersonal limitations to the therapy room. We can easily misjudge whether any given instance of client behavior represents a psychologically flexible or inflexible response. Thus, it can be useful for the clinician to maintain a general therapeutic stance that tends to instigate and reinforce psychologically flexible responding on the part of the client. The core competencies in this chapter are intended to describe the therapeutic stance that flows from the ACT model.

We present the core competencies related to therapeutic stance a little differently than we did the competencies in previous chapters. Here, the competencies are in bold and are followed by relatively brief explanations. At times, we list several competencies in a row, followed by information about those competencies, because they are intricately related and the explanation addresses their interconnection. Finally, we provide opportunities for practicing using a process unique to this chapter.

The first core competency perhaps sums up the ACT therapeutic stance better than does any other single statement:

1. **The ACT therapist speaks to the client from an equal, vulnerable, compassionate, genuine, and sharing point of view and respects the client's inherent ability to move from unworkable to workable responses.**

This most basic part of the ACT therapeutic stance naturally flows from a therapist's application of the ACT model of language and human functioning to his or her professional and personal life. The contextual philosophy underlying ACT holds that concepts such as sick/well, whole/broken, weak/strong, disordered/ordered, dysfunctional/functional are not inherent in any person, but rather are all ways of speaking or thinking propagated by our culture that are more or less useful depending upon the context. ACT therapists are encouraged to adopt a stance consistent with the phrase "there but for fortune go I," cognizant of the possibility that, given a slightly different history, the therapist could easily be the one with problems similar to those of the client and could be sitting in the client's seat. This ACT emphasis on context also implies that radical or even transformational change is possible for anyone, given a shift in the verbal, social, or historical context of that person's life. We do not need to rewrite our history, have different thoughts, or have better feelings before a full, deep, meaningful life is possible.

2. **The therapist is willing to self-disclose about personal issues when it serves the interest of the client.**

Although inappropriate and poorly timed self-disclosure can harm the therapeutic relationship (Ackerman & Hilsenroth, 2001), well-timed and well-crafted self-disclosure made in response to a therapeutic issue can be helpful (Safran & Muran, 2000). ACT therapists are emotionally accessible and responsive and are willing to use self-disclosure judiciously in the service of the client. If carefully done, self-disclosure tends to have an equalizing effect on the therapeutic relationship, can decrease the divide between therapist and client, and can bring the therapist's own humanity into the room. This is particularly important for ACT because it allows therapists to model an accepting stance toward their own struggles, while also modeling the ability to be effective in the living of their values.

3. **The therapist avoids the use of canned ACT interventions, instead fitting interventions to the particular needs of particular clients. The therapist is ready to change course to fit those needs at any moment.**

4. **The therapist tailors interventions and develops new metaphors, experiential exercises, and behavioral tasks to fit the client's experience and language practices, and the social, ethnic, and cultural context.**

Both of these core competencies reflect the need for behavioral and psychological flexibility on the part of the ACT clinician. ACT therapists are responsive to client needs and behaviors and do not rigidly follow protocols or rules about what is to be done. The key is to respond to client complaints and the unworkability of behaviors in terms of their underlying function, which often necessitates new and creative ways of responding. Any techniques that foster psychological flexibility are considered ACT consistent. Artful application of the ACT model means that therapists are creative in making up new metaphors and exercises and in adapting existing techniques to fit the needs of their clients, and are able to pull from their existing skill base whenever doing so would be supportive of an ACT process.

When learning the model, it is generally helpful to follow one of the available protocols and carefully practice the metaphors and exercises before working with a client in a given session. However, because following the ACT principles is more important than using any particular metaphor or exercise, it is usually helpful to leave topographical treatment protocols behind when entering the therapy room and to seek functional adherence instead. The client can get lost in the therapist's attempt to get a metaphor or exercise correct.

Tailoring your ACT intervention to match the needs of your client can enhance the relationship and allow the therapy to flow in a natural manner. For instance, you can choose to spend more time on control as the problem and less time on creative hopelessness. Or you can decide, given the client's needs, to drop creative hopelessness almost entirely. You can choose to start with values or bring in values later in the therapy. Awareness of the client, yourself, and the function of behavior in the session can help guide the movement and application of ACT principles.

5. **The therapist models acceptance of challenging content (e.g., what emerges during treatment) while also being willing to hold the client's contradictory or difficult ideas, feelings, and memories without any need to resolve them.**

It is important for the therapist to directly practice willingness in the room, remaining present to content and experience. This can pose some difficulty because many therapists have been taught that good therapy means resolving difficult emotions. For instance, when a client is confused, the therapist can prematurely slip into problem solving and give lots of information to get the client unconfused, without adequately considering whether more fully experiencing confusion would be the better long-term course. The key is for therapists to be willing to experience their own anxiety that arises when they don't try to fix the difficult content.

As we noted in the introduction, beginning ACT therapists tend to be anxious about the counterintuitive nature of the model, a reaction that ACT effectiveness research shows changes only slowly. Fortunately, good outcomes can be achieved by beginning ACT therapists even though this anxiety remains high (Lappalainen et al., in press), perhaps because it helps the therapist model and be in touch with ACT processes, rather than simply to transmit theoretical material to a client.

6. **The therapist introduces experiential exercises, paradoxes, and/or metaphors as appropriate and de-emphasizes literal sense-making of the same.**

7. **The therapist always brings the issue back to what the client's experience is showing, and does not substitute his or her opinions for that genuine experience.**

8. **The therapist does not argue with, lecture, coerce, or attempt to convince the client.**

Competencies 5 through 8 all emphasize the adoption of a nonliteral, defused, present, accepting stance, in which the growth possible in uncertainty is prized and in which literal understanding is observed with a skeptic's eye. Sense-making, in particular, exerts a powerful pull on human behavior, sometimes to the detriment of being and doing. The point of ACT exercises, metaphors, and stories is not so much that clients will understand their problems in a new light, but rather that ACT therapists are challenged to keep the goal of psychological flexibility square in the clients' vision—helping clients develop the ability to change or persist in behavior in the pursuit of their values. Often, trying to understand how they landed in a particular problem, and then working to understand how to get out of it, are part of the process that has gotten clients stuck in the first place. For example, a sufferer of chronic PTSD can believe he or she needs to know a lot more about PTSD to be able to solve the problem of PTSD and can spend years in therapy pursuing understanding, rather than learning more flexible ways of living with a trauma history. Thus, ACT therapists want to be careful not to add to this process. If you find yourself attempting to change a client's mind rather than trying to liberate the client's life, stop: you are not doing ACT.

## EXPERIENTIAL EXERCISE: THERAPEUTIC STANCE

Think about your current set of clients. If you have used ACT with any of them, have you ever found yourself working overly hard to help the client understand the exercises and metaphors rather than simply doing them?

Take a moment to reflect on the answer to this question. Close your eyes and think about what emotional experience arises when you are working hard to get your client to understand. See if you aren't working to escape some emotion during those times.

Write a few sentences about what you experience:

What do you imagine would happen if you stopped trying to get the client to understand?

Would you be willing to contact that emotion and just do the exercise or metaphor with your client?

The final and perhaps broadest competency is:

9.    **ACT-relevant processes are recognized in the moment, and when appropriate, are directly supported in the context of the therapeutic relationship.**

The rest of this chapter focuses on how to implement this competency through examining ACT theory as it relates to the therapeutic relationship and through providing the opportunity for practice.

# ACT PROCESSES AT THREE LEVELS: CLIENT, THERAPIST, RELATIONSHIP

In order to build an ACT model of the therapeutic relationship, we need to distinguish three levels, or aspects, of the relationship: the psychological processes of the client, the psychological processes of the practitioner, and the nature of the interaction between the practitioner and client.

## The Client

Because most of this book focuses on the level of the psychological processes of the client, we will not focus much on this level here. This level refers to issues such as the following: What processes are harmful to psychological growth? How can these processes be altered clinically? The processes in the hexagon model of ACT are a good summary of what our research and clinical work suggest is helpful to the client.

## The Practitioner

ACT researchers and clinicians have long argued that all of these processes apply to the psychology of the therapist, and that in order for therapists to most flexibly adopt the basic ACT therapeutic stance, they must necessarily be working with the six ACT processes in regard to their own psychological experience in the room. This book does not focus heavily on all the steps that need to be taken to establish greater psychological flexibility on the part of the practitioner. The ACT community has a tradition of using experiential workshops to help therapists work on these processes as they apply within the therapist, and it is common for ACT therapists to learn ACT by using books such as *Get Out of Your Mind and Into Your Life* (Hayes & Smith, 2005) to help with their own difficulties. Ongoing practice with and use of the six core processes in regard to the therapist's own psychology is essential if he or she is going to keep his or her therapeutic instrument in tune. For more guidance about how to develop greater psychological flexibility as a therapist, see appendix B.

Here we consider each of the core processes as applied to the therapist.

### ACCEPTANCE

When doing clinical work, painful feelings or memories emerge at times for the therapist. It hurts to watch others hurt, and furthermore the pain clients are experiencing regularly overlaps with and touches similar pain experienced by the therapist. Clinical work can be frightening or challenging in other ways, as well—such as the pain that comes from not being certain about how to help someone you are being paid to assist. A therapist who is unwilling or unable to sit with his or her own discomfort will tend to structure sessions in order to avoid them. Clients can detect this, consciously or not, and the resultant inconsistency can readily undermine therapy. For example, suppose an ACT therapist is asking a client to sit with anxiety, but is unwilling to sit with the anxiety of not knowing if things are getting better. The client may rescue the therapist by hiding his or her level of anxiety in session. In this case, we see that while the client is encouraged verbally to sit with anxiety, he or she is encouraged functionally to control it. That is an impossible situation for the client. Thus, the ACT therapist needs to have a good level of acceptance skills in order to do ACT effectively.

## COGNITIVE DEFUSION

Defusion presents the same problem. Therapists are tempted to defend the correctness of their thoughts in much the same way as are clients. These can include personal thoughts, but they also include thoughts about therapy itself. Suppose the therapist is asking the client on the one hand to simply notice thoughts, instead of treating them as true or false or as events to be believed or disbelieved, but on the other hand is subtly demanding the client treat clinical interpretations as factual, not as merely useful to the extent that they are useful. This, too, puts the client in an impossible situation because, in effect, he or she is being asked to "just notice your thoughts as thoughts, except when they disagree with me, in which case I'm right." For these reasons, ACT therapists need to know how to treat their own thoughts as thoughts, and to be willing to do so when it serves a valued purpose in therapy.

## BEING PRESENT

Attending to and residing in the present moment with the client is essential to effective ACT work. The present moment includes contact with the client (e.g., what is being said, how it is being said) and includes contact with the therapist's own feelings, thoughts, memories, and sensations. If the therapist is not able to consistently return to the now, therapy will have a distant, predictable, rule-governed quality that is likely to undermine its effectiveness.

## SELF AS CONTEXT

ACT seeks to undermine attachment to the conceptualized self and build contact with a transcendent sense of self. According to RFT, when a person learns to see experiences from the viewpoint of I/here/now, he or she also learns that others (you/there/then) see the world differently and develops a sense of what that perspective might look like or feel like (i.e., empathy). Contacting self as context can also facilitate acceptance on the part of the therapist and help therapists to be more flexible in the service of their clients, and to let go of limiting self-concepts and model this for clients.

## DEFINING VALUED DIRECTIONS

Valuing on the part of the therapist is a part of effectively doing ACT. Values dignify and make coherent the other aspects of the ACT model. The goal is not acceptance for its own sake, but acceptance that empowers values-based living. Clarity about and dedication to their own values in therapy and in life empower practitioners to step into psychologically difficult places in the service of the client.

## COMMITTED ACTION

The ability to actively pursue chosen values is the bottom line of the ACT model. The commitment about which we are speaking is not the commitment to a topography of action, but to a function; namely, the linkage to chosen values. The therapist's commitment to act on his or her therapy-relevant values can imply either persistence in or change in therapist behavior, depending on the situation. The key factor is the good of the client, not therapy techniques per se.

## The Relationship

Finally, the third level of analysis involves applying all six ACT core processes to the context and content of the therapeutic relationship as it occurs in the moment of the session. To give one example, the ACT therapist is not just targeting acceptance in the client, and is not just accepting his or her own feelings as they come up while doing therapy, but the ACT therapist is also accepting of the client in moment-to-moment interactions. The context and content of the therapeutic relationship give vital, moment-to-moment expression to this key process. The other parts of the hexagon model are expressed similarly through ACT therapeutic interactions that are defused, present, conscious, values-based, active, and flexible.

As we review some of the core processes of an effective therapeutic relationship in ACT, you will notice that some of them are probably important regardless of the type of therapy being done. For example, therapists need to be able to be present, use their own reactions as input, and respond flexibly to the situation, regardless of the model of treatment being pursued. Other core therapeutic processes are especially important in the context of ACT. For example, clients can benefit when the therapist models the ACT processes in his or her own behavior. Furthermore, targeting acceptance in an avoidant way or defusion in a fused way would be counterproductive. This chapter is informed by work on a sister technology that focuses on creating effective and curative therapy relationships, called Functional Analytic Psychotherapy (FAP; Kohlenberg & Tsai, 1991).

# AN ACT MODEL OF THE THERAPEUTIC RELATIONSHIP

The ACT model of a powerful therapeutic relationship is shown in figure 9-1. You can see all three levels of the therapeutic relationship simultaneously: that of the therapist, the client, and the social interactions between them. All of these levels acting together constitute an effective therapeutic relationship because a relationship is between two people, each with his or her own psychological processes brought to the table.

*Psychological flexibility* is discussed in chapter 1 as a kind of coming together of the six core ACT processes. It is represented as a circle at the center of the hexagon that emerges from all the processes (the points on the hexagon) and their interactions (the lines between them). As we extend this model to a dyad, the number of interactions within and between these processes increases exponentially, as seen in figure 9-1. Basically, it is the task of ACT practitioners to *detect instances of psychological flexibility and inflexibility in their clients, and to use psychologically flexible responses to establish a therapeutic relationship that models, instigates, and reinforces client psychological flexibility.*

# Figure 9.1: A Model of the ACT Therapeutic Relationship

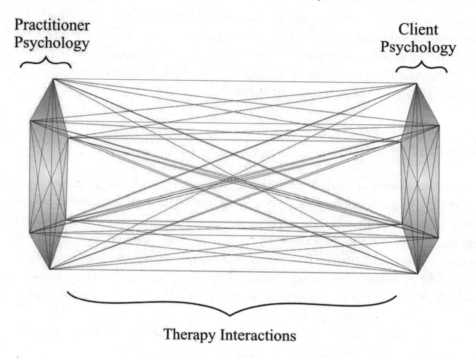

**Practitioner Psychology**

**Client Psychology**

**Therapy Interactions**

## Applying ACT to the Therapeutic Relationship

No practitioner could possibly hold all of the relationships in figure 9-1 in his or her head. That is not the point. Rather, our general message is that ACT can be applied to the therapeutic relationship itself. Here we provide a model of how ACT therapists can detect instances of psychological flexibility or inflexibility in client behavior in the session and can reinforce or challenge that behavior in the moment. Through this process, we hope to enhance your sense of how ACT-consistent therapeutic relationships feel. If you carry this sense into your clinical work, clients can become your teachers and trainers, while greater psychological flexibility in those clients supports your actions that produce it.

Applying ACT to the therapeutic relationship requires that you first are able to detect instances of psychological flexibility and inflexibility in your clients. We spend some time discussing how to detect these processes, but perhaps less time than might otherwise be the case because this part of the model is covered extensively throughout the rest of the book, including chapter 8.

If the client's action is a step forward with respect to psychological flexibility, the ACT therapist's job is to reinforce that step forward, while simultaneously modeling and instigating additional flexibility, by using psychologically flexible therapist responses. Conversely, if the client's action is psychologically inflexible, the ACT therapist's job is to not reinforce that inflexibility, while simultaneously modeling and instigating flexible client responses through psychologically flexible therapist responses. This analysis is a core focus of much of the rest of the chapter.

## When Do You Focus on the Relationship Itself?

Although all ACT methods in psychotherapy occur in the context of a therapeutic relationship, that does not mean you need to focus on the relationship per se in any given case. In the case conceptualization chapter (chapter 8), we noted at least four dimensions of responding that can be tracked in any given interaction. A client's statement can be addressed in terms of content, as a sample of social behavior, as a statement about the relationship between the client and therapist, and in terms of symbolic functions. For each of these tracks, an ACT analysis is possible.

Every single statement or action on the part of a client can be tracked at these four levels, but some are more interesting than others in a given situation. Focusing on the relationship per se seems most useful when the relationship level maps onto other levels, or when the therapeutic relationship level needs to be worked on for the therapist to be effective in other domains. For example, if a client is anxious and avoidant and shows such processes in the therapeutic relationship itself, working on them at that level has an immediacy and directness that cannot be otherwise attained. Similarly, if the degree of avoidance in the relationship could interfere with or prevent other therapeutic work, then the therapist needs to focus on the relationship at least enough so that it does not overly interfere with other therapeutic processes.

Focusing on the relationship itself can also be helpful when psychological inflexibility that shows up in the therapy relationship is functionally related to psychological inflexibility in other domains of the client's life. For example, clients can respond to the therapist in the same way they respond to other important people in their lives. If the therapist is able to have an impact on fusion in a client's relationship with him or her, for example, this can be generalized to corresponding changes in similar relationship contexts.

The relationship can also be used as a type of assessment when targeting other levels. If a client is claiming significant progress in willingness to have social anxiety, for example, but anxiety in the therapeutic relationship is actively avoided, it seems reasonable to look more closely at these verbal reports.

# TARGETING THE THERAPEUTIC RELATIONSHIP

In this section, we bring together the theory discussed so far in this chapter by unpacking a single characteristic moment in clinical practice. Later in the chapter you have an opportunity to work through additional examples. Because the ACT model of the therapeutic relationship is not limited to times when the relationship level is specifically targeted, some of the examples here do not have an exclusive relationship focus. However, all of them have a bearing on the therapeutic relationship. Parenthetically, given the primary focus of the book, we emphasize psychotherapeutic applications of ACT, but the same processes apply to ACT workshops, to consultations in work or educational settings, and to other settings.

## The Client Says It Is Not Going Well

For our first example, let's consider the situation in which a client challenges a therapist about how the course of therapy for an anxiety disorder is going. She says the following to the therapist.

*Client:*    I'm not getting any better in here. This just seems like psychobabble to me.

This challenge could easily contain within it aspects of psychological flexibility. For example, if the client's method of experiential avoidance is agreement with authority, or denial of all difficulty, she could be stepping into new and healthier territory by admitting to upset of any kind, including upset with the therapist.

Conversely, the challenge could be a predictable and psychologically inflexible expression of avoidance or fusion. The client could be engaging in a corpus delecti maneuver (Hayes et al., 1999, p. 253) of trying to prove she is right by pointing to the intractability of her problems. This would suggest fusion with a conceptualized self. Or the client could be challenging the therapist because she is not yet willing to step into the anxiety that would come by rising to the challenge of change. In the following pages we show how each of the ACT processes could be the primary source of a clinical response. The sample responses we give often target more than one ACT process; to give responses targeting only one ACT process would be artificial and unnecessary because most clinical responses in ACT have multiple functions due to the interrelatedness of the model.

## THE CLIENT'S STATEMENT IS AN IMPROVEMENT

Let's begin by supposing the therapist views the complaint as a small step forward in the ability of the client to admit to difficult feelings. In this case, the goal of the therapist's response is to reinforce that step forward, while at the same time modeling and strengthening ACT processes.

So, again, the client says, "I'm not getting any better in here. This just seems like psychobabble to me."

**Acceptance response:** "Thanks for telling me that ... What do you feel as you put that into this room?"

**Analysis:** A number of commonsense responses could be problematic from the ACT perspective. The therapist could try to explain away or at least resolve the sense that this is psychobabble, assuming the client is confused and what was misunderstood needs to be clarified. This kind of heavily fused response would take seriously the idea that thinking "this is psychobabble" is necessarily a content problem that needs to be resolved. Alternatively, the therapist could try to determine whether the sense that it is not getting better is justified, or could defend against that idea. For example, a response such as "Actually, your anxiety scores are way down; why do you feel you aren't getting any better?" would probably be seen by the client as a defense. The client knows that hearing a statement such as the one she made is probably upsetting to the therapist, and any move by the therapist to undermine or question the literal truth of that statement could be seen as—and, in fact, could be—a way to keep the therapist from feeling inadequate. A therapist response of that nature could be additionally troublesome if it invalidates the client's upset, and fuses with the idea that thinking "I'm not getting better" is necessarily a barrier to success.

"Thanks for telling me that" indicates the therapist is willing to feel upset. This response is designed to reinforce the emotional opening up the therapist thinks he or she detects. The instigation "What do you feel?" invites the client to explore the domain the therapist is trying to support.

**Cognitive defusion response:** "Ouch. That must be a painful thought to have."

**Analysis:** Done crudely, defusion in this situation is quite likely to be emotionally invalidating. That would undermine the whole purpose. In this case, the therapist has put in just enough defusion to make the point that the client is expressing a thought, not necessarily an event that has to be objectively true or false, and at the same time, the therapist is supporting the step forward. This statement also has an acceptance aspect: by acknowledging the pain, the therapist hopes to validate and support the client's expression of emotionally difficult material.

**Being present response:** [pause] "That must have been hard to say. Let's both just take a second to get present with what it feels like to be here with that in the room."

**Analysis:** This response acknowledges that both the client and the therapist have a challenge in the present moment: it is hard to say what the client said, and it is hard to hear it as a practitioner. By suggesting they both come back into the present together, while actively embracing the challenge, the therapist models acceptance and the importance of the present moment, and hopefully reinforces the client's step forward into a difficult feeling.

**Self-as-context response:** "If I felt like that, it would be really difficult. It would be hard for me to say what you just said to a therapist."

**Analysis:** A transcendent sense of self is based on deictic relational frames. In the RFT lab, one of the ways children are trained to use these frames is by asking them, for example, "If I were you and you were me, what would you have?" The simple act of the therapist putting himself or herself in the client's shoes appeals to the client's sense of consciousness and also has the desirable effect of supporting the client's step into psychological pain.

**Defining valued directions response:** "I hear you. And before we even unpack that, let me just say that what I'm in here for is you and what you really want in your life, not me getting applause for saying clever things."

**Analysis:** This response puts the therapist's values on the line. It defines therapy in terms of a contract that is about the client, not about the therapist's comfort or getting to be right. It also explicitly eschews an attachment to psychobabble (e.g., saying clever things).

**Committed action response:** All of the responses presented thus far can be thought of as committed actions on the part of the therapist because they are designed to put the client's needs first. A therapist could construct a response that emphasized this even more, although more context would probably be needed to do so in this case.

All the therapist responses assume the client's statement represents a positive clinical step that needs strong clinical support. Suppose, however, that the therapist does not see a positive step within the complaint. Suppose the therapist detects nothing but avoidance and fusion. What would the therapist then do? This depends very much on the therapist's overall strategy. Thus, in what follows, it is especially important for the therapist to link his or her response to the analysis, rather than to see the model responses provided as a correct (and especially not *the* correct) response in each area.

## THE CLIENT'S STATEMENT IS PROBLEMATIC

If the client's statement is seen by the therapist as psychologically inflexible, the therapist's goal would be to model and instigate positive processes without reinforcing negative processes. In the case of experiential avoidance, the presumed reinforcer is avoidance of difficult private experiences; thus, it is important the therapist not be deflected into a response that provides that functional outcome. For example, if the therapist goes into an extended analysis of why the client feels progress has not been made, the avoided emotions might never be contacted. Avoidance is at times difficult to address clinically because if the avoidance works, what is functionally important is not directly present. Thus, the therapist has to make astute determinations about what is going on. Suppose, for example, the client's statement is designed to avoid anxiety. In that case, it is important the therapist not inadvertently respond in a way that would forestall feelings of anxiety.

Similarly, in the case of fusion, the presumed reinforcer is defense of an extended, coherent relational network: being right. In this case, any therapist response that draws the client and therapist deeper into the relational network is undesirable. Disagreement and agreement both can have that effect, as can logical challenges, compliance, resistance, analysis, and the like.

For these reasons, some of the responses that follow may appear to be non sequiturs. This occurs when the clinical response is designed to step out of a normal but unhelpful contingency stream, and to step into certain ACT processes instead. We assumed in constructing these responses that the same avoidant and fused patterns that are hypothesized to be expressed in the form of the client complaint are also evident in the therapeutic relationship itself. Therefore, in some of these responses, the therapist shifts levels from the content to the relationship per se.

Again, the client says, "I'm not getting any better in here. This just seems like psychobabble to me."

**Acceptance response:** "I'm guessing you've felt like this before with other therapies. Yes? Okay, so could I ask you this: What did you do in the past when you felt like this? And how did that work for you?"

**Analysis:** This response asks the client to look at the function of the statement by going back into past instances. It is a kind of acceptance-based question because it points a beacon on experiential avoidance. Note that the therapist does not defend himself or herself but rather checks first to make sure there were past instances, and then links the client's response to workability for the client, not to truth or falsity in a literal sense. The therapist is not tilting the answer; he or she wants to know.

**Acceptance response at the level of the relationship itself:** "Are you feeling afraid I will disappoint you and let you down?"

**Analysis:** The therapist parses the complaint as a statement about the therapeutic relationship itself. By guessing about the possible function, the therapist both models and instigates the acceptance of difficult emotions. Even if the guess were incorrect, the client would probably see and appreciate the risk the therapist has taken and would define the relationship as a place in which difficult feelings can be stated.

**Cognitive defusion response:** "Could I ask you this: How close is that thought to you right now? Does it feel as if it is right on top of you, or does it feel as if it is floating out here in the space between us a bit? If this piece of paper were the thought 'I'm not getting any better,' could you show me how far away it is from you right now?"

**Analysis:** This is a straightforward defusion response because it looks at the process of thinking, not just from the products of that response. We have put it into this chapter, in part, because defusion is sometimes seen by relationship-oriented therapists as inherently invalidating because it is so outside of normal social interaction. But this response seems very unlikely to have such an effect, which is part of our point.

**Defusion response at the level of the relationship itself:** "Interesting. Well, if we take that thought literally, I suppose we would need to deal with whether you are in fact progressing. And we can do that if your gut level sense is that it really would have value. But I wonder if another area would be to look at our relationship and at what we plan to do when we have thoughts about the process itself that are scary or difficult."

**Analysis:** This response is another one based on the idea that the therapeutic relationship itself is part of the focus of the client's statement. It specifically links defusion to flexibility in being able to address the worry in multiple ways—literal or not—and to position this process inside the relationship.

**Being present response:** [moving the therapist's chair next to the client's so they both look back in the same direction] "Would it be possible for us both to get into contact with what it feels like to think therapy is going nowhere, right here right now? And let's put that thought out there on the floor in front of us and both of us watch in more detail what then comes up as we look at it."

**Analysis:** This response mixes defusion and contact with the present. At a literal level, the client's complaint is an apparent barrier between the therapist and client. The two chairs together, combined with putting the material out in front of them both, is a metaphor for a defused, present-focused therapeutic alliance. It is as if the therapist is saying, "Our worries and judgments are not a barrier to our relationship; they can instead be part of our legitimate focus of therapeutic work." This move also pulls the work from talk about another time and place and puts these reactions into the present moment.

**Self-as-context response:**

*Therapist:* I have something that may sound like a strange question, but how old do you feel right now?

*Client:* [pause] About seven.

*Therapist:* Okay, can we just take a moment to climb into the skin of that seven-year-old? Tell you what. Would it be okay if we do that as a kind of eyes-closed exercise?

*Client:* Okay.

*Therapist:* Good, let's do that, and we can unpack this more afterward. I'd like you to picture where you lived when you were seven, and in your mind's eye … [continues with the Little Kid exercise, in which the client is taken through a detailed examination of what it felt like to be seven and is asked to talk to the child and hear what he or she needs]

**Analysis:** This move treats the avoidance as a historically situated event. By moving the client into the body of the seven-year-old, the exercise moves I/here/now into a different context that then allows a greater sense of perspective on the current struggle.

**Defining valued directions response:** "And let's just go with that. Let's go with 'This is not working.' What do you want in your life that you'd be losing if that were true?"

**Analysis:** Inside our values we find our pain and inside our pain we find our values. This move situates the struggle in values, which can then give a different meaning to the struggle itself.

**Committed action response:** "Okay. Let me just ask you this: What do you suspect would have to be let go of to move therapy along? And if it were painful, but you saw what needed to be done, what would it take for us to move together in that direction?"

**Analysis:** This response, in essence, asks if the client is willing to commit to a therapeutic relationship that would be effective if she could see how it could be useful.

## SUMMARY

To some degree, this is an artificial exercise, especially in the sense that a single ACT-relevant process is given the most dominant position in each of the examples. Most clinical responses during the course of ACT are a mix of many ACT-based processes. But forcing the issue to some extent allows us to describe areas of application that might otherwise be avoided or misunderstood.

Building an effective therapeutic relationship is at the heart of ACT. Fortunately, the beginning skills needed to do so exist within ACT itself. In essence, the strategic rule is this: apply ACT in the process of creating a context in which you can do ACT, and apply ACT to the therapeutic relationship itself as you model, instigate, and support psychological change.

It should be noted that the examples in this section provide a template to use when dealing with ruptures in the therapeutic relationship. The therapist needs to take responsibility for his or her role, fully and without defense. This needs to be done in a way that models ACT processes and that does not attempt defensively to shift the focus to the client. Then, based on shared values, the therapeutic contract needs to be reassembled and reaffirmed, again modeling and instigating ACT processes at each stage of the process.

# CORE COMPETENCY PRACTICE

We encourage you to do your best to generate responses to the client statements in this section before looking at the model responses. If you struggle and still do it, you will learn the most. Feel free to look back at the examples in the first part of this chapter as you work to generate your own responses.

## The Client Says Things Are Going Well

A depressed twenty-three-year-old female comes to therapy with a history of bulimia. She tends to be self-critical and to hide herself behind a wall of superficial positive statements (e.g., "I'm just fine"). In the last session, the therapist worked hard on the client being honest in session about where she really is, rather than trying to look good.

Client:     This has been a great week, and I think it is due to our work together. I feel good, I'm more open, and my eating problems are under control.

Assume that the client's statement reflects progress (given her baseline) toward greater psychological flexibility. The therapist is pretty sure that "I feel good, I'm more open" is not a way to speak about avoidance. Based on knowledge of the client and the current context in therapy, the therapist thinks she primarily means she is more open to her own thoughts and feelings, but the therapist has a slight worry that "I feel good" might be focused on emotional content more than just on doing a good job of feeling emotions.

## EXERCISE 9.1

You want to model, instigate, and reinforce positive ACT processes. In this exercise, first read a list of responses, each of which illustrates primarily acceptance, cognitive defusion, being present, self as context, defining valued directions, or committed action. Be aware that some of the responses contain multiple ACT processes. Your job is to pick out the most dominant process.

Response 1: "Neat. And what shows up here as you say that?"

Response 2: "Thanks. I actually see you not just feeling *good*, but *feeling* good based on what we've done together. That's what is especially meaningful to me—to see you stepping into places that are difficult and then finding new things to do there."

Response 3: "Well, I see how you've been stepping forward. I want you to know I will be there for this next stage of work, as well, whatever it takes."

Response 4: "Sometimes my mind gives me a lot of things to worry about in here ... I know that has happened with you, too, *and* I think we're starting to see what is possible if we give ourselves some room to work above and beyond all of that chatter."

Response 5: "What is important to me is that this is about you and what *you* want in your life. It's just neat to see that happening and to see you let what you care about, instead of what your history is giving you, be your guide."

Response 6: "There is a part of you that has the capacity just to notice all of this programming and still make choices, yes? If you can stand with yourself, it's 'first we win, then we play' because that part of you is perfect to begin with. I don't know, but that seems to be part of the changes you are noticing: you're allowing yourself to show up as a conscious person."

Match the responses to the ACT processes by writing the response number in the blank space.

____ Acceptance

____ Cognitive defusion

____ Being present

____ Self as context

____ Defining valued directions

____ Committed action

The answer key is upside down at the bottom of the page.

---

Now assume a different context that suggests the statement primarily reflects psychological inflexibility. In this case, the therapist thinks the client's statement "This has been a great week, and I think it is due to our work together. I feel good, I'm more open, and my eating problems are under control" is the same old thing of presenting a falsely positive front—to herself and especially to the therapist. The therapist guesses "This has been a great week" means she did not face many challenges, and "I think it is due to our work together" is a carrot to keep the therapist from looking more closely. The therapist thinks "I feel good, I'm more open" is just the old emotional control agenda in new ACT clothing, and "my eating problems are under control" contains more than a hint of suppressive avoidance.

In the exercises that follow, you want to build the relationship while modeling and instigating positive ACT processes, but without reinforcing unhealthy processes. Each exercise provides a list of therapist reactions, one of which is the best instance of the process that is the focus of that exercise. Sometimes the least preferred response is adequate but does not exemplify the ACT process. At other times, it fits the ACT process but allows the source of inflexibility to be reinforced. At yet other times it is simply a weak response. In each case, remember the purpose and then pick the one that seems best.

Again, the client says, "This has been a great week, and I think it is due to our work together. I feel good, I'm more open, and my eating problems are under control."

[2, 4, 1, 6, 5, 3]

## EXERCISE 9.2

Place a check before the response that best exemplifies acceptance:

_____ "Yeah, I also feel great when things are going well."

_____ "Hmm. I'm a bit nervous when I hear that. Is feeling good what we are trying to do in here?"

_____ "You just need to accept your feelings. If you don't do that, the research suggests that nothing good is going to happen in here."

Check your favorite response before you continue to read.

**Explanation:** The third response is preachy. It is about acceptance, but seems fused and critical, and does not model or instigate acceptance. The first response reinforces avoidance, given the initial analysis. The second response acknowledges a difficult therapist emotion and undermines the hypothesized avoidance function; thus it is the most ACT consistent of the three.

## EXERCISE 9.3

Place a check before the response that best exemplifies cognitive defusion:

_____ "If you had the thought 'things are not going well,' would you be able to say that to me, as well? It could be hard. You'd probably run into that habitual 'I'm fine' thought, for instance."

_____ "Hmm. I'm noticing two thoughts. One is all about how great we've been doing. The other is wondering whether I should dig into this a bit more because I have a sense some of what you're saying is linked to wanting to please me. If you take a moment to look, what thoughts come up as you look at this overview of the last week?"

_____ "Would you mind saying what your evidence is for the idea that this was a great week?"

Check your favorite response before you continue to read.

**Explanation:** The last response asks for evidence to prove a thought is true. This is not prohibited by ACT, but you would use it rarely and it is not a defusion technique. Both of the other responses are focused on defusion, and both seem to confront the hypothesized avoidance. They both appear to be reasonable responses from an ACT perspective.

## EXERCISE 9.4

Place a check before the response that best exemplifies being present:

_____ "What is it about our work that you think is most helpful?"

_____ "So, how are you feeling right here, in the present, about getting your eating under control?"

_____ "Before we even get into that, let's just take three deep breaths and show up to what it feels like to be here and working together. Would that be okay?"

Check your favorite response before you continue to read.

**Explanation:** The first response is relatively fused and assumes that, in fact, things are going well, so it might reinforce what you are guessing is an avoidance move. The second response is a somewhat awkward attempt to get to the present. It links to the idea of getting eating under control, so it also could reinforce what you fear is a form of suppressive avoidance. The last response is not especially elegant, but it does situate whatever comes next in the present moment and avoids specifically reinforcing the negative aspects of what was said. It is the best of the alternatives given.

## EXERCISE 9.5

Place a check before the response that best exemplifies self as context:

_____ "And who is saying that? Is this coming from the part of you that likes to present a positive front even when things are difficult or is this coming from a more core aspect of you that is open to whatever you experience, whether it is called good or bad?"

_____ "If I were you and you were me, I'd want to please my therapist and it feels like you are just trying to impress me with how great things are even though they aren't great."

_____ "Is this the people pleaser talking?"

Check your favorite response before you continue to read.

**Explanation:** The first two responses both contain an appeal to a contextual self. The second one does so through a deictic relation ("If I were you and you were me"), but it is also quite a bit riskier because it moves strongly toward the correctness of the therapist's guesses about motivation rather than trying to help the client contact a more open sense of self. Unless it is part of a long pattern that was worked on repeatedly in therapy, the therapist probably would be wisest to say something softer, such as the first response. The third response could be fine, but is linked to self as context in the sense that it might encourage defusion from a conceptualized self.

## EXERCISE 9.6

Place a check before the response that best exemplifies defining valued directions:

_____ "I see how important it is to you to move forward. *And* when you thank me for the progress, I get a feeling I'm being held at bay. I could be way off, but that is what comes up. I'm in here for you, not me. I want to know what your actual experience is, whether or not it is easy for me to hear."

_____ "It seems important to do what works in your life right now, and openness is a more workable value than is being closed. So, are you being open with me right now?"

_____ "Okay. Could I ask you to look at something? As you say that to me, what do you think it is in the service of? That very statement. Don't answer right away. See if you can open up to what it is you are reaching for—what you really want, as reflected in that small moment."

Check your favorite response before you continue to read.

**Explanation:** The second response has the therapist telling the client what to value, which is a serious error in ACT. Workability here is with respect to chosen values, so the second response puts the cart before the horse. The first and third responses are better choices. The therapist could pick among them according to context. The first is more definitive and directed, the third more tentative and exploratory.

---

## EXERCISE 9.7

Place a check before the response that best exemplifies committed action:

_____ "If you are committed to you recovering from your eating disorder, you really need to be committed to following the eating plan we've devised."

_____ "Could we do something in here? I'm not saying this is true and what you said is not, but I want to see if together we can go into hard places. I'm going to move my chair up close to you, and I'd like you to look me right in the eye and see what it feels like to say—and for me to hear you say it—'I try to make you think I'm fine even when I'm engaging in old patterns.'"

Check your favorite response before you continue to read.

**Explanation:** These responses are a bit more difficult to write and to envision because committed action is not just a statement, it is a pattern of action. The first response pushes the client to commit to an eating plan, but it is preachy and probably would result in the client continuing to try to please the therapist. The second response confronts this issue directly, and thus, while bold and a bit risky, is a better response.

---

# The Client Wants Something Explained

The next series of exercises is perhaps among the most difficult in the entire book. In these exercises, you need to generate responses for each of the core ACT processes, both when the client response indicates increased psychological flexibility and when it does not.

You may find yourself struggling to respond in what seems like a fluid and effective manner (we did). It is dangerous to include such an exercise because readers may notice their struggles and presume that means they are not doing well or do not understand, or that ACT is not for them. Such metacognitive information can be misleading. You need to know that, like a complicated scale for a musician, this is a somewhat artificial exercise designed to broaden and smooth out your repertoire. Such a goal is just inherently difficult.

The general target of this process is to increase the psychological flexibility of the client by responding effectively to client expressions of flexibility or inflexibility that occur in the moment of the psychotherapy relationship. The therapist can respond at a level that involves modeling psychological flexibility on the part of the therapist (e.g., "I'm noticing that I'm thinking that I don't know what to say. You don't need to rescue me; I can sit with it. Still, I wanted to share that. Do you sometimes feel that way with this?"); targeting the relationship directly (e.g., "And what feelings about our relationship are associated with that thought?"); or responding to the relevant instance of behavior in an ACT-consistent manner (e.g., being accepting of a challenging remark).

Here are some hints about completing these exercises. One way to generate responses is to look at the models presented earlier in this chapter. Imitating these responses fairly directly can give you an initial idea for an approximation of an effective response. Now, although this can be an easier route to an ACT-consistent response, it is also likely to result in less learning and in less of a sense of what it means to do ACT "in the moment." To build more flexibility, we encourage you to generate responses that are less like the models in form, but that still target the same process. Try to bring your own voice into it. One resource for doing this is to refer to the list of competencies for the particular process under consideration (see appendix C for a list of all the competencies). These competencies provide some general guidance without overly restricting creativity. You can also consider generating responses that model psychological flexibility in terms of your own psychological process (this needs to be genuine). Consider generating multiple responses in order to further expand your flexibility.

We decided not to provide model responses for this last series of exercises because we felt that a large variety of responses could be appropriate, and any particular responses we might provide could inadvertently lead to a narrowing of therapist behavior. If you do want feedback on your response, you can discuss these exercises on the bulletin board at www.learningact.com.

A substance-abusing thirty-nine-year-old male, who was recently in a twenty-eight-day program for detoxification and substance abuse treatment, comes to therapy. Married, with two teenage children, he abuses alcohol, marijuana, and speed. In the past, he has tended to over-think things, and in this almost obsessive state, he tends to use drugs. He presents himself as being hardworking and motivated to change.

Client:     I'm doing it. I'm doing it. One day at a time. I'm even using that *Get Out of Your Mind* book. That is a real trip. This week I was reading that part about values. But I have a question. It seems to me that goals are more important than values because goals are things you can really achieve—and I'm clear about what mine are—but values are kind of off in the distance, and I can't be sure what mine really are. And I don't understand how I can choose them. Could you explain to me why values are so important? And how do I know what my values are, anyway?

## EXERCISE 9.8

Assume the client's statement contains within it progress (given his baseline) toward greater psychological flexibility. For example, you are pretty sure the client is really opening up to the possibility of values as a choice. In this case, you want to model, instigate, and reinforce positive ACT processes. Your responses can contain multiple ACT processes, but write six different responses, each of which emphasizes one of the core ACT processes.

Acceptance:

Cognitive defusion:

Being present:

Self as context:

Defining valued directions:

Committed action:

## EXERCISE 9.9

Now assume the same client's statement mostly indicates psychological inflexibility. In this case, you think that the client is becoming enmeshed in trying to figure out values, but you doubt he is really acting in a values-based way. You think the intellectual question is a ruse to fill in therapy spaces by figuring things out, rather than by stepping up to change.

Again, your responses can contain multiple ACT processes, but write six different responses, each of which emphasizes one of the core ACT processes.

Acceptance:

Cognitive defusion:

Being present:

Self as context:

Defining valued directions:

Committed action:

---

## EXERCISE 9.10

Identify a client statement you have encountered that you think is interesting, but that also was difficult for you, and work through the same process. Decide whether you are attempting to reinforce a step forward, while simultaneously modeling and instigating ACT processes, or to avoid reinforcing ACT-inconsistent steps, while still modeling and instigating ACT processes. Examples of statements include things clients have said that you feel put you on the spot, statements you didn't know how to respond to, and actions in session that were challenging to manage.

Think of one particular statement from a past clinical encounter and write it in the space provided. The client says:

Now write down an ACT-consistent response that reflects the process specified. In each case, consider also the level of the response you are choosing to address. In other words, you could track the content, the statement as a social sample, the statement in terms of the therapeutic relationship, or the statement in terms of the symbolic and functional processes it instantiates.

Acceptance:

Cognitive defusion:

Being present:

Self as context:

Defining valued directions:

Committed action:

---

## EXPERIENTIAL EXERCISE: FINDING LEVEL GROUND

This exercise is aimed at practicing the stance that you and your clients are not fundamentally different, but rather are cut from the same cloth.

Who was the most difficult client you ever had? Write his or her initials here: ____

Create a list of adjectives that describe this person (try to name at least six to twelve):

Look at your family, childhood, and history, and consider whether any of these attributes remind you of your own past. Write about that for a minute or two.

Look at yourself and ask yourself: Is any of this somewhere in me? Could any of this be said about me? If so, write about that for a minute or two:

After you have finished, consider the following questions:

How was it to do this exercise?

Did you notice any hesitance or resistance in doing it? If so, what were you resisting feeling? Can you open up to that?

If you see parts of this other person in yourself, how are you toward these parts in yourself? Are you warm, welcoming, or compassionate, or is it something you have worked hard to change or have given up on?

Write about your answers to these questions here:

## FOR MORE INFORMATION

For more on the therapeutic relationship, see Hayes et al. (1999), chapter 10 (pp. 267–280), "The Effective ACT Therapeutic Relationship."

For a more theoretical treatment of the therapeutic relationship in ACT, see Pierson and Hayes (2007).

For a behavioral analytic take on creating powerful therapy relationships, see *Functional Analytic Psychotherapy*, by Kohlenberg and Tsai (1991).

# CHAPTER 10

# BRINGING IT ALL TOGETHER

*Given the distinction between your self and the stuff you are struggling with and trying to change (self as context), are you willing to have that stuff—fully and without defense (willingness/acceptance), as it is, not as what it says it is (defusion)—and do what takes you (committed action) in the direction of your chosen values (values), in this time and this situation (being present)?*

—Wilson, Hayes, Gregg, & Zettle (2001, p. 235)

Learning ballroom dancing begins by repeatedly practicing the basic parts of a dance: spinning, leading, resting lightly on the balls of your feet, the basic steps, keeping a beat. After you have developed some skill with each of these aspects, you learn how to put them together into a coherent pattern. As you improve, you begin to improvise—adding a spin here, a flourish there—until the whole dance is an improvisation, created from these smaller parts. Eventually, you're able to respond fluidly and quickly, effortlessly weaving among other dancers on the floor, staying within the skill of your partner, matching the song that is playing.

This metaphor also describes the process of learning ACT. Throughout most of this book, we focus on the parts of the therapeutic dance that is ACT. Each needs to be understood on its own, and each practitioner needs to develop a basic fluency in each part. Increasingly, ACT researchers have shown that each of the ACT processes is effective in its own right. However, these individual moves only make a dance when they are put together.

In chapter 8 you had a chance to practice conceptually integrating all the ACT processes in a comprehensive case conceptualization, and in chapter 9 we began to consider how the various processes come together in the therapeutic relationship. Now we carry that one step further to help you to see how the various ACT processes are integrated and sequenced in the course of a typical ACT session. You are provided with some examples of the interwoven processes and also with practice exercises we hope will help you to improvise, experiment, and intervene using these basic patterns.

For the convenience of your learning, the six ACT processes have been presented largely as if they were separate processes. In practice, they are often densely interwoven, with the therapist rapidly and responsively shifting from process to process, interweaving them in response to the current context. That being said, ACT often focuses more heavily on a single process in particular sessions.

ACT has typically been conducted in one of two basic patterns. In one pattern, work begins with a focus on undermining the current psychological system or on creative hopelessness, in order to create an initial openness in that system so something new can be introduced. This is usually followed by initial willingness work, focused on the idea of control as the problem. Next follows a good deal of introductory defusion work, illustrating the basic concepts and moves. Throughout this process, homework is liberally used. Self as context is then introduced and developed. Values assessment and clarification occur. Then the idea of committed action is introduced, and willingness is reintroduced in a new light as something that allows action toward valued ends. The remainder of therapy is a process of systematic behavior change—components of which are often taken from behavior therapy and behavior analysis, in which commitment, willingness, values, and action are intermixed into exposure, skills development, and active behavior change. This final phase is presented in the context of practicing ACT processes introduced earlier in therapy. For example, formal exposure is done as a willingness and flexibility exercise, in the context of a defused, present-focused, conscious, and flexible expression of a valued path. This is the pattern according to which the original ACT text (Hayes et al., 1999) and *Get Out of Your Mind and Into Your Life* (Hayes & Smith, 2005) were written. Indeed, it fits with how the present volume is structured.

A second typical pattern has also been used for ACT. In this pattern, values assessment and clarification are conducted at the start of therapy. Committed action begins shortly thereafter, and all the other ACT processes are contextualized in terms of their relationship to valued action. Values work is revisited throughout therapy so the fusion and avoidance aspects that can sometimes be seen early in values work are systematically weeded out as clients understand more about how to create psychological flexibility. In this pattern, it is rare to see a whole therapy session focused on any one process; rather the focus is on multiple processes in each session. Books such as *ACT for Chronic Pain* (Dahl et al., 2005) and *ACT for Anxiety Disorders* (Eifert & Forsyth, 2005), and the chapter by Wilson and Murrell (2004), were written in this style. *ACT for Anxiety Disorders* is a particularly well-written protocol and is worth reading to supplement the present volume because it gives many examples of how to weave several processes together in a single session.

Research protocols have been written in both formats, and they each appear to be effective in moving ACT processes and in creating positive outcomes. However, research has provided no clear indication about when using one of these two patterns is better. The general clinical view—so far not evaluated with formal research—is that clients with little motivation for change (e.g., coerced clients, drug and alcohol abuse clients who are in early stages of change) can benefit from a strong focus on values at the beginning of therapy.

Additional formats are available, as well. For example, some extremely short protocols use a psychoeducational approach to the problem of control, and then proceed to willingness, defusion, and values work in rapid sequence. Prevention protocols often add relatively large doses of formal mindfulness homework as a way of practicing acceptance and defusion.

In the absence of more information, we consider it wise at this point to learn multiple styles, emphasizing those that fit your clinical style, and approximating those that clinical research has shown to be effective for the particular problems being treated. For downloadable manuals see www.contextual psychology.org/treatment_protocols.

# SAMPLE TRANSCRIPT ILLUSTRATING ALL SIX PROCESSES

An annotated transcript of a session illustrates how the therapist integrates work from all six core processes of ACT into a relatively short section of therapy. In the central part of the transcript, an eyes-closed exercise is conducted. ACT usually includes a fair number of exercises in which the therapist leads the client through a process of getting present and then guides him or her through an imaginal scene or exercise. Many therapists are not familiar with or comfortable with conducting this type of work, and therefore need to be mindful of their own concerns and discomfort with such an exercise and learn to make room for this discomfort while practicing these exercises. This transcript is presented as a model for therapists to study how they can improve their eyes-closed exercises.

This transcript is from an eighth session with a thirty-three-year-old male who has mixed anxiety and depression as well as problems with assertiveness. In the current session, he has presented a problem of feeling intimidated by a person he supervises, who he says is saying bad things about him to his other supervisees, but who does not directly say anything to him. He feels he needs to talk to this person in order to maintain his effectiveness as a supervisor, but is scared to do so.

# TRANSCRIPT 10.1

| | **Commentary** |
|---|---|
| *Client:* Yeah, I don't even walk by his office anymore, and I make sure I don't go into the lunchroom between noon and one so I don't have to see him. I've even started to keep my lunch in my office instead of the shared refrigerator. | |
| *Therapist:* And what is it like for you to do that? | |
| Client: Well, I feel a little like a wimp. But I also don't know what to do. When I get around him, it always turns out badly. I freeze up and can't talk. I feel like a little baby. | |
| *Therapist:* Yeah, you feel small. Can you touch that feeling right now, that feeling small, scared—is it here right now? | *Being present and acceptance:* assessing whether the client is currently experiencing the barrier; helping him to get present to it |
| *Client:* Sure. It's here right now. | |
| *Therapist:* So that passenger isn't just visiting you when you're around this guy, he's doing it even at other times. When he's not around, when you just think about him, this smallness—feeling like a wimp, wanting to shrink—shows up, yes? | *Cognitive defusion:* noticing automaticity; referring to the feeling as a passenger |
| *Client:* Yeah. | |
| *Therapist:* And when you feel this way, what does your mind say you should do about it? | *Cognitive defusion:* referring to his thinking as "What does your mind say?" |
| *Client:* I want it to go away, to do something to relax, distract myself. | |

*Therapist:* So your mind says to get it to go away, that if you can relax and feel less anxious, that would help. And as we've talked about before, you do often feel a little bit better right away. But let me ask you this: In your experience, has this really solved the problem? Has following what your mind has to say about this resulted in this problem shrinking over time? What does your experience say?

*Acceptance:* noticing the link between thoughts and the pull to avoid

*Client:* No, it's just gotten worse.

*Cognitive defusion* and *acceptance:* comparing what his mind has to say with what his experience has to say

*Therapist:* So, if trying to manage it, to get it to go away, and to feel better haven't worked, are you willing to do something that's probably going to make your mind scream or have a tantrum? Would you be willing to do an exercise in which we invite that passenger, the anxiety, to get really close to you if doing the exercise means you might be able to have something new in your life, such as being the kind of supervisor you want to be?

*Acceptance:* asking client if he is willing

*Values clarification:* connecting willingness and valuing

*Client:* Okay, maybe. What are we talking about?

*Therapist:* Well, I'd like to do an eyes-closed exercise involving a memory of interacting with this guy from work. Something in which you imagine that happening and do various things with it. Are you willing to do that?

*Acceptance:* getting permission to step into something difficult

*Client:* Okay.

*Therapist:* To start off, why don't you go ahead and get comfortable in your seat. [pause] I want you to become aware of the fact that you are here now, in this room, across from me. See if you can psychologically, in your mind's eye, see where you are in the room—visualize yourself, where you are seated, across from me, exactly where you are in the room. [pause] Then bring your awareness down and into your physical body and the sensations you feel there. See if you can become aware of the position of your body from the inside out. Become aware of air coming in and out of your nose and what it feels like to breathe in, the path that the air takes, [pause] and then to breathe out, and the path that the air takes. [pause] Notice the slight difference between the temperature of the air you breathe in and the temperature of the air you breathe out.

*Being present:* guiding the client to get in contact with the present through attending to his body

And see if you can become aware of the space behind your eyes. And then I want you to notice that there's a part of you that is aware of all these things. Sometimes people say there is a sense that they're behind their eyes. See if you can catch the sense that there is a person here called "you" who is aware of what you are aware of. [pause]

And I want you to think of something that happened last summer. Take a few moments to find one. [pause] Let's go back into that memory from last summer as if you were right back in your skin looking out from behind those eyes again. And in your mind's eye, look around you and see what was happening, who else was there. What were you hearing and seeing? See if you can catch maybe a little bit of what you were feeling and thinking.

*Self as context:* asking the client to notice that a part of him is aware of what he is aware of; then continuing with a short exercise to help the client contact a sense of self as observer, and with the continuity of that, sense across long time periods

And then I want you to notice that you were there then, and that the same person who is listening to me now in some sense was there then. As you notice the person who was behind those eyes, notice there's a continuity, a continuous line, between that person and the person who's here now. You've been you for your whole life. You were there last summer just as you are here in this circle now, even though lots of things have changed. Your body, emotions, and thoughts have changed—but in some deep sense, you are still you. This is not a belief, and I'm not making an argument; I just want you to catch the experience of being a person aware of what you are aware of. To have a word for it, I'll call it the "observer" you, the part of you that observes or is aware of what you're aware of. So, that kind of deep sense of you—I want you to connect with that, and say good-bye to the memory from last summer.

Now, I want you to find a memory of a time when you were around this guy at work, a time when you felt small and insignificant, intimidated. Take a few moments and find a memory. When you've found one and can picture it clearly, raise your right finger.

*Client:* [raises right finger]

*Acceptance* and *being present*: helping the client vividly recall the memory and emotions for a willingness exercise; learning only occurs when one is in the present moment

*Therapist:* Take a few moments and look around in that memory. What do you see? Where were you? [pause] Who was there? [pause] Feel your feelings. [pause] I'm going to ask you some questions as we go along, but let's not get into a conversation here. So, if you can, please keep your eyes closed and make your answers brief, okay?

*Client:* Okay.

*Therapist:* So, from the perspective or point of view of the observer, I want you to look at some parts of this experience. So, first, what are you noticing in your body?

*Being present*: bodily sensations only occur in the present, so having the client observe his bodily sensations can bring him into the moment

*Client:* Anxiety.

*Therapist:* Well, anxiety is an emotion, not just a bodily sensation. So, let's first look at the part of anxiety that is a bodily sensation. Notice where you feel it in your body. [pause] We just want you to spend some time sitting with it, getting familiar with it. What do you feel in your body?

*Client:* A tightness in my stomach.

*Therapist:* Okay. So just notice that. See if you can let go of any struggle with that sensation. Is that tightness something you have to stop?

*Willingness*: sometimes it helps to work on more specific minor areas first

*Client:* I can have it.

*Therapist:* Good. Now let's come back to the emotion of anxiety. Take a moment to notice your posture toward that emotion. What does your mind say about it? Do you like it? Do you want it to go away? How do you feel about it? You can answer me.

*Client:* I don't like it. I want it to go away.

*Therapist:* If you had to rate on a scale from zero to ten how willing you are to have the feeling of anxiety, just as it is, without changing it or doing anything about it—where zero is completely unwilling and ten is completely willing and welcoming—what would you say?

*Client:* Three. I don't like it and I want it to stop.

*Therapist:* Yeah, you don't like it. *And*, willing is not liking. You can be willing to have what you do not like. You remember that?

*Client:* Right, yeah.

*Therapist:* I want you to see if we can renegotiate your relationship with this feeling a bit. You said you were a three. Can you move that up a little more, open yourself up a little bit to the feeling? [pause] And then a little more. [pause] So, if you can, treat it kind of the way you might clear a spot at the table for a newly arriving guest, whether the person is your favorite or not. [pause] And where are you in terms of your openness to it?

*Client:* I'm at a six.

*Therapist:* Good. Keeping in touch with the scene with your coworker, visualize it. He's there. And then see if you can open up even a bit more. You can't stand this guy and you're not sure what to do. Notice the feelings, where you feel them in your body. [pause] Notice what your mind gives you. And the pull to do something, to avoid or run away. [pause] How intense is the anxiety from zero to ten?

*Client:* Six.

*Therapist:* I want you to see if you can hold this feeling lightly, as you might hold a butterfly that has just landed on your finger. Take a few moments to do this. [pause] Must this feeling be your enemy, something you need to struggle against, or can you let it be there just as it is? You don't need to like it or want it, just let go of struggling against it. [pause] And for a little while here, I'm going to be silent, but I want you to keep looking for what your body does, and dispassionately, as that observer, watch what your body does. And as you notice each sensation, see if you can simply acknowledge it, welcome it, say hi to it. And as you do all this, see if you can notice, just for a second, that there's a part of you that stands back from all this, noticing it all. [long pause] [at this point, the therapist can continue the exercise with other dimensions of responding, such as evaluations, behavioral predispositions, other images, or associated emotions; see the Tin Can Monster exercise in Hayes et al., 1999]

So, to wrap up, I'd like you to picture the room and what it will look like when you open your eyes. And when you are ready to come back, open your eyes

[pause] Okay, so what was your experience with that?

*Client:* Um. Well, it was kind of intense at first, I didn't really want to be doing the exercise. But ... I mean, I did it anyway. I felt a little better as we went along. It got less intense.

*Willingness:* when direct requests are not enough, use of metaphor can sometimes help clients find a mindful, accepting stance to take because most people know how to be willing and welcoming even without liking in some contexts, such as when a guest arrives who is not their favorite

*Self as context:* adding a little cue in an attempt to bring back the observer perspective for a moment (And as you do this ...)

*Therapist:* Okay, so it got less intense. For what we're doing, it's not really important whether it got less intense or not. Sometimes feelings are intense, sometimes not. They're always changing. What's more important here is your struggle against it. Did you notice any difference between when you were more willing later and at first when you were less willing?

*Client:* Yeah, I felt more tense at first. It was hard work. It was easier, somehow, later when I was more willing. I was more open I guess ... even though it was scarier in some way.

*Therapist:* Neat. So, let me ask you this: Is there a way you could bring a greater degree of willingness to do this in your real life? What is something you could do that would be about being the kind of manager you want to be, that would require some willingness such as this?

*Client:* I guess I could go confront him.

*Therapist:* Yeah, you could do that. My sense is that maybe we need to lay a little more groundwork before we get to that, so maybe we're not there yet. I wonder if there's anything else you've been thinking about doing that is kind of scary that would feel like a step in a positive direction?

*Client:* Well, I know I don't even walk by his office. I mean, if I even think of walking by his office, I get anxious.

*Therapist:* So you avoid walking by his office because that makes you anxious. One thing we might do is have you walk by his office while watching what shows up for you as you do that; to do it with willingness, not with struggling, but maintaining this sense of openness and willingness you practiced here in this exercise. What we're working on here is your ability to stay present with yourself even as you do some things that are difficult; to learn to make room for whatever part of your history shows up in the moment and to keep your feet moving in your valued direction. And what's doing this hard work about? What's your value that you're trying to live out here?

*Client:* Letting them know I care, making my workplace fun, and building a sense of teamwork.

*Therapist:* Does spending some time practicing getting more familiar with—practicing willingness with—these feelings seem like a step in that direction?

*Client:* Yeah, because I need to be able to talk to him; he's hurting our morale at work.

*Therapist:* So maybe you could spend some time sort of purposely walking into that feeling of being intimidated by him, feeling anxious about what might happen, as you did today. If you were to spend some time each day walking by his office, would that do it?

*Client:* Yeah, that would be a good start. How about I do it twice a day?

*Cognitive defusion*: not taking feeling better literally

*Willingness*: helping the client contrast struggle and willingness

*Committed action*: introducing the idea of translating this willingness into real life and briefly linking that to values

*Willingness*: seems like a pretty big willingness leap, one the client probably can't do with 100 percent willingness at this point; asking the client to think of something smaller

*Values clarification*: tying this back to the valued direction

*Willingness* and *committed action*: linking willingness and action to values

*Committed action*: making a commitment to action that is about moving toward this valued direction

*Therapist:* Sounds great! And remember, as you do it, try to bring a mindful, welcoming posture to whatever reactions show up for you. Watch your willingness as you do it, and watch what passengers show up and welcome them in. Treat your own reactions kindly. *And* remember this is not about making this stuff go away; it is about learning to carry your own history forward into a more powerful and effective life at work.

*Psychological flexibility:* summarizing the whole model, bringing all six core processes together in a few sentences

*[Therapist and client spend the rest of the session solidifying the between-session practice and developing a method to track what happens]*

# TROUBLESHOOTING ACT: SEVEN COMMON PITFALLS

Knowing how to detect common mistakes in applying ACT is essential in monitoring your own skill and learning over time. Developing competency with ACT is the result of a learning process. ACT therapists do not strive to provide the perfect metaphor or exercise, but rather attempt to contextualize these interventions to the lives of their clients, and in the process often even the best therapists make mistakes. Being able to detect common pitfalls can help you avoid inconsistency that could lead to client confusion or that could result in a disruption to the therapeutic alliance, which in turn could lead to premature termination of therapy.

**Pitfall 1:** Feeding avoidance and fusion

ACT defusion techniques require a therapist to step outside of the normal, literal way of speaking and to say and do things that would not ordinarily be considered acceptable in social discourse. This history of social training can be difficult to overcome. The challenge for an ACT therapist is to join clients in their subjective verbal reality, while at the same time remaining aware of the ongoing process of languaging and simultaneously using words to help clients defuse. The difficulty is in teaching clients the behavior of defusing, without attempting to convince them to defuse (which would happen inside the system of literal language). Ideally, therapist speech within ACT is oriented primarily toward supporting nonliteral experiences, such as metaphors or experiential exercises.

For example, in most situations, when someone asks you a question, you respond directly. However, fairly often, clients' information seeking can be an avoidance behavior. For example, clients who worry (e.g., as in the case of generalized anxiety disorder) often seek as much information as possible before making decisions, to the point at which even simple decisions can become overly burdensome and complicated (Eifert & Forsyth, 2005). Other clients spend a great deal of time trying to understand their history and why someone did something in the past, or why they are the way they are—and all the while their lives are passing them by. Sometimes, rather than more information, clients need to simply make room for whatever mind chatter and emotions are present and to take action toward their values. However, therapists, having been trained in the same social community, feel pulled to answer clients' legitimate and sometimes heartfelt questions. It can be difficult for the therapist to not answer these questions directly and rather to defuse from them. One way therapists sometimes get stuck is through responding literally to content that would best be sidestepped. Literally, a client's statements seem to be a way to seek information, but functionally they serve as a way to avoid or escape difficult or painful material.

Here's an example of a therapist feeding fusion, with the pitfall identified at the point in the dialogue where it occurs. This was taken from the twelfth session with a thirty-five-year-old male who expresses a great deal of confusion and uncertainty about who he is and what he wants to do with his life. The therapist has conceptualized this as a way for the client to avoid responsibility for his life and to be able to avoid memories and feelings related to a chaotic and unpredictable childhood. The client has committed to telling his wife how important she is to him. The following transcript occurs at the beginning of the session.

*Therapist:* So, what happened when you attempted to engage in your commitment from last week?

*Client:* Well, I'm not sure I understood what I was supposed to do. I thought about doing it, then realized I didn't know what I was doing.

*Therapist:* Okay, so let's break this down. What came up that stopped you from talking to your wife about how you feel about her?

*Client:* I was thinking about doing what we talked about, then I realized I don't really know how I feel about the situation: sometimes I want to leave, sometimes I want to stay. So I thought I'd hold off on that until I work it out a bit more in here.

*Therapist:* Where do you think that ambivalence comes from?

This last response by the therapist can be considered a pitfall in the sense that it probably will lead to more causal explorations, which is exactly what the client tends to do already (i.e., look for resolution to ambivalence before moving on with his life). In other words, this response simply feeds the avoidance. It also takes the client's analysis literally, as if ambivalence must be resolved before living one's values. Instead of the pitfall, imagine the therapist said this instead:

*Therapist:* Okay, so let me check out what happened. Last week we talked about your values in relation to your wife, and how your values meant you want to be more caring toward her, correct? And you made a commitment to that? Then, when it came time to put that value into action, your mind started talking to you. It started saying things such as, "Well, I'm not sure you really feel that way" and "Maybe you are being fake" and "Let's wait until next therapy session to work on this." And it's not that these are wrong or incorrect, but notice that meanwhile another week has gone by, and here we are again, right?

*Client:* Right.

*Therapist:* So, could I ask you this: would it be possible to have exactly those thoughts, as thoughts, and still do something caring?

*Client:* I guess. I'm not sure I can, though.

*Therapist:* Well, that's the same issue. Would it be possible to think, "I'm not sure I can, though," and thank your mind for that thought, and still do something caring? Would you be willing to see? What is something you could do that would involve being caring toward her?

Other forms of this pitfall include:

✓ *Getting caught up in explaining defusion to clients.* This usually results in the session feeling somewhat logical and removed from the client's experience. Fewer defusion exercises and metaphors are seen, and more talking *about* situations occurs. The main time it is relatively safe to talk about an ACT process is when there already is a sense of connection with that process in the room, and talking about it is a matter of briefly verbally encapsulating the benefits. As a means to produce benefits, it rarely works well to talk about defusion, with the possible exception of problems that call for brief psychoeducational intervention.

✓ *Slipping into a one-up position*, in which the therapist comes across from a place of arrogance and knowing what the right answer or solution is. One solution is for the therapist to remain humble and aware of whether he or she is being too sure of the correctness or rightness of defusion, of ACT, or of whatever is occurring in session. Therapists should use defusion on themselves and hold themselves lightly.

**Pitfall 2:** Using ACT metaphors and exercises in a fashion insensitive to timing, the client's in-session behavior, personal history, and other contextual factors

In this pitfall, a therapist can cram several metaphors and exercises into a session without a coherent context or without connection to the client's experience. Unfortunately, when we get a new hammer, we may have a tendency to make everything a nail. Thus, the therapist can be seen rambling from one ACT technique to another, while the client is lost with respect to what the therapist is doing. Ideally, ACT techniques are contextualized to the client's specific verbal behaviors in session, and metaphors and exercises are modified and tailored to fit them. Often this pitfall can negatively affect the therapeutic alliance, resulting in clients feeling disconnected from the therapist or feeling the therapist is not understanding them or is not on their team. Because ACT has a number of stock metaphors and exercises, it can be very important to repeatedly check in with a client's present moment experience, rather than rapidly shifting from exercise to exercise.

Other forms of this pitfall include:

✓ *Appearing dismissive of client concerns.* This is especially common with irreverent exercises and with comments that are poorly timed and are experienced as ridicule. Badly timed defusion exercises are a classic example, but any of the ACT processes carry this risk.

✓ *Ineffectively making light of clients' worries.* Therapists can inadvertently give the message that clients just need to "get over it."

✓ *Coming across as unnecessarily indirect or possibly disingenuous when using metaphors.* Sometimes clients push for direct answers to questions, and sidestepping these questions can lead to the impression the therapist is being evasive. If you find yourself searching for another exercise or metaphor to use and feeling unsure of yourself, examine whether this mirrors in some way how the client is feeling, and let your work be humanized by that.

**Pitfall 3:** Getting ahead of the client when conducting willingness/exposure exercises

This pitfall comes in a variety of forms. In one form, the therapist is not sensitive to the size of the step for the client and suggests exercises beyond the level of willingness with which the client currently is approaching these exercises. Exposing clients to situations in which they are unable to sustain a high level of willingness is unproductive at best and retraumatizing at worst. If a client is unable to approach an experience with willingness, then the situation at best will be another chance for the client to practice experiential avoidance or fusion—something he or she already has practiced plenty.

This situation can be avoided by following three steps. First, always ask the client's permission before doing an exercise that might evoke difficult or unpleasant private events. This gives the client a sense of choice in the situation and the opportunity to intentionally practice willingness. Second, conduct willingness exercises in a graded fashion, starting with relatively easier situations and gradually increasing in difficulty, while always keeping within the client's level of willingness and choice. Therapists can usually safely control the level of commitment by choosing the length of time for an exercise and choosing the situation (e.g., having a socially anxious client speak to a role-played stranger before speaking in front of a real stranger). On the other hand, setting a criterion for the level of intensity of the feelings, thoughts, or images that will willingly be experienced (e.g., "I'll be willing unless my anxiety goes above a seven out of ten") is asking for trouble, and therapists should generally not agree to this because it can undermine the quality of the process on which the client is working. Third, it is usually important to do training in defusion and self as context before doing willingness exercises. Without these processes, willingness exercises can turn into brute force exposure, potentially retraumatizing clients.

**Pitfall 4:** Using values coercively

Values can sometimes be used as a way to coerce clients into following through on things therapists want them to do. Values are not about having another way to "keep your client in line." They are not to be used coercively. Consider an example in which, relatively early in therapy, a twenty-two-year-old male client says he is going to call his father and tell him about an abuse incident that happened some years before with his older brother. The client had tried to tell his father at the time, but felt dismissed. This transcript takes place in the following session.

Client:      I just can't face him. It's too hard.

Therapist:   You said your value was to tell your father about what happened. Why don't you just accept your anxiety and go do it?

Client:      I know, but I'm afraid of what he'll say. I'm not sure I could handle it if he didn't listen to me again.

Therapist:   Well, you could give in to your fear, but that wouldn't be following your value. Haven't you suffered enough? If you don't do what you value, life is simply not going to change. So that is the real choice here: move ahead or not.

Client:      I want to move ahead.

Therapist:   Then stop messing around. Get your feet moving. Just do it. If you don't, nothing different is going to happen.

What appears to be occurring in this dialogue is that the therapist's agenda to create overt behavioral movement is dominating the client's. The therapist may be caught up in defending his or her idea of what the client needs to do, and may honestly want to produce change. However, the problem is that even if the client does achieve the goal the therapist has set out for him, it may not increase the client's psychological flexibility because, rather than the behavior being values directed, it is emerging out of pliance (i.e., social pressure from the therapist). Values are a choice, not a club to be used on the client.

It is not that the words are wrong; every single therapist statement in this transcript could fit into an effective ACT intervention. But, especially early in therapy, this kind of dialogue is almost certainly more indicative of social pressure than of reflecting back client processes. The therapist needs to make sure values clarification skills are being used, and to focus more on getting the client to move, based on what he really values, not based only on a social pressure to behave (done in the name of values).

Sometimes therapists can find themselves blaming a client (either out loud or in their heads) for breaking a commitment or for doing something counter to that client's values. Sample responses to this kind of stuckness include, "Why doesn't Marvin do what he says he is going to do? This client is so frustrating" or "Arlene has no motivation. I don't think there's much I can do, it's a biological thing. Maybe when the meds kick in, her motivation will get better" or "Jose doesn't care about his life." Behavioral psychologists sometimes say, "The rat is always right," and that joking statement holds an important core idea. Applied to clients, it conveys that the client is feeling, thinking, and acting exactly as he or she should be, given his or her learning history and current context. The job of the therapist is not to blame clients for their learning history, but to work to change the verbal and situational context to create new, effective behavior.

When a client is not doing what you as the therapist want that person to do, blame your own behavior and be glad because now you are in the same boat as the client and this can humanize your work. Blaming yourself for not arranging the right learning opportunities is an empowering place to stand because you can do something about your own behavior. Be assured the client is doing exactly what he or she should be doing, given his or her learning history and current context. Consider again your plan of action and change course if needed. Be open to taking risks and obtain consultation.

**Pitfall 5:** Being overly focused or not focused enough on goals

Sometimes the therapist and the client can become too focused on the accomplishment of particular goals or actions. While helping clients with committed action, it's important to keep in mind that the overarching goal of this process is developing psychological flexibility. We are trying to systematically build this capacity in our clients, not simply help them accomplish particular goals. Helping them accomplish particular goals is like giving people fish to eat, whereas helping them develop greater psychological flexibility is like teaching them how to fish. We want to empower clients to have a sense of effectiveness and real control over their own actions in life in the long run. However, we do not depend on this sense in the short run, but rather expect it to develop in the long run with repeated patterns of effective behavior. In this case, the harder the therapist pushes the client, the more resistant the client is likely to become. Motivation can instead be created by helping the client contact the costs of not following the value or the importance of the value.

On the other side of the coin is a lack of focus on goals. This can show up in the form of being vague about specific goals or actions that would instantiate values. It can also show up in not getting a firm commitment to accomplish a goal. It's usually best to get a clear statement from the client, with a specific time frame to complete the task. Often, therapists do not provide adequate structure or feedback in terms of translating values into a concrete action plan. A client cannot be expected to know how to develop a positive action plan for his or her life because this skill is not usually taught in the culture. The therapist's job is to help the client develop workable goals and actions in which the client is willing to engage.

**Pitfall 6:** Not connecting behavioral exercises/willingness exercises to deep/heartfelt values

It is important to attend to the context in which acceptance and defusion occur. Acceptance and defusion are not ends in themselves, but are only useful to the extent they help clients bring their values into their lived experience. Acceptance and defusion can be difficult, and what sets these apart from wallowing or masochism is that they are for a purpose. We might choose to wade through a swamp of misery if that was what stood between us and the life we wanted to live. The link to values is what dignifies and transforms our suffering from something potentially meaningless and purposeless into something of worth because it is part of a life with purpose. Exposure and willingness in ACT create pain for a purpose. While working on this, it is also important to avoid any connotation of "getting through" or "getting over," rather than "getting with."

**Pitfall 7:** Experientially avoidant clinician behavior

ACT is a challenging therapy for clinicians. In order to be done well, therapists have to step up to quite a challenge: being human, present, and in pain with their clients—all in the service of the clients. Many techniques and moves in ACT can evoke considerable discomfort and anxiety in therapists. Defusion can often lead to a sense of uncertainty because literal language has broken down somewhat, so it's unclear what to do or say next. Sometimes the only thing the therapist can do is simply be present and show up and see what happens. It can be very difficult in our appointed role as experts to not know the answers. For example, willingness exercises ask clients to experience difficult emotions, memories, and thoughts, without the therapist helping the clients feel better, think more rationally about themselves, and so on. The uncertainty created by effective creative hopelessness is often both anxiety provoking for the therapist and essential to the effective use of this method. Discussing and contacting values can lead clients to contact a huge sense of loss and pain in a life not lived, a pain the therapist would be wise not to take away. Clients who fully contact self as context sometimes have the experience of "falling into the void" as their attachment to their self-concept slips away.

Many aspects of ACT require considerable willingness on the part of the therapist to tolerate and accept uncertainty, not knowing, anxiety, and pain. Therapists are often tempted to try to reassure, rescue, and comfort their clients. If you feel this, check with yourself to see whether comforting, reassuring, or helping the client settle down is really in the best interest of the client or whether it is more about helping yourself feel better. See if you can wait a moment and consider what is really the most compassionate move in the service of the client.

# PRACTICE IN FINDING PITFALLS

The following transcripts provide examples of therapist and client interactions in which the therapist steps into one or more of the pitfalls described in the previous section. For each example, identify the pitfall in table 10.1, write a response explaining why this pitfall might be negative from an ACT perspective, and suggest an alternative response. Some of these pitfalls are deliberately subtle, so don't be alarmed if you think the therapist's response is pretty good. Look again, and from an ACT model, see if you can see a possible problem.

## TABLE 10.1

| Pitfall | |
|---------|---|
| 1 | Feeding avoidance and fusion |
| 2 | Using ACT metaphors and exercises in a fashion insensitive to timing, the client's in-session behavior, personal history, and other contextual factors |
| 3 | Getting ahead of the client when conducting willingness/exposure exercises |
| 4 | Using values coercively |
| 5 | Being overly focused or not focused enough on goals |
| 6 | Not connecting behavioral exercises/willingness exercises to deep/heartfelt values |
| 7 | Experientially avoidant clinician behavior |

## EXERCISE 10.1

This dialogue comes from the sixth session with a fifty-six-year-old male who spends a great deal of time stuck in depressive rumination. The therapist has just presented a number of exercises and metaphors related to the issue of contact with the present moment when the following dialogue occurs:

*Client:* I'm more confused than ever. I feel you won't answer my questions directly. You just keep telling me these stories and doing these exercises, but I don't see how they relate to my life.

*Therapist:* Well, I think I know another metaphor that might help you understand it better. What if your situation is like being stuck in quicksand …

What is the error here?

What might be the negative consequence of this error from an ACT perspective?

How might you respond instead?

**Problem with the above response:** The error is pitfall 2 and could also reflect pitfall 7 because the therapist may be sensing the session isn't going well at this point and using yet another metaphor as a way to escape his or her own anxiety. The client seems to be expressing frustration with the therapist and that probably needs to be addressed directly.

**Suggested response:**

*Therapist:* You sound frustrated.

*Client:* Yeah.

*Therapist:* It's as though I'm not listening to you and certainly not being helpful. It's possible I got off track for a little while here and got caught up in my own thoughts. My intention is always to be present with you here and to connect with where you are coming from, so it's neat to have your reactions put on the table, even if they might be hard for me to hear. [pause] So could I ask you this: this feeling of confusion, of frustration, of not understanding, or of not getting answers—could we just sit with that for a second? Maybe there is something inside that feeling that is really important for us. Could we just go there for a moment? [pause] Is there something familiar about this place?

**Explanation:** This response models acceptance and defusion, but then rolls the issue right back into the present moment, rather than into explanation, understanding, and technique.

## EXERCISE 10.2

The client is a nineteen-year-old female who is fairly psychologically aware and generally active and involved in sessions. The therapist has just finished the Taking Your Mind for a Walk exercise (Hayes et al., 1999, pp. 162–163) with the client when the following dialogue occurs:

*Client:*    Okay, so my mind is constantly chattering. But I don't get it. I'm not sure how that's helpful.

*Therapist:*    The point is that you don't need to listen to everything your mind tells you to do. Just ignore it.

What is the error here?

What might be the negative consequence of this error from an ACT perspective?

How might you respond instead?

**Problem with the above response:** The error is pitfall 1. This response operates inside the literal system, and thus supports fusion. The rule implied by the therapist's statement is "If you don't like something —> ignore it." This is not the point of the exercise. The purpose of the exercise is to practice a new skill, defusion. We cannot do that if we don't listen. Ignoring our minds is not defusion at all, in the same way that ignoring our feelings is not acceptance. Facility with defusion only develops through practice, and the therapist's response could promote more of that.

**Suggested response:**

*Therapist:*    Cool. And there it goes right now. Your mind is still talking to you. So just notice that. As for "helpful," that depends: where do you want to go?

**Explanation:** This response deliberately parallels the Take Your Mind for a Walk exercise. If the client's "I don't get it" statement is fused and avoidant, this response undermines these processes and brings the issue right back to values, action, and fusion as barriers.

## EXERCISE 10.3

The client is a forty-three-year-old mother of two who has been diagnosed with panic disorder with agoraphobia. She has lost her ability to be there for her family while she has struggled with her anxiety. The following dialogue occurs during an exposure exercise at a local department store:

*Client:*    I need to get out of here. I can't do it. The anxiety is too much.

*Therapist:*  Just stick with it. Don't leave. Anxiety comes and goes. You need to stick to your commitment to be in here for five minutes. You only have one more minute to go.

What is the error here?

What might be the negative consequence of this error from an ACT perspective?

How might you respond instead?

**Problem with the above response:** The error is pitfall 5 and pitfall 6. The goal of exposure is not simply staying somewhere for X amount of time. The goal is to live a more accepting and flexible life, linked to the client's values, not to pass five minutes per se. The clinician is communicating an excessive focus on the clock and not enough on the process and purpose of exposure.

**Suggested response:**

*Therapist:*  Good. So, notice that your mind is screaming at you. And as you feel that anxiety, as you touch it, see if you can also touch for a second that being in here is not just about anxiety. You came in here to learn how to be there for your kids and for your life, yes? What if opening up to Mr. Anxiety would serve that—would you be willing to do it? Let that question sit here, too, and notice that life is asking you this question right now. What if learning to be present and to let go is part of the process of learning how to be the mom you really want to be? Now, take that purpose right down into your body. Where are you feeling anxiety right now? Where in your body do you feel it?

**Explanation:** This response dances in and out of defusion, acceptance, and valued action. It contextualizes the work. The clinician is de facto encouraging the client to reach the five minute goal, but is keeping the focus on the key processes.

---

## EXERCISE 10.4

The client is a twenty-five-year-old depressed male in the fourth session.

*Client:*    I'm feeling so overwhelmed by work right now. It incapacitates me.

*Therapist:*  Okay, so let's work on that. Can we problem solve how to deal with this feeling? Why do you think you feel overwhelmed?

What is the error here?

What might be the negative consequence of this error from an ACT perspective?

How might you respond instead?

**Problem with the above response:** The error is pitfall 1. Working with this client to problem solve how to deal with this feeling is probably supporting the emotional change agenda, and thus supporting experiential avoidance.

**Suggested response:**

*Therapist:* What exactly does that feel like, and what does your mind do when you feel it? Can we create that feeling in here right now?

**Explanation:** Going into feeling overwhelmed communicates that the feeling itself is not the enemy, and gives the client a chance to create more flexible responses while feeling overwhelmed.

---

## EXERCISE 10.5

A fifty-seven-year-old female with chronic OCD is afraid of contamination with chemicals. During the previous session, she shared that she was afraid Drano crystals would pass from her to her children. The topic comes up again in the fifth session, and this time the clinician has the props needed to do exposure.

*Client:* Drano is harmful. It's a poison. It can kill. I'm afraid of what will happen to me and to my kids if I touch it. But my husband insists on keeping it in the garage ... so I have to drive my kids crazy telling them not to go near the garage. We fight about it, but he says he can't solve all my fears.

*Therapist:* Actually, the crystals need water to be dangerous. Look, I can pour some of them right into my hand and nothing bad happens because my hands are dry. [demonstrates]

What is the error here?

What might be the negative consequence of this error from an ACT perspective?

**Problem with the above response:** The primary error is pitfall 3, but the clinician is also risking fusion and is not linking exposure to willingness, flexibility, and values. One of the authors (SCH) of this book made this exact error with a client early in his career, and the client never came back. Always ask permission before doing exposure and willingness work. And keep the work focused on the key processes.

**Suggested response:**

*Therapist:* So, Drano is pulling a lot of difficult thoughts and feelings, and it is causing some difficulties in your relationship with your husband and with the kids, which is a pretty high cost, yes?

*Client:* For sure.

*Therapist:* It might be worth going into those difficult places in here so we can work on them directly. We've done enough acceptance and mindfulness work that now might be a good time to practice with real things. Would you be willing to have my secretary bring an unopened jar of Drano into the room? We could have her set it over there on the floor and start with what the jar itself evokes in your mind and your body, and how to be with these reactions in a more open and flexible way. That might be too high a place to start, though ... What do you think?

**Explanation:** This response gives the client a choice and focuses the work. ACT is an exposure-based approach, but brute force exposure is never the goal.

## More Practice in Finding Pitfalls

For more practice in identifying pitfalls, you can go back to your answers in this and the previous chapters and examine them to see if they exhibited any of the pitfalls. If so, what could have been problematic about what you said? For example, if your response was different from the model response, you can identify what impact your response might have on the client and whether it might feed a negative process from an ACT perspective.

# PRACTICE: BUILDING FLEXIBILITY WITH THE ACT MODEL

A major way to avoid stepping into pitfalls is not to try to avoid pitfalls at all, but rather to work to develop the same kind of psychological flexibility clients are asked to develop. One way to do this is through practice in developing multiple alternative responses to a single therapy situation. Sometimes it seems there is only one right therapeutic move to make in response to a given therapy situation. Books can foster that impression because they are inherently not flexible tools. But, in fact, 99 percent of the time, multiple ways forward exist within an ACT model. Without the flexibility to see multiple options, these other avenues never become apparent and ACT therapists can be tracked into narrow streams of behavior, along with their clients.

In this section, we challenge you (as we did in the last chapter) to build more flexibility with the ACT model by generating multiple responses to a single client verbalization. In each of these exercises, you are presented with a transcript and are asked to generate a response that corresponds to one of the six core processes on the hexagon model. As with other exercises, do your best to generate your own response before looking at the model responses. For the purpose of the exercise, you may want to look at the core competencies for each of the processes to prompt you if nothing comes to mind immediately (see appendix C for a list of core competencies). Even if you are unsure about how to generate a response based on the core processes, you will get the most out of the exercise if you generate one anyway, even if seemingly unskillful or inelegant.

## Practice Exercises: Building Flexibility

The therapist is in the fourth session with a fifty-four-year-old male who has struggled with alcohol problems for most of his adult life. He has had many periods of sobriety, followed by many periods of relapse. At the time of this session, he has had thirty days of sobriety, just enough time that he is beginning to come back to major areas of pain he covered up with alcohol. The therapist is concerned that he is getting close to a relapse. This transcript comes from a dialogue the therapist initiates about the client's values.

*Therapist:* You said you wanted to be about living your life sober. I hear from that statement there is something really important to you about being sober. What would being sober allow you to do? What would you hope your life to be like if you were able to maintain your sobriety?

*Client:* At this point, I just want to focus on my sobriety. I'm not thinking about anything else. I need to slow down and keep my eye on my sobriety, or I won't even make it a year. I feel as if my emotions are getting the best of me. Right now I'm working on slowing down. [pause] I just need to slow down.

*Therapist:* It seems as though your life is going too fast right now? Sort of like it's not headed where you want it?

*Client:* Not so much my life, more my mind. And my emotions. Before I know it, I'm racing along and then I'm off on a bender. It can be weeks or years before I stop again.

---

## EXERCISE 10.6

If you were going to work on *cognitive defusion*, write here what you would say:

What are your thoughts in saying this? What are you responding to and what core competency are you illustrating?

---

## EXERCISE 10.7

Using the same client statement as in the previous response ("It can be weeks or years before I stop again"), if you were going to work on *being present*, write here what you would say next:

What are your thoughts in saying this? What are you responding to and what core competency are you illustrating?

---

## EXERCISE 10.8

Using the same client statement ("It can be weeks or years before I stop again"), if you were going to work on *acceptance/willingness*, write here what you would say next:

What are your thoughts in saying this? What are you responding to and what core competency are you illustrating?

## EXERCISE 10.9

Using the same client statement ("It can be weeks or years before I stop again"), if you were going to work on *self as context*, write here what you would say next:

What are your thoughts in saying this? What are you responding to and what core competency are you illustrating?

## EXERCISE 10.10

Using the same client statement ("It can be weeks or years before I stop again"), if you were going to work on *defining valued directions*, write here what you would say next:

What are your thoughts in saying this? What are you responding to and what core competency are you illustrating?

## EXERCISE 10.11

Using the same client statement ("It can be weeks or years before I stop again"), if you were going to work on *committed action*, write here what you would say next:

What are your thoughts in saying this? What are you responding to and what core competency are you illustrating?

---

## Model Responses

### Sample 10.6a

*Therapist:* So your mind is racing along, and one of the things your mind says is to "slow down." It sounds like quite a struggle … On the one hand, your mind is the one speeding up; on the other hand, your mind's telling you to slow down. It's almost as if you were caught in the middle between these two parts of you that are sort of bossing you around.

*Client:* Yeah, I guess that seems kind of right. Sometimes I'm doing one, sometimes the other.

*Therapist:* It's as if you had all this programming, some of it telling you one thing, some telling you another, and there's a lot of stuff you don't want in there, right?

*Client:* Yeah.

*Therapist:* And this other part is telling you to slow down. What I'm suggesting is something a little bit different from that. What if what we needed is to step back a bit and watch the mental ping-pong without getting all entangled with it, either way? Let's take a deep breath here [does so] and let's watch your mind go for a bit. Just say out loud what your mind is giving you … but don't jump into it on either side.

**Explanation:** This dialogue illustrates the core competency: the therapist works to get the client to experiment with "having" difficult private experiences, using willingness as a stance. The client sees the danger of entanglement with a racing mind, but misses entirely the danger of entanglement with "I have to slow down." The therapist moves the process to defused mindfulness.

### Sample 10.6b

*Therapist:* Yeah, seems as though your mind is whacking you with scary thoughts—even to the point that it feels frightening to recall why sobriety matters. It's suggesting that something is wrong because emotions and thoughts are coming up, but this is the same mind that was there all along. You might remember, I warned you when we started that sobriety would bring up even more difficult things to face—especially all the stuff that drinking covered up. So this looks as though it's right on schedule.

**Explanation:** This dialogue illustrates the core competency: the therapist identifies the client's emotional, cognitive, behavioral, or physical barriers to willingness. The therapist is using defusion with the client's anxious struggle, noting the barriers that are emerging, and noting the costs of fusion occurring in the moment. The therapist is normalizing the struggle, but not minimizing it.

**Sample 10.7a**

*Therapist:* A minute ago, you said, "I just need to slow down." Can you remember that?

*Client:* Yeah.

*Therapist:* Can I get you to say that again, slowly?

*Client:* [said moderately slowly, with a flat affect] I just need to slow down.

*Therapist:* Can I get you to say that again, just one more time, but even more slowly and with some feeling?

*Client:* [said slowly and with a frustrated tone] I ... just ... need ... to slow down.

*Therapist:* Okay. And when you say that, how does it feel inside?

*Client:* I feel frustrated, like ... like ... I've been working so hard at it.

*Therapist:* Yeah, as you get really behind that, as if you really need to slow down, how does that feel? Does it feel as though you're relaxing and sort of backing off, or is it more as though you're actually picking up the struggle and working harder?

*Client:* Um, working harder, yeah. Weird.

**Explanation:** This dialogue illustrates the core competency: the therapist can defuse from client content and direct attention to the moment. The therapist directs the client to the latter's experience in the moment, as directly experienced, and away from the content about which the client is speaking (and incorporates a bit of acceptance at the end).

**Sample 10.7b**

*Therapist:* As you say this, that you need to slow down, I get a sense of desperateness there, as if your life depends on it.

*Client:* Yeah. [pause] It feels like it does.

*Therapist:* Can we sit with this a bit, this feeling of your life being on the line? What's it like inside as you sit with this?

**Explanation:** Same as previous.

**Sample 10.8a**

*Therapist:* I want you to consider something. What if it's the case that the problem isn't that your mind goes fast—all minds go fast—but the problem is your struggle with it, your attempts to get it to slow down? Tell me, what are the kinds of things you do to try to slow down?

*Client:* Well, I play it kind of safe and avoid heated conversations. I try to relax every day so I don't get too tired. I quit my last job and I'm going to look for something low stress this time out.

*Therapist:* And as you have done this, have you found in your experience that you have been able to slow down your mind, in a long-term way? Or is it the case that these things only work for a little while?

**Explanation:** The dialogue illustrates this core competency: the therapist actively uses the concept of workability in clinical interactions. The therapist shifts out of the pull to elaborate on the client's difficulties and directs attention instead to the workability of the client's efforts to slow down.

**Sample 10.8b**

*Therapist:*  The feeling that comes up right before you think, "I'm going too fast"—can we go there? How old is that feeling? How familiar is it?

*Client:*  It's anxiety. Like forever. I feel out of control.

*Therapist:*  Right. And so you try to get back into control by getting out of that feeling called "out of control." But what if that's where the growth lies? Maybe we need to go into that feeling.

**Explanation:** The dialogue illustrates this core competency: the therapist actively encourages the client to experiment with stopping the struggle for emotional control and suggests willingness as an alternative. The next step might involve asking permission to do an exercise in which the client practices willingness to experience the feeling of anxiety.

**Sample 10.9a**

*Therapist:*  I get the sense it feels as though you are in a war here with your own thoughts.

*Client:*  Yeah.

*Therapist:*  Do you know chess? [the therapist picks up a pad of paper and holds it up as if it were a chessboard]

*Client:*  Uh-huh.

*Therapist:*  Let's say this situation here is like a chess game. You've got the black pieces and the white pieces at war. [the therapist places various items on the notepad to illustrate "pieces"] All the pieces in this metaphor are your various thoughts, feelings, and memories—all the stuff you experience inside your skin. And so you go to war to try to have the white pieces win. You get aligned with the white pieces; you get down there on the back of the horse, the knight, and go out to battle. But what happens then is that you're really aligned with the thought, "I'm taking it slow enough." So that thought is the white pieces, and you need those pieces to win, so then the black pieces seem really threatening. And, you know, you have lots of those black pieces, right? Those pieces are within you. As soon as you get into this stance with those pieces, you are at war with huge parts of yourself. Your life turns into a war. And they try to knock each other off the board. But what's been your experience? As you've tried to get rid of these black pieces in your life—pieces you don't like, such as your urges to drink and your feeling that you're worthless—have you been able to win the battle? What if, in this metaphor, you're not the pieces at all, but you're more like the board, the arena, the context in which all this takes place? See, the board doesn't need to do anything; the board just holds all the pieces. It doesn't care whether there are a lot of them or few of them; it just holds them. And the board can move—just as I'm moving it back and forth in my hands right now. Would you be willing to do an exercise with me that can help you contact this board level? [suggests a mindfulness exercise, such as Leaves on a Stream]

**Explanation:** The dialogue illustrates this core competency: the therapist uses metaphors to highlight the distinction between the products and contents of consciousness and consciousness itself. Adding the experiential exercise at the end gives the client a way to have a direct experience of the distinction that was illustrated through the metaphor.

**Sample 10.9b**

*Therapist:* So, let's just go back and get the word machine doing its thing. See if you can get your mind yelling at you to slow down.

*Client:* That's easy.

*Therapist:* Okay. Then, when you really get into that space of noisy struggle, when you really hear it, raise your finger, and I want to ask you something. [pause]

*Client:* [after a while raises his finger]

*Therapist:* Who's hearing the noisy struggle?

**Explanation:** The dialogue illustrates this core competency: the therapist utilizes exercises to help the client make contact with self as context and distinguish this from the self as conceptualized. The therapist guides the client to get strongly into contact with the content of his experience and then utilizes this as an opportunity to help the client contact that part of himself that is conscious and an observer.

**Sample 10.10a**

*Therapist:* I get the sense there is something really important to you in this struggle to slow down. Something really important is on the line.

*Client:* Yeah, there is.

*Therapist:* What is it that you want in your life that is important, that you feel you don't have now? Can you tell me about that?

**Explanation:** The dialogue illustrates this core competency: the therapist helps the client clarify valued life directions. The client is focused on the problem and the solution to the problem (i.e., his life is going too fast and he needs to slow down). The therapist wants to bring in some of the larger picture related to what the client is attempting to accomplish by slowing down.

**Sample 10.10b**

*Therapist:* I get the sense you've been working to slow down for a long time. What is that about for you? Is it something you'd want on your tombstone? "Andy worked really hard to slow down"? Even sobriety: "Andy worked really hard to not drink alcohol"? Is that what this is really all about? That's life? If you could have something else on your tombstone, what would it be?

**Explanation:** Same as previous.

**Sample 10.11a**

*Therapist:* One problem with slowing down as a goal is that it's what we call a "dead man" goal. A dead man goal is a goal that a dead person can do better. For example, here, who can do a better job of slowing down his mind: you or a dead man? The dead man is going to win each time. What's one goal you've been putting off so that you can slow down? What have you been thinking about doing, but are afraid of doing, maybe because you think it will result in your mind speeding up?

**Explanation:** The dialogue illustrates this core competency: the therapist is helping the client identify valued life goals and build an action plan. The next step might be to work with the client to take action on whatever direction or goal he identifies and see whether slowing down is a solution or part of what stands in the way of his really living his life.

**Sample 10.11b**

*Therapist:* I think your instinct to slow down is right on. And maybe not just as a technique; maybe it's more important than that. Let's do it. Let's slow down right here, right now, and see if we can open up to what is here. Let's do that. [pause]

*Client:* [spontaneously takes a deep breath]

*Therapist:* Did you notice the urgency in your voice just a moment ago?

*Client:* I won't lie. I'm scared. I feel I have to do something.

*Therapist:* Right. That's how it works. So notice that pull to do something quickly. Then let's suppose there is deep wisdom in your wanting to slow down and get present. Here you can be real. Here you can live. Still, sometimes here is scary. How have you tried to get away from here?

*Client:* I numbed out. I drank. A lot.

*Therapist:* Yeah. And all mixed in with "I need to slow down and get present" is "quick, I have to deal with my mind and my emotions." Well, you had a way to do that, and look what it cost you. [pause] What I hear is that you want to live, you want to be you, you want to be here. And you can only do that if you're—?

*Client:* Sober. My drinking was costing me my life. It was costing me *me*.

*Therapist:* So let's not find a new way to run away quickly, supposedly in the name of sobriety, because that is just another way not to be you. Maybe sobriety is about something after all: it's about—?

*Client:* Me being me … [spontaneously takes another deep breath] I'm not running. I'm done running. I'm going to live right here.

**Explanation:** The dialogue illustrates this core competency: the therapist encourages the client to make and keep commitments in the presence of perceived barriers. Ironically, the client was mixing acknowledgment of the importance of living life in an intentional, conscious way with justification for yet another round of fused avoidance. By doing that, slowing down became a mere technique for self-manipulation, rather than an important indication of a wiser and deeper desire to show up to his life and live it in an honest and self-respectful way. A value was being covered up: the value of being present, alive, and authentic. His drinking became a violation of that value; but focusing just on sobriety in a closed-off, fused, urgent, avoidant, and self-manipulative way would be a violation of it as well.

# CONTEXTS THAT INFLUENCE THE SELECTION OF THERAPISTS' RESPONSES

The exercises in the previous section are somewhat artificial in the sense that the clinical encounters on which they are based are presented with relatively little context and therefore call for a great deal of interpretation from the reader. With the limited information, almost any process could be justified as useful. In the real world, the information that goes into selecting the appropriate technique is much richer and tends to favor the use of some processes over others. Nevertheless, we hope the exercises in this chapter are helpful in showing you that many options for responding are usually available in a given clinical situation. It is important for the therapist to have available the flexibility to utilize different ACT processes, depending upon clinical need. The selection of the exact intervention depends on the therapist's particular conceptualization of the client and his or her needs, the larger framework of the therapy, and the context of the therapist's own behavior.

## Understanding of Client Behavior

The specific client behavior in the moment defines the most immediate context that affects the therapist's response. Ideally, a client's behavior is responded to based on the therapist's in-the-moment functional analysis of that behavior. For example, is the client behavior a sample of avoidance, fusion, self-evaluation, or getting caught up in the past or future? This is the same as the in-the-moment functional analysis discussed in chapters 8 and 9.

In addition to client behavior in the moment, the therapist's interventions are determined by more extended patterns of client behavior that emerge across sessions. This is the realm of formal and informal case conceptualization. For example, case conceptualization might reveal a client weakness that warrants the development of a particular process across multiple sessions. As a result, the therapist would give greater focus to that process, regardless of the client's specific behavior in a given session.

## Larger Framework of Therapy

Therapists also select interventions based on parts of the ACT model they have already addressed in therapy and based on what they intend to do in the future with a particular client. For example, a therapist may do only a limited values assessment for a client who is being seen for no more than two sessions. On the other hand, a therapist who is seeing a client for longer term therapy may plan to help the client develop defusion skills prior to conducting willingness/exposure work with that client. How the larger framework of therapy affects what the therapist does in a specific session can be illustrated through numerous examples, such as the following:

✓ Previous work on developing agreement around goals and targets of therapy helps determine which interventions are selected.

✓ The therapist's knowledge of a client's values is usually important to develop prior to working on committed action.

✓ A therapist who is following the framework laid out by a particular manual may follow the form of that manual rather than respond to a particular client statement that could lead in another direction.

## Immediate Therapist Behavior

Effective ACT therapists learn to sequence and pattern therapeutic processes in complex arrangements that unfold rapidly across time. Often, one process sets the immediate context for a focus on another process. For example, contact with the present needs to occur during or immediately before values work, otherwise such work is dry and intellectual. Defusion that is not interwoven with acceptance is usually intellectual, invalidating, or both. Effective exposure-type exercises depend upon having at least some basic defusion skills in place and actively used so they do not become an example of the client white-knuckling through difficult experiences. Willingness exercises are often linked to values work because values provide the reasons that make willingness worthwhile. Contact with the present moment provides the experiential material that can allow the client to notice the person who is noticing (self as context). These contexts and patterns usually unfold over minutes, with the therapist dancing from process to process. This type of knowledge, often largely implicit, grows from practice. As therapists practice particular sequences of complex behaviors, they develop self-knowledge about the patterns of behavior they can access and which patterns tend to work.

# FREQUENTLY ASKED QUESTIONS

In this section, we review a number of common questions posed by therapists new to the ACT approach and provide brief responses. If you have any additional questions, you can post them on www.learningact .com or to the general ACT listserv maintained by the Association for Contextual Behavioral Science (links are at www.contextualpsychology.org).

**Question:** How do I introduce an experiential exercise or metaphor?

**Answer:** The extensive use of experiential exercises and metaphors that is characteristic of ACT can be anxiety provoking for therapists not accustomed to this approach. Because it is an experiential therapy, exercises and stories—as well as less didactic, more second-order forms of change—are important and occur frequently in sessions. Ideally, metaphors and exercises are contextualized to the specific nature of a client's difficulties. For example, the therapist can incorporate into a metaphor thoughts or feelings the client has expressed in the past or can let one of the client's comments evoke a particular exercise. Contextualizing metaphors and exercises helps avoid the problem of the therapist squeezing several metaphors or exercises into a session without adhering to a coherent theme. On the other hand, it can sometimes be hard to see how to directly connect a metaphor or exercise to a client's experience, even if the therapist senses that a particular exercise or metaphor could be helpful. In this case, it can still be worth doing the exercise in a more general form. We recommend that therapists get permission from their clients before introducing any exercises. A therapist can simply say, "I'm thinking of an exercise that might be helpful for you. Are you willing to do a short eyes-closed exercise with me?"

A beginning ACT therapist can take a number of steps to help sessions be more experiential. One is to follow a specific treatment manual. Manuals generally use a step-by-step approach and guide therapists to prepare for sessions by studying the appropriate session until they are able to deliver it consistently. If you are not following a manual, but are integrating ACT into work you already do or are using ACT in a less structured way, we recommend developing a loose plan for the ACT processes and exercises you could use in the next session. This way you can review the relevant metaphors and exercises (e.g., pick three or four) several times prior to the session to ensure you can deliver them accurately and understand their intended effect. A good way to prepare is to read them aloud because you will be speaking and listening in therapy, not reading silently. The DVD that comes with this volume is also helpful. Generally, it is not a good idea to read the text of the actual exercises in session with a client, although this can be done when learning an extended eyes-closed exercise, such as the observer self exercise.

**Question:** How do I explain ACT to clients and get informed consent?

**Answer:** Developing an adequate description of the process of therapy and general agreement on goals and tasks can be a bit difficult for a nonliteral therapy such as ACT. Because ACT is experiential and nonliteral, the process of therapy cannot be directly described. When clients come to therapy, their very understanding of their situation and of their change efforts is often part of the problem. However, it may not be helpful to immediately and directly share that with the client because it could be misunderstood as implying the client needs to get over the problem or be resigned to it. The solution most ACT therapists use is to speak metaphorically about the purpose of ACT.

The following transcript is a model of how the therapist can discuss informed consent with a client who has chronic worry.

*Therapist:* So, you've given me a picture of the concerns with which you've been dealing, and I also have a beginning sense of the larger picture of your hopes and dreams for your life. I want to give you an outline of what we might do in treatment and develop a contract for treatment before we actually get going. First, I can see how hard you worked to change yourself, to overcome the worry you have in your life. I can also see how this chronic worry seems to have gotten in the way of your relationships, particularly with your family. You've been working hard to get your worry and anxieties under control for years and yet it seems that hasn't panned out.

Some therapies help you develop more tools to try to get your worry in check, under control. My approach is not like that. It's as if a war has been going on with your worries … and some therapies give you more tools to fight that war. That is one approach. If you want to pursue that, I can get you a good referral to someone who uses that approach. The therapy work I do is more like learning how to leave the field of battle. The war may still go on, and you can see it, but you won't be living in a war zone. We'll work on ways to step out of this war with your anxieties, fears, and concerns in order to free up your hands and feet and energy to really live the kind of life you want to live. But you have to decide if this is the direction you want to go.

*Client:* [indicates being okay and wanting the therapist to continue]

*Therapist:* If therapy could be about helping you be the kind of mother and wife you most want to be, would that be worth doing? The depth of your commitment to your family and your willingness to acknowledge the places where you've been distracted by your worries and fears inspire me. If stepping out of the war with anxiety could make it possible for you to be the mother you most want to be, would you be interested in being in a therapy that is about that? [If the client wants more description about content, that can be talked about as well, but it also needs to be metaphorical.]

*Client:* What will take me out of the war zone?

*Therapist:* Well, one of the reasons it's difficult to answer that is that part of what keeps us in the war zone is literal language. I assume you've been doing what seems best, what seems logical. But I assume that hasn't been good enough: otherwise, why would you be here? To step out of the war, we may need to do something outside of simple logic. I'm not talking about doing anything crazy; I'm talking about changing the whole task ahead of you—what our normal mode of mind provides. So I can't answer your question inside that normal mode and still be understood. The closest I can come in this moment is this: stepping out of the war will involve changing how you relate to your own thoughts and feelings, and operating more on the basis of direct experience and your deepest yearnings. What that means concretely—well, that's what therapy will make clear. But I want to affirm that, ultimately, the person who will say if we are moving ahead or not is you, not me. So, I will need some time to work this through with you, but I'm not asking for a blank check.

Generally, it is a good idea to talk about what the empirical evidence has to say about the effectiveness of various alternative treatments, and about ACT. In addition to describing the general approach to therapy, ACT therapists usually ask clients to commit to an initial number of sessions of therapy and to put off evaluation until the end of this period. At the same time, therapists reaffirm the absolute importance of direct progress, as viewed by the client. In other words, we need a commitment for a reasonable but limited period of time, but we aren't saying "just trust us."

It is also good to warn about possible ups and downs. For example, ACT can be compared to riding a roller coaster that is gradually going uphill, but that at some points in time may appear to be lower than when the client came into therapy. If experiential avoidance has been assessed and the client has relatively high scores, it is helpful to predict that avoidance-based urges to drop out can develop during intense therapy processes, to normalize these urges, and to suggest how to bring them into therapy. Doing these things early in therapy, before the glue of the relationship has had time to set, can help reduce the chance of premature dropout and can give the therapist time to lay out this somewhat counterintuitive and often unusual approach, which can at times seem confusing, evocative, and painful to the client.

From an ACT perspective, the core of a treatment contract is a sense of shared values and a general description of the direction of therapy, as well as a stated choice to work together in these directions. Clients usually come to therapy implicitly espousing the dominant cultural story, which is that they need to feel better in order to live better. Living inside this story, they may find themselves endlessly pursuing feeling better, while living is put on the back burner. Because ACT is oriented toward freeing clients up to move in the direction of their chosen values, it is essential for the ACT therapist to have an initial sense of what really matters to the client (i.e., values), which may or may not be linked to feeling better. The treatment contract is built around this shared sense of the client's values and must be consistent with the client's larger life goals and dreams.

**Question:** Is experiential avoidance always a bad thing?

**Answer:** The short answer is no. The long answer is it depends. On the one hand, the ACT stance on experiential avoidance is pragmatic; in other words, experiential avoidance is "bad" when it doesn't work as defined in the context of a client's values. If experiential avoidance is not harmful to the client's life, then according to the ACT model, there is no reason to target it. And, for sure, some instances are not necessarily harmful. On the other hand, research over the past couple decades seems to suggest that experiential avoidance as a broad pattern of coping is one of the most destructive and harmful psychological processes in existence (Hayes et al., 2006). It has been related to many bad outcomes, from high-risk sexual behavior to pulling one's hair out, from panic attacks to burnout, and from depression to being unable to learn. Thus, it is reasonable to assume experiential avoidance is generally unlikely to be positive behavior when seen in clients as a broad response pattern. Ultimately, however, it is the client's experience that determines what is workable for that client.

**Question:** Come on, what's this stuff about "being in the same boat as the client?" You can't really mean that I and my client with schizophrenia are both equally dysfunctional.

**Answer:** ACT seeks to promote nonhierarchical, humanizing relationships between therapists and clients. We do not seek to deny the existence of differences between therapist and client, but rather to minimize those that do not serve the interest of the client. The ACT model assumes that because suffering is ubiquitous, the cause of suffering must be something that is ubiquitous. ACT/RFT suggests that the culprit is language itself and both the therapist and the client with schizophrenia have "the language disease." Although ACT recognizes that specific or abnormal factors can contribute to the form of a client's problems (e.g., a genetic predisposition to schizophrenia), that does not preclude a strong contribution by general processes based on language (e.g., experiential avoidance, fusion). In fact, two randomized, controlled studies have shown that ACT can result in a significant reduction in rehospitalization of patients with psychotic disorders, and that this result appears to be related to changes in ACT processes (Bach & Hayes, 2002; Gaudiano & Herbert, 2006).

**Question:** What is the role of psychopharmacology with ACT?

**Answer:** In most cases, medications do not eliminate thoughts and feelings. They moderate their impact. In cases in which medications make empirical sense, a soft stance is useful. Something such as the following statement often works well:

*Therapist:* As you know, medications do not 100 percent solve the problem for everyone, or you would not be in here today. But they do give us a peek at what it might be like to be less entangled with our thoughts and feelings. We will be working on another way. At some point, you may want to put the issue of medications on the table directly, but let's get some progress in here before we get to that.

In areas in which evidence shows medications can limit progress (e.g., the blocking effect of benzodiazepines on the benefits of exposure), the issue can be dealt with at the appropriate time. It is rare to start a course of therapy in ACT by trying to eliminate medication use, even under these circumstances; openness to continue to look at workability based in direct experience is all that is needed.

**Question:** I don't really like experiential exercises. Why can't I just explain to clients what they need to do?

**Answer:** Therapists can indeed do some good with ACT-based psychoeducation. However, we know that following verbal rules is not the same as behavior born from experience, which tends to be more flexible. Thus, we know that *how* the client learns can make a difference. The evidence and needs and values of the clients are the primary guides. As the therapist, your liking or disliking of approaches is worth noting. Accepting discomfort and doing what needs to be done is exactly what ACT is all about, so discomfort with ACT elements is not necessarily bad. Indeed, it can inform therapy greatly.

**Question:** Can you use creative hopelessness with hopeless or suicidal clients?

**Answer:** This question comes from a misunderstanding about terminology: creative hopelessness is not about making clients feel hopeless. The creative hopelessness phase of therapy is about validating the client's direct experience, letting go of what does not work, and preparing for real change. The result is typically hopeful and empowering, not depressing and hopeless.

**Question:** Is ACT not appropriate for some clients?

**Answer:** Because ACT is an evidence-based approach, the best answer is to follow what the current evidence suggests. However, something more specific can also be said. Sometimes this question is a way of asking, "What syndromes did you develop ACT to treat?" Usually the idea behind the question is that any treatment not targeted at specific syndromes is not empirically focused. That is false. The syndromal model is one way to do clinical science; it is not the only way. Indeed, we argue that this model has been relatively unhelpful, despite the enormous resources poured into it. ACT comes from an inductive, principle-focused tradition (i.e., behavior analysis) that has had a huge impact on empirically supported treatments, despite the fact that it has had a tiny fraction of research resources, compared with the syndromal model. So, another way to answer the question is this: ACT is not appropriate for clients without problematic

ACT-relevant processes, such as experiential avoidance, cognitive fusion, entanglement with a conceptualized self, psychological rigidity, and so on. Who are these people? The best answer is, again, to follow what the current evidence suggests, but we doubt the empirical answer will be something you can capture in a set of syndromal names. Clients with simple skills acquisition problems could be one example, but because cognitive and verbal processes often impede the learning of a new skill and ACT is useful with verbal and cognitive barriers, ACT should be of value even for a simple skills acquisition issue.

**Question:** How can ACT be combined with other treatments?

**Answer:** ACT is a model. Any technique that fits the model can be used. Many things fit the model that some therapists may think do not. For example, relaxation training fits easily—just treat it as training in letting go and don't present it as a tool to be used to fight anxiety. Direct cognitive disputation does not fit, but little current evidence indicates this method is helpful.

When other techniques fit within an ACT model, in our view, this combination can be called ACT, provided the fit has been tested. You don't need to do so, however. This is not about politics or branding. The point is that it is more worthwhile to open the right doors than to build the right fences. This attitude is widely held throughout the ACT/RFT community, and thus it allows ACT to benefit from the good ideas of its thousands of practitioners.

**Question:** What is the evidence supporting ACT?

**Answer:** Research in this area is moving rapidly. As of this writing, the latest comprehensive review is by Hayes et al. (2006), but you should continue to check the Association for Contextual Behavioral Science (ACBS) website (www.contextualpsychology.org) and keep your eye out for more recent data.

---

# CONCLUSION

Human beings can become so fused with their habitual process of minding that they become machine-like. The result is a verbally distorted person, caught up in evaluation, living in the future or past, controlled by his or her programming, inflexible, unresponsive, and constricted. Instead of being dominated by or attempting to dominate the verbal machine, ACT suggests we can learn to embrace this collection of habits, responses, and relations and bring the verbal machine along for the ride—just like any tool, to be used when it is useful, and not when it's not. ACT aims to help people find a more balanced approach to living and to empower them to live into their dreams, rather than living out of a limiting and defeating history. The goal is the journey—the journey toward full, rich human lives, lived with meaning and depth.

If you resonate with this work, you should know that you are not alone and that many others are on this journey with you. Make contact with them (see the appendices), and see what you might be able to contribute to others on this path.

ACT is part of an effort to create a new form of psychology. It is linked to a philosophy of science, to a basic program of research on cognition, and to applied research and practice that go far beyond the clinic. It is a large territory to explore, and a great place to start is with your own clients. That truly is the bottom line. And it is why we wrote this book. If the model does not work with clients, all of the rest is unimportant.

This book is about the core skills needed to begin to see how an ACT model works with your clients. We hope it helps you to empower and embolden your clients to step out of the war with their own pain and to begin to live.

## EXPERIENTIAL EXERCISE: BRINGING IT ALL TOGETHER

This exercise guides you through a process similar to what we might recommend for a client coming to the end of ACT therapy.

Write down the three most important things you learned from this book that you plan to incorporate into your practice:

1.

2.

3.

What are three things you could do to continue learning ACT or developing your abilities as a therapist?

1.

2.

3.

What are three high-risk situations that might pull you off track from following through with the goals you listed above? You know yourself best: how do you ordinarily get off track from following plans you set for yourself?

1.

2.

3.

Develop plans for how you might respond to these barriers from an ACT perspective. How might you respond to each of these three barriers?

1.

2.

3.

If you dig into an ACT perspective, you can see it has broad implications for families, schools, organizations, and culture, to name a few. If you see any of these connections, write down at least one of personal importance to you and your values. Then write briefly about how you might learn to extend the model into this domain.

# FOR MORE INFORMATION

For information about the application of the complete ACT model to a variety of different client populations (e.g., anxiety, depression, psychosis), settings (e.g., workplaces), and formats (e.g., groups), see *A Practical Guide to Acceptance and Commitment Therapy*, edited by Hayes and Strosahl (2005).

# USING THIS WORKBOOK IN GROUP AND CLASSROOM SETTINGS

This section is intended to provide guidance about using *Learning ACT* in the classroom, peer supervision, practicum, or any cooperative learning setting. We provide information about how classes can be structured; hints about forming effective peer consultation groups; ideas about using experiential exercises and role plays in learning ACT; and advice about modeling, reviewing video or audio recordings, and using the core competency rating form. A few controlled studies have examined the process of learning ACT (we mention some of them here), but most have not tried to break down the learning processes into specific components, so in this section we rely primarily on our history of using these training methods.

## GENERAL ISSUES IN USING THIS BOOK IN A GROUP LEARNING SETTING

One way this book can be used is as a core text in a course or study group focused on developing knowledge, skills, and competency in ACT. In contrast with ongoing supervision in ACT, which tends to incorporate experiential work with the therapist's barriers into the supervision process, study groups tend to focus more on learning the conceptual background and effective responses of an ACT therapist. There are ACT/RFT study groups around the world, both online and in person. Non-English-language communities have used such study groups to create a core of indigenous ACT-trained professionals.

In a course focusing on ACT, we recommend including at least one other comprehensive ACT text that is more theoretically and philosophically oriented, such as the original *Acceptance and Commitment Therapy* volume (Hayes et al., 1999). In classroom-based study groups, about three hours of class time per chapter is usually adequate to develop an introductory understanding of the material in this book. One session or class outline we have used is:

Start with an opening experiential exercise, often some sort of mindfulness exercise. For example, each week, a mindfulness exercise can be conducted that includes some aspect of the ACT process that is being focused on that week.

Briefly discuss reactions to the exercise, if any.

Have a discussion about the readings for the week and create an opportunity for questions to be asked and answered. Discussion questions for this book can be found at www.learningact.com.

Look for opportunities to conduct role plays as a way to respond to questions or issues brought up in class. For example, if a class didn't seem to understand a particular competency, the leader can decide to do a role play to illustrate that competency. Alternatively, a participant who has expressed uncertainty about the competency can try to role-play it as well as he or she understands it.

It is important for each participant to have read over the relevant chapter for that week and wrestled with the exercises before coming to class. Instructors are wise to check on this or test for it. It is helpful if each participant identifies questions or issues he or she has discovered during the process of reading the chapter and completing the exercises. One common issue worth discussing is the content of practice responses. Often, participants generate responses that do not appear formally similar to the model responses, and the question that emerges is whether these illustrate the competency. Similarly, the quality, appropriateness, and effectiveness of model responses can be discussed. Discussion of such issues can help the group better refine its understanding of the theory and technology. For example, if a participant has produced a response that is consistent with the competency but appears different from the sample responses, this can be an opportunity to help participants see how responses can be quite different in form while still being functionally similar. On the other hand, a response that reflects a misunderstanding of the competency provides an opportunity to improve the participants' understanding of the ACT model. Especially if participants have read different aspects of the ACT/RFT and contextualism literature, we have noticed that this process tends to weed out gross misunderstandings and to evolve toward a sensible center, even if none of the participants is truly an expert. An internal consistency in the work seems to produce this effect because idiosyncratic understandings are checked by the group.

We caution against turning such discussions into entirely verbal enterprises because they will devolve into almost definitional matters. Another error is to allow a single right answer to emerge too quickly. Getting at the heart of ACT/RFT requires some loosening of language at one level (e.g., higher level clinical terms focused on changing normal language functions) and tightening at another (e.g., RFT principles and philosophical assumptions). In addition, the model makes more sense when all of its elements are put into place. Thus, especially early on, participants need to live with some degree of ambiguity as they work through the model.

Study groups can also be conducted online. If done on a listserv, usually someone will summarize a chapter and an online written discussion of the material will take place on the listserv. These discussions can be helpful, and a vast library of such material is available on the main ACT and RFT listservs (see appendix B). A new book has summarized elements of these discussions (Gentry, in press). If done through an Internet or phone-based conference call, study groups are run in the same manner as a face-to-face group. Internet-based courses are commercially available.

# ISSUES SPECIFIC TO PEER CONSULTATION GROUPS

Peer consultation groups are an important part of the ACT approach to training and dissemination, which tends to be open, functional, and nonhierarchical. It truly is possible for a group of people to learn ACT, even though none of them are expert in it. Based on experience with starting and participating in such groups, we have a few tips to provide to those considering starting ACT peer consultation groups.

In order for a group to succeed, it is usually important to have at least one person who takes responsibility for organizing meetings and doing the necessary coordinating to make sure the group meets regularly. We have found that groups as small as two people can meet effectively and do useful work. Some peer consultation groups are more personal and tend to include experiential aspects in their training, while others are more focused on skill building and function more as a study group.

If experiential components are to be included in the group, it is imperative to spend some time during early meetings discussing whether experiential components should be included, how this would happen, and members' hopes and fears regarding the expression of personal material. In addition, the discussion needs to acknowledge that participation in experiential aspects of the group process should be completely voluntary. Developing a sense of shared values and trust is needed to conduct good experiential work, and confidentiality must be assured.

# EXPERIENTIAL WORK IN SUPERVISION, PRACTICUM, AND TRAINING SETTINGS

Traditionally, experiential work has been an important part of training for ACT therapists. By experiential work, we mean the application of the six ACT core therapeutic processes to the therapist as a person. This aspect of training is fairly unique to ACT, compared with training for other CBT approaches. The difference comes from the model. Therapists are assumed to swim in the same verbal soup as their clients and to struggle with the same basic issues of nonacceptance, entanglement with difficult thoughts, lack of values clarity, and lack of committed action.

The experiential aspects are included in training for two major reasons. First, addressing ACT processes in therapists should help them to be more committed, engaged, flexible, and effective in their work with clients. For example, it is difficult to guide clients to be accepting of themselves if the therapist is not accepting of his or her clients and of his or her own reactions to clients. It is inconsistent for the therapist to fluently practice defusion with clients if the therapist is fused with his or her own ideas that a right or wrong way exists to practice defusion or is attached to a particular idea about what a client needs to do. In fact, several studies (some early studies are summarized in Hayes et al. [2006], and others are currently under review) already have shown that ACT training focused on therapists is helpful in producing more flexibility, less entanglement, less burnout, and a greater ability to learn.

Experiential training is also thought to provide a metric for a functional understanding of ACT processes; for example, when a therapist learns to be more sensitive to the signs of his or her own cognitive fusion or defusion, it may be easier to sense these processes in clients and to use that feedback to detect the difference between topographical adherence to an ACT model and functional competence in implementing it.

Experiential supervision targets these sorts of barriers to clinician competence through engaging the supervisee in the same processes that are used with clients. It can take the form of helping trainees contact their present moment reactions to clients or to supervision (being present) or helping them contact a sense of self as context while observing harsh self-judgments (self as context). Trainees who feel stuck with clients can be guided through a physicalizing exercise with their own sense of stuckness and any other thoughts or feelings that arise (cognitive defusion). Trainees can be asked to notice the sense of struggle in the room with a client and helped to develop a more accepting and willing stance with their own reactions (acceptance). Trainees who are unclear what they are working for with clients can be guided to identify their own therapy-relevant values through an exercise in which they imagine their clients attending an imaginary retirement party (defining valued directions). Finally, trainees can be coached to a commitment to engage in a discussion or exercise with a client while simultaneously making room for their own anxious or uncomfortable reactions (committed action). When working in an experiential mode, the issue is less one of teaching and more one of establishing the conditions that allow learning.

In order for experiential work to be part of the supervision process, it is important to explicitly discuss its role and how it fits with the experiential focus of ACT. Supervision that includes experiential techniques needs to be built around an agreement with the trainee about the inclusion of his or her internal experiences and struggles as part of the supervision process. The trainee's willingness to disclose and desire for privacy need to be respected because it is critical that the experiential aspect of this work not be coerced in any way. Some of these key experiential processes can be done without a great deal of self-disclosure, which allows cautious supervisees to see over time that something can be gained by opening up to this level, even though dealing directly with emotional reactions, struggles, and concerns can be anxiety provoking and difficult. Sometimes it is useful for a trainee to engage in a trial period of supervision before launching into a more extended course of supervision.

For both supervisors and trainees, a focus on the experiential level of supervision can feel artificial, uncomfortable, or constraining at first. The supervisor usually needs to work hard early during supervision, whether in a group or individually, to focus on experiential aspects, until a norm of experiential work has been established. Once this norm has been established, sessions generally flow fairly smoothly between a focus on experiential learning and a focus on conceptual learning. It is very important that the supervisor be part of the experiential process. This model is not one of enlightened experts sitting in judgment of others. The model is recursive and horizontal; thus, if the supervisor is closed, defended, or attached to being right, he or she will not be able to create a sense of open exploration with trainees.

One way to foster an experiential focus in supervision is to begin each session (group or individual) with a mindfulness exercise. Mindfulness exercises can be modified to focus on a specific ACT process, depending upon the needs of the situation. Another way is to ask trainees (and the supervisor) periodically to put their own values and barriers on the table. A way to do this at the start of an ACT training group, or after a transition in membership, is to have all the participants take turns reporting one thing they want from the group and also one psychological barrier that could prevent that goal from being accomplished. Sometimes participants are asked to say how that barrier could manifest in the group. For example, one person might say, "What I want to accomplish within the group this semester is to learn to be bolder in trying out new things with my clients. A barrier to doing that is that I get afraid and I start having the thought, 'You will see how incompetent I am.' The way that would manifest in here is that I would start making jokes, and I would try to find a way to change the subject if the discussion got close to areas about which I feel uncomfortable." As each person in turn puts his or her aspirations, fears, and avoidance moves on the table, the group tends to come together as the members see how many of their barriers are shared. Usually, the supervisor asks the group members to give permission to others to verbalize any barriers they see emerging as the group proceeds.

One very common barrier to developing the trusting, open, and exploratory group process needed for effective experiential supervision is the creation of a norm whereby members compete to give the most insightful or correct response to a given supervision topic. Although this attempt to look good and be right can lead to the modeling of effective responses that can be useful for therapists in training, it can also stifle important experiential work if it is functionally attached to the avoidance of common fears. Supervision groups that want to include an experiential focus need to work hard to create a context in which "not knowing" and expressions of internal emotional experience are as important as being right or being smart (Safran & Muran, 2000). The supervisor can foster this by both modeling and instigating. If the group becomes entangled in this process, simply asking each member to put one currently present difficult thought or feeling on the table (without attempting to change it) can help ground the process in the present moment.

# USING AUDIO AND VIDEO RECORDING

In conjunction with this workbook, audio and video recordings of sessions are among the most important training tools. These are now common practice in many training settings. However, for established professionals in a group, recording is often an uncomfortable experience. They may not have had anyone watch their work for many years and may fear the judgment of a consultant or peers. They may fear clients' reactions and express concern with those reactions interfering with the therapy relationship. These fears can create a significant barrier to a powerful supervision method if not addressed directly. With a bit of willingness and effort, however, most therapists find that getting direct feedback on their work in ACT is an extremely valuable experience. In addition, the vast majority of clients are open to the process of recording sessions, as long as recording is presented in a matter-of-fact manner and the purpose and boundaries of confidentiality are explained.

Watching video or listening to audio recordings of sessions is highly recommended for supervision purposes. Recordings of sessions can keep supervisors and peers much closer to the actual experience. In addition, having another set of eyes and ears paying attention to the material of therapy can allow for the identification of particular aspects of the client's and therapist's behavior they were not aware of themselves. This would not be possible without the ability to watch or listen to sessions.

Videos of ACT experts also are available. The Association for Behavioral and Cognitive Therapies has a 1.5 hour video of Steve Hayes illustrating ACT in a role-played session with a client who has social anxiety. Although it is a bit rushed and the audio quality is not high, this video can give you a good idea of what ACT is like. Commercial ACT videos are beginning to appear from other sources. New Harbinger Publications has a tape series appearing in 2007, and APA has an ACT tape appearing in 2008. Videos also are available on the ACBS website (see appendix B).

# USING ROLE PLAYS IN TRAINING

Another way to re-create the richness of information only present in an actual session is through the use of role plays. Role plays can be conducted in multiple ways and for multiple purposes. One purpose of role-playing is to unpack an example of a particularly troubling, difficult, or puzzling interaction with a client. Role plays also can bring to life a conceptual issue that, if discussed conceptually, has the danger of turning into a dull, lifeless exercise. Often, conceptual issues in supervision are really a combination of conceptual and experiential barriers. Doing a role play that illustrates the conceptual issue can provide a way to work with both types of barriers and also provides the opportunity for modeling alternative in-session responses.

Role plays can be conducted by having the trainee role-play the client, the therapist, or both, depending upon the situation and need of the therapist. Often, role plays are used as ways to experiment with and model alternative ways of intervening with clients, but they are not as often used as opportunities for exploring and working with thoughts, feelings, and sensations related to the clinical situation. These internal therapist experiences can be the most important element in need of in-session work, yet trainees may not even notice or think of obtaining supervision relating to their internal emotional experiences. Role plays can help reinstantiate the trainee's initial reaction to the clinical situation and allow him or her to work with material closer to the original behavior. This is particularly helpful when recordings of sessions are not available.

Role plays in which the trainee plays the client can also have the benefit of helping the trainee be more empathic to the client's experience and better understand the client's viewpoint. When doing role plays in a group, it can be helpful to have multiple trainees take on the role of the therapist. This can help defuse some of the competitiveness that can occur. In addition, it can foster an empathic stance on the part of group members toward the trainee who is the primary recipient of supervision.

One way to help role plays be less artificial is to take a trainee through a brief eyes-closed mindfulness exercise, focusing it on the trainee's caring for the client, the values the trainee brings to the sessions, and the difficulty in feeling the pain of the client and not being sure what to do or how to help. The trainee is told to go inside the body of the client to feel the client's pain; and at the end of the exercise, as the trainee opens his or her eyes, the trainee is asked to picture being that client. In only a few minutes, what was an artificial, highly intellectual exercise can become a role play that is intensely focused on the reality of being with someone who is suffering.

# PROVIDING MODELS

Therapists in training rarely have the opportunity to observe expert models at work. Few supervisors allow their students to watch them work. However, studies have suggested that watching expert models conduct therapy is one of the most rapid ways to learn new therapy techniques (Baum & Gray, 1992). Thus, we strongly encourage including modeling as a method of learning ACT.

If trainees are going to learn by watching a model, they need to have access to the covert behaviors of that model. If a supervisor is performing as the model, this access can be obtained in several ways. The supervisor can review a clinical situation with the trainees, while discussing his or her own internal process and awareness of his or her own response to that clinical situation. The purpose of this dialogue is less about providing a model response and more about giving the trainees an opportunity to hear the internal process of an expert model.

If the model is a video recording of an expert (e.g., the DVD attached to this workbook), it can be helpful for the supervisor to periodically stop the video and lead a discussion about what was seen. What did the trainees see the client and therapist do? What do they think was the relevant client behavior that led to what the therapist did? What do they think were the purpose and rationale behind the therapist's intervention? The supervisor can ask the trainees to reconstruct the relevant verbal dialogue related to the expert's performance. Without an understanding of how ACT theory is guiding the expert's behavior, trainees will not have the desired ability to generalize the modeled behavior to related situations.

# APPENDIX B

# RESOURCES AND REFERENCES FOR FURTHER DEVELOPMENT

The ACT/RFT and contextual behavioral science community is rapidly growing and rapidly changing, so some of the resources in this section will undoubtedly change over time and many new resources (e.g., books, tapes, online resources) will emerge. Thus, we suggest you search online for the various terms relevant to ACT and RFT and supplement any advice given here.

Begin by putting the Association for Contextual Behavioral Science (ACBS) website (www .contextualpsychology.org) in your bookmarked list and consider joining the society. The ACBS is the central organization supporting the development of ACT, RFT, and other forms of contextual behavioral science. The website forms the nexus of an online community of clinicians, researchers, developers, and nonprofessionals interested in ACT and RFT. The whole community of ACT developers and researchers contributes to this website by adding webpages, files, and multimedia presentations and by voting and holding discussion groups. New materials are added on a regular basis.

Members of ACBS can download forms to use in their practice, as well as treatment manuals, publications, measures, audio recordings, videos, visual aids, PowerPoint presentations, and a large amount of other information that can be helpful in learning or using ACT. Training workshops are posted on the site, and you can also check for peer consultation groups in your area. If one isn't already available, consider posting a request to the ACT listserv or to one of the discussion forums on the website.

ACBS holds large training events (i.e., summer institutes and world conferences) annually, with hundreds of people attending. At these events, you can experience the essence of ACT work and learn it more thoroughly than you can simply through reading a book. Workshops also are regularly scheduled at the annual conventions of the Association for Behavioral and Cognitive Therapies and the Association for Behavior Analysis.

ACT trainers are located all around the world. A list of trainers is posted on the ACT website, including an agreed-upon values statement that is meant to ensure that the training delivery process is not excessively focused on money or needlessly hierarchical. If no trainer or supervisor is located in your area, consider phone consultation. This can be an excellent method for learning ACT, and some research data support it (Luoma, 2006).

The ACBS website provides links so you can join the many available ACT and RFT listservs. ACT and RFT have general lists; lists for many specific language communities (e.g., French, Spanish, German, Swedish, Portuguese, and Dutch); lists for specific countries or regions (e.g., the United Kingdom, and Australia and New Zealand); lists for specific topics (e.g., measurement, research, eating disorders); lists for specific professions (e.g., psychiatrists in ACT); and also a list for clients and the general public. These lists are notably collegial and helpful. The ACBS website also has threaded discussion boards where you can post questions and receive responses from the ACT community. There are also online events and online workshops.

The *Learning ACT* website (www.learningact.com), was created to go along with this book. It is a place to ask questions related to this book or to get feedback related to practice responses. It has discussion boards where you can interact with other people using this book as well as with the authors. Updated lists of all the ACT books and videos are available on both the *Learning ACT* and ACBS websites. Two publishers that have been especially active with ACT books are New Harbinger Publications and Context Press, both of which have websites in their names (www.newharbinger.com and www.contextpress.com).

# ACT CORE COMPETENCY RATING FORM

The Core Competency Rating Form describes the primary competencies of a therapist who is working in an ACT-consistent manner. It can be used for supervision of self and other. The competencies were developed through consensus at a meeting of ACT trainers. It also includes some competencies that were addressed indirectly in this book, but that were not specifically described in the previous chapters.

## USING THE FORM FOR SELF-SUPERVISION

If you are learning ACT, you can use this form to advance your learning by periodically rating yourself and then considering the following questions and guidelines in relation to your self-ratings (these are just suggestions; you can always add others). Engaging in this process can help you determine where to focus next as you learn ACT.

✓ Notice in which areas you rated yourself low. Do you understand what the competency means? If not, you may want to figure out what it would mean to engage this competency. What reading materials would you need? Could you post a question to the ACT listserv or www.learningact.com asking for advice or talk to colleagues?

✓ Outline what you are doing that is ACT inconsistent in areas in which you have low ratings. In other words, analyze why your behavior is inconsistent and what you are doing instead, and see if an ACT model can help illuminate this very process. In this way, you can decide whether you want to continue your current pattern of responding or practice something new. Trying something new has the advantage of building flexibility, even if you don't decide to continue it. So, if you have an immediate resistance to this new activity, it is worth digging to see if that resistance is itself fused or avoidant. For example, imagine you obtained a low rating on several items in defusion and self as context. You might consider what you do currently when clients express negative self-evaluative thoughts. Do you challenge these, do you look for evidence, or do you help them explore the historical roots of these thoughts? After you consider what you already do, try to see what functions your attachment to this approach serve. You may have the powerful experience that your approach is helpful or you may conclude the research literature clearly supports your approach. But sometimes neither of these may be happening and you will want to consider trying something new. In this case, it may be wise to address barriers to flexibility (e.g., fear, lack of confidence, being right).

✓ Consider some options for changing your behavior in relation to a competency for which you rated low. What can you do to improve your skills in that area? Is there something you can read? Is there a skill to practice? Are you willing to make room for the possible failure and sense of inadequacy or incompetence that can go along with practicing a new technique or skill, and still do it? Perhaps you can rehearse the new skill with a colleague before going into a session. Perhaps you can focus a whole session on that one process so you have a chance to practice it. Perhaps you can post a question on the ACT listserv about how to improve your practice in that area. What other ideas do you have about how to address this competency?

✓ A great place to start is to pick one action, commit to it, and get started on it. Which one will it be? As you try this one action, apply ACT to yourself as you do it. Be open to difficult thoughts (e.g., "I'm no good at this, and my clients will see that") and difficult feelings (e.g., "I feel so incompetent doing these strange things") and carry these thoughts forward while doing the actions.

✓ Go back and repeat this process with other competencies for which you rated yourself low.

# USING THE FORM IN SUPERVISING OTHERS

The rating form can also be used when providing supervision to others. If the supervisor is already familiar with a trainee's work, he or she can rate the trainee's consistency on all the relevant competencies on the form. Then the supervisor can develop a plan with the trainee to further develop flexibility and to practice any areas in which the trainee had low ratings.

Alternatively, the form can be used to rate individual sessions of therapy. This can help identify behaviors that are inconsistent with an ACT model and also behaviors for which frequency or skill level can be increased.

# CORE COMPETENCY RATING FORM

A number of statements are listed on the competency rating form. Please rate how true each statement is for you when you (or the person you are rating) use ACT, by writing the number next to it. Use the numbers on the scale to make your rating.

# RATING SCALE

| 1 | 2 | 3 | 4 | 5 | 6 | 7 | ? |
|---|---|---|---|---|---|---|---|
| never true | very seldom true | seldom true | sometimes true | frequently true | almost always true | always true | don't know |

# THE ACT THERAPEUTIC STANCE

| 1 | The ACT therapist speaks to the client from an equal, vulnerable, compassionate, genuine, and sharing point of view and respects the client's inherent ability to move from unworkable to workable responses. | |
|---|---|---|
| 2 | The therapist is willing to self-disclose about personal issues when it serves the interest of the client. | |
| 3 | The therapist avoids the use of canned ACT interventions, instead fitting interventions to the particular needs of particular clients. The therapist is ready to change course to fit those needs at any moment. | |
| 4 | The therapist tailors interventions and develops new metaphors, experiential exercises, and behavioral tasks to fit the client's experience and language practices, and the social, ethnic, and cultural context. | |
| 5 | The therapist models acceptance of challenging content (e.g., what emerges during treatment) while also being willing to hold the client's contradictory or difficult ideas, feelings, and memories without any need to resolve them. | |
| 6 | The therapist introduces experiential exercises, paradoxes, and/or metaphors as appropriate and de-emphasizes literal sense-making of the same. | |
| 7 | The therapist always brings the issue back to what the client's experience is showing, and does not substitute his or her opinions for that genuine experience. | |
| 8 | The therapist does not argue with, lecture, coerce, or attempt to convince the client. | |
| 9 | ACT-relevant processes are recognized in the moment, and when appropriate, are directly supported in the context of the therapeutic relationship. | |

# DEVELOPING WILLINGNESS/ACCEPTANCE

| 10 | The therapist communicates to the client that he or she is not broken but using unworkable strategies. | |
|----|--------------------------------------------------------------------------------------------------------|--|
| 11 | The therapist helps the client make direct contact with the paradoxical effects of emotional control strategies. | |
| 12 | The therapist actively uses the concept of workability in clinical interactions. | |
| 13 | The therapist actively encourages the client to experiment with stopping the struggle for emotional control and suggests willingness as an alternative. | |
| 14 | The therapist highlights the contrast between the workability of control and willingness strategies. | |
| 15 | The therapist helps the client investigate the relationship between willingness and suffering. | |
| 16 | The therapist helps the client make contact with the cost of unwillingness relative to valued life ends. | |
| 17 | The therapist helps the client to experience the qualities of willingness. | |
| 18 | The therapist uses exercises and metaphors to demonstrate willingness as an action in the presence of difficult internal experience. | |
| 19 | The therapist models willingness in the therapeutic relationship and helps the client to generalize these skills outside therapy. | |
| 20 | The therapist can use a graded and structured approach to willingness assignments. | |

# UNDERMINING COGNITIVE FUSION

| 21 | The therapist identifies the client's emotional, cognitive, behavioral, or physical barriers to willingness. | |
|----|--------------------------------------------------------------------------------------------------------------|--|
| 22 | The therapist suggests that attachment to the literal meaning of these experiences makes willingness difficult to sustain (helps clients to see private experiences for what they are, rather than what they advertise themselves to be). | |
| 23 | The therapist actively contrasts what the client's mind says will work with what the client's experience says is working. | |

| 24 | The therapist uses language tools (e.g., get off your "buts"); metaphors (e.g., Passengers on the Bus); and experiential exercises (e.g., Thoughts on Cards) to create a separation between the client and the client's conceptualized experience. | |
| --- | --- | --- |
| 25 | The therapist works to get the client to experiment with "having" difficult private experiences, using willingness as a stance. | |
| 26 | The therapist uses various exercises, metaphors, and behavioral tasks to reveal the hidden properties of language. | |
| 27 | The therapist helps the client elucidate the client's story and helps the client make contact with the evaluative and reason-giving properties of the story. | |
| 28 | The therapist helps the client make contact with the arbitrary nature of causal relationships within the story. | |
| 29 | The therapist detects mindiness (fusion) in session and teaches the client to detect it, as well. | |
| 30 | The therapist uses various interventions to reveal both the flow of private experience and that such experience is not toxic. | |

# GETTING IN CONTACT WITH THE PRESENT MOMENT

| 31 | The therapist can defuse from client content and direct attention to the moment. | |
| --- | --- | --- |
| 32 | The therapist brings his or her own thoughts or feelings in the moment into the therapeutic relationship. | |
| 33 | The therapist uses exercises to expand the client's sense of experience as an ongoing process. | |
| 34 | The therapist detects the client drifting into past or future orientation and teaches him or her how to come back to now. | |
| 35 | The therapist tracks content at multiple levels and emphasizes the present when it is useful. | |
| 36 | The therapist practices and models getting out of his or her own mind and coming back to the present moment in session. | |

# DISTINGUISHING THE CONCEPTUALIZED SELF FROM SELF AS CONTEXT

| 37 | The therapist uses metaphors to help the client distinguish between the content and products of consciousness, and consciousness itself. | |
| --- | --- | --- |
| 38 | The therapist utilizes exercises to help the client make contact with self as context and distinguish this from the self as conceptualized. | |
| 39 | The therapist utilizes behavioral tasks to help the client notice the workings of the mind and the experience of emotion while also contacting a self who chooses and behaves with these experiences, rather than for the experiences. | |
| 40 | The therapist helps the client recognize the distinction between the self who evaluates and the evaluation itself. | |

# DEFINING VALUED DIRECTIONS

| 41 | The therapist helps the client clarify valued life directions. | |
| --- | --- | --- |
| 42 | The therapist helps the client commit to what he or she wants his or her life to stand for, and focuses the therapy on that. | |
| 43 | The therapist teaches the client to distinguish between values and goals. | |
| 44 | The therapist distinguishes between outcomes achieved and involvement in the process of living. | |
| 45 | The therapist states his or her own therapy-relevant values and models their importance. | |
| 46 | The therapist respects client values and if unable to support them, finds a referral or other alternatives. | |

# BUILDING PATTERNS OF COMMITTED ACTION

| 47 | The therapist helps the client identify valued life goals and build an action plan linked to them. | |
|----|---------------------------------------------------------------------------------------------------|---|
| 48 | The therapist encourages the client to make and keep commitments in the presence of perceived barriers (e.g., fear of failure, traumatic memories, sadness, being right) and to expect additional barriers as a consequence of engaging in committed actions. | |
| 49 | The therapist helps the client appreciate the qualities of committed action (e.g., vitality, sense of growth) and to take small steps while maintaining contact with those qualities. | |
| 50 | The therapist keeps the client focused on larger and larger patterns of action to help the client act on goals with consistency over time. | |
| 51 | The therapist nonjudgmentally integrates slips or relapses into the process of keeping commitments and building larger patterns of effective action. | |

# GLOSSARY OF ACT TERMS

As you use this glossary, please keep in mind that these are mostly common language rather than technical definitions. Many of these terms, particularly those from behavior analysis and RFT, have technical definitions that are more accurate than these, but are also difficult to understand without a history of training in behavior analysis.

**Acceptance:** The active and aware embrace of private events that are occasioned by our history, without unnecessary attempts to change their frequency or form, especially when doing so causes psychological harm

**Appetitive (behavior):** Refers to behavior that is reinforced by achieving something or moving toward something, as contrasted with aversively controlled behavior, which is behavior controlled by avoiding or escaping an aversive stimulus

**Arbitrarily applicable:** Refers to contexts in which a response can be modified solely on the basis of social whim or convention

**Cognitive Behavioral Therapy (CBT) (traditional):** The branch of psychotherapy that applies information-processing cognitive models to the modification of dysfunctional beliefs; it is most strongly distinguished from ACT by its focus on changing the form or frequency of private events through processes such as cognitive disputation or testing and challenging irrational cognitions

**Cognitive defusion:** An invented word meaning to undo fusion, or "de-fusion"; the process of creating nonliteral contexts in which language can be seen as an active, ongoing, relational process that is historical in nature and present in the current moment

**Cognitive fusion:** The tendency of human beings to get caught up in the content of what they are thinking so that it dominates over other useful sources of behavioral regulation

**Committed action:** Series of actions that move in the direction of chosen values, regardless of internally experienced barriers (e.g. thoughts)

**Conceptualized self:** The descriptive and evaluative thoughts and stories we tell about ourselves

**Contingency:** A consequence that only occurs regularly in certain contexts; its appearance depends upon the behavior of the organism in that context

**Creative hopelessness:** Refers to a process of explicating and validating a client's experience of the unworkability of his or her behavior; creative hopelessness is often seen in a client's behavior as a posture of giving up previous strategies that are part of the person's current verbal system of problem solving, thus allowing for the creativity of truly new forms of behavior

**Deliteralization:** The original ACT term for cognitive defusion, which was replaced because it is so difficult to pronounce

**Depth (in theory):** Consistency or coherence across levels of analysis (e.g., the psychological, biological, sociological)

**Experiential avoidance/control:** The attempt to control or alter the form, frequency, or situational sensitivity of internal experiences (e.g., thoughts, feelings, sensations, or memories), even when doing so could cause behavioral harm

**Experiential exercise:** An activity or exercise in which the participant learns through practice or direct contact with events, rather than through conceptual learning

**Experiential knowledge:** Ways of knowing based on practice or direct experience (e.g., knowing how to play the guitar), as distinct from knowledge gained through conceptual understanding (e.g., knowing the notes on a scale)

**Function of a behavior:** The purpose of a behavior analyzed in terms of its history and current setting, as understood through the principles of operant, classical, or verbal behavior.

**Functional analysis:** The process of developing an understanding of the client's difficulties in terms of behavioral principles, in order to identify important relationships between variables that could be changed or influenced

**Functional contextualism:** A form of pragmatic philosophy underlying ACT and RFT, in which truth is defined on the basis of workability in achieving chosen goals; a scientific philosophy with the shared public goals of prediction and influence of behavior with precision, scope, and depth

**Language:** A socially conventional term for behavior that is at least in part influenced by relational framing

**Literality (context of):** Contexts in which symbols (e.g., thoughts) and their referents (i.e., what they seem to refer to or mean) are fused together, thereby lessening the distinction between the world as directly experienced and the world as structured through language

**Mind:** In ACT, the mind is not considered to literally exist as an entity, but rather is seen as the collection of verbal abilities we call thinking; sometimes it is useful to refer to the mind as if it were an entity because this can help create separation between thought and thinker

**Mindfulness:** Refers to the combination of the four processes on the left side of the ACT hexagon model; in mindfulness, one willingly and directly contacts the present moment without getting caught up in the content of thoughts and while maintaining a sense of being a conscious observer of experience

**Operant:** Classes of behavior defined by their functional effects in particular contexts; behaviors that occur in similar contexts and result in similar effects would be considered part of the same operant

**Pliance:** The habit of following a verbal rule, based on a history of being socially reinforced for rule-following, whether or not the rule-following is otherwise successful

**Principles:** Ways of speaking that have high precision and high scope

**Private events:** Thoughts, feelings, emotions, sensations, memories, and images are all forms of private behavior; in the tradition of which ACT is a part, public and private behavior are both considered to be behavior and neither is, in principle, privileged over the other

**Psychological flexibility:** The process of contacting the present moment fully as a conscious human being, and persisting or changing behavior in the service of chosen values

**Psychological inflexibility:** The inability to persist or change behavior in the service of chosen values, usually due to the domination of verbal regulatory processes

**Reason giving:** Verbal explanations for behavior

**Relational frame:** A relational frame is the most basic unit of language in RFT; more technically, it refers to a type of arbitrarily applicable relational responding that has the defining features in some contexts of mutual entailment, combinatorial entailment, and the transformation of stimulus functions; although used as a noun, it is always an action and thus can be restated as "framing events relationally"

**Relational Frame Theory (RFT):** A modern behavior analytic theory of language and cognition that underlies ACT; RFT is a much broader research program than ACT, and underlies not just ACT but any actions involving human language and cognition

**Rules:** Verbal formulae that guide behavior based on their participation in relational frames

**Self as content:** Viewing oneself from a literal perspective in which the thoughts, emotions, sensations, and memories that have been experienced are considered the self; the same as conceptualized self

**Self as context:** Experiencing events from I/here/now; self not as an object of reflection, but as the perspective or location from which observations are made

**Self as process:** The defused, nonjudgmental, ongoing awareness of and description of thoughts, feelings, and other private events in the moment

**Theory:** In functional contextualism, applications of sets of principles to a given domain for the purpose of predicting and influencing phenomena within the domain with precision, scope, and depth

**Thinking/thoughts:** Anything that is symbolic or relational in an arbitrarily applicable sense; this includes words, gestures, thoughts, signs, images, and some properties of emotions

**Topography of a behavior:** The form or appearance of a behavior

**Tracking:** Following a verbal rule, based on a history of correspondence between the rule and the non-arbitrary consequences contacted by following the rule

**Values:** Chosen qualities of actions that are personally important ways of living and that can never be obtained as an object, but rather are instantiated moment by moment; although used as a noun, the term *valuing* would be more fitting because values cannot be divorced from human action

**Verbal abilities:** Actions by a speaker or listener that depend upon relational framing

**Willingness:** Another term for acceptance; no technically important distinction can be made between the two terms; however, therapists sometimes use willingness to convey an active stance of acceptance because acceptance can carry a passive connotation in lay usage; thus, for example, exposure exercises are often called "willingness exercises" in ACT.

# REFERENCES

Ackerman, S. J., & Hilsenroth, M. J. (2001). A review of therapist characteristics and techniques negatively impacting the therapeutic alliance. *Psychotherapy: Theory, Research, Practice, Training, 38*(2), 171–185.

Addis, M. E., & Jacobson, N. S. (1996). Reasons for depression and the process and outcome of cognitive-behavioral psychotherapies. *Journal of Consulting and Clinical Psychology, 64*(6), 1417–1424.

Bach, P., & Hayes, S. C. (2002). The use of acceptance and commitment therapy to prevent the rehospitalization of psychotic patients: A randomized controlled trial. *Journal of Consulting and Clinical Psychology, 70*(5), 1129–1139.

Barnes-Holmes, D., Hayes, S. C., & Dymond, S. (2001). Self and self-directed rules. In S. C. Hayes, D. Barnes-Holmes, & B. Roche (Eds.), *Relational frame theory: A post-Skinnerian account of human language and cognition* (pp. 119–139). New York: Plenum Press.

Barnes-Holmes, D., Hayes, S. C., & Gregg, J. (2001). Religion, spirituality, and transcendence. In S. C. Hayes, D. Barnes-Holmes, & B. Roche (Eds.), *Relational frame theory: A post-Skinnerian account of human language and cognition* (pp. 239–251). New York: Plenum Press.

Baum, B. E., & Gray, J. J. (1992). Expert modeling, self-observation using videotape, and acquisition of basic therapy skills. *Professional Psychology: Research and Practice, 23*, 220–225.

Beck, A. T. (1993). Cognitive therapy: Past, present, and future. *Journal of Consulting and Clinical Psychology, 61*, 194–198.

Berens, N. M., & Hayes, S. C. (in press). Arbitrarily applicable comparative relations: Experimental evidence for a relational operant. *Journal of Applied Behavior Analysis.*

Blackledge, J. T. (2003). An introduction to relational frame theory: Basics and applications. *Behavior Analyst Today, 3*(4), 421–433.

Bodian, S. (2006). *Meditation for dummies.* Foster City, CA: IDG Books.

Chödrön, P. (1994). *Start where you are.* Boston: Shambhala.

Crits-Christoph, P., Connolly Gibbons, M. B., Crits-Christoph, K., Narducci, J., Schamberger, M., & Gallop, R. (2006). Can therapists be trained to improve their alliances? A preliminary study of alliance-fostering psychotherapy. *Psychotherapy Research, 16*, 268–281.

Dahl, J. C., Wilson, K. G., Luciano, C., & Hayes, S. C. (2005). *Acceptance and commitment therapy for chronic pain*. Reno, NV: Context Press.

Dimidjian, S., Hollon, S. D., Dobson, K. S., Schmaling, K. B., Kohlenberg, R. J., Addis, M. E., et al. (2006). Randomized trial of behavioral activation, cognitive therapy, and antidepressant medication in the acute treatment of adults with major depression. *Journal of Consulting and Clinical Psychology, 74*(4), 658–670.

Eifert, G., & Forsyth, J. (2005). *Acceptance and commitment therapy for anxiety disorders*. Oakland, CA: New Harbinger Publications.

Fletcher, L., & Hayes, S. C. (2005). Relational frame theory, acceptance and commitment therapy, and a functional analytic definition of mindfulness. *Journal of Rational Emotive and Cognitive Behavioral Therapy, 23*(4), 315–336.

Gaudiano, B. A., & Herbert, J. D. (2006). Acute treatment of inpatients with psychotic symptoms using acceptance and commitment therapy: Pilot results. *Behaviour Research and Therapy, 44*(3), 415–437.

Gentry, D. (2007). *Talking ACT*. Reno, NV: Context Press.

Gifford, E., Hayes, S. C., Kohlenberg, B., Antonuccio, D. O., Piasecki, M., & Pierson, H. (under review). Applying the acceptance and relationship context model to smoking cessation: An initial evaluation of acceptance and commitment therapy, functional analytic psychotherapy and bupropion.

Hanh, T. N. (1992). *Touching peace: Practicing the art of mindful living*. Berkeley, CA: Parallax Press.

Hardy, R. R. (2001). *Zen-master: Practical Zen by an American for Americans*. Tucson, AZ: Hats Off Books.

Hayes, S. C. (1984). Making sense of spirituality. *Behaviorism, 12,* 99–110.

Hayes, S. C. (1989). *Rule-governed behavior: Cognition, contingencies, and instructional control*. New York: Plenum Press.

Hayes, S. C. (1993). Analytic goals and the varieties of scientific contextualism. In S. C. Hayes, L. J. Hayes, H. W. Reese, & T. R. Sarbin (Eds.), *Varieties of scientific contextualism*, (pp. 11-27). Reno, NV: Context Press.

Hayes, S. C. (2004). Acceptance and commitment therapy, relational frame theory, and the third wave of behavioral and cognitive therapies. *Behavior Therapy, 35*(4), 639–665.

Hayes, S. C., Barnes-Holmes, D., & Roche, B. (Eds.). (2001). *Relational frame theory: A post-Skinnerian account of human language and cognition*. New York: Kluwer Academic/Plenum/Springer-Verlag.

Hayes, S. C., Luoma, J. B., Bond, F. W., Masuda, A., & Lillis, J. (2006). Acceptance and commitment therapy: Model, processes and outcomes. *Behaviour Research and Therapy, 44*(1), 1–25.

Hayes, S. C., Rosenfarb, I., Wulfert, E., Munt, E., Zettle, R. D., & Korn, Z. (1985). Self reinforcement effects: An artifact of social standard setting? *Journal of Applied Behavior Analysis, 18*(3), 201–214.

Hayes, S. C., & Smith, S. (2005). *Get out of your mind and into your life: The new acceptance and commitment therapy*. Oakland, CA: New Harbinger Publications.

Hayes, S. C., & Strosahl, K. D. (Eds.). (2004). *A practical guide to acceptance and commitment therapy*. New York: Springer-Verlag.

Hayes, S. C., Strosahl, K. D., Luoma, J., Smith, A. A. & Wilson, K. G. (2005). ACT case formulation in S. C. Hayes and K. D. Strosahl (Eds.), *Acceptance and commitment therapy: A practical clinical guide*. New York: Kluwer/Plenum.

Hayes, S. C., Strosahl, K., & Wilson, K. G. (1999). *Acceptance and commitment therapy: An experiential approach to behavior change.* New York: Guilford Press.

Hayes, S. C., Strosahl, K. D., Wilson, K. G., Bissett, R. T., Pistorello, J., Toarmino, D., et al. (2004). Measuring experiential avoidance: A preliminary test of a working model. *The Psychological Record, 54,* 553–578.

Hayes, S. C., Wilson, K. G., Gifford, E. V., Follette, V. M., & Strosahl, K. (1996). Experiential avoidance and behavioral disorders: A functional dimensional approach to diagnosis and treatment. *Journal of Consulting and Clinical Psychology, 64,* 1152–1168.

Heffner, M., & G. H. Eifert. (2004). *The anorexia workbook: How to accept yourself, heal your suffering, and reclaim your life.* Oakland, CA: New Harbinger Publications.

Herbert, J., & Forman, E. (2005, July). ACT *versus traditional CBT.* Paper presented at the ACT Summer Institute, La Salle University, Philadelphia, PA.

Jacobson, N. S., Dobson, K. S., Truax, P. A., Addis, M. E., Koerner, K., Gollan, J. K., et al. (1996). A component analysis of cognitive-behavioral treatment for depression. *Journal of Consulting and Clinical Psychology, 64*(2), 295–304.

Kabat-Zinn, J. (1994). *Wherever you go, there you are: Mindfulness meditations in everyday life.* New York: Hyperion.

Kohlenberg, R. J., & Tsai, M. (1991). *Functional analytic psychotherapy: A guide for creating intense and curative therapeutic relationships.* New York: Plenum Press.

Lappalainen, R., Lehtonen, T., Skarp, E., Taubert, E., Ojanen, M., & Hayes, S. C. (in press). The impact of CBT and ACT models using psychology trainee therapists: A preliminary controlled effectiveness trial. *Behavior Modification.*

Lewin, K. (1951). Problems of research in social psychology. In D. Cartwright (Ed.), *Field theory in social science: Selected theoretical papers* (pp. 155–169). New York: Harper & Row.

Lindsley, O. R. (1968). *Training parents and teachers to precisely manage children's behavior.* Paper presented at the C. S. Mott Foundation Children's Health Center, Flint, MI.

Lorde, A. (1997). *The cancer journals.* San Francisco: Aunt Lute Books.

Luoma, J. B. (2006, July). *Toward a more functional approach to the training and dissemination of ACT and other empirically-supported psychotherapies: Models, data, and future directions.* Address given at the Second World Conference on ACT/RFT and Contextual Behavioral Science, London, UK.

Martin, D. J., Garske, J. P., & Davis, M. K. (2000). Relation of the therapeutic alliance with outcome and other variables: A meta-analytic review. *Journal of Consulting and Clinical Psychology, 68,* 438–450.

McHugh, L., Barnes-Holmes, Y., & Barnes-Holmes, D. (2004). Perspective taking as relational responding: A developmental profile. *The Psychological Record, 54,* 115–144.

Moran, D. J., & Bach, P. (in press). *ACT in practice: Case conceptualization in acceptance and commitment therapy.* Oakland, CA: New Harbinger Publications.

Pierson, H., & Hayes, S. C. (2007). Using acceptance and commitment therapy to empower the therapeutic relationship. In P. Gilbert & R. Leahy (Eds.), *The therapeutic relationship in cognitive behavior therapy* (pp. 205–228). London: Routledge.

Ramnerö, J., & Törneke, N. (in press). *ABCs of human behavior: An introduction to behavioral psychotherapy.* Reno, NV: Context Press.

Rehfeldt, R. A., Dillen, J. E., Ziomek, M. M., & Kowalchuck, R. (2007). Assessing relational learning deficits in perspective-taking in children with high-functioning autism spectrum disorder. *The Psychological Record, 57,* 23–47.

Safran, J. D., & Muran, J. C. (2000). *Negotiating the therapeutic alliance: A relational treatment guide.* New York: Guilford Press.

Sheldon, K. M., & Elliot, A. J. (1999). Goal striving, need satisfaction, and longitudinal well-being: The self-concordance model. *Journal of Personality and Social Psychology, 76,* 482–497.

Strosahl, K. D., Hayes, S. C., Wilson, K. G., & Gifford, E. V. (2004). An ACT primer: Core therapy processes, intervention strategies, and therapist competencies. In S. C. Hayes & K. D. Strosahl (Eds.), *A practical guide to acceptance and commitment therapy* (pp. 31–58). New York: Springer-Verlag.

Twohig, M. P., Hayes, S. C., & Masuda, A. (2006). Increasing willingness to experience obsessions: Acceptance and commitment therapy as a treatment for obsessive-compulsive disorder. *Behavior Therapy, 37(1),* 3–13.

Walser, R. D., & Pistorello, J. (2004). ACT in group format. In S. C. Hayes & K. D. Strosahl (Eds.), *A practical guide to acceptance and commitment therapy* (pp. 347–372). New York: Springer-Verlag.

Walser, R. D., & Westrup, D. (2007). *Acceptance and commitment therapy for the treatment of post-traumatic stress disorder and trauma-related problems.* Oakland, CA: New Harbinger Publications.

Wenzlaff, R. M., & Wegner, D. M. (2000). Thought suppression. *Annual Review of Psychology, 51,* 59–91.

Wilson, K. G. (2003, April). *Introductory experiential workshop on acceptance and commitment therapy.* Symposium conducted in Oxford, MS.

Wilson, K. G., & Hayes, S. C. (1996). Resurgence of derived stimulus relations. *Journal of the Experimental Analysis of Behavior, 66(3),* 267–281.

Wilson, K. G., Hayes, S. C., Gregg, J., & Zettle, R. D. (2001). Psychopathology and psychotherapy. In S. C. Hayes, D. Barnes-Holmes, & B. Roche (Eds.), *Relational frame theory: A post-Skinnerian account of human language and cognition* (pp. 211–237). New York: Plenum Press.

Wilson, K. G., & Murrell, A. (2004). Values work in acceptance and commitment therapy: Setting a course for behavioral treatment. In S. C. Hayes, V. M. Follette, & M. M. Linehan (Eds.), *Mindfulness and acceptance: Expanding the cognitive-behavioral tradition* (pp. 120–151). New York: Guilford Press.

Zettle, R. D., & Hayes, S. C. (1986). Dysfunctional control by client verbal behavior: The context of reason giving. *The Analysis of Verbal Behavior, 4,* 30–38.

# INDEX

## A

acceptance, 17, 22, 23-56; core competencies related to, 41-55, 286; developing and practicing, 38-41; experiential exercise on, 33; as functional goal of ACT, 25; key targets for, 23; modeled by therapists, 219-220; practice exercises on, 41-55; responding to clients using, 226, 228; therapeutic relationship and, 221-222, 226, 228; undermining control related to, 27-38; use of term, 24-25. *See also* willingness

Acceptance and Action Questionnaire (AAQ), 205

acceptance and commitment therapy (ACT): beginning to use, 6-7; case conceptualization in, 183-216; combining with other treatments, 272; comprehensive treatment plan, 194-195; core therapeutic processes, 17-22, 243-248; definition of, 2, 22; evidence supporting use of, 272; explaining to clients, 268-270; model of psychopathology, 11-17; pitfalls encountered in, 248-258; resources and references, 3-4, 281-282; therapeutic relationship in, 217-239; traditional BT and CBT vs., 214-215

*Acceptance and Commitment Therapy: An Experiential Approach to Behavior Change* (Hayes, Strosahl, and Wilson), 3, 56, 90, 127, 155, 182

*Acceptance and Commitment Therapy for Anxiety Disorders* (Eifert and Forsyth), 4

Achebe, Chinua, 23

ACT acronym, 169

*ACT for Anxiety Disorders* (Eifert and Forsyth), 242

*ACT for Chronic Pain* (Dahl et al.), 242

*ACT in Action* DVD series (Hayes), 4

action: building patterns of, 168; values as, 144; willingness as, 40. *See also* committed action

action plans, 160-163

addiction, 168

anxiety: experiential avoidance and, 184; exposure and, 158, 165

assessment: case conceptualization and, 185; values clarification and, 139

Association for Behavior Analysis (ABA), 281

Association for Behavioral and Cognitive Therapies (ABCT), 279, 281

Association for Contextual Behavioral Science (ACBS), 4, 272, 281-282

audio recordings, 279

autobiographical rewrite, 69, 191

Automatic Thoughts Questionnaire-Believability (ATQ-B), 205

avoidance: pitfall of feeding, 248-250; thought/feeling, 186-187; three types of, 187. *See also* experiential avoidance/control

avoidant persistence, 17, 192

awareness. *See* present moment awareness

## B

barriers: committed action and, 163-166; internal vs. external, 166

basketball game metaphor, 166-167

behavior change processes, 22

behavior therapy (BT), 214-215

behavioral activation, 158

behaviors: avoidance, 187; functional analysis of, 184, 213-214; narrowed/constricted, 187-188; self-defeating, 192; understanding, 267

Berra, Yogi, 109

blaming, 191, 251-252

brief interventions, 115-117

building action patterns, 168

bus metaphor, 113, 165

## C

canned interventions, 219

case conceptualization, 183-216; assessment and, 185; experiential exercises on, 215-216; explanation of,

psychotherapists. *See* therapists
psychotic disorders, 270-271
public commitments, 161

# Q

Quicksand metaphor, 37-38

# R

rediscovering experience, 62-63
reformulating problems, 186
relapses, 169-170
Relational Frame Theory (RFT), 2, 10, 111, 162, 222
relaxation training, 214
resources and references: on ACT, 3-4, 281-282; on
    meditation/mindfulness, 108; on treatment plans,
    195
rigid thinking patterns, 189
Robinson, Edwin Arlington, 1
role plays, 279-280

# S

scheduled smoking, 158
secondary properties, 66
self: conceptualized, 15-16, 109, 110-111; observer, 113;
    transcendent, 111, 116
self as content, 110; brief interventions and, 115-117;
    distinguishing self as context from, 112, 126. *See also*
    conceptualized self
self as context, 19-20, 109-127; brief interventions
    and, 115-117; core competencies related to,
    120-125, 288; distinguishing self as content from,
    112, 126, 288; experiential exercises on, 117, 126;
    explanation of, 111; key targets for, 109; metaphors
    and, 113-115; method of, 113-120; model responses
    related to, 122-125; practice exercises on, 120-125;
    present moment awareness and, 99; responding
    to clients using, 227, 229; self-evaluations and,
    118-119; strategies for developing, 113; therapeutic
    relationship and, 222, 227, 229; triggers for using,
    112-113; valued living and, 119-120
self as process, 19, 95
self-concept, 15-16, 109; brief interventions and,
    115-117; distinguishing self as context from, 112,
    126; explanation of, 110-111
self-defeating behavior, 192
self-disclosure, 218-219
self-evaluations, 118-119
self-knowledge, 15, 189-190
self-observation, 99
self-supervision, 283-284
sense-making, 220
setbacks, 169-170
skidding metaphor, 170
skills training, 158, 214-215
slips and relapses, 169-170

smoking cessation, 158
social environment, 193
social interactions, 213, 223
social skills training, 158, 166
stories, undermining unhelpful, 67-69
strengths, harnessing, 193-194
study groups, 275-276
suicidal clients, 271
supervision: experiential, 277-279; providing to others,
    284; self-, 283-284
supportive listening, 103
syndromal model, 271
system: confronting, 27; drawing out, 27-28

# T

Taking Your Mind for a Walk exercise, 64-65
teaching: the limits of language, 62-63; what
    willingness is, 38-40
therapeutic relationship, 217-239; ACT model of,
    223-225; core competencies of, 218-221, 285;
    experiential exercises on, 220, 238-239; functional
    analysis and, 213; motivation to change and, 193;
    practice exercises on, 230-238; present moment
    awareness and, 98-99; responding to client
    complaints in, 225-230; targeting of, 225-230;
    therapy-relevant values and, 144-147; three levels of,
    221-223
therapeutic stance, 218-221, 285
therapists: contexts influencing responses of, 266-268;
    core competencies of, 218-221; experiential
    avoidance by, 252-253; flexibility of, 219, 221,
    234-235; modeling by, 219-220; self-disclosure by,
    218-219; in therapeutic relationship, 221-223
thoughts: avoidance of, 12; cognitive fusion and, 13,
    186; highly logical or rigid, 189; looking at rather
    than from, 65; mindfulness exercises and, 95-96;
    objectifying, 64-65
tolerance, 24
Tombstone metaphor, 133
training, experiential, 277-278
transcendent self, 111, 116
treatment manuals, 268
treatment plans, 194-195

# U

undermining control, 27-38; defining control as
    the problem, 36-38; drawing out the system,
    27-28; examining workability, 28-29; transcripts
    demonstrating, 30-33, 35-36; validating experience of
    clients, 29-30

# V

vague goals, 161
validating experience of clients, 29-30
Valued Living Questionnaire (VLQ), 133, 139

values, 21, 129-155; assessment of, 139; case conceptualization and, 191-192; choice of, 136-137; coercive use of, 251-252; contacting, 139; contextual purpose of, 133; conversations about, 134-138; core competencies related to, 147-155, 288; definition of, 131-132; denial of, 137-138; distinctions relevant to, 142-144; experiential exercises on, 129-130, 142-143, 146-147; exposure procedures and, 164-165; feelings vs. actions and, 144; goals distinguished from, 142-143; importance of, 131, 132-133; key targets for, 129; lack of clarity about, 16, 191-192; life directions related to, 140-141; linking goals to, 132-133, 161; methods for clarifying, 133, 139-147; model responses related to, 152-155; pain connected to, 25, 134; pitfalls related to, 251-252; practice exercises on, 147-155; present-oriented, 137; process vs. outcome and, 144; reasons for clarifying, 132-133; responding to clients using, 227; self as context and, 119-120; statements about, 140; taking a stand for, 140; therapeutic relationship and, 222, 227, 229; therapy-relevant, 144-147; triggers for clarifying, 134; vitality related to, 134-136; willing vulnerability and, 137

Values Compass method, 133

verbal conventions, 70

verbal problem solving, 10

video recordings, 279

vulnerability, 137

# W

willingness, 23-56; action of, 40; choice of, 39-40; client practice of, 40-41; cognitive defusion and, 26, 74; committed action and, 158-159; core competencies related to, 41-55, 286; definition/explanation of, 24-25; experiential avoidance and, 26-27; as functional goal of ACT, 25; integrated with ACT processes, 41; key targets for, 23; model responses related to, 48-55; pitfalls related to, 250-251, 252; practice exercises on, 41-55; process of developing, 27-41; reasons for using, 25; therapist modeling of, 219-220; triggers for using, 26-27; undermining control related to, 27-38; vulnerability and, 137. *See also* acceptance

workability, examining, 28-29

# Z

*Zen-Master: Practical Zen by an American for Americans* (Hardy), 108

**Jason Luoma, Ph.D.,** is a clinical psychologist, director of the Portland Psychotherapy Clinic, Research, and Training Center in Portland, Oregon, and a grant-funded researcher with the University of Nevada, Reno. His research focuses on the application of ACT to the alleviation of burnout in counselors, ACT as an intervention for the stigma of substance abuse, and the dissemination and training of evidence-based therapies. He also has an active clinical practice and is an experienced trainer in Acceptance and Commitment Therapy. This book is the result of this practical experience and research.


**Steven C. Hayes, Ph.D.,** is University of Nevada Foundation Professor of Psychology at the University of Nevada, Reno. He has authored nearly 400 articles and book chapters, and more than 30 books, including **Get Out of Your Mind and Into Your Life, Acceptance and Commitment Therapy,** and **Relational Frame Theory.** A past president of the Association for Behavioral and Cognitive Therapies, he has conducted hundreds of trainings in ACT around the world and supervised the clinical training of scores of graduate students.


**Robyn D. Walser, Ph.D.,** is a clinical psychologist who works as a consultant, ACT workshop presenter, and therapist in her private business, TLConsultation Services. She has been doing ACT workshop trainings, both nationally and internationally, since 1998, training in multiple formats and for multiple client problems. She also works at the National Center for PTSD at the Veterans Affairs Palo Alto Health Care System.. Dr. Walser has expertise in traumatic stress and has authored a number of articles and a book, **Acceptance and Commitment Therapy for the Treatment of Post-Traumatic Stress Disorder and Trauma Related Problems,** for use of ACT in treating PTSD and trauma related problems.